TERRORISM IN THE COLD WAR

TERRORISM IN THE COLD WAR

State Support in the West, Middle East and Latin America

Edited by
Adrian Hänni, Thomas Riegler and
Przemyslaw Gasztold

BLOOMSBURY ACADEMIC
LONDON • NEW YORK • OXFORD • NEW DELHI • SYDNEY

BLOOMSBURY ACADEMIC
Bloomsbury Publishing Plc
50 Bedford Square, London, WC1B 3DP, UK
1385 Broadway, New York, NY 10018, USA
29 Earlsfort Terrace, Dublin 2, Ireland

BLOOMSBURY, BLOOMSBURY ACADEMIC and the Diana logo
are trademarks of Bloomsbury Publishing Plc

First published in Great Britain 2021
This paperback edition published in 2022

Copyright © Adrian Hänni, Thomas Riegler, Przemyslaw Gasztold, 2021

Adrian Hänni, Thomas Riegler and Przemyslaw Gasztold have asserted their right under the
Copyright, Designs and Patents Act, 1988, to be identified as Author of this work.

Cover design by Adriana Brioso
Cover images © UWE MEINHOLD/DDP/AFP/Getty Images; jsteck/iStock

All rights reserved. No part of this publication may be reproduced or transmitted
in any form or by any means, electronic or mechanical, including photocopying,
recording, or any information storage or retrieval system, without prior
permission in writing from the publishers.

Bloomsbury Publishing Plc does not have any control over, or responsibility for, any third-party websites referred to or in this book. All internet addresses given in this book were correct at the time of going to press. The author and publisher regret any inconvenience caused if addresses have changed or sites have ceased to exist, but can accept no responsibility for any such changes.

A catalogue record for this book is available from the British Library.

A catalogue record for this book is available from the Library of Congress.

ISBN: HB: 978-0-7556-0027-4
PB: 978-0-7556-3655-6
ePDF: 978-0-7556-0029-8
eBook: 978-0-7556-0028-1

Typeset by Deanta Global Publishing Services, Chennai, India

To find out more about our authors and books visit www.bloomsbury.com and sign up for
our newsletters.

CONTENTS

Volume II
State Support in the West, Middle East and Latin America

Chapter 1
INTRODUCTION: STATE SUPPORT FOR TERRORIST ACTORS IN THE COLD WAR – MYTHS AND REALITY (PART 2)
Adrian Hänni   1

Chapter 2
GLADIO – MYTH AND REALITY: THE ORIGINS AND FUNCTION OF STAY BEHIND IN THE CASE OF POST-WAR AUSTRIA
Thomas Riegler   15

Chapter 3
THE BRITISH STATE AND LOYALIST PARAMILITARIES IN NORTHERN IRELAND
Andrew Sanders   43

Chapter 4
THE SECRET 1970 MORATORIUM AGREEMENT BETWEEN SWITZERLAND AND THE PLO
Marcel Gyr   63

Chapter 5
THE ROAD NOT TAKEN: CRISIS MANAGEMENT, DIALOGUES AND DEAL-MAKING WITH PALESTINIAN FEDAYEEN GROUPS IN THE CONTEXT OF THE JORDANIAN TRIPLE-HIJACKING INCIDENT OF SEPTEMBER 1970
Thomas Skelton Robinson   89

Chapter 6
THE LODO MORO: ITALY AND THE PALESTINE LIBERATION ORGANIZATION
Tobias Hof   153

Chapter 7
PACT WITH THE (UN)WANTED? THE WISCHNEWSKI PROTOCOL AS A SPOTLIGHT FOR AUSTRO-GERMAN 'AGREEMENTS' WITH TRANSNATIONAL TERRORISTS IN THE LATE 1970S
    Matthias Dahlke   175

Chapter 8
HEZBOLLAH AS AN IRANIAN PROXY IN THE AGE OF THE COLD WAR
    Ryszard M. Machnikowski   193

Chapter 9
THE PROPAGANDA CAMPAIGN FOR THE PFLP IN SWITZERLAND 1969–70
    Daniel Rickenbacher   207

Chapter 10
THE UNITED STATES AND NICARAGUA: STATE TERRORISM DURING THE LATE COLD WAR
    Philip W. Travis   223

Chapter 11
OUTLOOK: WRITING THE HISTORY OF MODERN INTERNATIONAL TERRORISM – WHERE ARE THE PUZZLES?
    Thomas Wegener Friis, Adi Frimark and Martin Göllnitz   237

About the Authors   247
Select Bibliography   250
Index   257

Chapter 1

INTRODUCTION

STATE SUPPORT FOR TERRORIST ACTORS IN THE COLD WAR – MYTHS AND REALITY (PART 2)

Adrian Hänni

There is a certain irony. While, overall, researchers on terrorism enjoy fairly good access to the historical archives of the socialist dictatorships in Eastern Europe, access to archival documents on the relations that Western states maintained with terrorist actors during the Cold War remains sparse. Therefore, the general findings presented in this introduction are to some degree preliminary. The aim is to give a brief synthesis of the current state of research, primarily as a guide for future studies. The United States as the Western superpower will be addressed first, followed by a summary discussion of the other NATO and Western European states.

As discussed in the introduction to the first volume, the US Central Intelligence Agency (CIA) has often been accused of supporting terrorist groups since the days of the East–West conflict. An early case of actual CIA involvement in international terrorist violence in Europe is the agency's cooperation with the West German anti-communist resistance group Kampfgruppe gegen Unmenschlichkeit ('Fighting Group against Inhumanity', KgU). While it had received support from various Western intelligence services since its foundation in 1948, the KgU was basically a CIA front from 1952 onwards. Besides intelligence collection and propaganda operations against the German Democratic Republic (GDR), the group also committed acts of violent sabotage and planned the assassination of an East German official. In some instances, the actions crossed the boundary to terrorism, for example, when department stores were attacked with incendiary compositions. The close relationship between the KgU and US intelligence is also demonstrated by the fact that the KgU's remaining undercover agents were handed over to the CIA when the organization dissolved in 1959.[1]

However, Jeffrey Bale is certainly correct in pointing out that the narrative that US intelligence services were secretly directing a major part of the individual terrorist groups against the world's 'progressive' forces was 'as much of a propagandistic, conspiratorial fantasy as the notion that the Soviets were controlling international terrorism'.[2] Nevertheless, the CIA and other US government actors gave active and passive support to a number of mostly right-wing/anti-communist armed groups that regularly committed acts of terrorist violence. Significant examples are the extensive support for Nicaraguan Contra organizations such as the Nicaraguan Democratic Force during the Reagan administration,[3] and for anti-Castro Cuban exile organizations during the 1960s and, to a lesser extent, the 1970s.[4] The CIA provided these groups with money, weapons, intelligence and training, as well as organizational and logistical support.

Another notorious example is a CIA covert operation launched in late 1984 with the objective of training 'hit teams' within the Lebanese intelligence service. At the time, the latter was dominated by the far-right Maronite Christian Phalange, whose militia had been responsible for the massacre of many hundreds of civilians in the Palestinian refugee camps of Sabra and Shatila two years earlier. On 8 March 1985, one of the 'hit teams' committed a major terrorist attack in South Beirut. Sheikh Muhammad Fadlallah, the spiritual leader of Hezbollah and intended target of the attack, survived the car bomb but eighty Lebanese civilians were killed and 200 more injured. Whether there was a direct involvement of the US government or individual representatives, such as CIA Director William Casey, in this act of violence is still unclear and disputed as of today. In any case, the CIA covert action was aborted after the terrorist attack.[5]

Another research question still not fully answered is how far the CIA was involved in terrorist violence that may have been perpetrated by some national components of the clandestine *stay-behind* networks, which the CIA had helped set up in various NATO and formally neutral European states to resist a potential Soviet occupation and which were run by intelligence services of their respective countries. As Thomas Riegler clarifies in his contribution to this book,

> evidence of an active and controlled involvement of stay behind in terrorism concerns mainly cases like Italy, Belgium, and military dictatorships such as Turkey, Portugal, Greece, and Spain. But even in Italy, which was most affected by right-wing violence and related deception by the intelligence services, no direct link between *Gladio* [the Italian stay-behind structure] and terrorism has been established.[6]

The question of possible CIA involvement in right-wing and neo-fascist terrorism that afflicted the First Italian Republic from the 1950s into the 1980s therefore still awaits clarification, although it is documented that as early as 1963 the CIA station chief in Rome, William Harvey, urged the counterespionage chief of the Italian military intelligence service Servizio informazioni forze armate (SIFAR) to sabotage the then ruling centre-left government. SIFAR should use its 'action squads' to carry out bombings of Christian Democratic party offices and newspapers, which would then be blamed on the left.[7]

The relations that the United States' allies, both the NATO countries and the formally neutral states in Western Europe, maintained with terrorist actors fall within a broad spectrum – from full state control to very loose contacts.[8] At the top end of the spectrum is the case of Le Main Rouge ('The Red Hand') and the Service de Documentation Extérieure et de Contre-Espionnage (SDECE). The

French foreign intelligence service used Le Main Rouge, a fictitious international terrorist organization from North Africa, as a cover for covert action, including several bombings and shootings in Germany, Switzerland and elsewhere during the Algerian War of Independence (1954–62). The attacks, which primarily targeted Algerian nationalists and European arms dealers who sold weapons to the Front de Libération Nationale, were carried out with the full approval of the highest political authorities in Paris.[9]

The documented cases somewhat further down the spectrum of state support are, for the most part, those involving the Southern European dictatorships. Whether this is the case because states with non-democratic forms of government were less hesitant to support terrorist groups,[10] or, rather, due to the fact that the collapse of these dictatorship enabled access to intelligence documents not accessible elsewhere, remains a question for further research.

In Portugal, during the last decade of the Estado Novo, the Lisbon-based anti-communist 'terrorist organization'[11] Aginter Press was allowed to use specially designated training camps of the Legiao Portuguesa and Policia Internacional e de Defesa do Estado (PIDE)[12] to provide military training to mercenaries and terrorists alike. The courses included unconventional warfare as well as training in sabotage and urban terrorist techniques such as the use of explosives.[13]

In Spain, the regime of Dictator Francisco Franco supported the Organisation Armée Secrète ('Secret Army Organization', OAS) in the early 1960s by providing the terrorist group with sanctuary and placing three training camps at its disposal.[14] With its bombings and assassination schemes in Algeria and France, the OAS was, despite its short life cycle, one of the most violent and deadliest terrorist groups in the Cold War era. In early 1961, the organization committed up to 120 bomb attacks a day in Algiers alone.[15] In the 1970s, Spanish intelligence services closely collaborated with Italian neo-fascists who had been involved in terrorist violence during the 'strategy of tension', including the notorious Stefano delle Chiaie, and provided them with weapons, funds, sanctuary and logistical support. In return, these foreign extremists contributed to the pro-Franco violence that erupted in Spain in 1971 with attacks against domestic opponents of the regime.[16]

In Greece, the Regime of the Colonels, which had come to power following the 1967 coup d'état, established close relations with Avanguardia Nazionale and other Italian neo-fascist organizations in 1968. As a result of the Junta's apparent desire to export its 'revolution' to Italy and beyond, militants of these groups received doctrinal education as well as unconventional warfare training on the Greek island of Corfu. Soon thereafter, their organizations became the principal actors in the terrorist violence that shook Italy starting in early 1969.[17] After the fall of the Junta in 1974, successive Greek governments continued to give passive support to terrorist organizations such as the left-wing nationalist Revolutionary Organization 17 November (17N). Evidently, other Western democracies granted passive support in a similar vein, for example, the United States to the IRA until the turn of the 1970s.[18]

Perhaps more significantly, several (if not a majority) of Western European states reached secret 'defensive agreements' with a range of terrorist actors, especially organizations of Middle Eastern origin. These agreements traded security for sanctuary: in return for a pledge to desist from attacks on the territory and against the interests of a particular state, the presence of a terrorist group in that country was tolerated and its members were allowed, to varying extents, to operate there. In some instances, the organization also received diplomatic support.

According to Marcel Gyr's chapter argued in this volume, one of the earliest of these agreements was reached, at least implicitly, between representatives of the Swiss government and the PLO/Fatah in late 1970. After a series of spectacular attacks against Swiss targets perpetrated by Palestinian commandos in 1969/70, some influential figures within the Swiss government and its foreign ministry, Gyr claims, reached an understanding with Fatah representatives that would spare Switzerland from further terrorist violence and in turn allow the PLO to operate an office in Geneva. While questions remain about the existence, character and scope of this agreement, negotiations about a PLO representation, indeed, started in early 1971 and, besides one minor exception, Switzerland did not suffer from further violent attacks by Palestinian militants during the 1970s.[19]

In contrast to this Swiss case, no reasonable doubt exists that the Italian government and its military intelligence service SISMI closed secret agreements with both Arafat's Fatah and the more militant PFLP of George Habash in the first half of the 1970s. As Tobias Hof shows in this volume, the so-called Lodo Moro, which was upheld into the 1980s, granted the two Palestinian organizations the right to move freely in and operate out of Italy, and assured them diplomatic support by the government in Rome, as long as they did not commit any attacks on Italian soil.[20]

Another interesting case is France. It has often been claimed, with good arguments, that until the mid-1980s its approach towards international terrorist organizations was guided by a 'sanctuary doctrine', trading tolerance of terrorists on French soil for their renouncement of violent attacks against French interests. According to these accounts, not only armed Palestinian groups but a broad range of organizations involved in terrorist violence, including ETA and the Armenian Secret Army for the Liberation of Armenia, also enjoyed the benefits of the sanctuary doctrine at one time or another.[21]

However, only one such deal, an accommodation with the Abu Nidal Organization (ANO) in the 1980s, can be backed up by primary source material and by applying rigorous academic standards. The initial spark for French action was the ANO attack on the Jewish restaurant 'Jo Goldenberg' in Paris in August 1982, which left six people dead and twenty-two severely wounded. In the months following this deadly attack, the French were engaged in intelligence diplomacy with Abu Nidal's state supporters to contain the terrorist organization. The director of the French foreign intelligence service Direction Générale de la Sécurité Extérieure (DGSE), Pierre Marion, held secret talks with Rifaat Assad, brother of the Syrian president Hafez Assad. Assad agreed to instruct Abu Nidal to refrain from carrying out terrorist attacks in France.[22] At about the same time, the French domestic intelligence service Direction de la Surveillance du Territoire (DST) sent Colonel Philippe Rondot to Baghdad to elicit the same commitment from the Iraqi regime.[23]

Subsequently, Abu Nidal signalled an interest in negotiations. From summer 1984 onwards, the DST and ANO held a series of secret talks that were sanctioned by leading decision-makers in the French government. A deal was eventually cut in 1985 and maintained at least until 1988. This non-aggression pact consisted of a pledge by Abu Nidal to commit no more attacks on French soil or against French interests. In exchange, ANO members would be allowed to come to France untroubled and the French government released two ANO operatives imprisoned in France for the killing of Ezzedine Kalak, the PLO representative in Paris, in 1978.[24]

Another Western European state that cut a deal with ANO is Austria. Austrian authorities had long chosen a law enforcement approach towards ANO and the country had been heavily targeted by the group in 1981 and 1985. French intelligence eventually brokered an agreement in 1988 that would remain in place until 1993. For its renunciation of terrorist attacks in Austria, ANO received safe haven, an unofficial office in Vienna and some medical aid. Additionally, family members of Abu Nidal, one of the most wanted international terrorists at the time, could undergo surgeries at a Vienna hospital.[25]

Several Western European states thus concluded secret 'defensive agreements' with terrorist organizations. The nature of these accommodations is comparable to the deals reached by Eastern European states with the very same groups. Additionally, while the interest in gaining intelligence has been a crucial factor for basically all socialist states, driving their support for terrorist actors, the exchange of intelligence was also a key component of the secret contacts between French and Austrian intelligence services and the notorious ANO.[26] In contrast to their counterparts in the East, however, there is, at least until now, no evidence in the scantly available official documents that Western European intelligence services went as far as to provide money, arms or training within these frameworks.

In many ways, these defensive agreements can be seen as complementary to a number of agreements that a range of Western states, including the FRG, France and Austria, concluded with the most active state supporters in the Middle East such as Libya, Syria and Iran from the mid-1970s onwards. As part of these secret agreements, the West European governments offered a range of 'carrots' – from technical support, training and security cooperation to economic aid, diplomatic support and arms – in return for pledges by their Middle Eastern counterparts to curb terrorist groups under their influence or to stop directing terrorist attacks on the soil of Western countries. Sometimes these deals also included the provision of intelligence on terrorist actors by the Middle Eastern regimes.[27]

The Cold War dimension of state–terrorism relations

As the two volumes of *Terrorism in the Cold War*, and the introductory chapters in particular, aim to demonstrate, the Cold War shaped state–terrorism relations, their perception and academic study in myriad ways. To summarize, three important dimensions can be distinguished.

(1) The various terrorist actors constituted at no point a monolithic movement exploited, or even directed, by the Soviet Union in order to gain victory over the West or support communist takeovers in Western Europe and the United States. The Cold War did, however, set the broader scope of action within which relationships between state and terrorist actors were formed and sometimes constrained. In some instances, as we have seen, both superpowers have supported organizations engaged in terrorist violence directly as part of their geopolitical rivalry. At times state actors also attempted to exploit such organizations for non-terrorist actions against the Cold War enemy. An interesting case, analysed by Isabella Ginor and Gideon Remez in this book, is the KGB's attempt in the early 1970s to use the PFLP to abduct a high-ranking CIA operative in Beirut in order to extract intelligence.[28] In other instances, Warsaw Pact states have used terrorist groups to collect intelligence on the Cold War enemy through less violent means. The MfS, for example, received documentation about a US military base in West Germany from the RAF as part of their periodical exchange of intelligence in the early 1980s.[29]

In a more systemic manner, the bloc system shaped by the East–West struggle led to forms of state–terrorism relations that have so far been widely ignored by academic research. Some of the Soviet Union's satellite states in Eastern Europe, locked into the economic straitjacket of the COMECON, established multidimensional cooperation with notorious Middle Eastern terrorist groups that allowed them to export arms and other goods in exchange for urgently needed hard currency.[30] In other instances, it was the fear that the terrorist actors could change into the camp of the Cold War enemy that motived the security services of these states to provide (mostly passive) support to some groups.[31] Yet the explanatory power of the Cold War is limited. Probably more often than not, Cold War rationales were not decisive for the establishment and continuation of state–terrorist relationships. Moreover, and importantly, the differences between the individual states of one bloc, both in the East and in the West, were at least as big as the differences between the blocs.

(2) On the material level, international terrorism was no conspiracy directed by either the KGB or the CIA. On the ideological level, on the other hand, terrorism has been integrated into a Cold War narrative on both sides of the Iron Curtain, especially between 1975 and 1985. As outlined in the first sections of this article, during this decade, encompassing what is sometimes referred to as the Second Cold War, the respective Cold War enemy's involvement in international terrorism became an important theme of propaganda and disinformation both in the West and in the East, put forward by intelligence agencies, politicians, mass media, book authors and popular culture. In Ronald Reagan's America, the imaginary Soviet-directed

terrorist offensive was even framed as an existential threat, seen by some influential intellectuals and government members as an ideological tool for 'moral rearmament' against communism. If the Cold War is understood primarily as an ideological contest, then the relationships between state and terrorist actors were, indeed, an important factor during the last decade of tensions – although not in the sense that it has usually been portrayed.

(3) The end of the Cold War with the collapse of the Warsaw Pact, the Soviet Union and the socialist regimes in Eastern Europe has been influencing research on terrorism and state support until today. The democratization of Eastern Europe led to a rare opening up of archives of the former security services in those countries, enabling researchers to gain broad knowledge on the socialist states' support for terrorism based on comprehensive primary source material. In Western Europe and the United States, on the other side, most of the respective records have remained classified. This leads to the somewhat paradox situation that today we have much more transparency and information on the socialist dictatorships than on the Western democracies, at least concerning their relations with terrorist actors. Thomas Wegener Friis, Adi Frimark and Martin Göllnitz therefore raise a crucial point in the concluding chapter of this book with their case for the release of respective archival documents kept by Western intelligence services.

Another epistemological heritage of the Cold War era concerns the terrorist actors that are selected as objects of scholarly research and are (partly cause, partly consequence) enshrined in the public historical consciousness. While much attention is given to terrorist actors that have challenged Western governments such as the Palestinian factions and leftist groups (e.g. the RAF, the Red Brigades, ETA and others), right-wing transnational terrorist groups and those fighting socialist regimes have received much less attention within terrorism studies. The different treatment cannot be explained by the significance of these organizations, considering the paramount ideological and tactical influence the OAS had on transnational neo-fascist violence,[32] the global modus operandi of Croatian émigré nationalists,[33] and the fact that anti-Castro Cuban exiles, like the OAS, were responsible for more terrorist attacks than all of European leftist organizations taken together.

Theoretical implications and outlook

The empirical historical findings presented in this book could further encourage a refinement of theorization on state–terrorism relations, particularly on the different types of support and the motivations of state actors. Theoretical explanations of state support for terrorist actors can be roughly categorized into three schools of thought: a first theoretical tradition, dating back to the late Cold War era, has conceptualized 'state sponsorship of terrorism' as a type of covert warfare and has put the analytical focus on external insurgency support and state actors' involvement in intra-state conflict through 'terrorist proxies' and 'surrogates'. A second theoretical tradition, which emerged in the mid-1990s and remained influential for about a decade, analysed state sponsorship within the larger framework of 'rogue states'. State support was closely tied to a specific regime type and understood as a threat to Western interests in geopolitical key regions.[34]

Particularly from the mid-2000s onwards, a more nuanced and differentiating theoretical tradition gained steam. An important step in this development was Daniel Byman's seminal work *Deadly Connections* (2005), laying out a broad range of types and motivations for state support. Byman and other authors also developed a better understanding of passive support,[35] started putting more emphasis on the domestic characteristics of state sponsors and conceived of domestic politics as an additional trigger of support besides strategic interest and ideology. In this tradition, a number of scholars developed theoretical models that, besides their various differences, all share the realist assumption that vulnerable states lacking the capacity to mobilize societal power resources due to domestic power fragmentation support terrorist actors against internal and external security threats as a substitute to alliance building with other states – either because they are unable to build interstate alliances or because they fear domestic repercussions of such formal alliances.[36]

While the increasing sophistication of theorizing is, of course, very positive and insightful, the various models and generalizations do not yet reveal the full picture. The findings presented in this book enable us to identify at least three missing puzzle pieces – important motivations for active or passive state support during the Cold War era that have so far been neglected by the literature. These missing puzzle pieces are (1) *accommodation*: state support motivated by a defensive desire to gain domestic security and/or protect interests abroad from the very same terrorist actors that are being supported; (2) *intelligence cooperation*: state support for terrorist groups in exchange for intelligence, which is, after all, the core business of the state actors that usually liaise with this type of organizations; (3) *economic interests*: state support motivated by the prospect of financial benefits or access to sensitive goods (technology, weapons) through mostly non-violent activities of a terrorist organization. These three puzzle pieces should find stronger consideration in future theory-building efforts. Scholars should attempt to figure out how they fit into the motivations that have previously been identified in the literature in order to gain a more comprehensive picture of state support.

However, this book not only attempts to inspire new theorization but also wants to encourage more historical investigations. It provides at best an interim result on state involvement with terrorist actors during the Cold War era, still leaving many gaps to fill.[37] Temporally, the two volumes, and terrorism research more broadly, remain heavily focused on the 1970s and 1980s. Geographically, with the notable exceptions of the chapters discussing North Korea, Middle Eastern states, Nicaragua, the United States and the Soviet Union, the contributions focus on European state actors. South Africa, arguably one of the most deeply involved states in the support of terrorist actors in the 1970s and the 1980s,[38] receives only one passing reference in this book and is almost entirely absent in scholarly discussions of state sponsorship. China is another elephant in the room that largely evades academic scrutiny on the subject. Future research efforts will therefore have to not only produce much more detailed knowledge about the relations Western European states maintained with terrorist actors but also further decenter Europe in this historiography. Accordingly, the aim of this book is much more modest than to produce a definite account on state-terrorism relations during the Cold War. We want to equip readers with an assessment of the state of research and, hopefully, provide a useful guide for researchers in the years to come.

While the first volume discusses the communist countries in Eastern Europe and beyond, the contributions to this volume provide an introduction and some major research findings on the relations that Western state actors maintained with terrorist groups during the Cold War. They are complemented with three articles on the Middle East and Latin America that present important recent findings on historical state-terrorism relations more broadly. Daniel Rickenbacher's case study explores propaganda as an important, yet rarely discussed, form of support states provide to terrorist organizations. Ryszard Machnikowski analyses the case of Hezbollah to show how the use of terrorist proxies by state actors was very effective and politically successful in some instances, for both the supporting state and the terrorist group. Finally, Philip Travis reminds us that allegations of state sponsorship of terrorism were often exaggerated and have served as powerful legitimations for particular foreign policies.

Notes

1 Enrico Heitzer, *Die Kampfgruppe gegen Unmenschlichkeit (KgU): Widerstand und Spionage im Kalten Krieg 1948–1959* (Köln: Böhlau, 2015); Enrico Heitzer, The Fighting Group Against Inhumanity: The Incarnation of Anticommunism in a Divided Germany 1948–1959, paper presented at the international conference 'Need to Know VII: The Hidden Hand of Intelligence', Budapest, 9–10 November 2017; Thomas Rid, *Active Measures: The Secret History of Disinformation and Political Warfare* (New York: Profile Books, 2020), 74–84.
2 Jeffrey M. Bale, *The Darkest Side of Politics, Vol. 2: State Terrorism, 'Weapons of Mass Destruction', Religious Extremism, and Organized Crime* (New York: Routledge, 2018), 7.
3 See, for example, James Bilsland, *The President, the State and the Cold War: Comparing the Foreign Policies of Truman and Reagan* (London: Routledge, 2015), 125–65; Malcolm Byrne, *Iran-Contra: Reagan's Scandal and the Unchecked Abuse of Presidential Power* (Lawrence, KS: University Press of Kansas, 2014); Abdelhak Boumaad, *La Politique Américaine en Amérique Centrale: La Présidence de Ronald Reagan et le Nicaragua* (Lille: Atelier National de Reproduction des Theses, 1999).
4 Don Bohning, *The Castro Obsession: U.S. Covert Operations against Cuba, 1959–1965* (Washington, DC: Potomac Books, 2005); Keith Bolender, *Voices from the Other Side: An Oral History of Terrorism against Cuba* (London: Pluto Press, 2010); as well as various documentations of primary source material by Peter Kornbluh of the National Security Archive.
5 Richard J. Chasdi, Counterterror Failure: The Fadlallah Assassination Attempt, in Richard Weitz (ed.), *Project on National Security Reform: Case Studies Working Group*

Report, Vol. 2, March 2012, 303–74, www.dtic.mil/get-tr-doc/pdf?AD=ADA558988 (accessed 1 January 2020); Timothy Naftali, *Blind Spot: The Secret History of American Counterterrorism* (New York: Basic Books, 2005), 147–52; Mattia Toaldo, *Origins of the US War on Terror: Lebanon, Libya and American Intervention in the Middle East* (London: Routledge, 2013), 112.

6 See the article by Thomas Riegler in this book.
7 David Talbot, *The Devil's Chessboard: Allen Dulles, the CIA, and the Rise of America's Secret Government* (London: HarperCollins, 2016), 475.
8 Useful classification scales for relations between state and terrorist actors are provided by Louise Richardson and Daniel Byman. Richardson represents relations as falling along a spectrum from very tight to very loose state control. At one end of this spectrum is covert action by intelligence agencies posing as terrorists, followed by the recruitment and training of operatives specifically for terrorist missions. The third level is reached when a government has close control over a terrorist organization and directs its operations. Further down the continuum is the provision of training, financing and safe haven to an autonomous terrorist group by a state actor. The fifth and final level according to Richardson consists of financial support for a terrorist group because of a perceived alignment of interests. See Louise Richardson, State Sponsorship: A Root Cause of Terrorism? in Tore Bjorgo (ed.), *Root Causes of Terrorism: Myths, Reality and Ways Forward* (New York: Routledge, 2005), 189–97. Byman's classification scale ranges from highly committed *strong supporters*, who offer significant resources to a terrorist group; to *weak supporters*, regimes that support a terrorist actor but have few resources to do so; to *lukewarm supporters*, including state actors that are sympathetic to a terrorist organization or their cause but do little to advance it directly; to *antagonistic supporters*, who support a terrorist group but in an attempt to control it or weaken its cause through their ambivalent relationship; to *passive supporters*, who do not support terrorist actors directly but knowingly turn a blind eye to their activities, which usually results in a safe haven; to *unwilling hosts*, (failed) states that are too weak to stop terrorist groups within their territories. See Daniel Byman, *Deadly Connections: States that Sponsor Terrorism* (New York: Cambridge University Press, 2005), 10–15.
9 Mathilde von Bülow, Myth or Reality? The Red Hand and French Covert Action in Federal Germany during the Algerian War, 1956–61, *Intelligence and National Security* 22/6 (2007), 787–820; Mathilde von Bülow, *West Germany, Cold War Europe and the Algerian War* (Cambridge: Cambridge University Press, 2016); Thomas Riegler, The State as a Terrorist: France and the Red Hand, *Perspectives on Terrorism* 6/6 (2012), 22–33.
10 There is some empirical evidence supporting this thesis. A large quantitative study by Belgin San Akca found that ceteris paribus autocratic states are significantly more likely to support non-state armed groups. However, the study also finds that 'even a highly democratic state that has allies, is not highly fragmented, and is not so vulnerable in terms of its external strength has a 14 per cent probability that it will support a NAG [non-state armed group] if the latter targets an external adversary'. See Belgin San Akca, Supporting Non-State Armed Groups: A Resort to Illegality, *Journal of Strategic Studies* 32/4 (2009), 589–613 (quote on p. 604).
11 According to the 1998 sentence of Milan investigative judge Guido Salvino. See Sentenza-ordinanza n. 9/92A del 3 febbraio 1998 nel procedimento penale contro Rognoni, Giancarlo + 32, Tribunale di Milano, Giudice Istruttore Guido Salvino, 369, cited in Jeffrey M. Bale, *The Darkest Sides of Politics, Vol. 1: Postwar Fascism, Covert Operations, and Terrorism* (New York: Routledge, 2018), 184.

12 In 1969, PIDE was renamed the Direçao-Geral de Segurança (General Security Directorate, DGS) by the government of Marcello Caetano.
13 Frédéric Laurent, *L'Orchestre noire* (Paris: Stock, 1978), 135–6; Giuseppe De Lutiis, *Storia dei servizi segreti in Italia* (Rome: Riuniti, 1984), 161.
14 Tramor Quemeneur, La Discipline jusqu'au l'Indiscipline, in Mohammed Harbi and Benjamin Stora (eds.), *La Guerre d'Algérie* (Paris: Laffont, 2004), 261; Matteo Albanese and Pablo del Hierro, *Transnational Fascism in the Twentieth Century: Spain, Italy and the Global Neo-Fascist Network* (London: Bloomsbury, 2016), 124.
15 Martin Evans, *Algeria: France's Undeclared War* (Oxford: Oxford University Press, 2012), 313–38.
16 Albanese and del Hierro, *Transnational Fascism in the Twentieth Century*, 146–53; Bale, *Darkest Sides of Politics*, Vol. 1, 145–75.
17 Ibid., 136–211.
18 For an overview of the Greek–17N and the US–IRA relations, as well as for a theoretical discussion of passive support, see Byman, *Deadly Connections*, 219–58.
19 Besides Gyr's article in this book, see also Marcel Gyr, *Schweizer Terrorjahre: Das geheime Abkommen mit der PLO* (Zürich: Verlag Neue Zürcher Zeitung, 2016). For the opposite standpoint, calling into question the existence of an agreement, see Sacha Zala, Thomas Bürgisser and Yves Steiner, Die Debatte zu einem 'geheimen Abkommen' zwischen Bundesrat Graber und der PLO: Eine Zwischenbilanz, *Schweizerische Zeitschrift für Geschichte* 66/1 (2016), 1–24. An inquiry commission of the Swiss government reported in May 2016 that it had been unable to find documentary evidence for the deal claimed by Gyr. See Interdepartementale Arbeitsgruppe '1970' (IDA 1970), *Schlussbericht*, Eidgenössisches Departement für auswärtige Angelegenheiten (EDA), Berne, 3 May 2016, https://www.eda.admin.ch/content/dam/eda/de/documents/publications/Geschichte/interdepartementale-arbeitsgruppe-1970_de.pdf (accessed 1 January 2020).
20 See the contribution of Tobias Hof in this book.
21 Jeremy Shapiro and Bénédicte Suzan, The French Experience of Counterterrorism, *Survival: Global Politics and Strategy* 45/1 (2003), 67–98; Michel Wieviorka, French Politics and Strategy on Terrorism, in Barry Rubin (ed.), *The Politics of Counterterrorism: The Ordeal of Democratic States* (Washington, DC: Paul H. Nitze School of Advanced International Studies, 1990), 61–90. For a brief discussion, see also the contribution of Thomas Wegener Friis, Adi Frimark and Martin Göllnitz in this book.
22 Terrorism Review, GI TR 82-004, Directorate of Intelligence, CIA, 26 November 1982, 3, in CREST, CIA General Records, 84-00893R, Box 1, Folder 4, Document No. 1–6.
23 Gilles Ménage, *L'oeil du pouvoir* (Paris: Fayard, 1999–2001), Vol. 3, 240f.
24 A triangulation of a number of different sources allows us to establish the existence of an agreement between France and ANO and its key details beyond reasonable doubt. Among these sources are, first, the memoirs and oral accounts of Yves Bonnet, the DST director at the time; Raymond Nart, head of counterespionage of the DST and personally involved in the negotiations with Abu Nidal; as well as Gilles Ménage, Chief of Cabinet of President François Mitterrand. See Eric Merlen and Frédéric Ploquin, *Carnets intimes de la DST: 30 ans au coeur du contre-espionnage français* (Paris: Fayard, 2003), 350–4; Ménage, *L'oeil du pouvoir*, Vol. 3; Vincent Gautronneau and Jérémie Pham-Lê, Attentat de la rue des Rosiers: Le pacte secret passé avec les terrorists, *Le Parisien*, 8 August 2019, http://www.leparisien.fr/faits-divers/attentat-de-la-rue-des-rosiers-le-pacte-secret-passe-avec-les-terroristes-08-08-2019-8130903

.php (accessed 1 January 2020). French officials have also confirmed constructive contacts with ANO in the mid-1980s in interviews with the British journalist John Follain conducted in the 1990s. See John Follain, *The Jackal* (London: Weidenfeld and Nicholson, 1998), 167–9. Second, a considerable number of interviews Patrick Seale has conducted with ANO defectors almost three decades ago (see Patrick Seale, *Abu Nidal: A Gun for Hire* (New York: Random House, 1992), 269–72). The findings from these interviews can be judged highly reliable, not least because those pieces of information on ANO's relations with Western European countries that can now be cross-checked with written sources prove to be accurate and astonishingly precise. Third, intelligence sources such as a range of recently declassified CIA documents, for example, the Terrorism Review of 26 November 1982 cited earlier, and, more importantly, records of the East German MfS held in the Berlin central office of the BStU archives, most prominently the report Darlegungen Abu Ayads zur Abu-Nidal-Gruppe, Berlin, 23 June 1987, in BStU Zentralarchiv, XV 3690/82 'Händler', 7116/91. However, the exact extent of the deal and the French concessions are still unclear. Patrick Seale claims, based on his interviews with ANO defectors, that the group made a commitment to refrain from attacking French targets, to launch no attacks from French soil and to bring no arms into France. In return, in addition to the release of Kalak's killers, the French allowed a secret ANO representative in France, handed out occasional visas, allowed the group to set up commercial ventures, provided it with some ambulances and Peugeot cars in Lebanon, enabled ANO members to receive treatment in French hospitals, and handed out three to four scholarships. While these modalities described by Seale are consistent with documentary evidence on ANO's relations with state actors in Austria and Switzerland during the 1980s, as well as the group's dealings in those countries, they need further confirmation from additional sources. (For documentation on Austria, see the following footnote; for Switzerland, consult the private archive of the author).

25 Thomas Riegler, *Im Fadenkreuz: Österreich und der Nahostterrorismus 1973 bis 1985* (Göttingen: V&R unipress, 2011), 279–342.

26 Ménage, *L'oeil du pouvoir*, Vol. 3, 242–5, 358.

27 On the German deals, see Eva Oberloskamp, *Codename TREVI: Terrorismusbekämpfung und die Anfänge einer europäischen Innenpolitik in den 1970er Jahren* (Berlin: De Gruyter Oldenbourg, 2017), 47–8. On the French deals, see Shapiro and Suzan, French Experience of Counterterrorism, 73–5; Wieviorka, French Politics and Strategy on Terrorism, 77–85; TREVI Group: Attitudes Towards Syria, EUR M86-20154, CIA, 2 December 1986, 4–5, in CREST, CIA General Records, 86T01017R, Box 5, Folder 477, Document No. 1–7; TREVI Group: Attitudes Towards Libya, EUR M86-20058, CIA, 22 April 1986, in CREST, CIA General Records, 86T01017R, Box 4, Folder 382, Document No. 1–3. On an Austrian deal with Libya made in 1975, see Thomas Riegler, *Tage des Schreckens: Die OPEC-Geiselnahme 1975 und der moderne Terrorismus* (E-book, 2015), 234–53.

28 There is further persuasive evidence that the Bulgarian intelligence service, working through an Italian agent of influence after the Red Brigades had kidnapped US General James Dozier in late 1981, offered to trade weapons and money for intelligence that the Italian group had obtained from Dozier. If such an offer was, indeed, made, it never led to a consummated arrangement and, in any case, it would demonstrate the lack of existing Soviet bloc ties to the Red Brigades. See The Soviet Bloc Role in International Terrorism and Revolutionary Violence, National Intelligence Estimate 11/2-86, August 1986, 16, www.cia.gov/library/readingroom/docs/CIA-RDP90T00155R000200050001-6.pdf (accessed 1 January 2020).

29 Tobias Wunschik, *Baader-Meinhofs Kinder: Die zweite Generation der RAF* (Opladen: Westdeutscher Verlag, 1997), 396.
30 See the articles by Przemyslaw Gasztold, Tobias Wunschik, Jordan Baev and Balazs Orban-Schwarzkopf in this book.
31 See, for example, Tobias Wunschik's article in this book for the case of the GDR. The opportunity to use intra-alignment leverage over terrorist actors to preclude a rapprochement between them and the state's adversary has been studied regarding Arab states such as Syria. See Hanna Batatu, *Syria's Peasantry, the Descendants of Its Lesser Rural Notables, and Their Politics* (Princeton, NJ: Princeton University Press, 1999), 301–5; Magdalena Kirchner, *Allianz mit dem Terror: Iran, Israel und die libanesische Hisbollah 1979–2009* (München: AVM, 2009), 36. For the post-Cold War era, a study on Pakistan and its relationship with the Afghan Taliban was conducted by Adrian Hänni and Lukas Hegi, Pakistanischer Pate: Der Geheimdienst Inter-Services Intelligence (ISI) und die afghanischen Taliban, 2002–2010, *Journal for Intelligence, Propaganda and Security Studies* 5/1 (2011), 46–60.
32 For a detailed discussion, see Bale, *The Darkest Sides of Politics*, Vol. 1, 136–211.
33 Mate Nikola Tokić, Landscapes of Conflict: Unity and Disunity in Post-Second World War Croatian Émigré Separatism, *European Review of History* 16/5 (2009), 739–53; Matthias Thaden, Radikal und transnational: Politische Gewalt von Exilkroaten in der Bundesrepublik Deutschland in den 1960er Jahren, in Adrian Hänni, Daniel Rickenbacher and Thomas Schmutz (eds.), *Über Grenzen hinweg: Transnationale politische Gewalt im 20. Jahrhundert* (Frankfurt: Campus, 2020), 205–29.
34 For a description of these two theoretical schools, see Magdalena Kirchner, *Why States Rebel: Understanding State Sponsorship of Terrorism* (Opladen: Barbara Budrich, 2016), 20–21.
35 See, especially, Daniel Byman, Passive Sponsors of Terrorism, *Survival* 47/4 (2005), 117–44.
36 San Akca, Supporting Non-State Armed Groups; Navin A. Bapat, Understanding State Sponsorship of Militant Groups, *British Journal of Political Science* 42/1 (2011), 1–29; Zeev Maoz and Belgin San Akca, Rivalry and State Support of Non-State Armed Groups (NAGs), 1946–2001, *International Studies Quarterly* 56/4 (2012), 720–34; Kirchner, *Why States Rebel*.
37 For some explicit suggestions for the direction of future research, see the final article in this book by Thomas Wegener Friis, Adi Frimark and Martin Göllnitz.
38 Richardson, State Sponsorship, 194–5; Truth and Reconciliation Commission of South Africa Report, Vol. 2, 29 October 1998, published online by the Department of Justice of the Republic of South Africa, www.justice.gov.za/trc/report/finalreport/Volume%202.pdf (accessed 1 January 2020).

Chapter 2

GLADIO – MYTH AND REALITY

THE ORIGINS AND FUNCTION OF STAY BEHIND
IN THE CASE OF POST-WAR AUSTRIA

Thomas Riegler

'NATO's secret armies'

In 2005 Swiss researcher Daniele Ganser published *NATO's Secret Armies: Operation Gladio and Terrorism in Western Europe*.[1] The book has since been translated into ten languages and has attracted widespread attention. The main reason 'NATO's secret armies' resonated with the public is that it presents a plausible explanation for some of the worst terrorist atrocities in Western Europe, which remain largely unsolved to this day. According to Ganser, outrages like certain bloody bombings in Italy during the 1970s and 1980s, or seemingly random attacks on supermarkets in Belgium in the 1980s, were, in fact, committed by sinister forces linked to NATO's 'secret armies', a term he has coined for stay behind – which, in turn, describes groups or individual agents placed or dropped behind front lines for intelligence collection, sabotage, escape and evasion. Ganser argues that the 'secret armies' fulfilled a wider role in the geopolitical context of the Cold War and suggests that 'false flag' terrorism was used as a means to influence public opinion to support tougher laws/security measures. Originally set up in the late 1940s and 1950s in each NATO member state and several neutral countries[2] as a guerrilla and partisan force against a Soviet invasion, the 'secret armies' were finally dissolved in 1990/1. While a war between the superpowers never occurred, in some NATO countries these secret structures were put to use against the internal enemy' – consisting mainly of Western Europe's communist parties. As Ganser emphasizes, terrorist crimes committed by 'secret armies' were 'wrongly blamed' on the communists in order to discredit the left at the polls: 'The operations always aimed at spreading maximum fear among the population and ranged from bomb massacres in trains and market squares (Italy), the use of systematic torture of opponents of the regime (Turkey), the support for right-wing coup d'état (Greece and Turkey) to the smashing of opposition groups (Portugal and Spain).'[3]

Ganser suggests that responsibility lay high up the chain of command in the transatlantic power structure: 'Most of these state sponsored terrorist operations, as the subsequent cover up and fake trials suggest, enjoyed the encouragement and protection of selected highly placed government and military officials in Europe and in the United States.'[4] Thus, the 'secret armies' functioned as 'an almost perfect manipulation system' that transferred the anti-communist fears of the US defence and intelligence apparatus on to the populations of Western Europe: 'By killing innocent citizens on market squares or in supermarkets and blaming the crime on the Communists the secret armies together with committed right-wing terrorists effectively translated the fears of the Pentagon into very real fears of European citizens.'[5] These claims have since been picked up by numerous publications, news portals and web pages.[6]

To prove his point, Ganser relies mainly on secondary sources. The most important documentary evidence he refers to is Supplement B of Pentagon Field Manual 30–31. It states that a critical moment comes when leftist groups 'renounce the use of force' and embrace the democratic process. It is then that 'U.S. army intelligence must have the means of launching special operations which will convince Host Country Governments and public opinion of the reality of the insurgent danger'. For Ganser, FM 30–31B is a blueprint for the 'false flag' terror campaign he associates with NATO's 'secret armies', namely a perfidious manoeuvre to strengthen the current order by creating a situation of fear and alarm.[7] FM 30–31B had first surfaced in Spain in 1976 and its authenticity is disputed. In 2006, the US State Department noted that a 'thirty year-old Soviet forgery' had been cited as one of the central pieces of 'evidence' for the notion that stay-behind networks engaged in terrorism at the instigation of the United States: 'This is not true, and those researching the "stay behind" networks need to be more discriminating in evaluating the trustworthiness of their source material.'[8]

Another of Ganser's primary sources is a document by the Italian Defence Intelligence Agency (*Servizio Informazioni Forze Armate*, SIFAR) from 1959, in which the focus of stay behind is specified as twofold against both internal and external threats: 'The possibility of an emergency situation, either through domestic upheaval or through military invasion forces, that involves all or some of the territories of the NATO countries, has for some time already been the subject of studies and preparations.'[9] In Italy, stay behind had been assigned the codename *Gladio*: officially established in 1956, it never amounted to more than 622 members, 'of which about half were selected between 1958 and 1967 and the rest in the period between 1967 and 1990'.[10] These agents were deployed from the north-eastern border down to Bologna. Most of them were in their forties; some were younger. The organization comprised five sections: information and propaganda, guerrilla, sabotage, escape and relief.[11] Furthermore, *Gladio* had 139 arms caches[12] at its disposal – comprising 'portable arms, ammunition, explosives, hand grenades, knives and daggers, 60 mm mortars, several recoilless rifles, sniper rifles, radio transmitters, binoculars, and various tools'.[13] Its headquarters, the Saboteurs' Training Centre (*Centro Adestramento Guastatori*, CAG), was located at Cape Marrargiu in Sardinia. The complex was equipped with underground bunkers, various training facilities and two small runways for planes.[14] Yet most of the evidence beyond this remains speculative: for example, on 24 February

1972, in Aurisina in north-east Italy, one of the secret arms caches of *Gladio* was discovered. Only three months later, the explosion of a booby-trapped car claimed the lives of three *Carabinieri* in nearby Peteano. There is widespread suspicion that the explosives used in the attack may have originated from the Aurisina dump. But when magistrate Felice Casson attempted to investigate the bombing in 1990, the *Carabinieri* claimed that all documentation relating to the findings had been destroyed.[15]

Apart from this episode, no specific link between *Gladio* and other unsolved bombings in Italy has been established. According to scholar Leopoldo Nuti, the documents released to the parliamentary committees investigating *Gladio* in 1991 'do not allow us to conclude that Operation "*Gladio*" was involved in any illegal activities connected with the terrorism of the late 1960s and of the 1970s. They do not help solving, in other words, any of the mysteries, which beleaguered Italian post-war history for more than a decade.'[16] Yet there is scattered evidence concerning parallel structures to *Gladio* set up by the Italian intelligence services and their links to anti-communist circles in Portugal and Greece as well as to officers of NATO bases in Northern Italy.[17] In particular, a paramilitary organization called *Nuclei for the Defence of the State* (NDS) was founded in 1966 and operated until 1973. While Ganser does not mention NDS in his study, this organization had not only been created with the explicit aim of fighting communist 'subversion' but also incorporated neo-fascist groups like *Ordine Nuovo* and *Avantguardia Nazionale*, whose members were later implicated in terrorist acts like Peteano.[18] According to a former member, the mission was 'to engage in the covert training of groups who in the event the leftists in our country made a move, would take to the streets to create a situation so tense as to require military intervention'.[19] On the other hand, despite the best efforts of the magistrates examining, for example, Milan's Piazza Fontana bombing of 12 December 1969, the leads provided by informer Carlo Digilio could not prove US/NATO involvement in this terrorist attack.[20] However, it is known by now that already in 1963 the CIA station chief in Rome, William Harvey, had urged SIFAR's counterespionage chief, Colonel Renzo Rocca, to sabotage the then ruling centre-left government – by using his 'action squads' to carry out bombings of Christian Democratic party offices and newspapers. The outrages would then be blamed on the left.[21] What is clear so far is that American and NATO networks were aware beforehand of actions and coup plots because of their informants inside the parallel networks and neo-fascist groups and 'that they rarely acted to prevent them'.[22]

What the numerous judicial inquests also revealed was that the right-wing bombers enjoyed a high level of complicity on the part of the Italian intelligence services. The judiciary was either obstructed or set on a false leftist track, while some of the main suspects were provided with passports to leave Italy in the meantime. In July 2015, a court handed down life sentences to two right-wingers in connection with Brescia's Pizza della Loggia bombing of 28 May 1974, which killed eight and injured 100 people. *La Stampa* called the verdict 'historic' – since for the first time both *Ordine Nuovo* and the intelligence services had been linked to a terrorist act of the 1970s.[23] The magistrates ruled that Carlo Maria Maggi, former head of *Ordine Nuovo*, organized the attack, while militant Maurizio Tramonte kept the intelligence services informed about the proceedings.[24] A new piece of evidence that surfaced in 2019 were protocols of training courses hosted by SIFAR at the Cape Marrargiu base in the years 1965–8, shortly before the Piazza Fontana bombing. According to these documents, the curriculum for *Carabinieri* officers included training in sabotage and 'unorthodox warfare', as well as in handling conventional and unconventional explosives.[25] Already in 1969, an article on the Piazza Fontana atrocity in the British newspaper *Observer* had introduced the metaphor of a 'strategy of tension': it postulated that the terrorist outrages coincided with peak times of labour unrest or critical election campaigns and, in effect, promoted conservative political and social tendencies. Italy is still coming to terms with the legacy of these *anni di piombo* (years of lead) and it remains to be seen whether *Gladio* had a part in it and if so, what exactly its role had been.[26]

Another significant case is Belgium, where between 1982 and 1985 the province of Brabant witnessed sixteen assaults on supermarkets and small businesses. Only small sums of money were stolen by the assailants, but they left a trail of twenty-eight people dead and forty wounded. The so-called Brabant Killers often wore carnival masks and long trench coats and were armed with tactical shotguns. They became notorious for using unprovoked extreme violence, even specifically targeting children.[27] According to rumours, the unidentified killers were extreme right-wingers and former members of the paramilitary *Gendarmerie*. Supposedly, their aim was to wreak terror, destabilize Belgium's democratic order and promote the establishment of an ultra-conservative government. However, a parliamentary inquiry (1990/1) found 'no indications' that would justify the conclusion that there was 'any link whatsoever' between Belgium's stay-behind force *SDRA8* and 'acts of terrorism and large-scale banditry'.[28] In 2017, the brother of a retired ex-member of an elite police commando unit came forward to claim that his dying sibling, Christiaan Bonkoffsky, had confessed to being 'the Giant', a member of the 'Brabant Killers'. The federal prosecutor's office stated that they were convinced this was not the case. Yet another ex-police officer was arrested on suspicion that he 'retained at least certain, possibly crucial, information' on the 'Brabant Killers'.[29] Charles Maurice, author of a 2018 study on the case, also emphasizes links between the perpetrators and the *Gendarmerie*, but at the same time debunks stay-behind-related explanations as inaccurate. Instead, he reached the conclusion that the 'Brabant Killers' were members of organized crime, initially pursuing an extortion scheme and then wanting to secure the reward money put up by the supermarket chains.[30] But because their suspected ringleader, the former gendarme Madani Bouhouche, was arrested for a different crime in early 1986, the 'Brabant Killers' suddenly disappeared.[31] Whether the motive was terror or robbery, the atrocities they committed, as well as the acts of left-wing terrorism that took place at the same time, had an 'undeniable political impact' by securing the victory of a law and order government in the 1985 elections.[32] Another theory advanced in 2020 by journalist Guy Bouten again speculates about a CIA-orchestrated conspiracy behind the 'Brabant Killers'. Bouten points to former mercenary and right-wing activist Roger Beuckels as the shooter who killed most of the victims. Allegedly, Beuckels was the subordinate of a key officer involved in *SDRA8*.[33]

There is a further incident linked to stay behind in Belgium: during the early hours of 13 May 1984 an army post in Vielsalm was attacked by three intruders. They critically injured the guard, Carl Freches, with four .45 calibre bullets and stole a large quantity of arms.[34] A former Belgian paratrooper, Lucien Deslaire, claimed that he had aided a stay-behind cell, including American Special Forces, just before the attack, and that the US troops had taken it too far by raiding the post. But investigators did not find proof of links between a secret NATO manoeuvre (*Oesling 84*), bombing attacks in neighbouring Luxembourg and the attack on Vielsalm. Already in 1993, the left-wing extremist group *Cellules Communistes Combattantes* (CCC) had declared itself responsible and criticized the 'grotesque fabrications' that had been reported in the media.[35] Furthermore, a few of the stolen firearms had turned up at hideouts used by the French left-wing terrorist group *Action Directe* in 1985 and 1987.[36]

From 2013 onwards a court in Luxembourg investigated a series of eighteen unsolved bombings between May 1984 and April 1986. Two members of the *Brigade mobile de la Gendarmerie*, an elite police unit, stood accused. Their alleged aim was to achieve increased funding for law enforcement. But it seems likely that the evidence was not sufficient for a successful conviction.[37] On 2 July 2014, the proceedings were suspended.[38] According to an alternative theory, the bombings – entirely directed against critical infrastructure like power poles or the radar at Findel airport – were a sort of psychological action aimed at a public that regarded the rearmament of the early 1980s too critically and therefore had to be re-convinced of the need to confront the Soviet threat.[39] Even the CIA's now declassified 'Terrorism Review' from early 1986 speculates that the bombers might be 'disgruntled civil servants who hold deep-seated grudges against the government'.[40]

In France, no clandestine actions were undertaken according to historian Charles Cogan: 'The network remained dormant, but was regularly kept up and trained. It was organized by a small team within *Service d' Action*,[41] and this very compartmented affair was known only to a very small number of people.'[42]

Things were different in neighbouring West Germany: between 1948 and 1954, the CIA organized several stay-behind networks in the southwest of West Germany and in West Berlin: LCPROWL, Kiebitz and Saturn. The latter was operated through the *Organisation Gehlen*, a forerunner of the West German foreign intelligence service *Bundesnachrichtendienst* (BND). LCPROWL APPARAT was the acronym for a large paramilitary asset – the Technischer Dienst (TD, verbatim 'Technical Service') of the right-wing *Bund Deutscher Jugend* (League of German Youth).[43] It became notorious for including former SS members and army officers with strong neo-Nazi connections.[44] For example, there is mounting evidence that the former Gestapo chief of Lyon, Klaus Barbie, who in 1948 spied on the Social Democratic Party (SPD) and the Communist Party (KPD), operated on behalf of the TD.[45] In order to provide intelligence in the event of a Soviet invasion, the stay-behind groups were equipped with buried radio sets, money and ammunition.[46]

A former TD member described how he received training from US instructors: 'The participants got American khaki-coloured fatigues, were only allowed to call each other by their forenames, and came from all over Germany, [...]. One was practically cut off from the outside world completely for four weeks. We learned to handle both American and Soviet weapons. Additionally, we received intensive political briefings and military instructions for the day "x".'[47] Planned for 7,000 members in the final phase of the build-up, the TD consisted one year after its approval in 1950 of 2,649 men and 55 officers.[48] But the organization was rendered useless already in 1952 after its unmasking in a high-profile public scandal, which was caused by a member who informed the police.[49]

Stay behind was, of course, not run solely by US intelligence. Former MI6 officer Anthony Cavendish revealed in his memoirs how he had managed the war planning activity in the British zone of West Berlin:

> In the event of Germany being overrun by war with the Russians, wireless sets, explosives and arms and ammunition were stashed all over Germany; both in the Soviet and the British zones, and in Berlin. Our agents in East Germany took their stores back piecemeal and these were then carefully hidden, generally underground but often in houses, barns or the other sort of places found secure by various resistance movements during the Second World War.

Cavendish's first priority was to cache a number of wireless telegraphy sets. He decided to bury them in the Grunewald (forest) of Berlin, which was in use for training exercises:

> We got the local Army workshops to fix up a jeep for us with RE [Royal Engineers] markings, and fit to it a large detachable spotlight with about twenty metres of cable. Dressed in civilian clothing, we reconnoitred the general areas during daytime, using as our excuse either a picnic or a birdwatching expedition, depending on the weather. When we located a suitable site we drew its position on large-scale map, adding the sorts of directions that would have done justice to *Treasure Island*. Four paces north of this oak, two paces west from large twin-pointed boulder, and so on.[50]

Overall, British stay-behind preparations comprised 1,000 partisans and over 400 tonnes of war material, which were shipped back to Great Britain during the 1990s. The whole programme was kept secret from both the West German army and the BND.[51]

When NSC-10/5 ('Scope and Pace of Covert Operations') of 23 October 1951 called for the development of resistance forces in areas under Soviet control, the CIA created stay-behind assets in East Germany[52] – 'clandestine operatives who would be equipped with radios and would remain inactive unless war actually came'. But these networks were rounded up in the wake of the 1953 riots in East Berlin. A subsequent analysis revealed that nearly all members of the various cells had known the identities of everyone else. Thus, the Soviets were able to arrest the entire operation after identifying one participant.[53] In 1951/2 the staunchly anti-communist and CIA-funded West German *Kampfgruppe gegen Unmenschlichkeit* (literally: 'Battlegroup against Injustice') had tried to develop structures from its own set of informers inside the German Democratic Republic (GDR) and was envisaged itself 'for resistance actions in event of a hot war', according to a CIA paper.[54]

In 1956, the numerous initiatives were taken over by the Stay Behind Organisation (SBO), effectively run by the BND.[55] There has been much speculation about a possible involvement of the SBO in the Munich Oktoberfest bombing of 1980, so far the bloodiest act of terrorism in recent German history.[56] The conclusion of the initial inquiry, which placed responsibility on a lone perpetrator, is contradicted by new evidence pointing to a group action of right-wing extremists. But experts like journalist Ulrich Chaussy, who investigated the Oktoberfest bombing since early on, caution against simply applying the Italian model of the 'strategy of tension' to the West German situation.[57]

A sober analysis of the inner workings of the US Army's stay-behind capability in West Germany can be found in James Stejskal's 2017 book *Special Forces Berlin: Clandestine Cold War Operations of the US Army's Elite, 1956-1990*. The retired officer and military historian provides a unique account of the inner working of *Security Platoon, Detachment 'A'*,[58] a select group of Special Forces soldiers, deployed in West Berlin from 1957 till 1990.[59] It was specifically tasked with counterterrorism and unconventional warfare, which included stay-behind missions to disrupt Warsaw Pact forces in their rear areas. Two teams would sabotage critical rail, road and canal infrastructure to delay a takeover of West Berlin. Four outside teams would slip across the Berlin Wall,[60] where they would collect and transmit intelligence as soon as hostilities began.[61] Furthermore, they would set out to organize escape and evasion 'ratlines' for downed pilots and to rally a guerrilla force among the civilian population. But according to Sejskal, planners never got that far: 'The few SF [Special Forces] men dedicated to the longer fight behind the lines were a small appendix to the main plan.'[62] Just like the CIA directed groups, *Detachment 'A'* established so-called Mission Support Sites throughout West Berlin. These caches contained 'sterile' weapons (9 mm Sten sub-machine guns and Walther P-38 pistols), ammunition, medical gear, C-3 plastic explosives, fuses and igniters. 'The teams carefully waterproofed the gear and then sealed it in special aluminium containers. Locations were chosen and cased in remote areas of the Allied zones including the Grunewald and Spandau forests, as well as in built-up or "urbanized" parts of the city.'[63]

Generally, each of NATO's stay-behind branches should be understood in its national context as there were great variations between the member states of the alliance. Black operations and human rights violations were more prevalent in some NATO countries than in others. In 1971, after a military coup, the Turkish offshoot *Kontrgerilla* (Counter-Guerrilla) was turned into an 'instrument of terror against the left'. During the 1980s, it found a new target: the militant Kurdistan Workers' Party (PKK), which it fought even after the dissolution of the Soviet Union.[64] Likewise the dictatorships in Southern Europe utilized their units for colonial warfare in Africa (Portugal) and for supressing dissent on a large scale (Spain, Greece). But the virulent anti-communism and the inherently repressive nature of these regimes differ from the situation in Northern and Western Europe and direct comparisons are therefore of limited value.

Assessing stay behind

In any case, the sketchy evidence available does not add up to support Ganser's central claim of a top-down Atlantic conspiracy. Scholar Olav Riste, who investigated the origins and development of Norwegian stay behind based on archival material,[65] points out that, cooperative links with British and American intelligence services notwithstanding, national control was a distinctive feature.[66] As Riste stresses, stay behind was a 'purely national responsibility': 'The plans were only to be put into effect after an enemy occupation of the country was an established fact, and the arrangement and control of the organisation was solely Norwegian business.'[67] Likewise, Dick Engelen concluded in his case study that 'the Dutch stay behind capacity would only report to a Dutch government in freedom, and never be subordinated to allied command, NATO or otherwise'.[68] Far from being controlled by the dominant Western powers, the respective stay-behind forces 'retained in every way their independence and national control even as they cooperated with and received advice and assistance from allies'.[69] All parties involved refrained from interference 'beyond attempts at coordination and joint planning that was mutually advantageous'.[70] Approximately in 1952, the Clandestine Planning Committee (CPC) was formed. Linked to NATO's Supreme Headquarters Allied Powers Europe, it coordinated the various stay-behind programmes run by the national intelligence services. The Allied Clandestine Committee (ACC) was founded in 1958 to relieve the CPC of some of its tasks. It was a 'technical organ', bringing the representatives of the various national stay-behind organizations in contact with each other. The ACC received directives from the CPC and had to organize international training exercises.[71] As veteran Thomas Polgar put it: 'They would meet every couple of months in different capitals, have wonderful lunches and discuss having compatible communications equipment, I.D. procedures, codes, food and, if the Russians advance, [ways] to overcome bureaucratic barriers to take people across borders [escape and evasion]. Each national service did it with varying degrees of intensity.' Polgar, who was CIA station chief in West Germany in the late 1970s, recalled: 'I don't think anybody took this very seriously. [...] I think a lot of the American taxpayer's money was sunk into the ground, as well as the German taxpayer's money and Italian taxpayer's money.'[72]

The exact figures may be disputed, but in regard to personnel, stay behind remained a small affair – that's why the popular term 'NATO's secret armies' is all but misleading. A former CIA officer told journalist Jonathan Kwittny: 'The more people who were involved, the worse your security would be.'[73] But there were also shortcomings in recruitment. For example, on paper, the Swiss *P-26* network consisted of roughly 800 cadres during the 1980s, but never reached that ambitious target. Instead, only between 250 and 300 members would have formed the resistance organization, if it had been activated.[74] Even in case of a major frontline state like West Germany, at the end of the 1950s stay behind was comprised of 500 intelligence assets, but had only seventy-five full-time members.[75] During the following decades, the numbers dropped further. In 1979, the network counted eighty-five agents. Only forty-six of them were equipped with modern radio sets.[76] During this period, in the 1970s and 1980s, stay behind had lost its significance: 'The "action" part of their mission, and especially sabotage and other forms of paramilitary parts of their activities, were eliminated or at least strictly curtailed – or passed on to each country's special forces.' Already by around 1970, the Belgian government decided 'definitively to abandon the sabotage mission'.[77] In 1979, the West German SBO eighty-one-strong reconnaissance and sabotage unit (*Lehr- and Ausbildungsgruppe für das Fernspähwesen*,) was dissolved.[78] When Wolbert Smidt took charge of SBO in the early 1980s, he came across an essentially outdated institution, which was still characterized by diehard Cold War ideology. Whereas stay behind had not evolved, NATO strategy had been radically revised: 'There would have been no large stay behind area [Überrollgebiet], because NATO assumed that once it could not withhold an attack near the border conventionally, it would employ artillery – and short-range rockets to destroy armoured enemy units nuclearly – and thereby naturally killing also its own stay behind organization.'[79] This growing irrelevance further expressed itself in the fact that although the ACC held meetings once a year and its subcommittee two or three times a year until 1987, stay-behind activity was mainly composed of joint exercises in cross-border infiltration and exfiltration of agents.[80]

The majority of documents concerning this late period of stay behind's history is still classified and an assessment thus difficult. However, one pool of primary sources exists and presents the subject from an alternative viewpoint: the East German Ministry for State Security (MfS), commonly known as 'Stasi', was well informed about the stay-behind activities on the part of the BND. Besides many high placed agents in the NATO apparatus, the MfS signal intelligence unit had managed to decode approximately 18 per cent of 16,000 messages sent from the BND to its stay-behind agents between 1976 and 1987. Based on this information, the MfS identified twenty-nine different receivers and recognized nine groups of agents with a main operational focus on Southern Germany.[81] This meant that in case of armed conflict, a substantial part of the SBO would have been in sight of the enemy from the outset.[82]

The MfS also analysed the SBO's assignment in detail:

Observation of all troop movements within the respective area – with special attention to details like

> nationality of the enemy troops,
> used fighting equipment
> information about quantity and mobility of fighting equipment

registration and reporting of the public's mood and morale
clearing and compiling of dead letter boxes
realisation of preparation measures for airborne-landings of individuals and small groups behind enemy lines. Thereby stay behind agents realise activities like

- placing light signals
- receipting of dropped persons and materials
- shunting of persons and material to predestined spots [...]

realisation of sabotage actions in enemy hinterland
securing connections, basically the radio connection with the BND. Stay behind agents are an important liaison link between the BND and autonomous groups (sabotage commandos et al.), who operate in the operational area of the stay behind agent.

The MfS remarked that personnel generally was composed of both male and female West German citizens:

They live on the territory of the FRG [Federal Republic of Germany], along the border with the GDR and the CSSR [Czechoslovakia]. They act as individuals or in groups of three to four people. Within that group, they know each other or in one case are related. [...]. Stay behind agents are capable of moving relatively free in the operational area even in case of a military occupation. Tasks have to be completed within a distance of 40 km from the residence.[83]

The numbers provided by the MfS material once again disprove the narrative of 'secret armies' put in place. Yet, in the absence of contextualizing Western sources, the picture of stay behind during this period is far from complete.

In contrast, the earlier years are better understood today. Recent research puts stay behind firmly in the context of the Cold War. Its raison d'être stemmed from the trauma of the German invasion of Western Europe during the Second World War and the initially costly build-up of anti-fascist resistance. In the face of a new threat from the Soviet Union, Western governments feared that their countries would again be vulnerable: 'This time they were determined to prepare as best they could, avoid the mistakes that had decimated their inexperienced wartime resistance groups, and seek assistance from allies willing and able to help.'[84]

The blueprint to achieve these aims was provided by unconventional warfare developed on several Second World War fronts. One of the earliest models for stay behind were the British Auxiliary Units established in early summer 1940 against a looming invasion: 'Having been provided with firearms and explosives, and with development of skills in their use well under way, they were to stay behind in Operational Bases. Once the enemy has passed by, they would emerge, preferably at night, and commit mayhem among his armed forces. The objectives were both tactical and defensive.'[85] From 1940 on, the Special Operations Executive (SOE) conducted espionage, sabotage and reconnaissance in occupied Europe. Although dissolved in early 1946, the SOE's experience was drawn upon when stay behind was built. Personnel was employed by a Special Operations Branch of the Secret Intelligence Service, commonly known as MI6. Shortly after the war, veteran leaders of the SOE proposed that skeleton elements of underground resistance ought to be formed in the British-occupied zones of Germany and Austria.[86]

Precursors of stay behind were also noted on the Eastern front: in the wake of the German invasion of the Soviet Union in 1941, partisans introduced the means of leaving behind a network of sleeper agents, who would strike at key enemy installations and relay information back.[87] Likewise, in 1944 the SS formed the *Jagdverbände* – literally 'hunter units' – who were tasked with sabotage behind enemy lines and the nurture of anti-communist resistance forces in previously German-occupied territories.[88] In Germany itself, from 1944 on, the SS initiated *Unternehmen Werwolf* (Operation Werwolf) to organize a partisan force. Its mission was to assassinate 'defeatists' and hamper the Allied advance with sabotage and guerrilla attacks. Yet, the Werwolf groups were poorly led, armed and organized, and thus doomed to failure.[89] In 1951, the former commander of the SS-*Jagdverbände*, Otto Skorzeny, even drafted a war plan for the Western allies based on his knowledge. Therein he stressed the need for a cadre of saboteurs drawn from veterans of his units:

> In order to hold off strong enemy forces in the West and in Eastern Europe, it will be necessary to develop, within enemy territory, military action concentrated against defined objectives. These specific objectives include the nerve centers and especially the supply points of the enemy forces, their communications and their munitions plants. The targets for such military undertakings on the part of the commando forces would be specific industries such as for example, ammunition factories, oil refineries, steel mills blast-furnaces, uranium mines, explosive factories, munition dumps, strategic bridges, power plants, etc.[90]

While the 'Skorzeny plan' was eventually discarded, stay behind was, indeed, reintroduced as a vital component for waging the Third World War. It came into play as a means of training and equipping of small networks for the eventuality of a Soviet invasion and a general retreat of the Western allies – in this situation, the agents would literally 'stay behind' in occupied territory to conduct sabotage and organize the escape and evasion of VIPs, downed pilots or informants. Additionally, stay-behind personnel would act as instructors and recruiters of local partisan units or, if these already existed, liaison with them.[91] They would also collect intelligence and transmit it via clandestine radio sets previously buried in waterproof containers. Already in 1978, former CIA director William Colby, who had organized stay behind in Scandinavia in the early 1950s,[92] revealed a great deal on the programme. In contrast to earlier wartime operations, this time 'we intended to have that resistance capability in place before the occupation, indeed before an invasion; we were determined to organize and supply it now, while we still had the time in which to do it right, and at minimum risk'. The 'stay-behind nets' were put in place throughout those Western European countries 'that seemed likely for Soviet attack'. According to Colby that meant 'clandestine infrastructures of leaders and equipment trained and ready to be called into action as sabotage and espionage forces when the time came'.[93]

Case study: Stay behind in Austria

Post-war Austria is a vivid example illustrating both stay-behind's purpose and initial layout. The examination presented in the remaining section of this chapter is based on documents released from 1998 onwards under the *Nazi War Crimes Disclosure Act*. Although Austria declared itself neutral to gain full sovereignty in 1955 and was not a member of the NATO alliance, stay behind was introduced in 1948/9, when the country was still under occupation. Thus, as a front-line state, Austria was among the first arenas where such structures were implemented by both the CIA and British intelligence. This was done with the knowledge and consent of many high-ranking government officials, yet under the utmost secrecy. Fritz Molden, a close assistant to Foreign Minister Karl Gruber (in office from 1945 to 1953) and son-in-law of CIA director Allen Dulles, stated in 1996 that the programme had, in fact, been instigated by Austria: 'It was part of a broad-based resistance strategy in case of a Soviet occupation and was initiated in a top-secret operation by the Austrian government.' Richard Helms, who acted as chief of CIA Special Operations in the early 1950s, has also revealed: 'What the Americans have done here was highly welcome to the Austrian government. The government was not only informed of the arms caches but also ... of the stay behind operations.'[94]

In general terms, stay behind had been assigned a high priority in Allied war planning and preparations. It would counterbalance conventional weaknesses – since between 1945 and 1951, a withdrawal from continental Europe was expected, followed by a phase of strategic air war and re-conquest of lost territory. Guerrilla and partisan warfare would slow the Soviet advance and buy time for the build-up to a final counteroffensive.[95] In terms of practical implementation, in December 1949 the CIA started a broad guerrilla training programme codenamed *Easeful*, for which the US Army contributed weapons, logistics, instructors and training sites.[96] As mentioned, following the foundation of NATO (1949) stay behind was put in place in all member states, as well as in neutral Switzerland, Finland, Sweden and Austria.[97] However, this happened in different ways, as Colby described in his memoirs: in allied countries, the governments themselves would build their own nets and coordinate them with NATO's plans. In neutral countries like Austria, 'CIA would have to do the job alone or with, at best, "unofficial" local help, since the politics of those governments barred them from collaborating with NATO, and any exposure would arouse immediate protest'.[98]

The creation of stay behind *was* conditioned by the overall strategic context of the early Cold War, a period of severe tensions between the former allies of the Second World War. From a Western viewpoint, the communist takeovers in Czechoslovakia and Hungary (1947/8), the Berlin blockade and the split between Tito and Stalin (1948), the loss of the Western nuclear monopoly (1949) and the Korean War (1950–3) confirmed the widespread perception of an imminent threat.

In Austria, where the power blocs were directly opposing each other, a supposed communist putsch in October 1950 and a possible separation of the country along the demarcation line contributed to the uncertainty. As the former US intelligence officer James Milano, who was stationed in post-war Austria, states in his memoir, the Western allies felt increasingly vulnerable: 'Soviet troops occupied about a third of the country: the zone of occupation completely surrounded the capital. The southern borders of Austria were flanked by Yugoslavia, which was still a member of the Soviet alliance, and by Communist Hungary. After the coup in Czechoslovakia, the north-eastern border was in the hands of the enemy.'[99]

Nevertheless, Austria played only a peripheral role for the allies: the main priority was to counter a possible breakthrough of the Red Army towards the Atlantic. A forcible defence of Austria beyond the Alps was not considered a feasible option.[100] The so-called Pilgrim plans called for a strategic withdrawal of British and French troops to Western Italy or Triest if the Red Army were to advance via Austria or Yugoslavia. Therefore, until a counteroffensive could be mounted, guerrilla and partisan units would be activated in the occupied territories.[101]

For this purpose, weapons caches were installed by British Special Forces between 1950 and 1954 in the southern Austrian province of Carinthia and a single one on the outskirts of Vienna in wooded terrain.[102] In 1952, former Royal Marine Simon Preston was among four soldiers taking part in stay-behind operations in Austria. Their mission was to set up six arms caches.[103] In 1996, Preston told author Michael Smith:

> We spent a lot of our time up in the mountains, learning all about the terrain, learning German, meeting other potential agents, recruiting agents if possible, identifying and plotting dropping zones. The whole object was that we would all form the nucleus of a partisan or a guerrilla army should the Russians invade. It was thought that within five years there would be a conventional war. We would be dropped back into the area we knew and immediately we would be among friends. The food, arms and explosives would be all there in the bunkers.

Yet Preston had no illusions about his chances of survival: 'It doesn't take much imagination to work out that the Russian Army would have hunted us from pillar to post. It would have been a short but interesting life I suspect. But I can't remember worrying about that.'[104] At the end of the 1950s and in the early 1960s most of the British caches had been detected and plundered. When the Austrian army's intelligence branch investigated the incidents in 1965, it concluded: 'These depots had the purpose of supplying local resistance forces behind enemy lines or agents dropped by plane with the necessary equipment for the setup of partisan- and underground-movements after those areas had been evacuated.'[105]

The already mentioned MI6 officer Anthony Cavendish had been transferred from West Berlin to Vienna in 1951. Again, he was charged with arranging caches of supplies for stay-behind personnel, this time in the Russian zone in Lower Austria. Cavendish purchased a large second-hand Chevrolet, changed the plates, took it to a garage and fitted 'a false boot within the enormous boot that American cars then had'. Then a secret compartment was placed behind that boot: 'When finished the compartment was approximately three and a half by one and a half by one and a half feet, so the car had to make three or four journeys for each cache.' When the job was done, the car was returned to its 'pristine' state and even sold for a profit.[106]

Yet, the American effort easily surpassed the British efforts. Between 1949 and 1954, seventy-nine weapons caches were installed, most of them in the US occupation zone. Sixty-five of these depots were recovered after US ambassador Swanee Hunt officially informed the Austrian government of their existence in 1996. They comprised 300 pistols, 50 anti-tank grenade launchers, 250 carabiners, 270 machine pistols, 65 machine guns, 20 silencer pistols, 2,700 hand grenades, 230,000 rounds of ammunition, 1,150 armour piercing shells and 3,400 kilograms of explosives. According to an official report by an Austrian government commission, in most of the caches manuals for guerrilla warfare in German were found as well as landing spotlights, Welrod silenced pistols, combat knives, and 'plenty' of explosives: 'This implies that the caches were also put in place for Austrian resistance fighters. Its purpose was to support a guerrilla war with eventual air support (supply of weapons and gear).' The exact function of the caches, as well as a possible Austrian involvement, could not be specified by the commission, since the documents provided by the US government only referred to the location and the content of the depots. The enlisted historians reached the conclusion that the arrangement of the caches correlated 'with concrete US plans for a withdrawal from Austria in case of a direct confrontation'.[107]

In 2006 John F. Richardson published an investigative memoir about his father, John ('Jocko') Richardson, who had been CIA station chief in Vienna between 1948 and 1952. In this book, the practicalities are described as follows:

> Jocko and his team concentrated on developing a stay-behind program, recruiting Austrian radio operators and sealing transmitters in gasoline cans, burying them at selected spots just inside the Soviet lines through the Vienna woods. Nater [Jean Nater, a co-worker from the CIA station] and a few others volunteered to stay behind and walk out after a Soviet invasion, and Jocko authorised the proper gear. Austrian mountain boots made to measure, rucksacks and Austrian clothing, dirndls for the women. [...] They also made plans to train and equip a core of resistance fighters, burying weapons in the forests. Every so often a gardener or game warden uncovered a cache, but the Austrian government never got very excited.[108]

CIA records concerning this specific *Operation Iceberg* were finally made available through the *Nazi War Crimes Disclosure Act*. Starting in the spring of 1948, fourteen SSTR-1-units ['Suitcase Radio'] as well as signal plans, ciphers, and generators were buried in Western Austria, mostly in the Vienna woods. Four additional SSTR-1-units were given to the CIA station in Salzburg for the same purpose.[109] The programme was initiated at a time of crisis in Central Europe, when the outbreak of hostilities 'appeared to be imminent'.[110] As a monthly progress report from February

1949 states, the implementation of *Operation Iceberg* was rash and improvised: 'It is clear that, had Austria been overwhelmed by the Soviets at or shortly after the imposition of the Berlin blockade, our W/T [Wireless/Telegraphy] efforts would have been entirely inadequate. Security considerations have been responsible for our painful slowness in acquiring W/T operators.'[111] A short undated internal note also expresses frustration about *Operation Iceberg*'s slow progress:

> We were under extreme pressure to develop this program as long as the Berlin crisis was current. We shall be under similar pressure should another such crisis occur. [...] Should we be forced out of Austria without leaving adequate W/T networks behind, the organisation as a whole and the station in particular would be liable to extreme and justifiable censure.[112]

Only by 1953, six Austrian radio operators with wartime experience had largely finished their training and had been fully briefed. In the event of an actual invasion and the loss of Eastern Austria (Vienna and the Soviet-occupied zone), the recruited Austrian stay-behind agents were supposed to get in contact with the allies and transmit information – concerning military, political and economic matters – but were not expected to engage in sabotage and resistance acts. They were assigned the following targets for intelligence collection:

- 'Road and rail movements on the secondary route from Wiener Neustadt to Graz via Aspang and perhaps observation of the main Wiener Neustadt-Kapfenberg route through the Semmering Pass.
- Observation of Wiener Neustadt airfield. [...]
- Operational intelligence on document, travel, and mail controls. [...]
- Political and economic information overtly available in the area.
- Small amount of industrial intelligence on Wiener Neustadt
- Political intelligence on the KPOe [Communist Party of Austria] and the puppet government – personalities, organization, policies and intentions as known to him through his position as a KPOe functionary in Vienna.
- Observation of OB [operational base] and bomb damage in Vienna.'[113]

One of the agents was a twenty-six-year-old medical student at Vienna University, who had served as a private in the German infantry during 1945. Assessing his personality, the CIA handlers remarked:

> 6 is a very quiet, introverted type. He leads practically no social life, but spends all his time either studying or helping his parents in their milk shop. [...] He does not enjoy dealing with people, giving cover stories, and the like. He appears to be a slow, methodical thinker, and has not done particularly well in his medical studies. Although lacking the drive and outgoing personality which are desirable, he appears strong on reliability. He has been brought up with a strong Catholic, bourgeois morality which should hold him firmly in the anti-Communist camp.[114]

A more promising candidate was a forty-six-year-old former Master Sergeant, who had already been recruited for an 'American-sponsored Austrian resistance group' in 1952: 'He is truly the "little gray man" type who never attracts any attention to himself. He cannot be considered a member of the bourgeoisie and possesses no property the Soviets might desire to confiscate. His knowledge of radio repair work and the fact that he has frequent American customers (although never American social contacts) could conceivably be a source of Soviet suspicion.'[115]

According to an earlier document from 1951, the CIA aimed to cooperate with the Austrian authorities in exchange for financial and material help: 'Equipment for another 10 circuits, using SSTR-1's, and other material assistance, may be placed at the disposal of the Austrian Ministry of Interior for stay-behind operations directed by this Agency if a mutually satisfactory agreement can be reached. The Austrian political situation has not yet reached the point where Austrian officials can be approached. Preparatory discussions have been held.'[116] In regard to equipment at this stage, a small quantity of medical supplies had been handed out to a particular agent:

> At last report, the station was planning to prepare packets of tinned food, clothing, and medical supplies to be held for issuance at the time of an emergency. [...] Required: An as yet indeterminate amount of medical supplies, tinned food, clothing and other items to be cached by stay-behind networks, to be secured on the local economy from non-American origin, including bicycles or motorbikes, skiing and climbing equipment and small arms and ammunition of European origin for active stay-behind personnel.[117]

All stay-behind activities in Austria were combined under the code name GRCROOND. The aim was to develop and strengthen the Austrian paramilitary programme along the following lines:

> To develop the existing and potential paramilitary assets of 1) a labour union having assets situated throughout Central and Eastern Austria, 2) detached indigenous groups in the Salzburg-Tirol areas, and 3) individual assets (indigenous) located throughout Austria; to select and cache-equip suitable operational bases from which these groups may operate during hostilities; to establish an evasion and escape line from Eastern to Western Austria with feeder lines from the Czech and Hungarian borders and connecting links to the Swiss, Italian and German borders.[118]

From the early 1950s on, the mentioned labour organization operated under the cover of the *Österreichischer Wander-, Sport- und Geselligkeitsverein* (OWSGV, literally: Austrian hiking, sports and social club). Its leader was the later union leader and minister of the interior, Franz Olah (in office from 1963 to 1964). In his memoir, he explained that the OWSGV had installed communication centres in several regions of Austria as well as an arms store in a trade union office in Vienna. 'Two or three' arms caches had been established in Western Austria, outside the

Soviet zone. 'Special units' were trained in judo, and in the use of weapons and plastic explosives.[119] The latter had 'no legitimate use in sports- or labor organizing, even in the most bitterly-fought contests. Its function could only be sabotage and guerrilla warfare', US historian Christopher Simpson noted.[120] According to Olah, 'there must have been a couple of thousand people working for us. [...] Only very, very highly positioned politicians and some members of the union knew about it.'[121] The mission of the OWSGV was twofold: it would be activated against a Red Army invasion or as a 'systematic defence force' in the event of a renewed coup attempt by the Austrian communists.[122] Financing of the OWSGV came from the CIA and the anti-Communist American Federation of Labor and Congress of Industrial Organizations (AFL–CIO).[123]

The CIA placed its trust in Olah and his organization, codenamed GRDAGGER, and had high expectations: 'The Principal Agent's organisation has a completely valid peacetime *raison d'être*, a cordial relationship with powerful elements in the Government, and a legitimate anti-Communist [cause?] which provides motivation and "cover" for much of the work done in KUBARK's [cryptonym for the CIA itself] interest. Moreover, the Principal Agent has strong political reasons for desiring to make a name for himself as a resistance leader if war should come.'[124] By the end of 1955, GRDAGGER consisted of twenty people, who the CIA expected to form an immediate wartime nucleus for guerrilla warfare: 'We estimate that the GRDAGGER organization will expand to approximately 250 persons six months after war starts. GRDAGGER is formed of members of an SPOe [Social Democratic Party of Austria] oriented trade union of 40,000 members, many of whom can be considered as potential candidates for resistance groups in time of war.'[125]

When Austria gained full sovereignty on 15 May 1955, the CIA began discussions with Olah regarding the future of the programme – 'strong arm squads' were no longer seen as necessary, because of the 'improbability of a Communist putsch or Communist demonstrations of significance'. Nonetheless, the paramilitary assets of GRDAGGER were to be maintained because of the continuing 'possibility of Soviet aggression'. Furthermore, the CIA was willing to grant Olah's organization the 'responsibility for sabotage of targets which would repel Soviet forces in the event of aggression'. While six agents would be given training each year, GRDAGGER would also be utilized 'to a greater extent to combat Communist Party activity in Austria'.[126]

Despite the fact that Austria declared itself permanently neutral on 26 October 1955, stay-behind operations continued. A CIA document from 1957 lists the number of secret weapons and equipment caches that had been installed up to this point: twelve (1951), fourteen (1952), three (1953) and thirty-five (1954).[127] During 1955, a further twelve sabotage and ten 'air-reception' caches were planned to be set up.[128] Austrian stay-behind agents even received training from US experts in guerrilla and partisan warfare. From 1953 onwards, the 10th Special Forces Group was stationed in Bad Toelz in Bavaria. In early 1962, its commander agreed to organize a one-week course for selected Austrians. The training covered various subjects:

a. Weapons familiarization, including firing those weapons that could be expected to be employed in the agent's area. b. Demolitions, to cover the placement and handling of various types of explosives. Live shots will be conducted. c. Land navigation, to include map reading and compass manipulation. d. Air supply, to include the selection of LZ's [Landing Zones] and DZ's [Drop Zones] leading up to and including a live drop. e. Fundamental survival adapted for alpine regions.[129]

Agent GRBLAMED-31, who undertook the training between 20 and 27 August 1962, turned out to be 'an apt and diligent student': 'His week with the 10th Special Forces not only bolstered his self-confidence, but increased his confidence in our ability and intentions to be of service to him and his country.'[130] When agent GRIMPASTE took the course in May 1962, his survival training included the preparation and cooking of a live rabbit – but as a CIA dispatch noted, when the same fate was planned for a chicken, 'it leapt from the box and rapidly departed the area with a guerrilla fighting Special Forces sergeant in hot pursuit with axe in hand. The chicken won!'[131]

A status report from 1958 lists eighteen agents recruited for the Austrian stay-behind programme: the youngest was thirty, and the oldest, fifty-eight. It was a mixed lot: two skiing instructors, a medical doctor, the business manager of an automobile dealership, an English teacher, an assistant to a law professor, an electrician, a foreman, a chauffeur, a trade-school instructor, a warehouse keeper, two officials in the county government and three local politicians from the conservative party. The latter were of particular importance to the CIA: the forty-year-old agent GRREPAIR-7 was a municipal secretary, chief of the local Farmers Exchange Association, president of the Veterans Association, and an insurance salesman. 'Under the Communists he might be arrested as an "Enemy of the People", but more likely would simply be removed from his official positions', the CIA noted. In the event of war, it was expected that GRREPAIR-7 would quickly recruit and organize those individuals he had previously identified for wartime activities. He would carry out instructions, 'which may include obtaining and transmitting information on particular targets, recruiting additional agents for specific purposes, organizing and directing sabotage and guerrilla activities'. Not everybody was of great use to the CIA: the English teacher, for example, demonstrated 'little apparent interest' in clandestine activity and progressed slowly in training: 'His motivation seems to consist of a desire to work against Communism, maintain cultural contact with English-speaking persons (probably for professional reasons) and gain some financial remuneration.'[132]

As in West Germany, stay-behind personnel also included former members of the Nazi intelligence services and the Waffen SS: by 1948/9, the US Army's Counterintelligence Corps (CIC) had recruited Wilhelm Höttl, a high-ranking officer from the SS, to build up networks for intelligence collection in Hungary and the Soviet zone of Austria – 'network Montgomery' trained a cadre of several dozen Hungarian refugees for guerrilla warfare, while 'network Mount Vernon' would have acted as an 'anti-bolshevist underground movement' in the event of war.[133] But Höttl's networks were dissolved in 1949 since their output was often 'pedestrian, sometimes dead wrong, and occasionally even bogus'.[134] Although the CIA severed its ties to Höttl in 1953, because he was allegedly part of a Soviet spy ring, he was later contacted again to use his connections for the recruitment of 'reliable patriots' as radio operators.[135] In 1996, Höttl recalled: 'I knew about them [arms caches] but really the Americans were looking for local people to bury the weapons, guns and grenades, because they knew the best places.' Since former SS men were 'confirmed anti-Communists', US intelligence 'felt they could be relied on to fight the Russians'.[136]

Despite the availability of new documents, the full history of Austrian stay behind is still elusive – mostly because Olah, who had to resign as interior minister in 1964 and stood trial for corruption in 1969, had ordered the destruction of all records on the OWSGV. This force was finally dissolved in 1967. Since the Soviet invasion of Hungary (1956) had again instilled fears, it had been disbanded only over a lengthy period.[137] What is now clear though is that stay behind was a project of both the Western allies and the Austrian authorities – yet there is no evidence so far that neutral Austria was a formal member of NATO's stay-behind framework. Rather, the country's elites shared the same determination as those in other Western European nations to not experience the humiliation of an unopposed invasion again. Contrary to the annexation of 1938, this time there would be resistance. As Fritz Molden stated: 'It was clear for us, that in such a case we would have had to resist. We had to set an example.'[138]

Conclusion

Ganser concludes that the 'secret armies', in addition to their military function, were 'also a source of terror' and that this feature 'will need more investigation and research' in the future. But for him the available evidence already allows the conclusion:

> The White House and Downing Street feared that in several countries of Western Europe, [...] the Communists might reach positions of influence in the executive [branch] and destroy the military alliance of NATO from within by betraying military secrets to the Soviet Union. It was in this sense that the Pentagon in Washington, together with the CIA, MI6, and NATO, set up and operated stay-behind armies in a secret war as an instrument to manipulate and control the democracies of Western Europe from within, unknown to both European populations and parliaments. This strategy led to terror and fear.[139]

This quotation exemplifies the conspiratorial angle of 'NATO's secret armies', making far-reaching claims based on selected pieces of evidence while neglecting context or contradictory information. As laid out in this article, evidence of an active and controlled involvement of stay behind in terrorism concerns mainly cases like Italy, Belgium and military dictatorships such as Turkey, Portugal, Greece and Spain. But even in Italy, which was most affected by right-wing violence and related deception by the intelligence services, no direct link between *Gladio* and terrorism has been established.

The picture that has now emerged is far more complex, and as more disturbing facts on the connections between right-wingers and state forces come to light, they indeed paint a picture of anti-communist paranoia and a willingness to go beyond legal means. However, these insights should be cautiously contextualized and not fed into the fixed framework of a transatlantic conspiracy. No doubt, there remains a need for much further research into this ambiguous era in recent European history. Yet, as the example of post-war Austria has shown, stay behind was essentially a matter of unconventional warfare. Therein also lies its newfound relevancy in the wake of the Russian occupation of Crimea (2014) and the resulting Ukrainian civil war.[140]

Notes

1 A bibliography of the main research on *stay behind* includes Leo Müller (ed.), *Gladio – das Erbe des kalten Krieges: Der Nato-Geheimbund und sein deutscher Vorläufer* (Reinbek bei Hamburg: Rowohlt, 1991); Jens Mecklenburg (ed.), *Gladio: Die geheime Terrororganisation der NATO* (Berlin: Elefantenpress, 1997); Olav Riste, *The Norwegian Intelligence Service 1945-1970* (London: Frank Cass, 1999); Daniele Ganser, *NATO's Secret Armies: Operation Gladio and Terrorism in Western Europe* (London: Frank Cass, 2005); Daniele Ganser, Terrorism in Western Europe: An Approach to NATO's Secret Stay-Behind Armies, *The Whitehead Journal of Diplomacy and International Relations* 6/1 (2005), 69–97; Daniele Ganser, The Ghost of Machiavelli: An approach to Operation Gladio and terrorism in Cold War Italy, *Crime, Law & Social Change* 45/2 (2006), 111–154; Leopoldo Nuti and Olav Riste (eds.), Special Section: Preparing for a Soviet Occupation: The Strategy of 'Stay-Behind', *Journal of Strategic Studies* 30/6 (2007), 929–1024; Tobias von Heymann, *Die Oktoberfest-Bombe: München, 26. September 1980* (Berlin: Nora, 2008); Olav Riste, 'Stay Behind': A Clandestine Cold War Phenomenon, *Journal of Cold War Studies* 16/4 (2014), 35–59; Erich Schmidt-Eenboom and Ulrich Stoll, *Die Partisanen der NATO: Stay-Behind-Organisationen in Deutschland 1946-1991* (Berlin: Ch. Links, 2015); Gérard Desmaretz, *Stay-behind: Les réseaux secrets de la guerre froide* (Paris: Editions Jourdan, 2015); Michael Wala, Stay-behind Operations, Former Members of SS and Wehrmacht, and American Intelligence Services in Early Cold War Germany, *Journal of Intelligence History* 15/2 (2016), 71–79; Agilof Keßelring, *Die Organisation Gehlen und die Neuformierung des Militärs in der Bundesrepublik* (Berlin: Ch. Links, 2017); Titus J. Meier, *Widerstandsvorbereitungen für den Besetzungsfall: Die Schweiz im Kalten Krieg* (Zürich: NZZ Libro, 2018).

2 Despite their neutrality, Austria, Finland, Sweden and Switzerland prepared *stay-behind* measures. In comparison, little is known about the Finnish outfit, which was exposed already in June 1945. But its existence apparently dissuaded the Soviet Union and the revived Communist Party from attempting a coup. The Swedish network was established in 1946/47 and included in NATO's Northern Command in 1961. During the 1950s, it had counted about 200 members. See Ralf Lillbacka, The Murder

of Swedish Prime Minister Olof Palme: A Rebuttal of the 'Stay-Behind' Scenario, *Journal for Intelligence, Propaganda and Security Studies* 11/1 (2017), 112–25, 120–1. In Switzerland, first measures for organizing stay-behind resistance were taken between 1957 and 1965/66. In 1980/81, the so-called *Spezialdienst* (literally: 'Special Service') was dissolved in favour of a new unit codenamed *P-26*. Beziehungen zwischen der Organisation P-26 und analogen Organisationen im Ausland, Bericht an den Bundesrat, Neuenburg und Bern 1991, 9–10, https://www.newsd.admin.ch/newsd/message/attachments/52169.pdf (accessed 1 January 2020). *P-26* was one of the last stay-behind units raised and probably one of the most professionally designed. See Martin Matter, *P-26: Die Geheimarmee, die keine war: Wie Politik und Medien die Vorbereitung des Widerstands skandalisierten* (Baden: hier + jetzt, 2012), 28. In 2018, the Swiss Federal Council declassified a 1991 report on P-26, which also includes information on the role of NATO and on links of Swiss stay behind to other European organizations. The report details especially the 'relationship of trust' with the British secret service from 1967 on, with members of *P-26* travelling to the UK to learn sabotage tactics, including a practice run on how to blow up oil refineries. See George Mills, Switzerland Publishes Redacted Report on Top Secret Cold War Army, *The Local*, 26 April 2018, https://www.thelocal.ch/20180426/switzerland-publishes-redacted-report-on-top-secret-p26-cold-war-army (accessed 1 January 2020). In 2018, research by Titus J. Meier revealed many details on the inner workings of *P-26*: its members were mostly carefully selected civilians with military backgrounds. They were dominantly male (94.9 per cent), with only a little more than a dozen female participants. See Meier, *Widerstandsvorbereitungen*, 301. Recruits received instruction in intelligence matters, psychological warfare and pistol shooting. Radio operators and sappers got extra lessons, the later ones in handling explosives and sabotage actions (ibid., 318–21). But in peacetime, no member had access to weapons or explosives (ibid., 338). The whole undertaking cost the Swiss taxpayers 54.3 million francs between 1979 and 1990 (ibid., 353). According to Meier there is 'no evidence' for characterizing *P-26* as a 'secret army' since it had always remained a training outfit (ibid., 474).
3 Ganser, *Armies*, 2.
4 Ibid., 245–6.
5 Ibid., 247–8.
6 For example, the influential German nonfiction publisher Kopp jumped the bandwagon and distributed several 'Gladio' books. The common thread of these products is the mixture of scarcely available evidence with rumours and assumptions in order to underpin a firmly held opinion: that the United States uses *stay behind* to pursue its imperialistic agenda and does not hesitate to use false flag terrorism to manipulate public opinion. Generally, intelligence services are depicted as overly powerful forces, which stop at nothing to enforce the interests of Western elites. Generally, 'Stay behind' or 'Gladio' have become codewords for all kinds of alleged state-sponsored crimes, while becoming increasingly detached from their historical context and meaning.
7 Ganser, *Armies*, 234.
8 Misinformation about 'Gladio/Stay Behind' Networks Resurfaces, 20 January 2006, https://de.scribd.com/document/114855262/Misinformation-About-Gladio-Stay-Behind-Networks-Resurfaces (accessed 1 January 2020). In his 2020 history of disinformation and political warfare, Thomas Rid reached the conclusion that FM 30-31B was, in fact, "one of the KGB's most sophisticated and impactful forgeries", because it "provided a twisted but appealing rationale for why the CIA would secretly

engage in far-left terrorist attacks." See Thomas Rid, *Active Measures: The Secret History of Disinformation and Political Warfare* (New York: Profile Books, 2020), 233 and 236.
9. Ganser, The Ghost of Machiavelli, 139.
10. Leopoldo Nuti, The Italian 'Stay-Behind' Network – The Origins of 'Operation Gladio', *Journal of Strategic Studies* 30/6 (2007), 955–80, here 970.
11. Jack Greene and Alessandro Massignani, *The Black Prince and the Sea Devils: The Story of Valerio Borghese and the Elite Units of the Decima Mas* (Cambridge: Da Capo Press, 2004), 200–2.
12. In comparison, when stay-behind units were dissolved in the 1990s, sixty-five arms depots were recovered in Austria, fifty in Switzerland, twenty in the Netherlands and six in Belgium. See Markus Kemmerling, Kaltes Kriegsspielzeug, *Zoom: Zeitschrift für Politik und Gesellschaft* 4–5 (1996) ('Es muss nicht immer Gladio sein: Attentate, Waffenlager, Erinnerungslücken'), 6–9, here 9.
13. Ganser, The Ghost of Machiavelli, 121.
14. Ibid., 126.
15. Philip Willan, *Puppetmasters: The Political Use of Terrorism in Italy* (San Jose: Authors Choice Press, 2002), 153.
16. Nuti, 'Stay Behind', 977.
17. Alessandro Silj, *Verbrechen, Politik, Demokratie in Italien* (Frankfurt am Main: Suhrkamp, 1998), 118–25.
18. Anna Cento Bull, *Italian Neofascism: The Strategy of Tension and the Politics of Nonreconciliation* (New York: Berghahn Books, 2012), 71.
19. J. Patrice McSherry, *Predatory States: Operation Condor and Covert War in Latin America* (Lanham, MD: Rowman & Littlefield, 2005), 43.
20. Ibid., 61.
21. David Talbot, *The Devil's Chessboard: Allen Dulles, the CIA, and the Rise of America's Secret Government* (London: HarperCollins, 2016), 475.
22. Jeffrey M. Bale, *The Darkest Side of Politics, I: Postwar Fascism, Covert Operations and Terrorism* (London: Routledge, 2018), 177–8.
23. Italy Jails Far-right Militants for 1974 Brescia Bombing, *BBC News*, 23 July 2015, http://www.bbc.com/news/world-europe-33633872 (accessed 1 January 2020).
24. Oliver Meiler, Die Wahrheit ist schwer verdaulich, *Der Tagesanzeiger*, 24 July 2015.
25. Andrea Pasqualetto, Piazza Fontana, le carte segrete dei Servizi: 'In Sardegna esercitazioni con l'esplosivo prima dell'attentato', *Corriere della Serra*, 12 December 2019.
26. Ganser, *Armies*, 7.
27. Charles Maurice, *Insane Killers Inc.: The Brabant Killers Mystery* (Rayem Press, 2018), 197 and 201.
28. Ganser, *Armies*, 140.
29. Daniel Boffey, Deathbed Confession May Crack Case of the 'Crazy Brabant Killers", *The Guardian*, 24 October 2017, https://www.theguardian.com/world/2017/oct/24/deathbed-confession-may-crack-case-of-the-crazy-brabant-killers-belgian-gang (accessed 1 January 2020); Daniel Boffey, 'Crazy Brabant Killers': Ex-gendarme Arrested on Suspicion of Hiding Evidence, *Guardian*, 24 January 2019, https://www.theguardian.com/world/2019/jan/24/brabant-killers-ex-gendarme-arrested-on-suspicion-of-hiding-evidence (accessed 1 January 2020).
30. Maurice, *Killers*, 323.
31. Ibid., 228 and 322.
32. Ibid., 249.
33. Douglas de Connick, Auteur Guy Bouten: 'Ik weet wie de killer van de Bende van Nijvel was', *De Morgen*, 30 January 2020.

2. Gladio – *Myth and Reality*   37

34 Maurice, *Killers*, 148.
35 Dislaire, Stay Behind und die CCC, *Luxemburger Wort*, 4 May 2014.
36 Maurice, *Killers*, 149–50.
37 Cerstin Gammelin, 'Affäre Junker', *Süddeutsche Zeitung*, 27 January 2013.
38 Der Bommeleeër-Prozess geht in eine lange Pause, *Luxemburger Wort*, 3 July 2014.
39 Strategie der Spannung: Der internationale Kontext der Bommeleeër-Affäre, *Lëtzebuerger Journal*, April 2012, 34–45.
40 Terrorism Comes to Luxembourg, in Terrorism Review, CIA, 10 February 1986, https://www.cia.gov/library/readingroom/docs/CIA-RDP87T00685R000200320002-1.pdf (accessed 1 January 2020).
41 Service Action is a division of France's foreign intelligence service Direction Générale de la Sécurité Extérieure (DGSE) responsible for planning and executing covert operations.
42 Charles Cogan, 'Stay-Behind' in France: Much Ado About Nothing? *Journal of Strategic Studies* 30/6 (2007), 937–54, here 949.
43 Keßelring, *Organisation*, 276.
44 Timothy Naftali, New Information on Cold War CIA Stay-Behind Operations in Germany and on the Adolf Eichmann Case, http://fas.org/sgp/eprint/naftali.pdf (accessed 1 January 2020); Badis Ben Redjeb, The Central Intelligence Agency and the Stay-Behind Networks in West Germany: An Assessment, *British Journal of Humanities and Social Sciences* 14/2 (2016), 50–62.
45 Peter Hammerschmidt, *Deckname Adler: Klaus Barbie und die westlichen Geheimdienste* (Frankfurt am Main: S. Fischer, 2014), 116.
46 Naftali, New Information.
47 Dieter von Glahn, *Patriot und Partisan für Freiheit und Einheit* (Tübingen: Grabert, 1994), 47. Translation from German by the author.
48 Wala, Stay-behind Operations, 75.
49 Keßelring, *Organisation*, 277.
50 Anthony Cavendish, *Inside Intelligence* (London: Collins, 1990), 59–60.
51 Christoph Franceschini, Erich Schmidt-Eenboom and Thomas Wegener Friis, *Spionage unter Freunden: Partnerdienstbeziehungen und Westaufklärung der Organisation Gehlen und des BND* (Berlin: Ch. Links, 2017), 179.
52 In 1952, the CIA itself ran a small programme for sabotage and paramilitary activity inside the GDR (Project LCSTART). A further project (Temper) envisaged the instalment of escape and evasion networks and the creation of a nucleus for future resistance activities. Records on both projects are still classified. See Eenboom and Stoll, *Partisanen*, 67–8.
53 David E. Murphy, Sergei A. Kondrashev and George Bailey, *Battleground Berlin: CIA vs KGB in the Cold War* (New Haven: Yale University Press, 1997), 123–6.
54 Enrico Heitzer, *Die Kampfgruppe gegen Unmenschlichkeit (KgU): Widerstand und Spionage im Kalten Krieg 1948–1959* (Köln: Böhlau, 2015), 396.
55 Heymann, *Oktoberfest-Bombe*, 338–40.
56 Gunther Latsch, Die dunkle Seite des Westens, *Der Spiegel*, 11 April 2005, 48–9.
57 Reinhard Jellen, Ulrich Chaussy uber das Oktoberfest-Attentat und die NSU-Mordserie, *telepolis*, 26 September 2014, http://www.heise.de/tp/artikel/42/42857/1.html (accessed 1 January 2020).
58 Because of operational security concerns, Detachment 'A' was inactivated in 1984 and re-setup as 'Physical Security Support Element-Berlin' (PSSE-Berlin). Overall, some fifty 'A' teams from the 10th Special Forces Group at Bad Tölz were allocated to conduct unconventional warfare operation in West Germany and Eastern Europe.

See James Stejskal, *Special Forces Berlin: Clandestine Cold War Operations of the US Army's Elite, 1956–1990* (Philadelphia: Casemate, 2017), 26, 227.
59 Ibid., X.
60 Ibid., 26–7, 196.
61 Ibid., 224.
62 Ibid., 244.
63 Ibid., 35.
64 Lucy Komisar, Turkey's Terrorists: A CIA Legacy, *The Progressive*, April 1997, 24–7.
65 See Riste, *Intelligence*.
66 Olav Riste, With an Eye to History: The Origins and Development of 'Stay-Behind' in Norway, *Journal of Strategic Studies* 30/6 (2007), 997–1024, here 997.
67 Riste, *Intelligence*, 48.
68 Dick Engelen, Lessons learned: The Dutch 'Stay-Behind' Organization 1945–1992, *Journal of Strategic Studies* 30/6 (2007), 981–96, here 995.
69 Riste, 'Stay Behind', 58.
70 Ibid., 56.
71 Beziehungen zwischen der Organisation P-26 und analogen Organisationen im Ausland, Bericht an den Bundesrat, 21–3.
72 Jonathan Kwitny, The CIA's Secret Armies in Europe, *The Nation*, 6 April 1992.
73 Ibid.
74 Meier, *Widerstandsvorbereitungen*, 298.
75 Eenboom and Stoll, *Partisanen*, 142–3.
76 Ibid., 179.
77 Riste, 'Stay Behind', 56–7.
78 Eenboom and Stoll, *Partisanen*, 162–8.
79 Radio Feature 'Geheimarmee Stay Behind: Der Staat als Pate des Terrors? Eine Spurensuche von Ulrich Chaussy', BR/WDR, 5–6 October 2014 (manuscript). Translation from German by the author.
80 Eenboom and Stoll, *Partisanen*, 182–5.
81 Sachstandsbericht über Analyseergebnisse zum Funkverbindungssystem der in der BRD dislozierten Überrollagenten des Bundesnachrichtendienstes, Stand: 31. 12. 1987, in Die Behörde des Bundesbeauftragten (BStU), MfS – HA III Nr. 8117, 1–20, 3–4. Translation from German by the author.
82 Heymann, *Oktoberfest-Bombe*, 365.
83 Sachstandbericht über eine spezielle Agentenart des Bundesnachrichtendienstes (BND), in BStU, MfS XV 3040/80, AOP 22087/91, 46–73, 49–51. Translation from German by the author.
84 Riste, 'Stay Behind', 50.
85 John Warwicker, *Churchill's Underground Army: A History of the Auxiliary Units in World War II* (London: Frontline Books, 2008), 81.
86 Riste, 'Stay Behind', 41.
87 Eenboom and Stoll, *Partisanen*, 15.
88 Perry Biddiscombe, *The SS Hunter Battalions: The Hidden History of the Nazi Resistance Movement 1944–45* (Stroud: The History Press, 2006), 33.
89 Perry Biddiscombe, *The Last Nazis: SS Werewolf Guerilla Resistance in Europe 1944–1947* (Stroud: The History Press, 2000), 19–27.
90 CIA Electronic Reading Room, Nazi War Crimes Disclosure Act [henceforth CIA-ERR-NWCDA], 'Comments on the Political and Military Situation and The

Consequences Thereof', Official Dispatch, 21 December 1951, http://www.foia.cia.
gov/sites/default/files/document_conversions/1705143/SKORZENY%2C%20OTT
O%20%20%20VOL.%202_0041.pdf (accessed 1 January 2020).
91 Ganser, Terrorism in Western Europe, 69–97.
92 In Denmark, Colby identified a group of anti-communists who agreed to form the nucleus of a stay-behind net. A trainer was dispatched by the CIA to work with the cell, while Colby delivered a shipment of special crystal-powered miniature radios. He used his family as cover by telling them that they were going to take a tour of Denmark's castles: 'Colby recalled that the trunk of his car was so heavily laden with radios that it barely cleared the ground. […] Driving between sights, Colby abruptly turned off on a dirt road leading into the woods. There he rendezvoused with the CIA trainer.' Colby's children went for a stroll, while the Danish *stay behinds* uploaded the radios. See Randall B. Woods, *Shadow Warrior: William Egan Colby and the CIA* (New York: Basic Books, 2013), 91–2.
93 William Colby, *Honorable Men: My Life in the CIA* (New York: Simon and Schuster, 1978), 82.
94 Daniele Ganser, Secret Warfare in Neutral Austria during the Cold War, *Internationale Zeitschrift für Sozialpsychologie und Gruppendynamik in Wirtschaft und Gesellschaft* 34/119 (2009), 3–19.
95 Walter Blasi and Wolfgang Etschmann, Überlegungen zu den britischen Waffenlagern in Österreich, in Walter Blasi, Erwin A. Schmidl and Felix Schneider (eds.), *B-Gendarmerie, Waffenlager und Nachrichtendienste: Der militärische Weg zum Staatsvertrag* (Köln: Böhlau, 2005), 139–53.
96 Christopher Simpson, *Gladio-Type Guerilla Operations in Austria: A Report*, unpublished manuscript, 7–8.
97 Ganser, *Armies*, 1–2.
98 Colby, *Honorable Men*, 82–3.
99 James V. Milano and Patrick Brogan, *Soldiers, Spies, and the Rat Line: America's Undeclared War Against the Soviets* (Dulles: Brassey's, Inc., 2000), 155.
100 Bruno Thoß, Österreich in der Entstehungs- und Konsolidierungsphase des westlichen Bündnissystems (1947–1967), in Manfried Rauchensteiner (ed.), *Zwischen den Blöcken: NATO, Warschauer Pakt und Österreich* (Köln: Böhlau, 2000), 19–87.
101 Simpson, *Gladio*, 6–7.
102 Blasi and Etchmann, Überlegungen, 139–53.
103 Gerhard Hofer, Als Londons Agenten in Österreich landen wollten, *Die Presse*, 12 April 1996.
104 Michael Smith, *New Cloak, Old dagger: How Britain's Spies Came in from the Cold* (London: Victor Gollancz, 1996), 118.
105 Information für den Herrn Bundesminister, 15 November 1965, in Österreichisches Staatsarchiv/Archiv der Republik (ÖSTA/AdR), Bundesministerium für Landesverteidigung 22.099-17/66, Waffenlager. Translation from German by the author.
106 Cavendish, *Intelligence*, 74–5. See also Gordon Corera, *The Art of Betrayal: Life and Death in the British Secret Service* (Weidenfeld & Nicolson: London, 2011), 27.
107 Bericht der Regierungskommission zu den US-Waffenlagern, Bundesministerium für Inneres, 21 October 1997, private archive of the author. Translation from German by the author.
108 John H. Richardson, *My Father The Spy: An Investigative Memoir* (New York: Harper Collins, 2005), 102.

109 CIA-ERR-NWCDA, 'Status of Iceberg Operations in Austria', Memorandum, 31 January 1949, http://www.foia.cia.gov/sites/default/files/document_conversions/1705143/ICEBERG_0071.pdf (accessed 1 January 2020).
110 CIA-ERR-NWCDA, 'Iceberg', 15 July 1949, http://www.foia.cia.gov/sites/default/files/document_conversions/1705143/ICEBERG_0088.pdf (accessed 1 January 2020).
111 CIA-ERR-NWCDA, 'Extract for Iceberg Adm', Monthly Progress Report for December 1948, 7 February 1949, http://www.foia.cia.gov/sites/default/files/document_conversions/1705143/ICEBERG_0073.pdf (accessed 1 January 2020).
112 CIA-ERR-NWCDA, Undated Note Concerning Operation Iceberg, http://www.foia.cia.gov/sites/default/files/document_conversions/1705143/ICEBERG_0095.pdf (accessed 1 January 2020).
113 CIA-ERR-NWCDA, 'Vienna Operations Base Iceberg Program, Semi-Annual Status Report', 15 September 1953, http://www.foia.cia.gov/sites/default/files/document_conversions/1705143/ICEBERG_0096.pdf (accessed 1 January 2020).
114 Ibid.
115 Ibid.
116 CIA-ERR-NWCDA, Office of Special Operations, 'Outline of Stay-Behind Operations', Austria, Vienna Station, January 1951, http://www.foia.cia.gov/sites/default/files/document_conversions/1705143/ICEBERG_0094.pdf (accessed 1 January 2020).
117 Ibid.
118 CIA-ERR-NWCDA, Project Status Report, 1–31 January 1954, http://www.foia.cia.gov/sites/default/files/document_conversions/1705143/GRCROOND%20GRREPAIR%20%20%20VOL.%202%20%20%28GRCROOND%20SUPPORT%29_0008.pdf (accessed 1 January 2020).
119 Bruno W. Koppensteiner, Geheimarmeen im Nachkriegsösterreich: Aufgebot und ÖWSGV, *Pallasch: Zeitschrift für Militärgeschichte*, March 2013, 83–105.
120 Simpson, *Gladio*, 13.
121 Ganser, *Warfare*, 13.
122 Franz Olah, *Erlebtes Jahrhundert: Die Erinnerungen* (Wien: Amalthea Signum, 2008), 143.
123 Gerald Stourzh, *Um Einheit und Freiheit: Staatsvertrag, Neutralität und das Ende der Ost-West-Besetzung Österreichs 1945–1955* (Köln: Böhlau, 2005), 201–2.
124 CIA-ERR-NWCDA, 'Program for Preparation for Wartime Operational Activity in Austria', 6 October 1953, http://www.foia.cia.gov/sites/default/files/document_conversions/1705143/GRCROOND%20GRREPAIR%20%20%20VOL.%203%20%20%28GRCROOND%20OPERATIONS%29_0009.pdf (accessed 1 January 2020).
125 CIA-ERR-NWCDA, Project Status Report, November 1955, http://www.foia.cia.gov/sites/default/files/document_conversions/1705143/GRCROOND%20GRREPAIR%20%20%20VOL.%202%20%20%28GRCROOND%20SUPPORT%29_0030.pdf (accessed 1 January 2020).
126 CIA-ERR-NWCDA, Project Status Report, 7 August 1953, http://www.foia.cia.gov/sites/default/files/document_conversions/1705143/GRCROOND%20GRREPAIR%20%20%20VOL.%202%20%20%28GRCROOND%20SUPPORT%29_0025.pdf (accessed 1 January 2020).
127 CIA-ERR-NWCDA, Dispatch to Chief of Station, Vienna, 27 April 1958, http://www.foia.cia.gov/sites/default/files/document_conversions/1705143/GRCROOND%20GRREPAIR%20%20%20VOL.%202%20%20%28GRCROOND%20SUPPORT%29_0085.pdf (accessed 1 January 2020).

128 CIA-ERR-NWCDA, Project Status Report, August 1955, http://www.foia.cia.gov/sites/default/files/document_conversions/1705143/GRCROOND%20GRREPAIR%20%20%20VOL.%202%20%20%28GRCROOND%20SUPPORT%29_0027.pdf (accessed 1 January 2020).
129 CIA-ERR-NWCDA, 'GROOVY/GRCROOND', Dispatch from Chief of Base, Salzburg, 16 March 1962, http://www.foia.cia.gov/sites/default/files/document_conversions/1705143/GRCROOND%20GRREPAIR%20%20%20VOL.%202%20%20%28GRCROOND%20SUPPORT%29_0170.pdf (accessed 1 January 2020).
130 CIA-ERR-NWCDA, Dispatch from Chief of Base, Salzburg, 28 August 1962, http://www.foia.cia.gov/sites/default/files/document_conversions/1705143/GRCROOND%20GRREPAIR%20%20%20VOL.%204%20%20%28GRCROOND%20OPERATIONS%29_0067.pdf (accessed 1 January 2020).
131 CIA-ERR-NWCDA, Dispatch from Chief of Base, Salzburg, 5 June 1962, http://www.foia.cia.gov/sites/default/files/document_conversions/1705143/GRCROOND%20GRREPAIR%20%20%20VOL.%204%20%20%28GRCROOND%20OPERATIONS%29_0062.pdf (accessed 1 January 2020).
132 CIA-ERR-NWCDA, 'Status of SOB U/W Staybehind Assets', 30 November 1958, http://www.foia.cia.gov/sites/default/files/document_conversions/1705143/GRCROOND%20GRREPAIR%20%20%20VOL.%203%20%20%28GRCROOND%20OPERATIONS%29_0082.pdf (accessed 1 January 2020).
133 CIA-ERR-NWCDA, 'Nachrichtendienstliche Planungen des Dr. Wilhelm Höttl', 23 September 1948, http://www.foia.cia.gov/sites/default/files/document_conversions/1705143/HOETTL,%20WILHELM%20%20%20VOL.%203_0009.pdf (accessed 1 January 2020).
134 Eric Lichtblau, *The Nazis Next Door: How America became a Safe Haven for Hitler's Men* (New York: Houghton Mifflin Harcourt, 2014), 36–7.
135 Martin Haidinger, Wilhelm Höttl, Agent zwischen Spionage und Inszenierung, diploma thesis, Wien, 2006, 63. Translation from German by the author.
136 Ganser, Warfare, 17.
137 Olah, *Jahrhundert*, 150–1.
138 US-Waffenlager: Molden: Österreich bat um Anlegung, *Austria Presse Agentur*, 11 June 1996. Translation from German by the author.
139 Ganser, *Armies*, 246.
140 As a result of renewed fears over Russian expansionism, several Baltic and Eastern European members of NATO have bolstered their defence capabilities by setting up paramilitary organizations and militias that are trained in unconventional warfare against occupational forces.

Chapter 3

THE BRITISH STATE AND LOYALIST PARAMILITARIES IN NORTHERN IRELAND

Andrew Sanders

Collusion is evidenced in many ways. This ranges from the willful failure to keep records, the absence of accountability, the withholding of intelligence and evidence, through to the extreme of agents being involved in murder [...] The failure to keep records or the existence of contradictory accounts can often be perceived as evidence of concealment or malpractice. It limits the opportunity to rebut serious allegations. The absence of accountability allows the acts or omissions of individuals to go undetected. The withholding of information impedes the prevention of crime and the arrest of suspects. The unlawful involvement of agents in murder implies that the security forces sanction killings [...] My three Enquiries have found all these elements of collusion to be present. The co-ordination, dissemination and sharing of intelligence were poor. Informants and agents were allowed to operate without effective control and to participate in terrorist crimes. Nationalists were known to be targeted but were not properly warned or protected. Crucial information was withheld from Senior Investigating Officers. Important evidence was neither exploited nor preserved.[1]

The Stevens Enquiry: Overview and Recommendations, 2003

On 25 August 1989, Loughlin Maginn was shot dead by loyalist paramilitary gunmen at his home near Rathfriland in County Down. Over a period of a year and a half, Maginn had reported being detailed by British security forces on several occasions and being threatened with assassination. Reporting on the killing, Chris Moore, a reporter from the British Broadcasting Corporation, was taken to a secret location by members of the Ulster Freedom Fighters (UFF), a code name used by the Ulster Defence Association (UDA) when conducting acts of violence to preserve the legal status of the UDA itself. There, he was shown security documents and video tapes that contained information about suspected terrorists. Loughlin Maginn was one of those featured.[2]

The revelation that the UFF had obtained classified intelligence documentation was proof of different things to different groups. On one hand, it proved to the Irish nationalist community that the British state was acting as a puppet master to loyalist paramilitary groups. On another hand, it proved to loyalists that Loughlin Maginn had, indeed, been a member of an Irish republican paramilitary group. To the public, it demanded some form of official inquiry and in September 1989, Sir John Stevens, then the Deputy Chief Constable of Cambridgeshire Constabulary, arrived in Northern Ireland where he was appointed to head an inquiry into the killing of Maginn.

There was an immediate response to the threat of an external inquiry and four days before Stevens arrived in Northern Ireland, three men were charged with the murder. Two of them, Andrew Smyth and Andrew Browne, were members of the Ulster Defence Regiment.[3] It was said that Smyth had given documents concerning Maginn to Browne, who had, in turn, passed them to the UFF. Smyth and Browne were given life sentences in March 1992 along with two loyalists, who were also sentenced to life imprisonment.[4]

As the Stevens investigation gathered pace, fingerprints were discovered on some of the leaked documents that were seized after a raid on UDA premises. They belonged to former British soldier Brian Nelson. Nelson, in his role as the UDA's director of intelligence, had travelled to South Africa in 1985 to purchase weapons. Nelson had been recruited by British intelligence during the early 1980s and thanks to his newfound ability to supply high-quality intelligence to the UDA, he was appointed as the head of intelligence of the loyalist paramilitary group.[5] It was during this time as a British informer that he made the trip to South Africa, a trip that cannot have escaped the attention of his handlers.[6] As the investigation developed, questions emerged regarding the Force Research Unit (FRU), who had been acting as Nelson's handlers. Stevens and his investigators met with serious resistance from military intelligence about the existence and role of the FRU. It became apparent that many army personnel did not even know of the FRU's existence, while those in the Royal Ulster Constabulary (RUC) who were aware of the unit were uneasy over the way it was operating.[7]

These issues were compounded by a mysterious fire that destroyed the Stevens Inquiry incident room. Significant evidence was destroyed in the fire, though fortuitously the team had backed up much of it in a secure holding centre in England. One of the detectives participating on the Stevens team recalled the blaze: 'There were a number of fire alarm points in the building and I went to one and I smashed it with the heel of my shoe and nothing happened. I ran down to another one and smashed that and again nothing happened.'[8] Soon after, Brian Nelson was arrested and charged with conspiracy to murder, possession of information likely to be useful to terrorists and illegal possession of a sub-machine gun.

The arrest of Nelson was a significant step in our understanding of collusion in Northern Ireland, rather undermining allegations that all state forces were fully compliant with the policy. On the contrary, it was evidence of the enormous rift that had opened up between different security agencies over territory, intelligence sharing and overall strategy.[9] A former RUC intelligence officer described the Nelson affair as 'army incompetence […] it was a military intelligence cock-up. Those guys were prepared to do anything and it was their undoing over Nelson'.[10]

The Nelson case came to trial in 1992 with former FRU commander Colonel Gordon Kerr giving evidence in support of his agent. Nelson benefitted from a lenient court that dropped fifteen charges against him, including two counts of murder, and he ultimately was sentenced to only ten years in prison for conspiracy to murder, possession of a weapon and possession of information likely to be of use to terrorists. Kerr alleged that intelligence provided by Nelson had helped to prevent 217 murders.[11]

Nearly a decade later, *Sunday Herald* journalist Neil Mackay, now the editor of that newspaper, began further exploring the FRU and its role in collusion. In one of his articles, a former FRU operative claimed: 'There's no doubt […]. My unit was guilty of conspiring in the murder of civilians in Northern Ireland, on about 14 occasions.'[12] This raised questions about the role of Brigadier Gordon Kerr, then the British military attaché in Beijing. Mackay persisted in subsequent articles, which suggested that Kerr had given approval to loyalist killings as well as betraying former agents who had become compromised. A former FRU operative told Mackay that Kerr had removed protection from three Irish Republican Army (IRA) informers who were executed in Armagh on 1 July 1992.[13] The agent noted that 'if Kerr had done what he was supposed to do – protect agents working for him – none of these people needed to die. Instead the IRA were able to tape the confessions of these guys, and get masses of information about how we operated. It was a nightmare scenario.'[14]

Sir John Stevens returned to Northern Ireland to conduct two further inquiries, the most prominent of which was the April 1999 inquiry into the killing of Belfast lawyer Patrick Finucane on 12 February 1989, a murder which former FRU agent Brian Nelson was believed to have been involved in. The report into this third investigation was published in April 2003 and an excerpt is quoted here. Reviewing his series of investigations into collusion between the British state and loyalist paramilitaries in Northern Ireland, Stevens noted that the actions of Nelson had saved merely two lives rather than the 217 suggested by Gordon Kerr at Nelson's trial. One of those lives was that of Gerry Adams, the president of Sinn Fein and, at that time, the Member of Parliament for Belfast West.[15]

Following the publication of the Stevens Inquiry in 2003, Brigadier Kerr was reportedly set to be suspended by the Chief of the General Staff, General Sir Mike Jackson.[16] A subsequent report in the *Socialist Worker* alleged that Kerr had, in fact, been appointed by Prime Minister Tony Blair as the head of intelligence in Iraq when the conflict began there in March. This role saw him direct two secretive intelligence groups named the Joint Support Group and the Special Reconnaissance Regiment.[17]

The discrepancy between the 217 lives that Gordon Kerr alleged had been saved by Brian Nelson and the two lives that Sir John Stevens found had actually been saved is deeply symbolic of the utility of collusion. It seems highly unlikely that Kerr actually believed that Nelson had been so effective; rather, his statement was an attempt to justify the activities of the FRU by misleading the court. The condescending attitude of Kerr towards the process of law typifies one aspect of the collusion that occurred between the British state and loyalist paramilitaries, namely that British forces knew better than the law and found it necessary to operate outside the law in order to achieve their objectives.

Stevens' report concluded that 'the murders of Patrick Finucane and Brian Adam Lambert [a Protestant killed in 1987 by the UDA in a "mistaken identity shooting"] could have been prevented. I also believe that the RUC investigation of Patrick Finucane's murder should have resulted in the early arrest and detection of his killers. [...] I conclude there was collusion in both murders and the circumstances surrounding them.' He criticized the lack of information sharing between the security forces but focused on the role of British agents in the killings, which he suggested 'implies that the security forces sanction killings'.[18] The report concluded that Nelson was complicit in at least thirty murders.

Newspaper reports of the third and final Stevens Inquiry were published on Thursday, 17 April 2003. On that day, they shared column space with the obituary of Brian Nelson. The former agent and one of the key figures in the allegations of collusion between the British state and loyalist paramilitaries, Nelson had apparently died of a brain haemorrhage a few days before Stevens published his report. In September 2003, *Belfast Telegraph* journalist Chris Thornton reported that Nelson had indeed died, resident in Cardiff, where he had moved under an assumed identity since his release from prison during the mid-1990s.[19]

That collusion occurred in Northern Ireland is hardly a matter of debate any longer, but the extent to which it infiltrated British strategy in Northern Ireland and the utility of employing collusion with loyalist paramilitaries remain highly contentious. Ian Hurst, an ex-soldier who wrote under the alias 'Martin Ingram', has claimed that 'there is a firebreak between government and the work on the ground. Do you honestly believe that politicians would have allowed themselves to be implicated in murder? They just don't have the balls.'[20] He later wrote of his regret that 'certain lines, certain moral boundaries were stepped over too many times and innocent people died'.[21]

Hurst's book *Stakeknife* is one example of a relatively limited literature on the topic of collusion in Northern Ireland. This literature is largely limited to accounts from journalists who have investigated the topic, while scholarly literature is limited to wider studies of loyalism and the activities of the state. One of the leading experts on the issue is journalist Martin Dillon, who published his book *The Dirty War* in 1990.[22] The book covered all aspects of the security operation in Northern Ireland, in doing so covering issues such as military killings, counter-gangs, informers and, more generally, collusion. There were many instances of troops and police officers operating outside the law and continuing investigations into events may yet bring about further convictions. Maurice Punch's *State Violence, Collusion and the Troubles: Counter Insurgency, Government Deviance and Northern Ireland* is a rare example of a scholarly study on collusion, which largely attributes blame to the British government for failing to adequately respond to baiting on the part of the insurgent forces of the Irish republicans. It was this that set them on a path where collusion was one possible outcome.[23] Other books that cover the topic are Paul Larkin's *A Very British Jihad: Collusion, Conspiracy and Cover-up in Northern Ireland*, and Nicholas Davies's *Dead Men Talking: Collusion, Cover-Up and Murder in Northern Ireland*. More recent studies include two publications by researchers at the Pat Finucane Centre (PFC) in Derry. Anne Cadwallader and Margaret Urwin have published *Lethal Allies* and *A State in Denial*, respectively.[24] These publications reflect hours of painstaking research on the part of researchers at the PFC and add layers of information to discussions about the issue of collusion between the British state and loyalist paramilitaries. Both Cadwallader and Urwin contend that collusion was a top-down process, requiring high-level authorization from leading political and military figures. This chapter will explore this idea further, but will use the frames established by Martin Dillon, who produced both the first and one of the most objective studies on the topic.

Military killing and collusion

Of the issues identified by Martin Dillon as being most pertinent to a discussion of Britain's dirty war in Northern Ireland, military killing is one of the most significant when the conversation focuses on collusion. There have been several cases of controversial killings by the British military in Northern Ireland that have brought about inquiries. The most notable of these was the Saville Report into the Parachute Regiment killing of fourteen people in Derry on 30 January 1972, a day known as Bloody Sunday. Saville has, despite several calls since the report's publication in 2010, failed to prompt any prosecutions for the soldiers involved.[25]

There have been several instances of soldiers being convicted of crimes committed during their deployments to Northern Ireland. As recently as December 2016, two retired soldiers were charged with the April 1972 killing of Official IRA member Joe McCann. The Public Prosecution Service commented that 'the two defendants in the case are surviving members of the army patrol which shot Mr McCann. A third member of the patrol who also fired at Mr. McCann died in the intervening years.'[26] The soldiers accused of the murder were members of the Parachute Regiment, the same regiment that was responsible for the deaths of Bloody Sunday three months prior to McCann's death. The retroactive prosecution of British soldiers for actions in Northern Ireland has drawn controversy, notably from Conservative MP and former soldier Johnny Mercer.[27]

Prosecution of soldiers for murders committed during the conflict was rare but did occur. Perhaps most prominent was the case of the 'Pitchfork Murders', named after the agricultural tool by which the victims appeared to have been killed. The October 1972 murders of farmers Michael Naan and Andrew Murray were initially believed to have been committed by loyalists, but life sentences were given to two soldiers from the Argyll and Sutherland Highlanders in 1981, with a third serving four years for manslaughter and their commanding officer given a suspended sentence leading to his resignation from the army in disgrace. Lieutenant General Sir Alistair Irwin, who later served as the General Officer Commanding, Northern Ireland, considered the episode to have been 'a perfect example of rogue soldiers who got out of control'.[28]

The Naan and Murray murders had been committed while the soldiers responsible were off-duty but three years later Private Ian Thain became the first soldier convicted of a killing while on duty. Thain shot dead Thomas Reilly in West Belfast in August 1983 and was sentenced to life imprisonment, though he was later released on licence and returned to duty.[29] There followed, in the 1990s as the dynamics of the conflict continued to shift, a series of soldiers convicted for killing civilians in Northern Ireland and later being released and allowed back on duty.

In September 1990 Private Lee Clegg shot dead two teenage joyriders in West Belfast. He was sentenced to life imprisonment for murder in 1993, but was released on licence by Secretary of State Patrick Mayhew in 1995. Two years after the Clegg shooting, two members of the Scots Guards shot dead teenager Peter MacBride as he ran away from their patrol in North Belfast. Guardsmen James Fisher and Mark Wright were both sentenced to life imprisonment for the killing, ultimately serving six years before returning to their regiment. In each case, the shootings were ruled to have been in contravention of the yellow card, the rules provided to British soldiers for opening fire when on duty. In each case, the victims were ruled to have been moving away from the soldier or soldiers who had opened fire, and, in each case, the soldiers convicted of the killings were released and returned to duty.[30]

The issue with allowing these troops back on duty was one of legal consistency. Troops had been issued with a document that provided them with the criteria under which they could open fire. Operational strategy may have been aggressive, but soldiers were restrained throughout the period by the rule of law. A 'red card' had been issued to soldiers during operations in Kenya during the Mau Mau uprising between 1952 and 1960, which provided guidelines for opening fire with and without warning. In the latter case, paragraph thirteen did its best to provide guidance. Soldiers could fire without warning, they were told:

> Either when hostile firing is taking place in your area, and a warning is impracticable, or when any delay could lead to death or serious injury to people whom it is your duty to protect or to yourself, and then only: (a) against a person using a firearm against members of the security forces or against people whom it is your duty to protect; (b) against a person carrying a firearm if you have reason to think he is about to use it for offensive purposes.[31]

The yellow card was issued to soldiers following the killing of Daniel O'Hagan in Belfast on 31 July 1970. O'Hagan was alleged to have been in the process of throwing a petrol bomb, a claim denied by locals, and no legal proceedings were brought against the soldier who shot him. It was then amended in January 1971, permitting the opening of fire at anyone carrying a firearm and believed to be about to use it, as well as authorizing firing at petrol bombers provided a clear warning was issued.[32] This amendment would not have provided retroactive legislative justification for O'Hagan's shooting, but it did so for future similar incidents. Soon after the amendment, Gunner Robert Curtis became the first soldier to be killed in active service during Operation Banner when he was shot by an IRA sniper in North Belfast.[33]

Later, as rioting intensified and attacks on the army grew more violent, further amendments were made to the yellow card, evidence that the situation on the ground was often too complicated to legislate for. Following Bloody Sunday, the controversial Widgery inquiry considered that the rules for opening fire were still broadly satisfactory.[34] The establishment of 'yellow card principles' was tricky at a time when the British Army was under increased attack from the IRA; 238 soldiers were killed between 1970 and 1973. During this same period, 150 people were shot dead by soldiers.[35] Military strategy was aggressive throughout, with operations such as the 1970 Falls Curfew and 1972 Operation Motorman where military control was re-established over nationalist areas of Belfast and Derry as well as the policy decision to implement internment without trial in August 1971, each providing evidence for the fact that the British saw an opportunity for a quick resolution of Operation Banner.

There was an argument that consistent application of yellow card principles could put a soldier in serious danger. The March 1973 death of nineteen-year-old Private Gary Barlow was one incident that angered troops. Barlow became isolated in a nationalist area of West Belfast and was surrounded and taunted by a crowd, many of whom were women. He made no attempt to use his rifle on them and was quickly disarmed. Some tried to help him but others beat him before calling the IRA to shoot him dead.[36] The *Belfast Telegraph* praised Private Barlow as 'a brave young man, he died honouring the orders of his superior officers, he played the rules of the Yellow Card right to the end. Even as he was being mauled he did not forget to uphold the name of the British Army, for considering the terrible circumstances he did not open fire.'[37] Nobody was ever charged with Barlow's murder.

Soldiers on active duty during this period grew frustrated. They were under increased scrutiny, from both the media and the director of Public Prosecutions (DPP), and were finding the yellow card to be restrictive at a time when the IRA campaign was escalating. One former soldier considered that 'the Army as a whole would have been better used in the seventies if they'd been allowed to do the job properly; they knew who the "names" were and where to get them, but were told to go easy. PIRA would have been finished as an effective force by 1980 if the Army had had the gloves taken off'.[38] This does not reconcile with reports from the *Sunday Times* insight team, who published a book in 1972 entitled *Ulster*, which noted that the military had 'increasingly used violence in circumstances which did not warrant it'.[39]

The implementation of Direct Rule from London after Bloody Sunday brought the appointment of a DPP. One of the earliest considerations of the new DPP, Sir Barry Shaw, QC, judged that the existing system by which the Military Police investigated army shootings was 'far from satisfactory'. Information was apparently sought 'for managerial, not criminal purposes'.[40] The DPP revoked the RUC's discretionary powers, which had previously allowed the Constabulary to decide whether or not to institute criminal proceedings against soldiers. In his report, Lord Saville was also critical of an agreement between the army command and the RUC that in effect 'removed soldiers from the normal operation of the criminal justice system and involved the establishment of an alternative structure operated and controlled by the military'.[41] The report suggested that this contributed 'to a culture within which soldiers could shoot, and kill, with impunity' because they knew their use of lethal force would not be subject to scrutiny.

Earlier army killings were not investigated by Saville in his inquiry, but the 2005 establishment of the Historical Enquiries Team, a unit within the now rebranded Police Service of Northern Ireland, saw renewed investigation into the early years of the conflict. The Historical Enquiries Team worked alongside organizations such as the PFC in Derry to investigate controversial killings, notably the 150 people shot dead by the army between 1970 and 1973, for which very few soldiers were called to account.[42]

The PFC opened in May 1993 in honour of the late Belfast solicitor who had been shot dead in his home by loyalist paramilitaries in February 1989.[43] Finucane's killing drew allegations of collusion between the state and loyalist paramilitaries, allegations that have persisted well into the twenty-first century. The role of UDA double agent Brian Nelson in the killing, which was carried out by the UFF, suggested to many that the state had been complicit in it. It is important, first, to better establish the role of loyalist paramilitaries in the context of discussions about collusion in Northern Ireland.

Collusion and counter-gangs

In 1960 Frank Kitson published his first book *Gangs and Counter-Gangs*.[44] In it, he discussed his experiences serving with the British Army during the Mau Mau insurgency in Kenya. For Kitson, a pseudo- or counter-gang would be a locally recruited and covert militia, which could work alongside a police special branch. Kitson's second book *Low Intensity Operations* also offered guidance on counter-insurgency strategy and was published just as Kitson arrived in Northern Ireland to command the 39th Infantry Brigade, responsible for the Belfast area. In 2015, Mary Heenan, the widow of Paddy Heenan, served papers on both Kitson and the Ministry of Defence (MOD), seeking compensation for the death of her husband. Heenan had been travelling to work in a minibus when a loyalist paramilitary threw a hand grenade into the vehicle. Heenan died instantly and Albert Baker, known as 'Ginger', was given a life sentence for the killing, along with those of three other Catholics. Baker, a former British soldier who had gone absent without leave and joined the UDA had used a British-issue device in the attack and solicitors, acting on behalf of Heenan's widow, claimed that Kitson was 'liable personally for negligence and misfeasance', suggesting that he and the MOD had been 'reckless as to whether state agents would be involved in murder'.[45]

The idea that the British state could use loyalist paramilitaries to carry out covert operations has been persuasive among critics of British policy in Northern Ireland. More than a decade before Brian Nelson was recruited to serve as a double agent inside the UDA, there had been evidence of links between British security forces and loyalist paramilitary groups.

Loyalist paramilitaries were active in Northern Ireland three years prior to the arrival of the British Army in 1969. The fiftieth anniversary of the 1916 Easter Rising had prompted concern from loyalists that another Irish republican insurgency was to be launched and the loyalists, drawing inspiration from the Ulster Volunteers of 1912, struck pre-emptively. They began their campaign with a series of petrol bomb attacks, notably an attack on Holy Cross Girls School in North Belfast on 6 April 1966. The following month, they continued their petrol bomb campaign against Catholic schools with an attack on St Mary's Training College in West Belfast before an attack on Catholic-owned premises in the Shankill area of West Belfast killed Protestant pensioner Matilda Gould, who lived next door. An open verdict was returned in the inquest into the death of Gould, who died seven weeks after the attack.[46] The murders of John Scullion and Peter Ward were more direct; the two Catholics were shot dead by Ulster Volunteer Force (UVF) gunmen, led by former British soldier Gusty Spence, who was jailed for life for the Ward killing in October 1966.

The vigilante culture that was established by Spence and the co-founders of the UVF was mirrored in the UDA, which formed in 1971 out of a number of smaller, locally organized groups. Northern Ireland had a very active gang culture during the early 1960s that provided fertile recruitment ground for the paramilitaries. Gareth Mulvenna's groundbreaking study of the 'tartan gang' phenomenon details the transition of young Protestants from street gangs into paramilitaries as the conflict developed in Northern Ireland during the 1970s.[47] Mulvenna highlights the role of violence for these gang members and how that played a role in their transformation into paramilitaries as the conflict developed during the early 1970s.

Beyond the connections that existed in the B-Specials, ties between loyalist paramilitaries and state forces first became apparent during the mid-1970s.[48] This period coincided with the 'Ulsterization' strategy introduced by the British, named after the American 'Vietnamization' strategy in the Vietnam War. This strategy involved aspects like criminalization, where paramilitary prisoners were denied special category status, as well as police primacy, where control of security operations returned to the RUC and the military was restored to its role in support of the civil power. Criminalization was introduced on 1 March 1976, a few weeks after the Special Air Service had arrived in Northern Ireland, but over a year previously the actions of a deadly UVF unit in the southern border regions began to pose serious questions about the links between British security forces and loyalist paramilitaries.

The first killing of 1975 was that of IRA staff captain John Francis Green, who had escaped from the Maze prison in 1973. Green's body was found in County Monaghan near the home of an elderly republican sympathizer and he was believed to have been killed by a UVF unit based in County Armagh, which became known as the Glenanne Gang. They were led by Robin Jackson, who went by the nickname 'the Jackal'. The details of the killing were not known until 1999, when former RUC officer John Weir was released from prison having served a life sentence for the murder of Catholic shopkeeper William Strathearn in the small County Antrim town of Ahoghill in April 1977. Upon his release, Weir named the three men who had been involved in the killing of Green, Jackson as well as Corporal Robert McConnell from the British Army's Ulster Defence Regiment (UDR) and Harris Boyle. McConnell was killed by the IRA in April 1976 and Boyle was killed during the UVF ambush of the Miami Showband in July 1975. Boyle, the leader of the UVF unit that was carrying out the attack along with at least two UDR soldiers, died along with another UVF member when the bomb they were planting in the van belonging to members of the band exploded prematurely. Their apparent intention had been to frame the band as a covert IRA unit transporting explosives, and they had used the UDR members to establish a fake roadblock at which they attempted to plant the bomb while pretending to be conducting a search.[49]

During his 1999 revelation, Weir claimed that Green had not been the intended target of the unit, but he just happened to be at the house, which was apparently that of the group's real target, when the hit squad arrived.[50] Stumbling into the killing of an IRA volunteer is consistent with accounts that suggest that the Jackson-led UVF unit was merely interested in the random assassination of Catholic civilians. They allegedly struck, most notoriously, on 17 May 1974, when thirty-three people were killed in Dublin and Monaghan in a series of bomb attacks.

Recent research, most notably that carried out by the PFC and published by Anne Cadwallader in her book *Lethal Allies*, has suggested that the Jackson unit, believed to have been responsible for the Dublin and Monaghan bombs, was not in itself capable of carrying out such precision attacks.[51] The evidence of the Miami Showband attack points, rather, to a unit that was not capable of actually carrying out a deeply sinister attack involving one bomb and a relatively compliant civilian target, much less structuring a multiple bomb attack across a major city and coordinating it with a separate attack, nearly one hundred miles away. The three car bombs in Dublin exploded almost simultaneously, killing or fatally wounding twenty-six and injuring 140 people, while six were killed and one fatally injured in Monaghan.

Examining the Dublin and Monaghan bombings and the attack on the Miami Showband alongside one another, it hardly seems credible that these attacks could have been carried out by the same unit: on one hand, a callous but precise attack on a large number of civilians, on the other, a nakedly sectarian and recklessly brutal assault on a soft target. The Irish Government introduced the Commissions of Investigations Act 2004, which led to an inquiry into the Dublin and Monaghan bombings, led by Irish barrister Patrick McEntee. The McEntee report, published in May 2007, was critical of Gardai intelligence but did not find evidence of collusion between the British state and those responsible, though it did note that British authorities had not been fully cooperative in their investigation.[52]

The Glenanne Gang, which faded after the convictions of Weir and his colleague William McCaughey in 1980, was notable for the number of British security officers in its midst. Along with Weir, Jackson and Boyle, McCaughey was in the RUC Special Branch and had been a B-Special. Further, Jackson himself had been a member of the UDR, though he was discharged from the unit.⁵³ The problems that had beset the B-Specials continued to plague their successor, the UDR.

The B-Specials had been a predominantly Protestant unit of the RUC Reserve and, consequently, highly porous to loyalist infiltration. Following the 1969 Hunt Report, commissioned by the Northern Irish Minister of Home Affairs to 'examine the recruitment, organisation, structure and composition of the Royal Ulster Constabulary and the Ulster Special Constabulary and their respective functions and to recommend as necessary what changes are required to provide for the efficient enforcement of law and order in Northern Ireland', significant reforms took place.⁵⁴ The B-Specials were disbanded and replaced by the UDR, a locally recruited part-time force under the command of the General Officer Commanding, Northern Ireland, but the new regiment was also plagued by allegations that it was rife with loyalists.

Brigadier Charles Ritchie, the commander of the UDR when it was amalgamated into the Royal Irish Regiment in 1992, recalled:

> You could argue that with knowledge and hindsight that maybe the vetting procedures should have been much stricter, but they weren't. Take someone joining the British Army, unless you're going to a highly sensitive job you are not given security vetting. [...] We tried very much to keep out the ex B specials, they had a bad reputation for being very hard-line.⁵⁵

Ritchie's comments provide some indication that the problem of loyalist infiltration of the UDR was more of a bottom-up process. This would seem to indicate two major problems: first, that loyalists realized that membership of the UDR was possible and could be exploited; and second, that the UDR was either indifferent to their applications or unable to weed out the most troubling recruits. Neither of these problems necessarily suggests that the UDR was a vehicle for collusion in the top-down sense, that is, a deliberate strategy that was imposed from within military command. Rather, it was the loyalist infiltration of the UDR that allowed for this collaboration to take place.

It is also important to note that the UDA remained a legal organization until 1992, and the UVF, though illegal before and after, was itself legal between April 1974 and October 1975. The proscription was lifted to allow loyalists to take part in political talks.⁵⁶ During these periods, joint membership of either of the two organizations and a state body would have been entirely legal. The UDA, which used the cover name 'Ulster Freedom Fighters' to claim operations, continued to exploit its legal status throughout this period, despite involvement in some high-profile attempted assassinations.

Assessing the role of the UVF, and in particular the so-called Glenanne Gang, in the context of counter-gang culture is tricky. It seems clear that there was a steady supply of disgruntled security force personnel who were quite prepared to moonlight with the UVF in order to attack Catholic civilians. In that sense, the Glenanne Gang would be more appropriately understood within a discussion on the issue of military killings. Kitson's view that the counter-gang could work alongside a special branch unit does not necessarily apply to the relationship that developed between the RUC and the UDR in South Armagh and the Glenanne Gang, though it is possible that the relationship began as such.

With the Glenanne Gang effectively finished as of the 1980 convictions of John Weir and William McCaughey, our analysis of collusion shifts to a relationship that would seem to have clearer lines of demarcation.

Collusion in the 1980s: The UDA

The relationship between the UDA and the security forces was more formal than that of the UVF. Where the UVF often had RUC officers and UDR members within its membership, the UDA tended to maintain a looser organizational structure than the UVF and was therefore open to different forms of government interference, most notably informers and double agents. This was exemplified with the recruitment of Brian Nelson.

In recruiting Nelson as a double agent, who rose to prominence within the UDA, the British state forces took a more proactive role in loyalist paramilitary strategy. Formalizing collusion with loyalist paramilitaries would, in theory, limit the scope of loyalist operations to those that would meet with the approval of their handlers. The Glenanne Gang had proven itself reckless and unpredictable, which, as Anne Cadwallader has argued, was not without merit from the British perspective.[57] There was, however, the danger that if loyalist paramilitaries were simply around to run rampant, a bloody sectarian war would ensue.

Early in the 1980s, the UDA, using the UFF banner, came very close to killing Bernadette Devlin McAliskey and Gerry Adams, major figures in the Northern Ireland Civil Rights Association and Sinn Fein, respectively. Both were shot by loyalist hit squads and both were lucky to survive their injuries. In both cases, British security force personnel were close on hand to apprehend the would-be assassins, which raised questions over their presence in proximity to the attacks and their inability to halt them.

Early on Friday, 16 January 1981, a group of masked gunmen broke into the relatively remote Coalisland home of Bernadette and Michael McAliskey and shot the couple several times. The gunmen had cut the telephone line to the house before launching their attack in an attempt to maximize the chances of their victims being at least fatally wounded.[58] A patrol of British soldiers was in the area, apprehended the gunmen and administered emergency treatment to the McAliskeys, most likely saving their lives.

Raymond Smallwoods, himself shot dead by the IRA in June of 1994, had been one of the gunmen. He was sentenced to fifteen years in prison and, upon his release, became active in loyalist politics, notably the Ulster Democratic Party.[59] Quoted many years after the attack on the McAliskey's home, senior loyalist spokesman Jackie McDonald said that 'the attack would be seen as a failure but it was one hell of an effort'.[60]

McAliskey had been a member of what journalists Henry McDonald and Jim Cusack have labelled the 'UDA's "shopping list"', a list of prominent members of the anti-H blocks campaign that was drawn up in 1979 by UDA commander John McMichael.[61] McMichael's hand-picked pseudo-commando units killed John Turnly, a founding member of the Irish Independence Party, in June 1980, before killing Queen's University lecturer and founding member of the Irish Republican Socialist Party (IRSP), Miriam Daly, in her home in Andersonstown. As with the McAliskey home, the phone lines at the Daly house had been cut. They followed up Daly's killing with that of Ronnie Bunting, another founding member of the IRSP and its paramilitary unit, the Irish National Liberation Army, and the son of Major Ronald Bunting, an ally of Ian Paisley.

After the arrests of Smallwoods and the other two members of the unit, UDA rival Tommy Lyttle, who later became the West Belfast brigadier and was well known to have been informing on the organization, leaked McMichael's list to the press.[62] This leak did not stop the UDA from targeting high-profile figures, however, and in 1984 they came very close to killing Sinn Fein President Gerry Adams in a gun attack in central Belfast.

In an interview with historian Ian S. Wood, Jackie McDonald recalled that 'the boys were practically queuing up for the chance to do that one'.[63] Adams later commented that it was 'quite obvious that British intelligence were aware' of the operation and that 'they wanted myself and my comrades out of the way'.[64] Adams held a press conference five days after the shooting, upon his release from hospital. The day after Adams was released from the hospital, the three men who had been arrested in connection with the shooting appeared in court on charges of attempted murder, possession of firearms and membership of the proscribed UFF.

As the UFF unit left the McAliskey house, it was immediately apprehended by a British Army patrol, which also administered potentially life-saving treatment to the victims. A *Guardian* report noted that McAliskey's role in the hunger strike campaign had prompted the security forces to keep watch over their house.[65] McAliskey, who later claimed that the attempted murder could have been prevented by the units, stated that 'we are forever indebted' to the soldier and the military surgeon who operated on her and her husband.[66] One sergeant who was involved in the rescue recalled that 'she was close to death, the action of the army medic without a doubt saved her life. What sticks in my mind though was her attitude. Close to death and with the medic frantically trying to save her life, she was still ranting and raving at us in the foulest language. We all wished then that we had let the bitch die.'[67]

The notion that the loyalist hit squad had been permitted to enter the McAliskey house, with three young children inside who were ultimately physically unharmed in the attack, in order to carry out the attack raises serious questions about the ethics of the patrol. The above comment betrays a lack of compassion for the McAliskey family, whose protection had clearly been the task assigned to the army patrol. The circumstances of the attempted murder of Gerry Adams were somewhat less controversial, but still questions persisted about the security provided to the Sinn Fein president.

Adams was being driven from an appearance at a central Belfast courthouse when a UDA gang led by John Gregg ambushed him and his associates, shooting Adams several times. The loyalists' car was rammed by that of an off-duty soldier who just happened to be in the immediate vicinity. Gregg's view that an informer had compromised the attempted hit on Adams was shared within the UDA.[68] Gregg was sentenced to eighteen years in prison for his part in the attempted assassination, though he was released in 1993.[69]

Smallwoods and Gregg were both later victims of violence themselves. In 1994 Smallwoods was shot dead by the IRA at his house in Lisburn and Gregg was shot dead during a loyalist feud in 2003. They had achieved a certain notoriety for their respective roles in ultimately unsuccessful assassinations, with Smallwoods the chair of the UDA-aligned Ulster Democratic Party and Gregg the SE Antrim brigadier before their untimely deaths. The nature of these unsuccessful killings raised serious questions about the relationship between the security forces and loyalist paramilitaries and the idea that British intelligence had been aware of the intention to kill McAliskey and Adams and had intended to stand by while the attacks took place, but in sufficiently close proximity to effectively catch the perpetrators red-handed, so to speak, began to grow. John Gregg himself, along with fellow UDA members, believed that his operation had been compromised, with one suggestion being that the bullets used had been tampered with. These lower-velocity bullets had both reduced the risk of their target being killed, though not substantially, and minimized the risk of the informant being discovered.[70] That Gerry Adams required life-saving surgery did little to imply that the bullets were significantly less deadly than untampered bullets. There were also suggestions within the UDA that the attempted hit on the McAliskeys had also been compromised.[71]

In either case, there is an important point to be made about the opportunity that loyalists had to attack either victim. The operations were both compromised in the sense that the hit squads would be apprehended almost immediately after carrying out their attacks, but also effectively allowed to try to kill the politicians. From a strategic perspective, it makes little sense that the British would want to see two prominent nationalists murdered, unless they sought to provoke republican violence.

By 1981 McAliskey was largely marginalized and more active in community work, and by 1983 Adams was a Member of Parliament. The British had been aware of Adams' desire for a political solution to the conflict since they met him in June 1972 along with Daithi O Connail, noting that 'there is no doubt whatever that these two at least genuinely want a cease fire and a permanent end to violence'.[72] The fact that it was around this time that the FRU recruited Brian Nelson as their informer at the very heart of UDA operational strategy makes more sense if one follows the logic that the British were unaware of the McAliskey and Adams attacks and sought to exert more influence over the loyalists.

One prominent nationalist target that the UDA, again using the UFF cover name, was successful in killing was Belfast lawyer Pat Finucane. Finucane had been described as 'one of the Provisional IRA's regular lawyers and the go-to solicitor for the Belfast Brigade', and had family ties to republicanism.[73] During his career, Finucane had represented IRA volunteers, most notably Bobby Sands, as well as victims of alleged state 'shoot to kill' operations like the family of Gervaise McKerr.[74] His involvement in these cases drew the attention of the British state and comments such as those of Grantham MP Douglas Hogg shortly before Finucane was murdered were troubling. Hogg suggested that 'some solicitors were unduly sympathetic to the cause of the IRA', a comment highlighted in the third Stevens Inquiry. Stevens noted that 'Mr Hogg's comments about solicitors' support for terrorism made on 17th January 1989 aroused controversy. To the extent that they were based on information passed by the RUC, they were not justifiable and the Enquiry concludes that the Minister was compromised.'[75]

As Stevens returned for his third inquiry, UDA quartermaster William Stobie was arrested. Stobie, who was a RUC agent, had apparently told his handlers that a top republican was to be targeted in the attack and admittedly supplied the weapons to Finucane's killers.[76] He further accused his RUC handlers of tampering with UDA weaponry, which, in his job as quartermaster, he was responsible for.[77]

The judge at Stobie's trial was forced to declare a mistrial after a police witness accidentally referred to his previous convictions. The case against him ultimately collapsed in December 2001, but Stobie was shot dead by fellow loyalists less than two weeks later.[78] In 2004, loyalist Ken Barrett was convicted of the murder. Journalists Hugh Jordan and David Lister contended that Barrett had been the driver of the vehicle and an unnamed loyalist had been the assassin, but did note that Barrett 'would shoot just about anybody if given a gun and pointed in the right direction'.[79] Most pointedly, when asked about the Finucane murder, Irish Taoiseach Bertie Ahern commented to US diplomats that 'everyone knows the UK was involved'.[80]

Even with Barrett and Stobie arrested for the killing, the campaign for justice continued. In May 2002 Canadian judge Peter Cory was tasked with investigating six controversial murders that took place during the Troubles. These were the killings of Pat Finucane, fellow Catholic solicitor Rosemary Nelson, who was killed in a car bomb attack in 1999, as well as loyalist paramilitary leader Billy Wright, who was killed inside the Maze prison in 1997, and Catholic civilian Robert Hamill, who was beaten to death by a loyalist mob allegedly in full sight of an RUC patrol who did nothing to stop the attack. Further, Cory investigated allegations of collusion on the part of the Irish state with the IRA in the killings of Lord Justice and Lady Gibson in 1987 and those of Chief Superintendent Breen and Superintendent Buchanan in 1989. In each case except that of Lord and Lady Gibson, Cory recommended a state inquiry. His decision was somewhat hindered by the implementation of the Inquiries Act 2005, which attempted to establish the parameters under which any state-funded inquiry would proceed. Although the Finucane family refused to cooperate with any investigation in light of the 2005 act, Sir Desmond de Silva published a report in December 2012, which provided evidence of state collaboration with loyalist paramilitaries.[81] In particular, de Silva noted: 'I believe, on balance of probabilities, that an RUC officer or officers did propose Patrick Finucane (along with at least one other man) as a UDA target when speaking to a loyalist paramilitary [...] in RUC Castlereagh on either 8 or 9 December 1988.'[82]

Cory also recommended an investigation into collusion between An Garda Siochana and the IRA in the killings of two prominent RUC officers. On 20 March 1989 RUC Chief Superintendent Harry Breen and Superintendent Robert Buchanan attended a meeting at Dundalk Garda Station with senior Gardai. On their return journey to Northern Ireland they were ambushed at Jonesborough, close to the border, by the IRA, who used a heavy machine gun to fire upon their vehicle, striking it twenty-five times. Breen, the divisional commander of the South Armagh and Newry area, had acted as police spokesman after the Loughgall shootings of 1987, where SAS soldiers had killed many key members of the IRA's East Tyrone Brigade.[83] Sinn Fein publicity director Danny Morrison described the killings as 'a prestige attack and coup'.[84] This comment was somewhat at odds with the statement Gerry Adams had given when he claimed that he sought a 'non-armed political movement to work for self-determination' in Ireland. In 2000, using parliamentary privilege, Democratic Unionist MP, and cousin of two UDR soldiers who were killed by the IRA, Jeffrey Donaldson alleged that former Garda detective sergeant Owen Corrigan had colluded with the IRA in the killings.[85]

The Irish Government established a tribunal under Judge Peter Smithwick in 2005. Following five years of investigations, public hearings began in 2011 and Smithwick published his final report in December 2013. He concluded that members of the Garda had provided information to the IRA which facilitated the killings of the two RUC officers.[86] He did not, however, assign blame to any particular Garda officer.[87]

Conclusion

That British security forces colluded with loyalist paramilitaries during the Northern Ireland conflict, particularly during the period between 1976 and 1990, is clear. Crucial questions, however, remain about the extent to which this was an active British government policy. In many cases, loyalist paramilitaries, eager to wreak havoc on the innocent Catholic communities that they perceived to be harbouring the IRA, would have been willing participants. They would not have required financial compensation or some perverted notion of carrying out a task for queen and country.

Further key questions remain, notably on the utility of collusion. Anne Cadwallader makes a convincing case that the UK government could garner support from their counterparts in Dublin as a result of the Dublin and Monaghan bombs.[88] One of the major outstanding questions was addressed by former IRA volunteer and author Anthony McIntyre, who conducted a three-part interview with Bill Lowry, the former head of the RUC's Special Branch in Belfast, in his online journal *The Blanket*. One of the questions raised was why so many innocent Catholics were killed compared to republican paramilitaries. Lowry responded: 'If we colluded as much with loyalists as is often alleged by republicans why did they kill so many innocent Catholics and very few republicans? Would the purpose of collusion not have been to target senior republicans?' McIntyre, in turn, pointed out the argument made by journalist Ed Moloney that the security force's concern was to avoid loyalist killings of security force agents within the republican paramilitaries.[89] The murky web of British operations in Northern Ireland effectively created collusion as a means by which to protect itself.

Lowry's argument bears some comment. Seventeen IRA volunteers died at the hands of loyalists during the conflict, a figure that surely would have been significantly higher were loyalists operating with high-level intelligence. Many loyalist organizations may have adopted the Gusty Spence doctrine, cited in Martin Dillon's *The Shankill Butchers* as 'if you can't get an IRA man, you shoot a taig', referring to the pejorative term used to describe Catholics within loyalist communities.[90] This does not reconcile with the attempts that were made on the lives of Bernadette McAliskey and Gerry Adams, which leading loyalists noted were much sought after operations. An argument has been made, notably by Nicholas Davies, that haphazard but deadly violence on the part of loyalist paramilitaries within Catholic communities played a role in eroding support for the IRA.[91] This argument, while persuasive, rather ignores the limited support that the IRA enjoyed throughout the conflict from within nationalist communities.

Cowardice and incompetence are certainly allegations that can be levelled at loyalist paramilitaries, particularly in the later years of the conflict as criminality and the lure of financial gain and a sort of celebrity status became attractive to loyalist leaders who lacked the same principles that had marked their predecessors. Most famously, Johnny 'Mad Dog' Adair found it rather easier to order killings than to carry them out himself. The Adair era of loyalism was marked by internecine feuds over territory and prestige and loyalists found themselves once again on the outside as peace negotiations took place.[92]

Through the tireless work of the centre that was founded in his name and through continuing efforts on the part of his family to get to the truth of his killing, Pat Finucane remains the name most closely associated with collusion between British security forces and loyalist paramilitaries in Northern Ireland. His brutal murder in front of his family was one of the most shocking killings of the conflict. The work of the PFC researchers, particularly their ability to access previously classified documents under Freedom of Information requests, has opened up new avenues of research for future scholars as the issue of collusion and the degree to which the British state influenced the actions of groups like the UDA and UVF can be further researched and analysed. Even with the work of the PFC and scholars of the Northern Ireland conflict, the likelihood remains that a full understanding of collusion in Northern Ireland may never be possible.

Notes

1   The Stevens Enquiry: Overview and Recommendations, Sir John Stevens QPM, DL, Commissioner of the Metropolitan Police Service, 17 April 2003, available at http://cai

n.ulst.ac.uk/issues/violence/docs/stevens3/stevens3summary.pdf (accessed 1 January 2020).
2. Peter Taylor, *Loyalists* (London: Bloomsbury, 2000), 205–6.
3. *The New York Times*, 12 September 1989.
4. Taylor, *Loyalists*, 206.
5. *Irish Times*, 19 June 2016.
6. See Henry McDonald and Jim Cusack, *UDA: Inside the Heart of Loyalist Terror* (Dublin: Penguin, 2004), 165, 203–4.
7. John Stevens, *Not for the Faint-Hearted: My Life Fighting Crime* (London: Weidenfeld and Nicholson, 2005), 5, 162–3.
8. *Irish Times*, 19 June 2016.
9. See Andrew Sanders, Northern Ireland: The Intelligence War 1969–1975, *British Journal of Politics and International Relations* 13/2 (2011), 230–48.
10. Former E4A Officer, interview, 16 February 2009.
11. Nicholas Davies, *Ten-Thirty-Three: The Inside Story of Britain's Secret Killing Machine in Northern Ireland* (Edinburgh: Mainstream, 1999), 94–8, 129–35, 188–9; *The Guardian*, 17 April 2003; Taylor, *Loyalists*, 209.
12. *Sunday Herald*, 19 November 2000.
13. David McKittrick, Seamus Kelters, Brian Feeney, Chris Thornton and David McVea, *Lost Lives: The Stories of the Men, Women and Children Who Died as a Result of the Northern Ireland Troubles* (Edinburgh: Mainstream, 2008), 1290–1.
14. *Sunday Herald*, 16 February 2003.
15. *The Guardian*, 17 April 2003; *Irish Times*, 19 June 2016.
16. *The Daily Telegraph*, 20 April 2003.
17. *Socialist Worker*, 7 April 2007.
18. The Stevens Inquiry: Overview and Recommendations.
19. *Belfast Telegraph*, 3 September 2003.
20. *Guardian*, 16 April 2003.
21. Martin Ingram and Greg Harkin, *Stakeknife: Britain's Secret Agents in Ireland* (Madison: University of Wisconsin Press, 2005), 196; *Belfast Telegraph*, 21 December 2011. A wider study of the role of informers in the Northern Ireland conflict would certainly require further comment on Stakeknife, though for the purposes of this study, which focuses on loyalist paramilitaries, the case is only of tangential relevance.
22. Martin Dillon, *The Dirty War* (London: Arrow, 1990).
23. Maurice Punch, *State Violence, Collusion and the Troubles: Counter Insurgency, Government Deviance and Northern Ireland* (London: Pluto Press, 2012), 199.
24. Anne Cadwallader, *Lethal Allies: British Collusion in Ireland* (Cork: Mercier Press, 2013); Margaret Urwin, *A State in Denial: British Collusion with Loyalist Paramilitaries* (Cork: Mercier Press, 2016).
25. Report of the Bloody Sunday Inquiry, 15 June 2010, available at https://www.gov.uk/government/publications/report-of-the-bloody-sunday-inquiry (accessed 1 January 2020).
26. *The Guardian*, 16 December 2016.
27. *The Guardian*, 8 December 2016.
28. Lt. Gen. Irwin, interview, 16 February 2009.
29. *Irish News*, 4 August 2007.
30. Sanders and Wood, *Times of Troubles*, 196–7, 199, 200–3.
31. Instructions by the Director of Operations for Opening Fire in Northern Ireland, Restricted Document, November 1971, in Linen Hall Library, Belfast, Northern Ireland Political Collection, Army Cuttings, Box 2.

32 On the 'yellow card', see Sanders and Wood, *Times of Troubles*, 94, 171, 177, 185, 221.
33 Operation Banner was the codename given to the British military operation in Northern Ireland.
34 Michael Dewar, *The British Army in Northern Ireland* (London: Arms and Armour Press, 1985), 59.
35 For full details, see McKittrick et al., *Lost Lives*, 46–411.
36 McKittrick et al., *Lost Lives*, 337–8.
37 Desmond Hamill, *Pig in the Middle: The Army in Northern Ireland, 1969–1984* (London: Methuen, 1985), 137.
38 Former soldier, Royal Scots, interview, 1 September 2009.
39 Sunday Times Insight Team, *Ulster* (London: Penguin, 1972), 280–1.
40 Saville Inquiry, Vol. IX, Para 194:10, p. 234, available at http://webarchive.nationalarchives.gov.uk/20101017060814/http://report.bloody-sunday-inquiry.org (accessed 1 January 2020).
41 Ibid.
42 *Guardian*, 20 June 2011.
43 McKittrick et al., *Lost Lives*, 1159–62.
44 Frank Kitson, *Gangs and Counter-Gangs* (London: Barrie and Rockliff, 1960); also *Low Intensity Operations: Subversion, Insurgency, Peace-keeping* (London: Faber and Faber, 1971).
45 *Irish Times*, 27 April 2015. The implication of the device being British-issued was that it had either been given to the individual responsible or perhaps stolen.
46 *Irish Times*, 7 April 1966; 9 May 1966; 25 November 1966.
47 Gareth Mulvenna, *Tartan Gangs and Paramilitaries: The Loyalist Backlash* (Liverpool: Liverpool University Press, 2016).
48 The B-Specials were the part-time reserve unit of the Ulster Special Constabulary and were disbanded in 1970, with many of their members joining the newly formed Ulster Defence Regiment.
49 McKittrick et al., *Lost Lives*, 555–7.
50 McKittrick et al., *Lost Lives*, 511, 555–7, 716–17.
51 Cadwallader, *Lethal Allies*, 223.
52 Commission of Investigation into the Dublin and Monaghan Bombings of 1974, Final Report, March 2007, available at http://www.dublinmonaghanbombings.org/home/docs/CommissionOfInvestigationFinalReport.pdf (accessed 1 January 2020). An Garda Siochana is the state police force of the Republic of Ireland. Gardai is the plural of Garda.
53 *Irish News*, 11 February 2006.
54 Baron Hunt, *Report of the Advisory Committee on Police in Northern Ireland* (Belfast: Her Majesty's Stationery Office, 1969).
55 Brigadier Charles Ritchie CBE, interview, 26 August 2010.
56 *Guardian*, 3 May 2007.
57 Cadwallader, *Lethal Allies*, 227–32.
58 David Beresford, Devlin is 'very ill' after shooting, *The Guardian*, 17 January 1981.
59 Taylor, *Loyalists*, 168.
60 *Sunday Times*, 28 February 1999.
61 McDonald and Cusack, *UDA*, 116–18.
62 Ian S. Wood, *Crimes of Loyalty: A History of the UDA* (Edinburgh: Edinburgh University Press, 2006), 122; McDonald and Cusack, *UDA*, 118.
63 Wood, *Crimes of Loyalty*, 120.

64 *An Phoblacht*, 14 March 2014.
65 *Guardian*, 17 January 1981.
66 *Guardian*, 18 March 1981.
67 Sergeant Begg, interview with Ian S. Wood, 25 August 1992.
68 Ibid.
69 *The Guardian*, 24 August 2002.
70 McDonald and Cusack, *UDA*, 129–30.
71 Wood, *Crimes of Loyalty*, 119–20.
72 Note of a meeting with Representatives of the Provisional IRA, Ballyarnett, near Donegal Border, 3.00 p.m., 20 June 1972, in PREM 15/1009, National Archives of the United Kingdom, London.
73 Ed Moloney, *Voices from the Grave: Two Men's War in Ireland* (London: Faber, 2010), 415; *Guardian*, 13 June 2002.
74 Davies, *Ten-Thirty-Three*, 126.
75 Stevens Enquiry: Overview and Recommendations.
76 *Guardian*, 12 December 2001. Stobie was also questioned over the death of Protestant Brian Lambert on 9 November 1987, believed to have been a misdirected reprisal for the IRA's Enniskillen bomb.
77 Wood, *Crimes of Loyalty*, 120–1. This was also a claim of loyalists involved in the attempt to kill Gerry Adams, as noted on the previous page.
78 *Guardian*, 14 June 2002.
79 David Lister and Hugh Jordan, *Mad Dog: The Rise and fall of Johnny Adair and 'C Company'* (Edinburgh: Mainstream, 2003), 53–4.
80 *Guardian*, 17 January 2011; *The Times*, 14 September 2004; *Guardian*, 13 September 2004.
81 The Rt. Hon. Sir Desmond de Silva, *The Report of the Patrick Finucane Review*, December 2012, https://www.gov.uk/government/uploads/system/uploads/attachment_data/file/246867/0802.pdf (accessed 1 January 2020); see also Peter Cory, *Cory Collusion Inquiry Reports* (London: The Stationery Office, 2004).
82 De Silva, *The Report of the Patrick Finucane Review*, 16.
83 *The New York Times*, 10 May 1987.
84 *The New York Times*, 26 March 1989.
85 *Belfast Telegraph*, 3 December 2013.
86 Report of the Tribunal of Inquiry into suggestions that members of An Garda Siochana or other employees of the state colluded in the fatal shootings of RUC Chief Superintendent Harry Breen and RUC Superintendent Robert Buchanan on the 20th March 1989, Dublin, 2013, http://opac.oireachtas.ie/AWData/Library3/smithwickFinal03122013_171046.pdf (accessed 1 January 2020).
87 *Daily Telegraph*, 3 December 2013.
88 Cadwallader, *Lethal Allies*, 227–32.
89 Anthony McIntyre, Out From the Shadows, *The Blanket: A Journal of Protest and Dissent*, 11 July 2004.
90 Martin Dillon, *The Shankill Butchers: A Case Study of Mass Murder* (London: Arrow, 1989), xxi.
91 Davies, *Ten-Thirty-Three*, 211.
92 Jordan and Lister, *Mad Dog*; Ian S. Wood covers Adair in some detail, see *Crimes of Loyalty*, 171–2, 220–79, among many references to Adair and his activities.

Chapter 4

THE SECRET 1970 MORATORIUM AGREEMENT BETWEEN SWITZERLAND AND THE PLO

Marcel Gyr

Translation from German by Thomas Skelton-Robinson

A persistent rumour

In autumn 2015, shortly after his retirement from the University of Zurich, Professor Jakob Tanner published his *Geschichte der Schweiz im 20. Jahrhundert* ('The History of Switzerland in the Twentieth Century').[1] In his book Tanner discusses the series of terrorist attacks in 1969 and 1970 that set off public shockwaves in the country. Tanner's narrative begins with the shooting of an El Al Boeing on 18 February 1969 at Zurich's Kloten Airport by four activists from the Popular Front for the Liberation of Palestine (PFLP) in which a pilot died in the hail of gunfire. One of the attackers was shot dead by an Israeli security officer, the other three were arrested. Tanner's enumeration continues with the parcel bomb attack on a Swissair Coronado en route from Zurich to Tel Aviv by Ahmed Jibril's PFLP-General Command on 21 February 1970. The explosion, which, according to Tanner, was in fact intended to have targeted an El Al flight, caused the plane to crash close to Würenlingen in Canton Aargau, killing all forty-seven people on board. Finally, he refers to the hijacking of three civilian airliners, including one belonging to Swissair, in September 1970, with the aim, among others, of forcing the release of the three Kloten Airport assailants.[2] Tanner concludes his section on the series of Palestinian attacks with the following words: 'The actions of the Swiss authorities in the subsequent prosecution of the PFLP activists involved in the attacks remained passive: the persistent rumor, still current today, is that the investigations were shelved during the course of negotiations with the Palestinians.'[3]

A fierce controversy

Independently of Tanner's reference, a few months later, in January 2016, the book *Schweizer Terrorjahre – Das geheime Abkommen mit der PLO* ('The Terror Years in

Switzerland – The Secret Agreement with the PLO') appeared under the imprint of the publishing house of the *Neue Zürcher Zeitung* (*NZZ*).[4] In the account I, as the author, elaborated the thesis that Switzerland had sealed a secret moratorium agreement with the Palestine Liberation Organization (PLO) in September 1970. On the Swiss side, the negotiations had been orchestrated by *Bundesrat* (Federal Councillor, a member of the federal cabinet) Pierre Graber, the then head of the *Eidgenössisches Politisches Departement* (Federal Political Department, EPD), who had secretly established contact with Farouk Kaddoumi, a founding Fatah member and, later, the foreign affairs representative of the PLO.[5] Furthermore, I asserted that this contact had been mediated in the context of what is known in Switzerland as the Zarqa Crisis (and in English commonly as the Dawson's Field Hijackings, or in its larger context, the September crisis) by Jean Ziegler, a long-serving Swiss parliamentarian, world-renowned book author and one-time professor of sociology at the University of Geneva.[6]

In my book I also stated that there was no conclusive evidence for a causal connection between the moratorium and the failure to prosecute the suspects in the Swissair bombing over Würenlingen, the main perpetrator being one Sufian Kaddoumi. Nevertheless, I argued that there are a series of indications that would at least suggest that this conclusion could be drawn.[7] My theory concerning a secret agreement with the PLO was based largely on the spoken testimony of three sources: the previously mentioned Jean Ziegler and Farouk Kaddoumi as the directly and indirectly involved parties at the time, as well as a former ranking Swiss intelligence service officer, who requested anonymity. According to my findings the verbal agreement consisted of a promise to spare Switzerland from further terrorist attacks on the Palestinian side, while Switzerland undertook a pledge to support the PLO on the diplomatic stage, including in particular the opening of a PLO office in Geneva.[8]

Following the publication of my book, I continued my investigations. Based on various references in the final report of the *Interdepartementale Arbeitsgruppe '1970'* (Interdepartmental Working Group '1970', henceforth IDA 1970 or Working Group),[9] a telephone interview with Ilich Ramirez Sanchez (aka 'Carlos'),[10] follow-up conversations with Jean Ziegler and the inspection of further files in the *Bundesarchiv* (Swiss Federal Archives)[11] I would like to reassert the account presented in my book, but also to make certain modifications to it.

The leading Swiss figure in the negotiations with the Palestinians was, as I described in my original account, Federal Councillor Pierre Graber and the ministry he headed. From an early stage, *Bundesanwalt* (Federal Public Prosecutor) Hans Walder and André Amstein, the then head of the *Bundespolizei* (Swiss Federal Police, BUPO) were likewise involved in the project, although they probably played less active roles than I presented in my book. In 1970 the *Bundesanwaltschaft* (Federal Public Prosecutor's Office), including the BUPO, was, in contrast to nowadays, not an independent body. As the IDA 1970 outlined in their final report, at the time the Federal Public Prosecutor acted under the supervision and direction of the *Bundesrat* (Federal Council, that is, the Swiss government or cabinet). In other words, the Federal Public Prosecutor was obliged

4. The Secret 1970 Moratorium Agreement between Switzerland and the PLO 65

to accept instructions issued by the Federal Council.[12] Based on what has come to light so far, the picture that emerges is as follows. From the outset the head of the BUPO Amstein repeatedly registered his misgivings about the opening of a PLO office in Geneva,[13] but nevertheless 'grudgingly' complied with the various orders emanating from the EPD. The minister in charge of the EPD, Federal Councillor Pierre Graber, was the prime mover in the deal. His fellow Federal Councillor Ludwig von Moos, who as minister in charge of the *Eidgenössisches Justiz- und Polizeidepartement* (Federal Department of Justice and Police, EJPD) was formally responsible for the Public Prosecutor's Office and the BUPO, played in reality a subordinate role.

A second adjustment concerns the time frame in which the negotiations with the PLO took place. Although in several places in my book I set the parameters to September 1970, or, rather, to a date directly connected with the Zarqa Crisis, it is in the meantime evident that this time frame was too narrow. In fact, the establishment of contacts with the Palestinians had already commenced in summer 1970 as a reaction to the Würenlingen bombing, and, as a consequence, the negotiations may well have stretched until the end of 1970 or even, for that matter, the first days of 1971.

In the process a new name comes into play: Fuad al-Shamali, a Jordanian citizen who at the time was Fatah's informal representative in Switzerland.[14] According to my information Farouk Kaddoumi reached a basic understanding with the Swiss authorities in Geneva during a two- or three-day visit in autumn 1970 that was sealed with a handshake. The transaction was subsequently handed over to his fellow Fatah member al-Shamali, whose wife lived in Geneva, for detailed consultations. This point will be returned to later.

Following the appearance of *Schweizer Terrorjahre* in late January 2016 a public debate broke out, much of it heated. The assertion that Federal Councillor Graber had been responsible for a secret moratorium agreement with the PLO was first cast into doubt in French-speaking Switzerland, in particular by the former ambassador François Nordmann, who had entered service in the EPD in 1971 and from 1975 had served as Federal Councillor Graber's personal assistant until the latter's resignation in early 1978. In a column in the daily newspaper *Le Temps*, Nordmann ultimately came to the conclusion that the prevailing opinion was that there had been no secret deal – the *NZZ* was, in his opinion, unable to furnish the 'smoking gun', the irrefutable piece of evidence.[15]

With a slight time lag the controversy was then taken up in German-speaking Switzerland by the *Tages-Anzeiger*. On 6 February 2016 the title page of the newspaper quoted Franz Blankart, a former top diplomat and personal assistant to Federal Councillor Graber, with the words: 'There was no secret deal with the PLO.'[16] In an interview printed the same day Blankart asserted that he could not find the evidence for a deal in the book; the whole thing sounded fictitious to him. It was impossible that something of such impact was not in writing somewhere. And even if nothing had been put into a protocol, he, Blankart, would have known about any such agreement. Admittedly Federal Councillor Graber had been power-hungry, but he had been a person of absolute loyalty and integrity – he would never have deceived the Federal Council. Moreover, during the Jordan hijackings Graber had been preoccupied night and day in Berne with the efforts to free the hostages.[17]

A few days after this assessment I met Blankart in Berne for a personal conversation. He emphasized that he stood by his statements. His only qualification related to the fact that he was unable to say with certainty whether he had been in the EPD in Berne until the very end of the Zarqa Crisis. It might have been the case that he had been posted to Brussels in the course of September 1970, in other words prior to the ending of the hostage drama. This conjecture is confirmed in the final report of the IDA 1970. An entry in Federal Councillor Graber's private agenda for 22 September 1970 reads 'Départ Blankart' ('Departure Blankart').[18] Therefore, Blankart, in fact, left Berne over a week before the Zarqa Crisis came to an end with the deportation of the three Kloten Airport attackers to Cairo on 1 October 1970, and as such he was no longer a first-hand witness to the events in the EPD in these crucial closing days.

Following Blankart's transfer to Brussels his position as Federal Councillor Graber's personal assistant was filled by Pierre-Yves Simonin. I originally approached Simonin for information in summer 2015 during the research for my book, but he wrote back that he was unable to oblige due to a 'blurred memory' of the period in question, ending his email rather brusquely with the words: 'A telephone call would therefore be a pure loss of time for you (and for me).'[19] What is evident, however, is that Simonin was involved at the heart of negotiations in February 1971 when deliberations regarding a PLO office in Geneva entered into their decisive stage: he and a second EPD representative discussed for over three hours with two Palestinian functionaries, one of whom was the later office head Daoud Barakat.[20]

The IDA 1970, to which I have already repeatedly referred, was formed following the publication of my book based on a mandate issued by the Federal Council. It began its work in February 2016. Operating under the auspices of the EPD's successor, the *Eidgenössisches Departement für auswärtige Angelegenheiten* (Federal Department of Foreign Affairs, EDA), the Working Group also included representatives from other departments, the Federal Archives and the Federal Public Prosecutor's Office.[21] The Working Group's remit was, in particular, to pursue two questions:

- Did Switzerland, indeed, finalize an agreement with the PLO in September 1970?
- Did federal law enforcement agencies undertake serious clarifications and thorough investigations following the Würenlingen plane crash in February 1970?[22]

In May 2016, the Working Group presented its final report. It had consulted almost 400 dossiers and a series of files (known in Switzerland, due to their physical form, as *Fichen*, derived from the French *fiches* or index cards) from six departments and the *Bundeskanzlei* (the Federal Chancellery). All the federal administration documents that were reviewed are listed in the final report.[23] As far as oral testimonies were concerned the Working Group was of the opinion that their use was permissible only within clearly defined terms. The upshot was that both persons who had already publicly stated that they knew nothing and those who had publicly stated what they did know were not even recontacted. In addition, as opposed to the book's author, the Working Group chose not to publish anonymous witness testimony.[24]

Set against this background, the Working Group contacted the following three individuals: Walter Buser (who as vice chancellor had been responsible for the minutes of the meetings of the Federal Council), Pierre-Yves Simonin and Farouk Kaddoumi. Nevertheless, these three people were, in fact, not questioned in person orally by the Working Group, as is implied in the final report, but rather in writing. In Kaddoumi's case this took the form of a questionnaire, passed on to him by the Swiss Embassy in Amman (after thirty years in Tunisia, Kaddoumi was in the meantime living in Jordan).[25] Regarding my claim of a meeting between Kaddoumi and a delegation from Berne in Geneva in September 1970, the final report states: 'The written answers provided by Farouk Kaddoumi, the last remaining alleged participant, demonstrate that he does not recall such an encounter.'[26]

An examination of the questionnaire, reproduced in the appendixes to the final report, reveals the following: Farouk Kaddoumi answers all four of the Working Group's queries with the stereotyped words 'I do not remember'. Even at the end of the list of questions, in response to the confirmation 'Read and approved on 20.04.2016 in Amman, Hashemite Kingdom of Jordan', Kaddoumi wrote 'I do not remember'.[27] As such, taken literally, he cannot recall having even read the Working Group's questionnaire.

Furthermore, the IDA 1970 final report records that Farouk Kaddoumi had verifiably visited Switzerland over twenty times, both officially and secretly, but not prior to 1976.[28] This fact is likewise referred to by Sacha Zala, Thomas Bürgisser and Yves Steiner from the *Diplomatische Dokumente der Schweiz* (Diplomatic Documents of Switzerland, DDS and the online Dodis database) in an academic article (henceforth DDS article).[29] According to their findings, the documents recording the arrivals of bearers of diplomatic or regular travel papers issued by the Arab states contain no mention of a man registered as entering Switzerland under the name Kaddoumi in the relevant period, nor for that matter any of the various phonetic transliterations of his name, or under his nom de guerre Abu Lutf or anything similar.[30]

This contradicts information given by my anonymous Swiss intelligence service source, by Ziegler and by Kaddoumi, who I met twice in person in Tunis together with the local *NZZ* reporter Annette Steinich. Kaddoumi, who was in poor health, failed to respond immediately to the catchwords 'September 1970, triple airplane hijacking to Zarqa', but later in the conversation unexpectedly returned to the subject of his visit to Switzerland himself. In response to my surprised queries he provided specific details, saying that at the time he had been invited to Geneva. He had been received by a delegation from Berne in a five-star hotel with a view of the landmark Jet d'Eau, the same delegation having taken leave of him at the end of his visit. He was unable to remember either names or the precise date. He had planned to attend a foreign ministers' meeting in Paris when Switzerland had asked him for assistance, so he had expressed his willingness to make a stopover in Geneva. After the talks his interlocutors had paid his taxi fare to Paris so that he could join the meeting on time.[31] Referring to this detail the authors of the DDS article raise the fact that the search for proof of Kaddoumi's sojourn in Paris had to date likewise been unsuccessful.[32]

Jean Ziegler, who claims to have mediated Kaddoumi's journey to Geneva, was, according to his own account, not personally present at the meeting.[33] At first glance this would seem somewhat surprising, but is perhaps explained by a detail in the IDA 1970 final report: in a confidential talk with a childhood friend in summer 1970 Federal Councillor Graber made it clear that he did not trust Ziegler and that under no circumstances did he want to have him present during possible talks or negotiations.[34]

As far as Kaddoumi's visits to Switzerland are concerned the Working Group's final report initially stated that police diligence could by no means guarantee that all of them had been documented – in addition to the numerous recorded visits there might be a certain number of non-registered stays.[35] Despite this, the conclusion reached is as follows:

> There is [...] no trace of al-Qaddumi having visited Geneva prior to the opening of the PLO office in Geneva [...]. A general overview of the information contained in these records allows such earlier visits to appear as a possibility, but for September 1970 as unlikely[;] a meeting [of] al-Qaddumi and Graber and a Swiss-Palestinian agreement in September 1970 can be ruled out with a probability bordering on certainty.[36]

The early Geneva PLO office

The first initiatives to open a PLO office in Geneva that occurred in early 1971 are described by the IDA 1970 in their final report with these words: 'Following the Zarqa Crisis the PLO approached the Swiss authorities via two intermediaries. A clergyman offered the Berne notary Hans Ellenberger, who was involved in promoting Swiss-Arab friendship, a type of deal along the lines of "less terror in exchange for the opening of an office in Geneva".'[37] With this proposal, the wording of which corresponds almost exactly to the secret accord alleged by me, Ellenberger visited Michael Gelzer, the EPD state secretary. Gelzer recorded the details of Ellenberger's visit, which took place at the latter's urgent wish,[38] in a memorandum on 14 January.[39]

The IDA 1970 evaluates Ellenberger's initiative in this way: 'This proposal for a deal, presented to the federal administration in 1971, was not connected to any prior deal of the same nature, and was met with resistance from the relevant authorities, in particular from within the EJPD and the Geneva Police.'[40] Although it is correct that the corresponding documents contain no reference to

4. The Secret 1970 Moratorium Agreement between Switzerland and the PLO   69

an earlier deal, nonetheless it is worth repeating that the contents of the proposal conspicuously mirror those outlined in my book.

In addition, the Working Group takes the view that the Geneva PLO office was officially opened only in 1975.[41] Consequently the demands set by the Palestinians in the deal outlined in my book were not even fulfilled. The authors of the DDS article similarly point to the fact that there was no corresponding Federal Council resolution in 1971,[42] although elsewhere in their article they concede that already in summer 1971 the Federal Council had in principle expressed its agreement to allow a Palestinian journalist to be accredited in Geneva.[43]

The PLO office was, as stated, indeed officially opened in 1975. It is equally pertinent, however, that the Swiss authorities and their Palestinian contact person Daoud Barakat had already reached a broad agreement to install an unofficial PLO agency in Geneva in the second half of 1971. With public feelings in mind, the agency was to be disguised as an office for a Fatah correspondent. These plans were only nullified by a bomb attack on the Jordanian UNO mission in Geneva on 16 December 1971 in which two police officers were slightly injured and a Geneva Airport fireman critically wounded. The attack remained unsolved, but in the aftermath the EPD suspended the plans for the opening of an unofficial office. Up until this point however, that is, around a year after the Zarqa Crisis, the EPD had explicitly signalled its approval for the opening of a PLO agency in Geneva. These circumstances are evident in the telling titles of the two corresponding dossiers: 'Eröffnung PLO-Büro in Genf, 1971–1975'[44] and, in particular, 'Bureau palestinien à Genéve (OLP/PLO) 1971–1973'.[45]

It was in this vein that EPD state secretary Gelzer wrote to selected Swiss Embassies on 6 August 1971: 'On 4 August we were verbally apprised of the fact that the Palestinians are willing to meet these guidelines for the activities of the office. As far as our side is concerned, as soon as the written confirmation of Palestinian consent is presented there are no further obstacles to the definitive authorisation for the opening of the office.'[46] On 8 August 1971, Gelzer again addressed a memorandum to the same ambassadors and to the *Fremdenpolizei* (the aliens' branch of the police) in response to a leak in the Egyptian press a few days earlier announcing the launch of the PLO office in Geneva. The item had been picked up by the Swiss press agency SDA, and the *NZZ*, for instance, reporting on 2 August 1971: 'The Palestine Liberation Organisation (PLO) has received permission from the Federal Political Department to open an information office in Geneva that is to nominally serve to maintain contacts with the UN Geneva headquarters.'[47] The communication from the EPD official contains not a single word either denying or even qualifying the report, and the sixteen Swiss daily newspapers that had reprinted it are listed minus any commentary whatsoever.[48]

Although by autumn 1971 the final confirmation from the Swiss authorities was still pending, the PLO had, as a report by the Geneva Cantonal Police noted, already rented a four and half-room premises at 31 rue du XXXI-Décembre that a member of Barakat's staff had spent a number of months arranging and furnishing.[49] In an EPD memorandum dated 10 December 1971, it was noted that Barakat had mentioned that the facility was ready for business, apparently since 1

December. At the same time, however, he explained that he would now probably forego an office – a move probably undertaken in response to the strict stipulations laid down by the EPD, according to which the office would be allowed to operate only under the brass-plate designation 'Correspondant du Fath, Journal et Radio'. Barakat interjected that the original intention had been to fill the post with someone of ambassadorial rank, but that in the meantime they would simply have to properly rethink their position. Strictly speaking, office space, a library and the other items were secondary. They were content to make do with more pragmatic arrangements elsewhere; for instance, in Paris where the PLO representative was a student. The notary Hans Ellenberger, who was likewise present during the encounter, disagreed. In his opinion the PLO should under no circumstances do without an office. An information official required a library, editorial space and so on.[50]

Apparently, Ellenberger won the argument, as shown by a lunch with a member of the EPD staff on 23 December 1971 when Barakat announced that the office was in the meantime ready, including a library and furnishings. The costs to date amounted to around 25,000 Swiss Francs, which had yet to be paid.[51] As early as 15 December 1971 Barakat had telephoned the EPD to inform them that the PLO had accepted the conditions for the approval for two PLO journalists.[52]

However, due to the bombing of the Jordanian UNO mission a day later the EPD informed Barakat during the lunch on 23 December that the finalization of the project would have to be postponed for at least a couple of months.[53] A few days prior to this, in an internal discussion on 20 December 1971 chaired by general secretary Pierre Micheli, the EPD had nevertheless come to the conclusion that despite the new situation it would be inadvisable to directly confront the Palestinians with a cancellation of the project. 'We must be aware that a refusal could have consequences.'[54]

The IDA 1970 likewise compiled a chronology of what they referred to as the 'pre-history of the Geneva PLO office' in their final report. Although their work on this aspect is based on other documents, their findings can likewise be interpreted to read that the well-advanced plans by the EPD to permit the PLO to maintain an informal office in Geneva were stymied by the bomb attack of 16 December 1971.[55] Despite this, the IDA 1970 drew the following conclusion to their overview concerning the Geneva office:

> There is not only no trace whatsoever of an alleged agreement concluded in September 1970, but the reading of these papers also makes it extremely unlikely in the sense that one side or the other, or indeed both, would most certainly have invoked it during the numerous controversies over minor issues. Moreover, had such an agreement existed then the Geneva bomb attack of 16 December 1971 would have represented a gross breach of it, which would have definitely resulted in a Swiss censure, of which there is no such trace.[56]

The second part of this conclusion is incorrect. It is curious to talk in terms of a simple Swiss reprimand in response to the bombing of the Jordanian UNO mission, when in fact the attack had far more drastic consequences, namely the suspension of the pending opening of the PLO office for years to come. But for the attack, which was never solved, an unofficial Geneva PLO office would have undoubtedly been opened.

What is correct, on the other hand, is the first part of the Working Group's conclusion in the section of their report dealing with the early history of the Geneva PLO office. There is no direct evidence of my claimed autumn 1970 moratorium in the documents consulted: in none of the numerous notes and memorandums does either party refer to a verbal agreement. This absence is likewise highlighted in the DDS essay: 'In the last resort, the question that poses itself is what sense and purpose a verbal agreement has if no reference is ever made to it and apparently no one knew about it.'[57] Considering the current information available I am unable to provide a convincing answer to this objection. The lack of written proof for my case for a deal with the PLO remains the weak point in my thesis.

Traces of a deal

Having said this, in this context I would like to raise an interesting point that has been neglected in the discussion up until now. In his 2013 dissertation, the Basle historian Jonathan Kreutner tackled, among other things, the subject of the early diplomatic relations between Switzerland and the Palestinians.[58] In exploring the topic Kreutner also examined the dossier concerning events surrounding the planned PLO office in Geneva from 1971 onwards, and concluded: 'A study of the files creates at least the subjective impression that the Swiss authorities considered themselves powerless in their exposure to the pressures exerted by Barakat.'[59]

In another passage dealing with the suspension of discussions regarding the PLO office following the bomb attack on the Jordanian UNO mission in Geneva, Kreutner notes:

> The Palestinian Daoud Barakat remained the PLO's contact person to the EPD, and time and time again he resorted to strong-arm tactics: in response to every Swiss action that displeased him he subtly intimated this or that would 'provoke risks' and that the 'extremists would now extend their desire for revenge to Switzerland again'. Reading the sources gives the impression as if the Swiss authorities' response to Barakat's attempts at intimidation was one of helplessness.[60]

On reading about the deal between Switzerland and the PLO in the *NZZ* Kreutner experienced what the *Basler Zeitung* in an article on 22 January 2016 described as something of a revelation: 'A number of things that I was unable to categorise up until now are now evident.'[61] What Kreutner had apparently sensed in the course of reading the documents was an invisible lever with which Barakat had been able to pressurize the Swiss authorities.

My claim of an agreement is also echoed in another important respect, namely in the form of a person who repeatedly and very publicly referred to a verbal deal between Switzerland and Arab underground organizations. This person is the French lawyer Jacques Vergès, widely known as the 'terror's advocate' or the 'devil's advocate' because he defended, during his illustrious career, figures such as the 'top terrorist' Carlos, the Nazi war criminal Klaus Barbie ('the Butcher of Lyons'), a leading member of the Cambodian Khmer Rouge and a number of African despots.

In 1982, Maître Vergès took on the defence of the Swiss Bruno Bréguet and Magdalena Kopp, Carlos's lover, following their arrest in Paris on 16 February. Bréguet and Kopp had been apprehended, having been found with five kilograms of explosives in the boot of their car. On 15 March 1982, a month after Bréguet's arrest, the French-Swiss magazine *L'Hebdo* ran an interview with Maître Vergès. Asked by the journalists whether the French judiciary would cave in to Carlos's threats, Vergès answered that the French criminal procedural code granted the Public Prosecutor's Office, under certain circumstances, the right to refrain from a prosecution. This course was not unique to France, stressed Vergès. Two weeks previously West Germany had deported three Syrians who had been arrested transporting explosives. No information had been issued about the case. At this point in the interview Vergès turned to the example of Switzerland: 'There is an unwritten agreement between the Swiss authorities and a certain number of Arab and Israeli organisations to ensure that these organisations refrain from attacks in Switzerland; and, in return for compliance with this condition, the authorities turn a blind eye to lesser offences.'[62]

On 15 June 1982 *Nationalrat* (National Assembly member) François Jeanneret submitted a minor parliamentary interpellation under the title 'Underground Organisations: Agreements with Switzerland'. With reference to the *L'Hebdo* interview Jeanneret asked the Federal Council whether it could confirm or deny the existence of such an agreement. Almost three months later, on 8 September 1982, the Federal Council gave its answer, stating that as far as Switzerland was concerned Maître Vergès claims were completely unfounded. 'The Federal Council assures that no agreement of this type between our nation and whatever organizations has been made.'[63]

For no immediately apparent reason the IDA 1970 points out in its final report that the answer given by the Federal Council had been drafted by the Federal Public Prosecutor's Office and had not been subjected to amendments by either the EDA or any other department.[64] With that, as far as the Working Group is concerned, the matter is closed. But why would Jacques Vergès, seemingly out of the blue, conjure up the claim in 1982 that Switzerland had made an unwritten agreement with Middle East underground organizations?

The Working Group's conjecture that Vergès' public intervention probably related to an agreement claimed by the PFLP at the end of 1970, in fact, makes little sense.[65] A more adequate explanation would appear to be Vergès' close personal acquaintance with François Genoud – an ominous if not sinister figure from French-speaking Switzerland. A lifelong avowed Nazi, early in his career Genoud served as a banker to the Algerian liberation movement, a cause in which the young lawyer Jacques Vergès was active. In the late 1960s Genoud's fluid affiliations led him to lend his support to the Palestinian cause,[66] with which he shared a common enemy in Israel, bringing him into the same political orbit as Maître Vergès. In 1969, Genoud summoned the later French star lawyer to Switzerland, where Vergès was to support the official defence of the three surviving Palestinian commando members from the attack on the El Al flight at Zurich Airport.[67]

Following the 1982 arrest of Bruno Bréguet, who saw himself as a fighter for the Palestinian cause, Genoud turned once again to Vergès and mediated him as a defence lawyer for the Swiss terrorist.[68] This, therefore, constitutes the proper background against which Maître Vergès' mention of a secret agreement between Switzerland and Middle Eastern groups in his interview with *L'Hebdo* should be set. This, in turn, raises two questions: Did Genoud have knowledge of Switzerland's deal with the Palestinians? And did he confide his information about this deal to his long-standing companion Vergès?

Ilich Ramirez Sanchez answers the first question with a clear 'yes'. Carlos, the now 69-year-old Venezuelan, is currently serving a triple life imprisonment for numerous murders in a prison on the outskirts of Paris. Via his Zurich lawyer Marcel Bosonnet, I was able to conduct a long telephone interview with him in early March 2016. In the course of the conversation Carlos stated that as a *fedayeen*, in other words as a Palestinian fighter, he had been able to move freely in Switzerland in the 1970s. This freedom was due to a deal that had been negotiated following Farouk Kaddoumi's handshake in Geneva, the contact to the Swiss authorities having been established at the time by François Genoud.[69]

According to Carlos, therefore, Genoud not only knew about the deal but also, in fact, participated in bringing it about. With this in mind it can no longer come as a surprise that Jacques Vergès, mediated in 1982 by Genoud to act as Bréguet's lawyer, referred in his *L'Hebdo* interview to a verbal agreement with Middle East underground organizations. Carlos's lawyer Bosonnet, for his part, confirmed to the *NZZ* in writing that Carlos had already described these facts to him in 2011. 'My client spoke at the time of a type of non-aggression pact between Switzerland and the Palestinian commando groups. Based on his description one was able to conclude that he assumed that he had enjoyed the protection of the Swiss authorities.' Carlos had wanted to make this information public at an earlier stage but the Swiss journalist he had entrusted the story to at the time had failed to pursue it.[70]

By his own estimate, Carlos travelled to Switzerland ten times or so. The episode that particularly stuck in his mind was the route he took in early December to take part in the OPEC hostage attack in Vienna. Instead of travelling directly to Austria he had travelled from Beirut to Zurich, due to the fact that he felt that he enjoyed an impunity granted by the Swiss authorities. On the train to Vienna he had by pure chance encountered two members of the West German Revolutionäre Zellen (Revolutionary Cells) involved in the OPEC attack,[71] namely Wilfried Böse and Hans-Joachim Klein, who were likewise making their way from Zurich to Vienna on the same day. This sequence of events is confirmed in Klein's confessional 1979 book *Rückkehr in die Menschlichkeit*.[72]

Asked by telephone who had recommended Switzerland to him as a safe haven, Carlos gave two names: his then employer Wadie Haddad, the commando leader of the PFLP and, again, François Genoud. Both of them had assured him that he, together with his fellow comrades-in-arms, could move freely in Switzerland. The only thing he was warned about was to not attract unnecessary attention to himself and not to undertake any attacks – conditions that he naturally stuck to.

Farouk Kaddoumi's handshake in autumn 1971 did not represent the end of the negotiations, said Carlos, instead they marked their beginnings. Kaddoumi, described by Carlos as a dutiful diplomat, was succeeded at the negotiation table by a representative from an operationally active commando group.[73] In order to exclude any misunderstandings about the spoken form of this new figure's name Carlos added that the man in question had died of cancer in a Geneva hospital shortly afterwards.

A second explosive name

Carlos the Jackal's reliability is – needless to say – limited. For this reason, I initially took the decision not to publicly name the man said to be responsible for the negotiation of a 'non-aggression pact' on behalf of the Palestinians with Switzerland. However, the archival material I subsequently consulted contained nothing that would refute the claim. Therefore, I made the man's name public in the *NZZ* in late December 2016: Fuad al-Shamali.[74]

There is one contemporary witness who verifies the key role played by Fuad al-Shamali, namely Jean Ziegler. 'Yes, that's correct: al-Shamali negotiated the details of the agreement' said Ziegler to the *NZZ*. 'But it was Farouk Kaddoumi who continued to hold the reins in the background.' As far as the Swiss side was concerned, Ziegler's assumption is that the negotiation partner was the Geneva diplomat Pierre Micheli, the then EDP general secretary. Micheli was considered to have been a close confidant of Federal Councillor Graber. He retired in late 1970 and died in Geneva in 1989.[75] There is, to date, no written evidence for Micheli's mandate to bargain with the Palestinians – Ziegler remains the only oral witness.

The personal index card file (*Fiche*) compiled on Fuad al-Shamali by the Swiss Federal Police consists of thirteen index cards, closely written on both sides. His full name is written as 'Foad Assad El Shamali'.[76] According to the details in the index card file, al-Shamali had been born in 1935 in Lebanon, where he had taken part in a failed coup attempt in 1961, forcing him to flee to Jordan. From 1962 onwards he had been in possession of a Jordanian passport.

The first entry in his index card file is dated 22 August 1968 and consists of a harmless notification by the aliens' branch of the police.[77] In the mid-1960s al-Shamali studied in Paris, and from 1968 onwards he repeatedly spent time in Geneva where his wife worked as a translator for the Saudi Arabian UNO mission.[78] In Switzerland he took on the role of an unofficial Fatah representative.[79] He maintained close ties to the *Comité suisse de soutien au peuple palestinien* (Swiss-Palestinian Support Committee) and other pro-Palestinian groups. On 15

December 1968, the Geneva Cantonal Police informed the Federal Police in Berne that al-Shamali was ill, and that according to his doctor he would probably never fully recover.[80]

Al-Shamali suffered from Hodgkin's lymphoma, a cancer of the lymph glands.[81] His treatment took place at regular intervals in Switzerland in Geneva and Lausanne. But al-Shamali was apparently not as ill as he professed to be, according to an entry in his index card file made by an official on 10 September 1969, and was politically active in Switzerland.[82] At this point al-Shamali was subjected to criminal proceedings by the Federal Public Prosecutor's Office, accused of having engaged in political espionage, specifically that he had lifted the interrogation protocol of the Israeli security officer Mordechai Rachamim from the files of the *Bezirksanwaltschaft* (District Prosecutor's Office) in Bülach, Canton Zurich, following the Kloten Airport attack and had then published it under the title *Livre blanc* ('White Book').[83]

It was presumably in connection with these criminal proceedings that the Federal Police began on 17 July 1969 to tap al-Shamali's telephone. The relevant entry reads, in technical terms: 'An GD-PTT Anhebung TK gg. S. u. Gattin' – 'To General Direction Post Telephone and Telegraph Agency instigate telecommunications monitoring against S. and wife'.[84] An initial evaluation of this telephone surveillance from mid-July to the end of October 1969 revealed 'very numerous contacts to Genoud François'.[85]

This aspect is mirrored in somewhat greater detail in Genoud's own index card file, which was evaluated by his biographer, the French journalist Pierre Péan. As of 17 July 1969, a new figure appeared on the stage in the form of Fuad al-Shamali, as cited by Péan from Genoud's file, and in the course of time Genoud, al-Shamali and his wife became friends. According to the Federal Police, during his numerous journeys Genoud met with 'three big terrorist fish': Wadie Haddad in Lebanon, the head of the Libyan secret service in Tripoli and Fuad al-Shamali on the shores of Lake Geneva.[86]

On 24 February 1970, a few days after the bomb attack on the Swissair flight over Würenlingen, the Federal Public Prosecutor's Office instituted an entry ban against al-Shamali.[87] The relevant directive read: 'In accordance with this decreed measure, undertaken for security reasons, the person named is prohibited from entering or remaining on Swiss territory without express permission.'[88] The reasons for the entry ban are not contained in his index card file, but it remained permanently in force and was formally lifted only after al-Shamali's death in August 1972.[89]

Following the initiation of the entry ban against al-Shamali, François Genoud approached the Federal Police in March 1970 to put in a word of support for his Jordanian friend.[90] A short while later, on 25 March 1970, an appeal was lodged against al-Shamali's entry ban with the complaints office of the EJPD. The sender was Dr Hans Ellenberger, lawyer and notary with chambers at Aarbergstrasse 46 in Berne.[91] This was, of course, the same Ellenberger who a number of months later, on the evening of 12 January 1971, would present himself in person to EPD state secretary Michael Gelzer, opening the discussion concerning the forming of a PLO office in Geneva.[92] An important aside at this juncture is that the wording of the original version of Ellenberger's proposal contains an interesting discrepancy when compared with the version given in the final report by the IDA 1970: according to the file note of 14 January 1971, the request originated not from the PLO as claimed by the Working Group, but, rather, from Fatah.[93] This detail is significant because as a *Fürsprecher* (the local description for a lawyer) Ellenberger had been retained with a mandate from Fatah representative al-Shamali.

Returning to al-Shamali's entry ban, Ellenberger's petition was successful. On 27 April 1970, the EJPD accepted Ellenberger's complaint and granted al-Shamali a so-called *sauf-conduit*, a type of entry permit with which he could travel to Switzerland. This document allowed the cancer-stricken Jordanian to receive treatment in Geneva and Lausanne until, initially, the end of June 1970.[94] This procedure was subsequently repeated over a dozen times over the coming two years: lawyer Ellenberger applied for a *sauf-conduit* for al-Shamali, which was always issued, sometimes on the same day as the application.[95] Petitions to revoke the entry ban, on the other hand, were refused by the EJPD up until the very end.[96] As late as July 1972, a month before al-Shamali's death, the commanding officer of the Geneva Cantonal Police reported to Berne that 'such an easing of restrictions on al-Shamali could have unforeseeable ramifications'.[97]

This makes an entry of 19 August 1970 in al-Shamali's index card file all the more extraordinary: the telephone surveillance was to be stopped – with immediate effect. Al-Shamali's illness made the original reasons for telephone tapping obsolete, noted a Federal Police official.[98] This argument appears unconvincing. A glance in the corresponding dossier, filing the respective documents on which an index card entry is based, reveals that the telephone monitoring of al-Shamali and his wife was annulled on the instructions of the Federal Public Prosecutor's Office. The order, signed by the head of the Federal Police, gives no explanation for the move.[99]

Therefore, it is not known what the Federal Public Prosecutor's Office's reasons were to rescind the tap, but a possible background does present itself. In summer 1970, as the IDA 1970 noted in its final report, Switzerland felt itself vulnerable to Palestinian attacks: 'Considering the profound effects of the Würenlingen airplane crash it is per se not surprising that the authorities, set against this background, deliberated what measures to take and perhaps sought out contacts.'[100]

Whether the authorities also sought to establish contact with Fuad al-Shamali during this threatening period in summer 1970 is not documented. What the records do show, on the other hand, is that the authorities were aware of al-Shamali's standing. When on 27 January 1971 Graber's department tabled the issue of the opening of a PLO office in Geneva, the wary Federal Police head André Amstein expressed his scepticism, saying that such an office should not be overrated. Switzerland had already its experiences with a Fatah representative, Fuad al-Shamali, who had done more harm than good.[101] Despite his presence, said Amstein, a Swissair airplane had crashed – presumably referring to the Würenlingen bombing of February 1970. While Amstein's objections did nothing to hinder the EPD from pushing ahead with the project for a PLO office in Geneva, they do make it all the more curious that it had been precisely the same Amstein who as head of the Federal Police had previously lifted the tapping of al-Shamali's phone.

What is important to know though, is that the Federal Public Prosecutor's Office, including the Federal Police, was not an independent body at the time. Instead, it was supervised and controlled by the Federal Council. Put differently, in the words of Franz Blankart – Federal Councillor Pierre Graber's personal assistant at the time – in an interview with the *Tages-Anzeiger*: 'The rules of the game were clear-cut: a civil servant does what his boss orders.'[102] In keeping with these facts, therefore, one scenario that potentially but logically presents itself is that the Public Prosecutor's Office effected the discontinuation of the telephone surveillance of al-Shamali on the orders of the Federal Council.

The shadow of Black September

Al-Shamali's card index file contains a final evaluation of his monitored calls dated 24 August 1970, significantly showing four meetings with Genoud for July alone.[103] As far as can be reconstructed from the details in his card index file, Fuad al-Shamali spent much of his time in the second half of 1970 in Switzerland, primarily for the medical treatment of his cancer. His arrival in Geneva was recorded on 1 June,[104] on 12 June he departed for Lebanon,[105] and on 20 July 1970 he returned to Geneva.[106] This was followed by various extensions of his *sauf-conduit* and al-Shamali did not depart again until 19 March 1971 'to attend to important political decisions by the Fatah' as his lawyer Hans Ellenberger informed the Federal Police.[107]

Fuad al-Shamali lost his battle with cancer on 3 August 1972, dying in the Geneva Cantonal Hospital at the young age of thirty-six. From the entry in his file of 6 August 1970 it would appear that the Federal Police learned of his death from the newspapers, given in the form of a reference to a report in the French-language Swiss daily newspaper *Tribune de Lausanne* with the title 'Demise of a Leader of the Black September Organization'.[108]

The Black September Organization (increasingly referred to in the literature by the acronym BSO, but here retained in full) was formed in the wake of the crushing of the Palestinian movement in Jordan by King Hussein in September 1970. Even for experts the contours of the organization are hard to delineate, but in general it is described as a militant spin-off from Fatah. The *Tribune de Lausanne* article quoted from a Fatah communiqué describing al-Shamali as the brains of the Black September Organization. Based on what was described as a well-informed Palestinian source, the paper added that right up until his death al-Shamali had been involved in the preparations of all the group's operations, including an attack on an oil refinery in Trieste in Italy on 4 August 1972, the day after al-Shamali's death.

These details were duly recorded in a further file note dated 23 August 1972, reporting that following al-Shamali's death the Black September Organization had spread information to the international press that his death had robbed them of one of their most commendable leaders. He had played a part in various different terrorist operations, among them the attack in Trieste.[109] The Federal Police confronted François Genoud with this information, which was obviously new and unexpected to them. The index card file entry noted that Genoud, who had long vouched for al-Shamali, had reassured the authorities that he had not been a militant, dismissing the recent reports as pure propaganda – al-Shamali would under no circumstances have been able to undertake any such attacks.[110]

On 7 March 1973 the Swiss television political programme *Rundschau* broadcast a television documentary about the Black September Organization made by the BBC.[111] The film sequences included images of al-Shamali's burial in his native Lebanon with thousands of people taking part in the funeral march in Beirut. According to the BBC, the deceased had been celebrated as a Palestinian fighter who had believed in the credo of revolutionary violence as the highest form of justice. Observers were said to be confused, stated the commentary: Berne was refusing to release their dossier on al-Shamali's political activities.

Having said this, were it to have been released the BBC reporters would have found very little to assist them. The indications of al-Shamali's leadership role in the Black September Organization that found their way into his index card file were essentially circular, all dating from after his death and all based on secondary media sources. Prior to that there is no mention of a possible militancy on al-Shamali's part in the thirteen closely typed double-sided index cards.

More information was apparently available in the Middle East. The obituary in one Lebanese newspaper celebrated him as one of the 'héros du Munich' (a hero of Munich).[112] It has been persistently rumoured that the Jordanian was involved in the preparations for the attack on the Olympic Games in Munich when on 5 September 1972 a Black September Organization commando infiltrated the Olympic village and took eleven Israeli sportsmen and functionaries hostage. A total of seventeen people, including all eleven hostages, were killed in what became the Munich massacre. Shortly before his death al-Shamali purportedly gave an interview to an Egyptian newspaper, quoted in part by the BBC documentary: 'We have to hit their weak spots. Bombing an El Al office does not serve our purposes. We have to kill the most famous. Since statesmen are difficult to kill, we have to kill artists and athletes.'[113]

A further first-hand witness comes forward

There is a further contemporary eyewitness who chose to publicly comment on my claims of a secret agreement following the publication of *Schweizer Terrorjahre*. This person is the Zurich business lawyer François A. Bernath, a member of the *Aufsichtsbehörde über die Bundesanwaltschaft* (Federal Public Prosecutor's Office's Regulatory Agency, AB-BA). Bernath approached the IDA 1970 of his own accord and put his recollections down in writing.[114] In his account he describes how, as a young adult, he had eavesdropped on confidential conversations between his father and his father's childhood friend Pierre Graber. According to Bernath, the names Jean Ziegler and Farouk Kaddoumi were mentioned in these secretly overheard conversations in the context of the Palestinian threat of 1970. Moreover, Federal Councillor Graber had been adamant that his government colleagues were not to be included in the explorations to find an 'arrangement discret' with the Palestinians. In a talk with the *NZZ* the bilingual Bernath translated the term 'arrangement discret' as 'a secret, non-written agreement'.[115]

Despite the obvious pertinence and implications of Bernath's recollections, the Working Group decided to accord them little weight in their final report. It is hard to escape the impression that the Working Group had difficulties with Bernath's submission, indicated not least at the outset in the cryptic formulation with which it is introduced into the final report: 'The spontaneous statement given by a member of the AB-BA was likewise accepted, who, based on the information he possessed, did not take part in the Regulatory Agency's inquiries.'[116]

François A. Bernath, born 1950, is a contentious person. In his long career as a corporate lawyer he has made a number of enemies. Following his selection to the AB-BA by both chambers of the Federal Assembly the *NZZ* described him as a 'colourful figure in the Zurich lawyers' scene' who was 'not an ideal choice' for such a responsible post.[117] Another Swiss newspaper accused Bernath, in late 2016, of having massaged his curriculum vitae. In his list of places where he had studied given on the AB-BA's website were institutions at which he had never been enrolled – details that had later been corrected.[118]

It is evident that the Working Group did not trust Bernath as a direct first-hand witness, but instead of saying so the IDA 1970 focused upon an ostensible chronological problem in order to dilute the relevance of his recollections: 'These first demarches [by Federal Councillor Graber] occurred, according to the source, in the period prior to Zarqa, in other words in a completely different context.'[119] This inference is false.

In the introduction to his statement François Bernath writes that he remembered two or perhaps even three meetings between his father Armand and Pierre Graber. Bernath, who was twenty at the time, dates the first of these meetings to summer 1970. 'Possibly early summer, I can no longer recall the precise month.' Somewhat later Bernath writes: 'It is likely that the meetings between Pierre and Armand took place between June and September 1970.'[120] Finally, in the course of writing down his recollections he comes to the realization that there definitely must have been a third encounter between Federal Councillor Graber and his father, 'Namely somewhat later [...] a week or two after the hijacking of the Swissair flight to Zarqa.'[121]

This passage demonstrates two things. The first aspect is that according to François Bernath's recollections the third meeting between his father and Federal Councillor Graber took place in approximately mid-September (the hijacking of the Swissair plane took place on 6 September 1970). Therefore, in chronological terms his observations are, indeed, relevant. The second aspect is that his dating of the first two conversations to summer 1970 reinforces François Bernath's credibility. In order to prejudice his recall of events as little as possible, Bernath had, as he explained in the preliminary remarks to his report, refrained from reading my book.[122] In

Schweizer Terrorjahre I erroneously stated throughout that the Swiss authorities had established contact with Farouk Kaddoumi in September 1970, meaning, therefore, that Bernath did not tailor his recollections to match my account.

Following the publication of the final report I contacted Jean Ziegler again, who confirmed that the initial contact with Federal Councillor Graber had, indeed, actually taken place in summer 1970. He was unable to specify a month, but he was certain that it had been in summer. During our conversation Ziegler explained that this relatively long time span between the first contact and the handshake with Farouk Kaddoumi in autumn 1970 was due to the complicated circumstances: communications had been undertaken via a contact man in Paris, sometimes the contact had been interrupted, and on other occasions Kaddoumi had made unfeasible demands. As Ziegler explained to me in summer 2016, all of this had proven very time-consuming.

Ziegler had already described the events to the *Matin dimanche* in late January 2016, in other words long before the publication of the final report.[123] According to his account Federal Councillor Pierre Graber had first approached him in the opulently marbled toilets on the third floor of the Federal Palace in Berne. He required Ziegler's assistance, said Graber, which had surprised Ziegler – although both were members of the Social Democratic Party, they represented opposing political agendas. Nevertheless, Graber had laid his misgivings aside in the knowledge that Ziegler possessed particular insights into the PLO. Graber had shown him a dossier complied for him – Graber – by the head of the intelligence service that lacked even the bare essentials such as an accurate organizational chart of the PLO or a characterization of its leaders. Ziegler had explained the correlation of forces within the PLO to Graber and encouraged him to make contact with Farouk Kaddoumi, who, in contrast to the PFLP, was willing to negotiate. The locations for the meetings with Graber had been deliberately chosen. Sometimes they had taken place in the Marzilibahn funicular between the terrace of the Federal Palace and the river Aare; they had ridden up and down, the clattering of carriages shielding their conversation from prying ears. On other occasions they had met in the corridor connections between train carriages. Once the contact with the Palestinians had been established, the intermediaries had rung him each time from a telephone booth. His most common contact had been Ezzedine Kalak, the PLO representative in Paris. He, Ziegler, could still clearly recall the day that he had met with Kalak and Kaddoumi in Paris. He had been approached by Kaddoumi on the Boulevard Haussmann, Kaddoumi telling him that he wanted to talk to the Swiss *Raees* – with him and nobody else. Ziegler had explained to him that there was no sole Swiss *Raees* in the Arabic sense of a leader, rather there were seven Federal Councillors; and he had recommended Pierre Graber, a man Kaddoumi could approach in trust.

Shortly afterwards Ziegler also talked to the *Basler Zeitung* about the subject, his account of this containing slight deviations vis-à-vis that given to the *Matin dimanche*.[124] In response to the prompt 'preliminary talks with the PLO', Ziegler said that there had been numerous meetings. Once, a female student called Malka had arranged a telephone contact with Ezzedine Kalak; he, Ziegler, had had to wait for a call in a public phone box in the Geneva municipality of Carouge; at some point Kalak had said that things were not going to work and the meeting had to be abandoned – Farouk Kaddoumi wanted to meet the *Raees*, not with some simple Graber or another. He had thereupon met with Kalak in Paris and explained the mechanics of the Swiss political system. The Palestinians had only been half convinced, but ultimately had accepted Graber as a bargaining partner. Under the subheading 'on the course of the discussions', Ziegler recounted to the *Basler Zeitung* that Graber had never told him what exactly he was negotiating, he had simply always confronted him with questions. While the exchanges with Graber had always been terse, the Palestinians had kept him better informed. The code word for Graber had been the 'grand-mère' (grandmother).

All of this played itself out in the period in which the meetings between Graber and his childhood friend Armand Bernath took place. His son François overheard the confidential conversations in the garden of the family's house in Cully close to Lausanne, the son lying, pretending to be asleep, in a deckchair slightly concealed behind a wall. During the meetings with his father Federal Councillor Graber had admonished his father to be absolutely discreet about the matter.[125]

During the first meeting with his father it emerged that Graber was endeavouring to talk to Palestinian leaders. It was evident that he had not yet informed his colleagues in the Federal Council: Armand Bernath raised his worry that the Federal Council knew nothing of the planned initiative, to which Graber responded that the Federal Council would never give him a green light to negotiate with terrorists. What he aimed for were simply unofficial explorations for an 'arrangement discret' (a secret accord) that would shield Switzerland against Palestinian terrorism. According to François Bernath's recollection, his father thereupon suggested that Graber should contact Jean Ziegler. Graber initially brushed the idea off – he did not trust Ziegler, and he reasoned that it was completely unpredictable what a man like Ziegler might make out of such an approach.[126]

It became clear from the second conversation that Graber had, in fact, been in touch with Ziegler and that the latter had agreed to mediate the appropriate contacts. The name Farouk Kaddoumi had been mentioned during the conversation. As François Bernath explained, he was able to remember the name well because the eponymous Egyptian king Farouk had owned a property in Cully. During this second meeting Graber rated the chances of finding a discreet arrangement with the Palestinians as realistic.[127]

Finally, in his recollections of a third meeting, which took place in approximately mid-September 1970, François Bernath was inclined to think that by this point contacts with the Palestinians had already been established. Graber was 'frantic' and discussed with his father how one could most reliably come to an accommodation with the Palestinians. Bernath was unable to say whether an 'arrangement discret' was later made or not, but based on his recollections it was clear that such an agreement had at least been initiated.[128]

During the second meeting, apart from that of Farouk Kaddoumi a second name had been mentioned that Bernath was initially unable to localize. 'Another name, presumably that of a Palestinian, was brought up – "Khaled": but I can no longer remember a surname', explained François Bernath in his written recollection, and added: 'I can remember the name Khaled because this was the name given to me in Arab circles.'[129]

Who could this 'Khaled' have been? Shortly before Christmas 2016, while reading through Fuad al-Shamali's personal index card file a second time, I discovered an interesting reference. A report by the *Service politique*, the intelligence branch of the Geneva Cantonal Police, recorded that al-Shamali had made a public appearance under the pseudonym 'Fouad Khaled'. The police officer referred to a number of pointers, including an interview in the *Tribune de Genève* on 20 September 1969 where al-Shamali had been introduced as 'Monsieur Khaled'.[130]

Shortly after this discovery in the Federal Archive in Berne, the British historian Thomas Skelton-Robinson, during a conversation, alerted me to a second lead. In a passage in his 1979 memoirs, the historian Saul Friedländer details an event in Geneva in 1969 during which an Arab had stood up and introduced himself as 'Fuad Haled'. Friedländer describes him in his memoirs as having been a highly educated and sensitive person, with a detailed awareness of life in Israel and a wide knowledge of Jewish history.[131]

Three years later, following the attack on the Munich Olympics in 1972, a friend informed him that 'Fuad Haled' was, in fact, the deceased Fuad al-Shamali, that he had belonged to the Black September Organization and that he had been one of the organizers of the Munich massacre.[132] And how does Saul Friedländer pronounce 'Fuad Haled'? In response to an email the 84-year-old historian explained that the question could only be answered by phone. I called him on 27 December 2016 on the West Coast of the United States and he explained that his pronunciation of 'Haled' was similar to that of 'Hamas', comparable with the Spanish 'jamás'. Rounding off his short phonetic discourse, Friedländer said that in terms of clarity he would nowadays spell the name as 'Khaled'.

François Bernath may be a contentious figure, but the Working Group has deliberately chosen to take the easy way out by simply invalidating his recollections on the supposition of an invalid time frame. There is a distinct possibility that Bernath's 'Khaled' is in reality Fuad al-Shamali, which would constitute a new link in the chain of evidence indicating that Federal Councillor Graber has sought out Swiss Fatah representatives and Fatah co-founder Farouk Kaddoumi for secret negotiations in summer 1970.

Despite this, the IDA 1970 comes to a different conclusion in its final report published in May 2016. On the basis of its 'exceptionally wide-ranging researches', the Working Group inferred that 'there was no "secret agreement" between Farouk Kaddoumi and one or more Swiss representatives in Geneva in September 1970'.[133]

A remarkable comment from intelligence circles

A few months later, in October 2016, the editor-in-chief of the *Bulletin* of the Vereinigung Schweizerischer Nachrichtenoffiziere (Association of Swiss Intelligence Officers, VSN) came to a decidedly different conclusion. In his book

4. The Secret 1970 Moratorium Agreement between Switzerland and the PLO

review of *Schweizer Terrorjahre* Lukas Hegi wrote: 'Gyr's research is meticulous and he can plausibly substantiate his thesis with interviews with contemporary eyewitnesses – even if in the last resort the evidence for a deal can never be produced due to the fact that there are no records of it.'[134] The VSN consists mainly of active and former intelligence officers from across Switzerland.

The final remaining question is why Jean Ziegler has decided to reveal his information incrementally, portioning out key details in successive salami slices. Although Ziegler repeatedly admitted – both in summer 2015 in the context of my research for the book *Schweizer Terrorjahre* and after its publication in January 2016 – that he had established the liaison to Farouk Kaddoumi, nevertheless, he at first chose not to disclose the crucial role played by Fuad al-Shamali, which he only confirmed when I concretely approached him about it at the end of 2016.

Ziegler's answer remains vague. A decisive factor may well be that al-Shamali maintained close contacts to the avowed Nazi and enemy of Israel, François Genoud. Even after the passage of so many years this remains – understandably – politically explosive terrain for a man of Ziegler's standing. Federal Councillor Graber and his department presumably faced a similar dilemma. Faced with the threat scenario it may have been politically opportune to make contact with a Fatah representative in 1970, especially when he was vouched for as a non-violent representative of the Palestinian cause; but this changed abruptly after al-Shamali's death when he was suddenly labelled as a leading Black September Organization member jointly responsible for the planning of the attack on the Munich Olympics.

Based on these allegations that al-Shamali was a high-ranking Black September Organization leader, two interrelated conjectures could be made, although written evidence for either of them has yet to be found. First, it would potentially explain why al-Shamali and the putative moratorium agreement negotiated by him became completely taboo subjects in Switzerland from autumn 1972 onwards, tainted as they were by this association. And second, this, in turn, might offer an explanation as to why the verbal deal continues to be kept secret by the authorities until the present day.

Notes

1 Jakob Tanner, *Geschichte der Schweiz im 20. Jahrhundert* (Munich: Verlag C.H. Beck, 2015).
2 Ibid., 387.
3 Ibid.
4 Marcel Gyr, *Schweizer Terrorjahre: Das geheime Abkommen mit der PLO* (Zurich: Verlag Neue Zürcher Zeitung, 2016).
5 Ibid., 161.
6 Ibid., 162.
7 Ibid., 164.
8 Ibid., 10 and 162.
9 Interdepartementale Arbeitsgruppe '1970' (IDA 1970), *Schlussbericht*, Eidgenössisches Departement für auswärtige Angelegenheiten (EDA), Berne, 3 May

2016, https://www.eda.admin.ch/content/dam/eda/de/documents/publications/Geschichte/interdepartementale-arbeitsgruppe-1970_de.pdf (accessed 1 January 2020).
10. Telephone call with the author, in the presence of lawyer Marcel Bosonnet, Zurich, 1 March 2016.
11. In particular, the dossiers 'Bureau palestinien à Genéve (OLP/PLO) 1971–1973', in Schweizerisches Bundesarchiv (Swiss Federal Archives), Berne (henceforth BAR), E4300C#1981/35#37; 'Foad El Shamali, 1968–1985', in BAR, E4320-01C#1996/202#52; 'El Shamali Fouad, 1968–1985', in BAR, E4320C#1994/120#334.
12. IDA 1970, *Schlussbericht*, 26.
13. For example IDA 1970, *Schlussbericht*, 123 and 124, both references referring to file note, 18 November 1971, in BAR, E2001E-01#1982/58#317.
14. IDA 1970, *Schlussbericht*, 74 and 76.
15. *Le Temps*, 1 March 2016, 10.
16. *Tages-Anzeiger*, 6 February 2016, 1.
17. Ibid., 3.
18. IDA 1970, *Schlussbericht*, 67.
19. Private email from Pierre-Yves Simonin to the author, 27 July 2015.
20. IDA 1970, *Schlussbericht*, 124.
21. Ibid., 3.
22. Ibid., 6.
23. Ibid., 29–46.
24. Ibid., 16.
25. Ibid., 16–17.
26. Ibid., 25.
27. Ibid., 135–6.
28. Ibid., 25.
29. Sacha Zala, Thomas Bürgisser and Yves Steiner, Die Debatte zu einem 'geheimen Abkommen' zwischen Bundesrat Graber und der PLO: Eine Zwischenbilanz, *Schweizerische Zeitschrift für Geschichte* 66/1 (2016), 1–24.
30. Ibid., 7.
31. Gyr, *Schweizer Terrorjahre*, 131–2.
32. Zala, Bürgisser and Steiner, Die Debatte zu einem 'geheimen Abkommen', 7.
33. Gyr, *Schweizer Terrorjahre*, 133.
34. IDA 1970, *Schlussbericht*, 144.
35. Ibid., 118.
36. Ibid., 121.
37. Ibid., 21.
38. Ibid., 74, citing 'Notice de Gelzer pour Micheli', 14 January 1971, in BAR, E4001D#1976/136#133.
39. Ibid., 22, referring to 'Aktennotiz Gelzer', 14 January 1971, in BAR, E2001E-01#1982/58#317.
40. Ibid., 22.
41. Ibid.
42. Zala, Bürgisser and Steiner, Die Debatte zu einem 'geheimen Abkommen', 15.
43. Ibid., 22–3.
44. Dossier 'Eröffnung PLO-Büro in Genf, 1971–1975', in BAR, E2001E-01#1987/78#409.
45. Dossier 'Bureau palestinien à Genéve (OLP/PLO) 1971–1973', in BAR, E4300C#1981/35#37.
46. 'Schreiben von Gelzer an ausgewählte Botschaften, 6 August 1971', in Ibid.

47 *Neue Zürcher Zeitung*, 2 August 1971, 14.
48 'Schreiben von Gelzer an ausgewählte Botschaften plus Fremdenpolizei', 8 August 1971, in BAR, E4300C#1981/35#37.
49 'Bericht Kantonspolizei Genf an Bundesanwaltschaft', 20 January 1972, in Ibid.
50 'Aktennotiz EPD zu Vorsprache Barakat bei Gelzer', 10 December 1971, in Ibid.
51 'Notiz EPD, Lunch mit Barakat', 23 December 1971, in Ibid.
52 'Notiz EPD', 15 December 1971, in Ibid.
53 'Notiz EPD, Lunch mit Barakat', 23 December 1971, in Ibid.
54 'Aktennotiz zu Aussprache EPD von 20. Dezember 1971', 21 December 1971, in Ibid.
55 IDA 1970, *Schlussbericht*, 122–7.
56 Ibid., 128.
57 Zala, Bürgisser and Steiner, Die Debatte zu einem 'geheimen Abkommen', 20.
58 Jonathan Kreutner, *Schweiz und Israel: Auf dem Weg zu einem differenzierten historischen Bewusstsein* (Zurich: Chronos Verlag, 2013).
59 Ibid., 83.
60 Ibid., 102.
61 *Basler Zeitung*, 22 January 2016, 4.
62 *L'Hebdo*, 15 March 1982, 10–11. In the French original: 'Q: En France, la justice s'incline-t-elle devant des menaces? A: Vergès: La justice doit tenir compte d'un rapport de forces et des opportunités. En France, le code de procédure donne au procureur de la République la liberté d'apprécier l'opportunité d'une poursuite. Cela n'est pas un cas particulier à la France. Il y a quinze jours, l'Allemagne fédérale a expulsé trois Syriens arrêtés alors qu'ils transportaient des explosifs. Il n'y a pas eu d'information ouverte. Il y a aussi un accord non écrit entre les autorités de la Confédération helvétique et un certain nombre d'organisations arabes ou israéliennes pour que ces organisations ne commettent pas d'attentats en Suisse, et, à cette condition, les autorités ferment les yeux sur leurs autres infractions mineures.'
63 *Amtliches Bulletin der Bundesversammlung*, 1982, 1489.
64 IDA 1970, *Schlussbericht*, 21.
65 Ibid.
66 Karl Laske, *Ein Leben zwischen Hitler und Carlos: François Genoud* (Zurich: Limmat Verlag, 1996), 224–5.
67 Willi Winkler, *Der Schattenmann – von Goebbels zu Carlos: Das mysteriöse Leben des François Genoud* (Berlin, Rowohlt, 2011), 177.
68 Magdalena Kopp, *Die Terrorjahre: Mein Leben an der Seite von Carlos* (Munich: Deutsche Verlags-Anstalt, 2007), 150.
69 *Neue Zürcher Zeitung*, 7 March 2016, 1 and 9.
70 Ibid., 1.
71 Ibid., 9.
72 Hans-Joachim Klein, *Rückkehr in die Menschlichkeit: Appell eines ausgestiegenen Terroristen* (Reinbek bei Hamburg: Rowohlt Taschenbuch Verlag, 1979), 55–6.
73 *Neue Zürcher Zeitung*, 7 March 2016, 9.
74 *Neue Zürcher Zeitung*, 29 December 2016, 14.
75 Marc Perrenoud, Micheli, Pierre, in *Historisches Lexikon der Schweiz*, http://www.hls-dhs-dss.ch/textes/d/D14870.php (accessed 1 January 2020).
76 Index card file cover, in BAR, E4320-01C#1996/202#52.
77 Initial index card file entry, in Ibid.

78 'PLO Representation in Geneva', Cable from U.S. Mission to the U.N. (Geneva) to the Secretary of State, U.S. Department of State, 12 April 1978, https://wikileaks.org/plusd/cables/1978GENEVA05490_d.html (accessed 1 January 2020).
79 IDA 1970, *Schlussbericht*, 74 and 76.
80 Card index file entry, 15 December 1968, side 1, in BAR, E4320-01C#1996/202#52.
81 Pierre Péan, *L'Extrémiste: François Genoud, de Hitler à Carlos* (Paris: Librairie Arthème Fayard, 1996), 337.
82 Card index file entry, 10 September 1969, sides 3–4, in BAR, E4320-01C#1996/202#52.
83 Card index file entry, 17 July 1969, side 2, in Ibid.
84 Card index file entry, 17 July 1969, side 3, in Ibid.
85 'Rapport Kantonspolizei Genf', 26 November 1969, side 8, in BAR, E4320C#1994/120#334.
86 Péan, *L'Extrémiste*, 321 and 337–9.
87 Card index file entry, 24 February 1970, side 5, in BAR, E4320-01C#1996/202#52.
88 'Verfügung der Bundesanwaltschaft', 24 February 1970, in BAR, E4320C#1994/120#334.
89 Card index file entry, 14 August 1972, side 12, in BAR, E4320-01C#1996/202#52.
90 Card index file entry, 24 March 1970, side 6, in Ibid.
91 Card index file entry, 10 April 1970, side 6, in Ibid.
92 IDA 1970, *Schlussbericht*, 74, citing 'Notice de Gelzer pour Micheli', 14 January 1971, in BAR, E4001D#1976/136#133.
93 IDA 1970, *Schlussbericht*, 74. In the French original: 'A la demande urgente d'Hans Ellenberger, Président de l'Association Suisse-Arabe, M. Gelzer le reçoit et apprend que le Fatha [sic] souhaite ouvrir un bureau à Genéve.'
94 Card index file entry, 27 April 1970, side 7, in BAR, E4320-01C#1996/202#52.
95 Card index file entry, 27 October 1970 and 8 November 1970, both side 9, in Ibid.
96 Card index file entry, 18 January 1972, side 11, in Ibid.
97 Card index file entry, 4 July 1972, side 12, in Ibid.
98 Card index file entry, 19 August 1970, side 8, in Ibid.
99 'Meldung der Bundesanwaltschaft an die Generaldirektion PTT', 19 August 1970, in BAR, E4320C#1994/120#334. In the French original: 'Messieurs – Nous vous prions de noter que nous avons décidé de supprimer le contrôle téléphonique (y compris envois exprès, télégraphiques contre Elisa et Fouad-Assad El Shemali.'
100 IDA 1970, *Schlussbericht*, 23.
101 Ibid., 74, citing 'Aktennotiz Meili', 27 January 1971, in BAR, E4300C#1981/35#37.
102 *Tages-Anzeiger*, 6 February 2016, 3.
103 'Rapport Kantonspolizei Genf', 24 August 1970, in BAR, E4320C#1994/120#334.
104 Card index file entry, 24 July 1970, side 8, in BAR, E4320-01C#1996/202#52.
105 Ibid.
106 Ibid.
107 Card index file entry, 16 March 1971, side 10, in BAR, E4320-01C#1996/202#52.
108 Card index file entry, 6 August 1972, side 12, in Ibid.
109 Card index file entry, 23 August 1972, side 12, in Ibid.
110 Card index file entry, 23 August 1972, side 12, in Ibid.
111 Schwarzer September: Politik des Terrors, *Rundschau*, Schweizer Fernsehen, broadcast 7 March 1973. The item was originally broadcast on the BBC programme *Midweek* on 6 December 1972. See Transcript of the BBC programme 'Midweek'

on 6 December 1972, in the National Archives of the United Kingdom, Kew, FCO 17/1625, 'Acts of Violence by Arab Terrorist Organisations', part D.
112 Péan, *L'Extrémiste*, 345, citing *Al Moharrer*.
113 Schwarzer September: Politik des Terrors.
114 IDA 1970, *Schlussbericht*, 141–6.
115 *Neue Zürcher Zeitung*, 14 May 2016, 17.
116 IDA 1970, *Schlussbericht*, 4.
117 *Neue Zürcher Zeitung*, 18 September 2014, 13.
118 *Tages-Anzeiger*, 13 December 2016, 4.
119 IDA 1970, *Schlussbericht*, 20–1.
120 Ibid., 143.
121 Ibid., 145.
122 Ibid., 141.
123 *Le Matin dimanche*, 24 January 2016, 1–2.
124 *Basler Zeitung*, 30 January 2016, 2.
125 IDA 1970, *Schlussbericht*, 143.
126 Ibid., 144.
127 Ibid., 144–5.
128 Ibid., 145.
129 Ibid., 144–5.
130 'Rapport Kantonspolizei Genf', 26 November 1969, 6, in BAR, E4320C#1994/120#334.
131 Saul Friedländer, *When Memory Comes* (Wisconsin: University of Wisconsin Press, 1979), 35–6.
132 Ibid.
133 IDA 1970, *Schlussbericht*, 25.
134 *VSN-Bulletin*, 25 October 2016, http://www.swissint.ch/?p=799 (accessed 1 January 2020).

Chapter 5

THE ROAD NOT TAKEN

CRISIS MANAGEMENT, DIALOGUES AND DEAL-MAKING WITH
PALESTINIAN FEDAYEEN GROUPS IN THE CONTEXT OF THE
JORDANIAN TRIPLE-HIJACKING INCIDENT OF SEPTEMBER 1970[1]

Thomas Skelton-Robinson

Introduction

Any discussion of contacts between Western governments and the Palestine Liberation Organization (PLO) in the 1970s inevitably labours under two main interwoven controversies. The first is the question whether the armed Palestinian nationalist movement, and therefore the alphabet soup of Palestinian fedayeen (literally 'self-sacrificers', in this sense guerrillas) and terrorist groups, both within and outside of the PLO umbrella organization, were monolithic, or whether they were riven by rivalries. The second is whether tendencies within the movement towards moderation, diplomacy and a territorially diminished two-state solution were genuine or were in fact nothing more than a calculated subterfuge behind which lurked the immutable aim of reversing history and erasing the state of Israel.

Minus the space to discuss these issues in full, it is nonetheless important to preface this essay by expressing the author's own views, which per se inform the following excursus. First, contrary to ideologically coloured perceptions, the Palestinian movement was by no means homogenous. On the whole – and even before the rise of Abu Nidal's splinter Fatah-Revolutionary Council in the mid-1970s drew the PLO into a destructive fratricidal cycle – ideological and tactical clashes between the groups were both real and occasionally lethal. Secondly, although it took a long time for it to gain an ascendency, and even, although when it did, its primacy was at times tenuous or indeed eclipsed, there is an unmistakable current of pragmatism and realpolitik that runs through the history of the thinking of both the PLO and its main constituent group Fatah that recognized that Palestinian nationhood could only ultimately be achieved with the support of the West, above all the United States.

This, however, is not to deny that at various junctures Palestinian groups and factions allied with each other in the use of terrorism or indeed resorted to fictitious nomenclatures in an attempt to disguise the true authorship of terrorist acts – most notoriously in the case of the Black September Organization (BSO) between 1971 and 1973. Neither is this to deny the widespread Palestinian adherence, based on the North Vietnamese model, to a two-stage strategy, namely the liberation of a rump territory to be followed by the campaign for complete national re-conquest. Instead, one of the key objectives in analysing Palestinian terrorism is to recognize the permanent flux within and between the groups and to map the shifting patterns that emerge.

A key factor hampering a proper examination of deals between Western governments and Palestinian groups is the circumstances of the archival sources. Unsurprisingly, these deals, by their nature, not only were secret and informal, but by the same token were considered too sensitive for public consumption, with both sides having vested security and credibility interests in them not becoming common knowledge. As British prime minister Edward Heath paternally admitted in his memoirs, referring to the British arrangement with Egypt and the Popular Front for the Liberation of Palestine (PFLP) in September 1970, 'our need to keep our tactics secret meant that it was difficult to explain our actions to the British public, who were in any case unused to incidents of this kind'.[2] On the other side of the equation, the stakes were somewhat higher. If, as a high-ranking Fatah representative noted to a US Central Intelligence Agency (CIA) case officer in November 1970, 'his own role in the current contact were ever to become known or widely suspected, he would be branded as an "American Agent" and might even be liquidated'.[3] These reciprocally tied political sensitivities are reflected in the state of the archival records, where key documents remain closed to historical scrutiny or for that matter lost forever.[4] The unavoidable conclusion is that such records are considered, decades later, to still be potentially incriminating and inimical to national security interests.

There is a further corollary that tends to obscure analysis, namely the widespread view that contacts and discussions with terrorist groups who maim and murder represent a capitulation to blackmail, encourage further acts of terrorism, and indeed project a corrosive weakness and pusillanimity in Western state power, its obverse encapsulated in the hyperbolic (and demonstrably hypocritical) mantra of the 1980s 'we don't talk to terrorists'.[5] This stance injects a righteousness, and hence more heat than light, into discussions about Western–Palestinian contacts, sensationalizing and blurring our understanding of them. In reality, the violent international ramifications of the Palestinian–Israeli conflict were (and indeed still are) ultimately governed – to use former CIA agent Miles Copeland's vivid and cogent phrase, coined specifically for the Arab world – by the pragmatic, strategic and amoral rules of the 'Game of Nations'.[6]

These blinkers explain some of the media controversy surrounding Marcel Gyr's 2016 book *Schweizer Terrorjahre* and his thesis of a secret deal involving Swiss Federal Councillor and acting Foreign Minister Pierre Graber and Fatah's Farouk Kaddoumi (nom de guerre Abu al-Lutf) following the so-called triple hijacking of September 1970.[7] Hued with a tone of innate scepticism, the media echo culminated in an official Swiss interdepartmental inquiry that concluded, albeit in self-imposed narrow parameters, 'there was *no* "secret agreement" struck in September 1970 between F. Kaddoumi and Swiss representatives in Geneva'.[8]

In fact, the vast majority of Palestinian hostage-taking incidents in the 1970s, however deadly, did see attempted or de facto 'deals' with terrorists, be it in the form of the release of imprisoned compatriots and free passage back to the Middle East and/or ransom payments; and almost all Palestinian terrorists arrested in Western Europe in the 1970s either were never prosecuted or were released and deported long before serving out their prison sentences. Too great was the overriding and justified fear that applying the rule of law to Palestinian combatants would simply invite further reprisal attacks. Moreover, any idea of a cordon sanitaire is a misnomer. Western governments, including the United States, regularly talked to the PLO and Fatah throughout the 1970s in one form or another; and conversely, from around 1974 onwards, elements within Fatah and the PLO actively assisted Western governments in security matters and in resolving or even thwarting terrorist incidents involving more extremist elements within their own ranks.[9]

This context also helps us locate the dual significance of Gyr's contention: in terms of timing it predates other documented cases by a number of years, and, as claimed, involved a substantive quid pro quo of a moratorium on terrorist attacks in return for a promise of future diplomatic recognition.[10] This ostensibly makes Gyr's scenario incongruous, although in terms of both timing and content it should be noted that allegations of at least one comparable deal between a European state and the fedayeen predate it, as is discussed below. Moreover, if one were to believe contemporary press reports, such deals were in fact part and parcel of European diplomatic exchanges in the Arab world throughout the 1970s.[11] Indeed, minus any other flanking documented cases it might be ventured that the only anomalous feature in the Swiss deal was that it involved direct contact between a serving West European minister and the PLO. The first such encounters that are publicly reported did not occur until 1974 in the context of the Middle East peace process. Prior to this date – and indeed afterwards too – the favoured avenue was a more discreet arm's length approach via an intermediary Arab state or other third-party actors. However, Gyr's scenario matches this pattern in substantial aspects too.

In April 2016, following the appearance of Gyr's book and in the midst of the controversy it provoked in the Swiss media, the author of this article gave an interview arguing that his thesis was intrinsically credible, adding the proviso that given the geo-strategic context 'it is unlikely that diminutive Switzerland would have risked so much without being aware of similar actions by their partners'.[12] This chapter provides the evidence on which this opinion is based. It sets out to demonstrate that analogous contacts between the PLO and diplomatic representatives from the United States and Great Britain likewise originated as early as 1969 to 1970, but that they were also substantive. In this sense the events of the multiple hijackings of September 1970 – also commonly known as 'Skyjack Sunday', the 'Dawson's Field hijackings' or in German the 'Zarqa Crisis' – is a lens that allows us to roughly perceive the lineage of such contacts and thus to recognize them as a given historical phenomenon. Their normalcy, of course, raises further questions. How do they dovetail not only with the known record of the Middle East conflict and the peace process but also with the overall cadence of political violence and assassination in the Palestinian–Israeli conflict in the 1970s? And given the fact, who were ultimately the players and who were the pawns?

The stage is set – September 1970

On 6 September 1970 the PFLP – which already had a deserved reputation as the pioneers par excellence of Palestinian attacks and hijackings against airline targets, in particular against El Al – pulled off their most spectacular coup de théâtre to date. In what is widely considered to be the most skillfully orchestrated multiple skyjacking prior to 9/11, the miniature Palestinian guerrilla faction commandeered a total of three international airliners: a TWA Boeing 707 from Bombay to New York via Tel Aviv after a stopover in Frankfurt with 153 people on board; a Swissair DC-8 from Zurich to New York with 155 people on board; and a Pan Am Boeing 747 from Brussels via Amsterdam to New York with 171 people on board.[13] Adept as they might have been, two things went wrong for the PFLP on 6 September. The Pan Am hijackers had been originally booked to board an El Al flight at Amsterdam bound for New York but were refused passage, with the result that they switched to the TWA flight instead.[14] More grievously, the simultaneous attempt to hijack another El Al flight, from Tel Aviv to New York via Amsterdam, failed spectacularly when US/Nicaraguan hijacker Patrick Arguello was shot dead by an Israeli sky marshal and his fellow assailant Leila Khaled, the poster girl of the Palestinian cause, was beaten unconscious and then detained after an emergency landing at Heathrow Airport in London. This mishap dragged Britain impromptu into the crosshairs of an operation in which it had hitherto not been a target.[15] The unforeseen forfeit to the British authorities was duly made good on 9 September when a BOAC VC-10 from Bombay to London via Bahrain with 155 people on board was hijacked.[16] While the TWA and the Swissair flights, and later the BOAC flight, were diverted to a remote former British military airstrip called Dawson's Field, located close to Zarqa in northern Jordan, because of its sheer size the Pan Am jumbo was directed to Cairo, where the hostages were evacuated and the $24-million plane was spectacularly blown up on 7 September. Meanwhile, in Jordan, the PFLP found themselves with over 350 hostages canned up in three planes in the scorching desert heat. Promptly surrounded by the Jordanian military, and a little later by the world's media, the PFLP was ready to play its hand.

The mastermind behind the operation was Wadie Haddad, the co-founder and operational brains behind the PFLP's so-called outside operations. Widely acknowledged by his devotees and enemies alike as a terrorist genius, the ambiguity of Haddad's role in the PFLP is encapsulated by former PFLP speaker Bassam Abu Sharif's description of him as the 'cuckoo' in fellow PFLP founder George Habash's 'nest'.[17] In this particular case Habash was – conveniently or not – absent from the scene at the time of the multiple hijackings, heading a PFLP delegation to North Korea and later China.[18] The outwardly stated goal of the operation was to free an initially unspecified number of fighters captured abroad, but the hijackings were also the most audacious example of the PFLP's belief in propaganda by deed, designed not only to jolt world opinion into an awareness of the fate of the Palestinians but also to mobilize and galvanize its own potential basis.[19] At the same time the operation had a specific two-pronged strategic component, namely to sabotage the ongoing US-led Middle East peace initiative and to incite a Palestinian uprising in Jordan.

Abridged, the background is such. Following the Six-Day War of 1967, the short-lived fedayeen operations within Israel and the newly occupied territories were ruthlessly crushed, leaving Lebanon and Jordan as the only bordering countries from which the Palestinian guerrilla operations could effectively be launched, with Jordan initially bearing the brunt of Israeli reprisals. The much-celebrated 'Battle of Karameh' of 21 March 1968, in which an Israeli incursion was repulsed, produced a general euphoria, with King Hussein of Jordan declaring at the time 'the day may come when we are all fedayeen'.[20] This was an inauspicious turn of phrase at a time the PFLP and other groups were acting under the slogan that Amman should become the Arab 'Hanoi' from which the Israeli-controlled 'Saigon' of Jerusalem would be liberated. By September 1970 relations between the Jordanian regime and the fedayeen were already at boiling point, the latter behaving as if Jordan was already theirs for the taking. An agreement brokered by multiple Arab states in July held briefly, only to degenerate into open fighting between the Jordanian army and Palestinian units in Amman, beginning on 29 August and renewed following a failed ambush on a convoy with King Hussein and his retinue on 1 September.

As Jordan toppled on the brink of civil war, the administration of US president Richard Nixon sought for a second time to revive the moribund UN peace initiative of November 1967, named after the UN's special envoy Gunnar Jarring and based on the eternal bone of contention of UN Resolution 242 of 22 November 1967 ('land for peace').[21] Under the auspices of US secretary of state William Rogers, the renewed American initiative of June 1970 – effectively a re-launch of the previous Rogers Plan of December 1969 – was surprisingly accepted by the Egyptian president Gamal Abdel Nasser on 23 July, and, after entreaties and promises from Nixon, by the Israeli government under Prime Minister Golda Meir on 4 August.[22] Followed by a provisional ninety-day ceasefire accepted in tandem by Egypt, Israel and Jordan, which came into effect at midnight on 7 August, the fragile consensus ended the two-year 'war of attrition' and allowed Jarring to hold preliminary talks with the three countries on 25 August. The Israeli decision led to the collapse of the ruling coalition in Israel, and it subsequently withdrew from the UN talks on the same day, 6 September, as the triple hijacking over perceived Egyptian violations in its military redeployments. To complicate matters, the Rogers Initiative and the position of the State Department were being eroded by behind-the-scenes manoeuvres by National Security Advisor Henry Kissinger, who in the words of Yitzhak Rabin, Israel's ambassador to the United States, encouraged Israel to treat the initiative as effectively 'non-existent'.[23]

In the midst of these developments, in early August 1970 US State Department official Talcott Seeyle reported internally on a discussion he had had with the

Lebanese journalist George Hishmeh. Seeyle explained to Hishmeh the expectation that (in Nixon's famous phrase) a 'silent majority' of Palestinians would support a solution based on UN Resolution 242 and an association with Jordan, adding significantly that formal contacts with and indeed recognition of the PLO were possible should they show a readiness to accept the UN resolution and take part in a negotiated solution.[24] Seeyle was the State Department's country director for Lebanon, Jordan, the Syrian Arab Republic and Iraq at the time, and as such his sentiments were presumably a low-level institutional broadcast. Whether tied to this or other murmurs, Israel would seem to have become aware of an undercurrent in the State Department to potentially factor in the Palestinians into the peace process, as indicated by a pointed public comment made by the Israeli ambassador Rabin in a radio interview two weeks later. 'The United States is sitting at a negotiating table with a "Fatah" which is killing Americans – with the Viet Cong', he declared, therefore 'we should not be surprised if they are prepared to accept a "Fatah" which is killing not Americans but Israelis'.[25] A week later, Israeli prime minister Meir felt prompted to declare on television that the Middle East issue could have long been solved by the Palestinians being absorbed into other Arab countries. 'We negotiate only with states, and heads of states', she stated, adding sardonically that just by virtue of being 'terrorist organizations' with the 'ideal […] to kill Jewish men, women and children and attack buses with children, does not make them eligible for negotiations'.[26]

For their part, the general response by the Palestinian groups to Egypt's acceptance of the Rogers Initiative and the subsequent ceasefire was one of deep consternation and anger, loudly denounced by left-wing leaders such as Habash of the PFLP and Nayef Hawatmeh of the breakaway Democratic Front for the Liberation of Palestine (DFLP). A PFLP-organized mass demonstration in Amman against Nasser's decision took place, scurrilously ceremonially led by a donkey with Nasser's picture attached to its head,[27] and at the close of the month, three PFLP members were arrested in Egypt and deported.[28] Early criticisms of perceived Egyptian treachery from Fatah and the PLO leadership likewise incurred Egyptian sanctions. In late July two Cairo-based Palestinian radio stations were closed down, and in face-to-face meetings Nasser warned the PLO of the dire consequences of forcing a split with Egypt or triggering a civil war in Jordan.[29] Despite deep Palestinian misgivings, an uneasy modus vivendi was met between the PLO and Egypt, apparent in the mixed messages that emerged from an emergency Palestinian National Council (PNC) meeting held in Amman in late August, with PLO chairman Yasser Arafat announcing the PLO's formal rejection of the 'American conspiracy' of the Rogers Initiative,[30] but at the same time trying to conciliate on behalf of Nasser with the more extremist delegates.[31]

The course of the hijackings – 6 September to 1 October 1970

At Dawson's Field the PFLP would seem to have quickly realized that they had bitten off more than they could chew, immediately releasing 127 women and children to the Intercontinental Hotel in Amman on 7 September.[32] At the same time, however, the hijackers selected a small group of 'star hostages', most of whom were Jewish (dual American-Israeli citizens), in an attempt to try and restore the crucial leverage over Israel (by proxy through the United States) forfeited in the two failed El Al hijackings. While President Nixon allegedly issued a dangerously harebrained order to immediately bomb fedayeen positions in Jordan, deflected by Secretary of Defense Melvin Laird,[33] less bellicose moves were afoot in Berne, Switzerland, where the countries affected by the hijacking – Switzerland, West Germany, Britain and later the United States and Israel – set up a permanent crisis committee (the 'Berne Five' or officially the 'Coordination Committee', referred to here as the Berne Group). As Kissinger records in his memoirs:

> We knew that Israel had a policy of never yielding to blackmail. It feared that if it ever yielded, no guerrillas could be held captive; terrorism would be encouraged. Our own view was roughly the same. The European countries involved did not believe that they could adopt such an uncompromising position. We urged them, at a minimum, to negotiate as a group.[34]

Ostensibly a joint coordinating body, the ambassadorial committee struggled throughout the course of the hijacking with the differing and irreconcilable agendas of its members.

In a first move the Berne Group installed a sanitary divide between themselves and the hijackers by agreeing that the International Committee of the Red Cross (ICRC) act as an intermediary.[35] The man who initially headed negotiations with the PFLP was the ICRC's Middle East delegate André Rochat, who arrived in Amman on 8 September. On the same day the PFLP issued its first concrete demands on the individual countries concerned: the release of three Palestinians involved in the attack on an El Al plane at Zurich-Kloten Airport on 18 February 1969 (during which the Israeli pilot and one attacker had been killed), three would-be hijackers arrested at Munich-Riem Airport on 10 February 1970 (one person killed and thirteen wounded),[36] the release of Leila Khaled and the return of Patrick Arguello's body from Britain, and a 'prisoner exchange' for an unspecified number of Palestinians held in Israel.[37] No direct demands were made on the United States, but it was obviously expected that the large number of American hostages would serve to compel it to pressure Israel.[38]

On 10 September the PLO actively stepped into the hijacking operation, when a meeting of the Central Committee out-voted the PFLP, assuming control of the situation and deciding to release all the hostages save American-Israelis 'with military status', as well as the planes, in return for the fulfilment of the PFLP's demands.[39] Later lauded as a first sign of the PLO's 'moderation', other motives are equally plausible, none of them necessarily precluding the other. One interpretation is that the move in fact saw Fatah embracing the PFLP's agenda, swept along by the wave of popular Palestinian and Arab enthusiasm for the hijackings.[40] Another is that the PLO intervention was due to the mounting sabre-rattling by the United States, Kissinger commenting:

> On 11 September the alert measures of the previous two days began to pay off. Rumors of our fleet movements were translated by the gossip mill in Amman into reports of imminent American intervention. Red Cross representative Rochat reported that 'fantastic tension' reigned at fedayeen headquarters, and he fully expected them to take some action to demonstrate that they would not be intimidated. All aircraft had been wired for bombing, but the passengers had been removed from them. That our threat was not without effect became apparent at the end of the day when the fedayeen suddenly released a group of eighty-eight hostages, including some Americans (but not dual-nationalists).[41]

On 12 September the PLO evidently held enough sway over the situation to secure the evacuation of the majority of the remaining hostages to Amman, and ultimately to freedom. However, in a sleight of hand the PFLP squirrelled away fifty-six hostages in four groups to Zarqa, Amman and Irbid, spectacularly blowing up the three planes against the barren desert skyline beforehand. Providing one of the most vivid images of Palestinian terrorism, the iconoclastic act also showed that brandishing the sword of military retaliation was double-edged. Abu Sharif recounts that 'rumours of a joint US-Israeli plan to attack us at Dawson's Field' had indeed reached them, but that the threats 'meant that we would have to raise the stakes even higher'. In response Haddad had ordered him on 11 September to take two journalists to Dawson's Field the next morning to record the detonating of the explosives. This was followed by a parade of the hostages, each of them flanked by a PFLP member with a gun pointed at their heads, Haddad apparently issuing a threat to the Jordanians that 'you can kill one or two of us [...] but we will kill the rest of them'.[42] According to other commentators, the destruction was also an act of defiance directed at the PLO, for which the PFLP was punished with the largely symbolic gesture of being suspended from the Central Committee, only for it to be promptly readmitted a few days later, 'thus demonstrating', in the estimation of the CIA, that the PLO 'did not have the power, or possibly the will, to enforce its own regulations'.[43]

Despite assurances from Fatah that the remaining hostages would not be harmed,[44] Britain, West Germany and Switzerland fretted over who now really had ultimate control of the situation. The blowing up of the airplanes was, in the words of ICRC vice president Jacques Freymond, 'proof that the PLO, at least in this respect, has been over-trumped by the PFLP', prompting him to break off his mission at what he saw as escalating and contradictory demands, amounting to a 'diktat'.[45] Meanwhile the Swiss Bundesrat (the Federal Council, or cabinet) considered the situation to have fragmented even more dramatically, based on information that the planes had been destroyed not only contrary to the will 'of the umbrella organization controlled by Arafat' but also 'without the knowledge of the key people in the Popular Front for the Liberation of Palestine'.[46]

5. The Road Not Taken

British, West German and Swiss attempts to forge direct contacts to the PFLP became largely academic when amidst all of this confusion a prevaricating King Hussein (who had already brokered three ceasefires after clashes between his troops and the fedayeen since 6 September) finally took action, declaring martial law and the formation of a military government on 17 September. This precipitated the onset of all-out warfare in Amman a day later, engulfing all other events. The ferocious ten-day civil war, causing thousands of casualties, has been long raked over by political commentators and historians as a model flashpoint among the proxy battles of the Cold War. However, whether this geo-strategic perspective in fact captures the true dimensions of events is moot. King Hussein's decision to militarily crush the fedayeen – his resolve steeled by the CIA chief of station Jack O'Connell and the newly arrived US ambassador Dean Brown – was followed by a Syrian armoured intervention, US and Israeli counter-mobilization (the latter, surprisingly, at King Hussein's request), a US-Soviet global standoff, unexpected Iraqi inertness, unexplained Syrian withdrawal and finally Arab League mediation and arm-twisting by Cairo. On 27 September an accord was hammered out between King Hussein and Arafat that, at least on paper, saw a return to the *status quo ante*, although in fact the Palestinian movement had suffered a defeat of truly historical dimensions from which it arguably never recovered. As if to crown the internecine Arab bloodletting, Egyptian president Nasser suddenly died aged fifty-two of a heart attack a day later, throwing Egypt and the Arab world into turmoil and robbing the Palestinian cause of its arguably mightiest supporter.

As far as the hostage situation was concerned, a first group of fifteen was found by the Jordanian army in Amman on 25 September, followed by the appearance of Swiss hostage Walter Jost, who had been released by his captors the same day. A day later the PFLP voluntarily gave up a further thirty-two hostages in Amman, followed by the release of the final six 'star hostages' on 29 September in Irbid. Although there was publicly no quid pro quo to release their prisoners, London, Bonn and Berne evidently felt they had an obligation to reciprocate. On 30 September a Royal Air Force Comet took off from the Lyneham base in Britain with Khaled on board, stopping in Munich and Zurich to pick up the other six prisoners, and landed in Cairo on the morning of 1 October to release them, seemingly marking the end of the Jordanian hostage crisis.

A taxonomy of contacts and deals during the September hijackings

Prior gentleman's agreements?

One of the intriguing details in the records of the British National Archives is that the hijackings of 6 September apparently represented the breach of a previous explicit agreement to suspend airline attacks. Among a series of personalities to present themselves as interlocutors to Western authorities during the hijackings was Knut Hammarskjöld, the staid director general of the airline industry's worldwide business organization, the International Air Transport Association

(IATA). In March 1970 Hammarskjöld had undertaken a widely reported trip to the Middle East that had included a meeting with PLO chairman Arafat.[47] On 9 September (the day of the additional BOAC hijacking) Hammarskjöld approached BOAC, who in turn promptly contacted the British Board of Trade on his behalf. The message – reportedly also communicated by Hammarskjöld to the chairman of Jordanian Airlines, the Jordanian prime minister and the government of the United States – was that in March he 'had had talks with the guerillas in Jordan and had secured an understanding that there would be no more hijacking on their part', an agreement that 'had continued until last weekend'. His query, which British mandarins judged should best be postponed until after the ongoing negotiations had been concluded, was whether the various parties 'thought it might be helpful for him to see the guerillas again, in particular Mr. Habbash'.[48] What the fedayeen had demanded and received in return for their agreement with the IATA is not recorded.[49] The only corroboration (of sorts) is to be found in a later British Foreign and Commonwealth Office (FCO) analysis, which stated that following the double airline bombing incidents of 21 February 1970 – in which an Austrian Airlines flight was damaged and a Swissair flight crashed close to the Swiss town of Würenlingen killing all forty-seven people on board – the 'moderate fedayeen' under Arafat had 'succeeded in getting an assurance from Dr. George Habash [...] that his organisation would not undertake further actions of this kind', leading to 'a lull of some five months' until the hijacking of an Olympic Airlines plane on 22 July 1970.[50]

Precisely why the hijackings of 9 September represented the abrogation of this agreement with the IATA while that of 22 July did not is unclear but may be tied to the outcome of the earlier episode. On 22 July 1970 the Olympic Airlines flight with fifty-eight people on board had been hijacked en route from Beirut to Athens by a six-person commando said to have belonged to the ephemeral Popular Struggle Front (PSF), led by Bahjat Abu Gharbiya, and/or the PFLP. The resulting standoff at Athens Airport was resolved via the intervention of ICRC representative André Rochat, who was by coincidence present in Athens that day. Rochat had secured the release of the hostages, voluntarily offering himself as a captive to accompany the hijackers to Cairo as a voucher for the promised later release of the seven fedayeen held in Greek prisons demanded by the hijackers.[51] This duly took place after a decent interval on 12 August, again accompanied by Rochat. The episode, however, may have involved more than just a simple hostage-for-prisoner exchange. On 14 August the semi-official Athens News Agency reported, in the words of the British Embassy, that as a corollary of the releases 'a diplomatic representative of an Arab nation had given the Greek government an assurance that the Arab commandos would never again utilise Greek territory and Greek interests in general for illegal activities'.[52] This scenario was also later given by journalist Stewart Steven, who states that the releases were tied, in his words, to a 'dubious immunity' whereby it was 'also pledged that "Arab commandos" would never again operate on Greek soil'.[53]

True or not, there is a further connection between the Olympic Airlines hijacking and the multiple hijackings of September 1970 that is of potential significance.

The link concerns ICRC representative Rochat, who publicly earned the enmity of Israel for his role in Athens – not only for having facilitated the prisoner release, but moreover for having apparently known the correct code word to prove his bona fides with the hijack commando.[54] In an unpublished manuscript detailing the hijacking dangers that beset his airline in the late 1960s and early 1970s, Swissair director Albert G. Fischer detailed a meeting with Rochat on 19 August 1970.[55] The background, as Fischer wrote, was serious intelligence from Olympic Airlines and BOAC security officials that following the success of the Olympic Airlines incident Swissair would be the PFLP's next target, this time to force the release of the three Palestinians from the El Al plane attack of 18 February 1969 at Zurich-Kloten Airport. Fischer, together with Dr Claude Baumann, the assistant commander of the Zurich Canton Police Department, met surreptitiously with Rochat in a secluded corner of a park in Geneva. Rochat explained that the ICRC had considered his actions in Greece as having been 'detrimental' to its 'standing' and that the only reason that he had been able to hold on to his position had been thanks to 'the Americans'. After accompanying the seven freed terrorists to Cairo on 12 August, Rochat had met with the leaders of the two groups responsible for the 22 July hijacking in Amman in person – Habash and the leader of PSF, whom Rochat refused to name other than describing him in awestruck terms as the head of 'a small group that is very dangerous'. According to Rochat (filtered via Fischer), Habash and the PSF leader had given him an unequivocal demand that the Kloten attackers be released in order to 'spare Switzerland eventual catastrophes like "Würenlingen"'. Rochat had refused to act as blackmail messenger to the Swiss government, whereupon he had anyway been told that the Swiss government had until 15 September to 'consider' the situation and that were they to agree in principle to release the Kloten attackers this deadline could be prolonged to 30 September.[56] These details were also circulating at higher Swiss official levels from 13 August onwards,[57] and on 16 August the Libyan government had likewise approached the Swiss government with a request to release the Kloten attackers to Tripoli in return for Libya's willingness 'to persuade the Palestinian resistance organizations to give an assurance and promise to no longer commit acts of terror in Switzerland'.[58] Five days later, the rough outlines were leaked in the Swiss Weltwoche in an article by Jean Ziegler, declaring: 'It is an open secret that Swiss authorities are attempting to keep up at least minimal contacts with the Palestinian guerrilla organizations.'[59] This sequence of events, and moreover Rochat's duplicate role, would suggest that Switzerland was in essence being offered a deal similar to the one that had apparently already been struck with Greece.

Israel turns up the heat

As it is, the events of September 1970 are a textbook example of the fundamental tensions and contradictions between Israel (and by affiliation the United States) and Western European governments over the Palestinian conflict at the time. These fissures already became apparent on day two of the hijacking crisis with the alacrity with which West Germany and Switzerland announced their willingness to free their prisoners,⁶⁰ coupled by Israeli irritation at the choice of André Rochat to head the ICRC delegation.⁶¹ Although the PFLP was pressing for individual negotiations with the countries concerned, by the night of 9–10 September the crisis committee in Berne had managed to establish a tenuous consensus that they would only act in unison in return for the release of all of the hostages. The innate centrifugal forces in this formula were expressed by the British Embassy in Tel Aviv. As perceived, Israel had two main objectives: to maintain the 'principle of non-discrimination' and 'to keep the price paid as low as possible, especially what they have to pay'. The thinking was

> that under pressure they would pay something, but it will not be easy to persuade them to make a substantial offer quickly. They have seen the PFLP put off their deadline once and there have been reports of the passengers being moved to Amman[;] the Israelis are likely to see these signs as reasons for tough bargaining.

Were Britain to go ahead with a separate deal, it would undoubtedly lead to bitterness and act as proof of Israeli suspicions – 'always near the surface' – that 'the West cannot be trusted to safeguard Israel's interests'. In response, Israel might see itself forced to 'strengthen its hand', the potential reactions being 'e.g. by hijacking an Arab airliner or kidnapping some important Arab'. After playing through the larger contingencies, including an Israeli military intervention, the British Embassy judged that Israel would probably 'play it long'. Whatever the outcome, however, 'the chances of a peace settlement would be seriously damaged and it would be optimistic to expect a resumption of the Jarring talks'.⁶²

On 12 September, with the blowing up of the planes at Dawson's Field and the PLO's apparent failure to rein in the PFLP, the unified front in Berne promptly fractured, the looming failure of the ICRC mission raising the prospect, as the US Embassy in Berne put it, of 'an immediate tendency to settle bilaterally with a potentially dangerous residue'.⁶³ The 'residue' referred to was the possibility that West Germany, Britain and Switzerland would break ranks and abandon the sworn-by but brittle consensus to find a 'global solution', leaving the United States and Israel to fend for their hostages themselves. On 11 September, Israel had repeated its adamant refusal to make a material contribution to a resolution to the hostage crisis by releasing any fedayeen held in Israel, leading to increasing recriminations. On 13 September Swiss foreign minister Graber went as far as to echo a sharp British rebuke of the same day, telling Israel that it could not afford the luxury of quarrelling with friends 'for the pleasure of maintaining her intransigence'. These sentiments were surprisingly also echoed by the US representative in Berne, who said that 'Israeli intransigence was being directed against her allies, not the *fedayeen*, and solidarity, on which the Israeli laid so much stress, could not be a one-way street'.⁶⁴

None of this was presumably helped by the fact that the same day Israel responded to the nebulous situation in its own muscular fashion by rounding up hundreds of Palestinians related to notorious fedayeen, including members of Habash's family.[65] In order to drive the point home, six of those detained were flown to a secluded spot in Jordan and left to make their way to Amman to deliver a clear message that harm to the hostages would entail severe reprisals.[66] The warning to the PFLP was:

1) The Arab–Israeli conflict had so far been relatively 'humane'. However, reports of possible ill-treatment of hostages would make the Israelis inclined to be 'inhumane' as well.
2) If any harm came to the hostages, PFLP members convicted by Israeli courts would be given death sentences instead of life imprisonment.
3) The property of persons linked in any way to the PFLP would be confiscated, their houses blown up and their relatives deported.

The messengers were not meant to persuade the PFLP to make concessions, nor were they to bring back an answer, the British ambassador to Jordan J. F. S. Phillips understatedly commenting that the Israel move was 'hardly calculated to calm the PFLP'.[67]

West Germany breaks ranks

Events were thrown into further disarray on 11 September with the arrival of the West German special emissary and Social Democratic Party (SPD) federal chairman Hans-Jürgen Wischnewski, whose legendary rapport with Arab revolutionaries and potentates alike had earned him the moniker 'Ben Wisch'. Although sanctioned by West German chancellor Willy Brandt, Wischnewski's presence was billed as a purely private initiative, and despite West Germany's assurances to the contrary it was not surprisingly seen by the other countries as an attempt to conclude a separate deal by the backdoor.[68] Against the admonishments of the United States to abort his mission or to negotiate only through the ICRC,[69] Wischnewski went straight to the source and undertook one-to-one talks. As well as a meeting with Arafat, he also met twice with PFLP leader Abu Maher (Ahmed al-Yamani) – the man, according to at least one commentator, with overall operational control of the PFLP in Jordan during Habash's absence in the Far East.[70] The first meeting with Abu Maher took place in the Hotel Intercontinental in Amman, Jordanian soldiers obligingly removing themselves from the building prior to his arrival. During their talks, Abu Maher informed Wischnewski that with the breakdown of the ICRC talks the PFLP now only wanted to negotiate on a country-by-country basis.[71] A day after the meeting West Germany felt obliged to clarify Wischnewski's moves, saying that his 'talks' had irrefutably 'contributed to an easing of the situation in Jordan' and that he could not have been expected to turn down the PFLP's offer to 'repatriate German hostages', but that Bonn would still abide by 'the common procedure'.[72] In overall terms, Wischnewski retrospectively justified his actions with the exculpatory claim that 'other states had in the meantime likewise established direct contacts'.[73]

Wischnewski's explanation is left hanging in his memoirs simply as a bald statement. However, faced with criticisms about his mission at the time, Wischnewski had pointedly raised the fact that 'a British journalist in Amman appeared to be very actively attempting to negotiate a separate deal'.[74] This figure was presumably the journalist Michael Adams, director of the London-based pressure group the Council for the Advancement of Arab-British Understanding (CAABU). The CAABU was the largest pro-Arab pressure group in Britain, described as being also the 'most closely related to the British "establishment"', while Adams was asserted to have played a 'forward role' in negotiations in Jordan.[75] Also said to have 'first class' relationships to the PFLP leadership, Adams had arrived in Amman on 9 September and apparently stepped into the gap left by ICRC representative Freymond's angered departure on 12 September. On 13 September Adams negotiated a signed-and-stamped 'contract' with Abu Maher for Leila Khaled's release, which was reportedly taken to the British Embassy and cabled to the government, only for it to be rejected. Nonetheless, the same day Adams successfully negotiated the token release of Dutch hostage Rudi Swinkels with Abu Maher on behalf of the Dutch ambassador.[76]

Further 'private' initiatives

Wischnewski and Adams were not the only players to insert themselves into the breach left by the ICRC's temporary withdrawal on 12 September. Likewise in Amman was a Swissair delegation, headed by the company's director Alexander von Crayen. According to the official 2016 Swiss Interdepartmental Inquiry, von Crayen and his team were on the ground from 14 to 16 September.[77] Yet newly available documents indicate that they had already arrived a number of days earlier and that von Crayen's presence in Jordan lasted far longer, trapped as he was by the outbreak of warfare on 17 September.[78] As von Crayen himself later detailed, the background to his approaches had been the withdrawal of the ICRC, and on 13 September he and the Swiss ambassador to Lebanon, Charles-Albert Dubois (who oversaw affairs in Jordan during the crisis and was likewise in Amman from 8 to 23 September), met with a PFLP 'representative' – in fact Leila Khaled's brother – who in von Crayen's words informed them that 'the option of separate negotiations was now available'.[79] Details of this opening were also picked up by the British Embassy in Amman, which reported that on 13 September the PFLP had offered Swiss ambassador Dubois a separate, bilateral deal – an offer that the British ambassador Phillips encouraged his own government to likewise pursue so as to 'not be left out on a limb'.[80] The content of Dubois and von Crayen's meeting with the PFLP was communicated to the Swiss cabinet a day later when Swissair representatives met with Swiss Federal Councillors Roger Bovin and Nello Celio. As a result of 'discussions with the fedayeen leaders' in Amman, the Swissair dignitaries urged the Swiss government to reconsider its position. 'Switzerland's readiness, as the first of the countries concerned to be willing to contribute to a positive resolution', they said, 'has generally left a very good impression in Amman', and appealed to the councillors not to back what was a losing horse. 'In Amman' – from the context a polite synonym for the PFLP – there was a 'conviction that the solidarity with the other affected states is a bad bargain for Switzerland'. The quintessence of the Swissair's audience was straightforward: the lives of the hostages were threatened and 'Switzerland up until now enjoys a special position, which should be exploited'.[81]

A day later von Crayen was informed (presumably by Swiss officials) that bilateral talks were off the cards and that the course being followed was for the ICRC to resume its role, leading to what Swissair representatives later described as a 'hardening of the PFLP's stance' regarding access to the hostages.[82] On 16 September von Crayen was able to hold a last meeting with three PFLP members, including Abu Maher (i.e. the same PFLP commander-in-chief in Jordan with whom Wischnewski was likewise negotiating) and a man named 'Bassam'.[83] With these figures, the Swissair's troubleshooters, and as a corollary the Swiss authorities too, were better-wired at this juncture in the crisis than is commonly thought.

Upon his subsequent return to Switzerland, von Crayen met with Swiss foreign minister Graber on 25 September as part of a renewed Swissair delegation. Fresh from the combat zone, he expressed his opinion that 'the men involved are recklessly extreme. They are of the view that Switzerland has joined forces in a front with the "Western capitalists"'.[84] Graber for his part assured the delegation that pressure was being applied on the various fedayeen groups by both 'Arab and non-Arab' parties. He expressed his sympathy for Swissair's plight, but said the government 'had the impression that it was dramatizing the situation somewhat'. The main problem was that there were 'many different opinions within the PFLP, but nobody has the authorization to speak in the PFLP's name on a binding basis'. Von Crayen, in response, admitted that his contacts 'haven't perhaps spoken the last word for the PFLP' but had – and here a crucial concession – 'nevertheless promised calm for Switzerland and Swissair if the three Kloten attackers are freed'.[85]

Imbroglio

With the outbreak of the civil war in Jordan on 17 September, the British reported: 'It has now become impossible to establish contact with the PFLP, or the overall organisation, the Palestine Liberation Organisation.'[86] Coupled with continuing reports of West German willingness to strike a separate deal, this deteriorating situation explains why nerves began fraying further. Just how much so became evident in an acrimonious telephone call on 18 September between the British permanent undersecretary of state for foreign affairs Sir Dennis Greenhill, Henry Kissinger and Assistant Secretary of State for Near Eastern and South Asian Affairs Joe Sisco to discuss West German proposals that, if necessary, negotiations should continue on a four-power or even three-power basis, that is, minus Israel and potentially minus the United States too. Sisco stated that such a move would cause an 'outcry' in the United States, to which Greenhill angrily retorted, referring to Israeli prime minister Golda Meir's presence in Washington, that there would be outrage in Britain too 'on the lines that your visitor won't lift a bloody finger and put any contribution to a bargain', especially if British hostages were to be killed and it was to emerge that they could have been freed 'but for the obduracy of you and the other people so to speak'.[87] This angry British refusal to put their hostages, as they expressed it, 'wholly at the mercy of the Israelis', and their willingness to entertain the idea of a 'tripartite or country-by-country' settlement with the fedayeen earned them a private warning via the British ambassador in Washington 'of the potentially very serious consequences for Anglo-American relations which would ensue if we were to take this course'.[88]

Although Israeli foreign minister Abba Eban had indeed informed London on 14 September that as a country it remained steadfast in its refusal to deal with terrorists,[89] Israel in fact at the same time signalled to Washington its willingness to at least marginally soften its stance, in particular were they to be able to 'cite overwhelming pressure (especially from the United States) forcing them to take part in the exchange'.[90] Prime Minister Meir met with Undersecretary Sisco in Washington on 18 September, both of them seemingly unperturbed by events to the point of being almost sanguine.[91] Meir complimented Sisco, saying that the United States 'had held out beautifully', and adding that the 'Swiss were good in this affair but [the] Germans and British were awful'. As to the possibility of 'partial deals', Meir responded that 'she was not sure about the British but she was sure that the Germans would never agree to a separate exchange for their people, which still left Jews as hostages. This would be too much and they would not do it'. While still refusing to release imprisoned fedayeen, Meir and her advisors acceded in principle to the PFLP's demands to free two Algerian intelligence officers forcibly removed from a BOAC flight at Lod Airport on 14 August and ten previously captured Lebanese soldiers, whereby Sisco advised against mentioning the ten Lebanese 'until [Israel] was sure of getting something in return'.[92] In addition Israel agreed not to object to any deal involving fedayeen held in European prisons.[93] Although not recorded in the Meir-Sisco meeting, in at least one subsequent State Department cable the Israeli concessions were recorded as including the release of a Swiss, unnamed in the document but obviously referring to the young Bruno Breguet, arrested by Israeli authorities after disembarking at Haifa harbour smuggling explosives for the PFLP on 23 June 1970.[94] These were exclusively US-Israeli discussions: when Greenhill again pressed Kissinger as to whether there had been any shift in the Israeli stance he was told that there had not.[95]

Considering the pressure of events, Israel's continuing refusal to put its cards on the table, and now the chaos and bloodshed in Jordan, the temptation in the second half of September for the members of the Berne Group to potentially start hedging their bets and either intervene in or indeed bypass the ICRC mechanism mounted exponentially, the mantra of the common front notwithstanding. On the face of things the options available looked slim, but three countries – Switzerland, the United States and Great Britain – each nevertheless sought out, found and used unorthodox channels through which to try and exercise a sway on the PFLP. Moreover, compared to the bustle and horse-trading at the Hotel Intercontinental in Amman in the frantic days of 13 to 16 September, these initiatives were not only more earnest and prolonged but also involved heavier hitters.

Swiss soft power

The first case concerns Switzerland. Despite playing dutifully by the rules of the game set out by their senior partners, in mid-September Switzerland did what Switzerland does best and undertook an astute and consummately circuitous attempt to have the PFLP's arm twisted on its behalf. The route taken was to the very top of the PFLP in the person of its leader George Habash, carried out via a proxy on the other side of the globe that Habash and the PFLP could ill afford to ignore, namely the People's Republic of China – a vital yet little-understood key player in the early years of the Palestinian struggle. The idea of approaching China as an intermediary was first raised in the Swiss cabinet on 13 September,[96] and two days later – propitiously coinciding with the arrival of Habash's PFLP delegation in Peking from North Korea[97] – the Swiss chargé d'affaires in the Chinese capital, on his government's instructions, visited the acting head of the Chinese Foreign Ministry's West European Department, Vice-Minister Lo Kuei-Po, to cordially request that China exercise their influence with the Palestinian guerrillas to effect the release of the Swissair hostages.[98] The Swiss venture bore fruit, the British ambassador to Switzerland reporting on 25 September that the Chinese government had issued a démarche to Habash following a Swiss entreaty for intervention on their behalf.[99] In early October, after the hostage crisis had blown over, the Swiss duly thanked Vice-Minister Lo Kuei-Po for the Chinese intervention, with Kuei-Po responding 'that the Chinese government strongly disapproved of this sort of activity and they had made this clear to Habash'.[100]

Whether the Chinese admonishments had any practical effects on the outcome of the hostage crisis in Jordan is unclear, but they certainly had an impact on Habash's longer-term thinking. The *Christian Scientist Monitor* reported on 15 November 1970 that the Chinese had told him that his operational and strategic methods were wrong, criticizing the PFLP's reliance on outside operations and urging him to concentrate his actions within Israel.[101] The details of the dressing-down that Habash received are worth citing in full. According to journalist John K. Cooley, the author of the article, 'there is strong evidence, supplied by diplomats in Peking during Habash's visit there and to North Korea while the hijackings were underway [...] that the Chinese sent considerable arms aid just before these events, but took him to task for using the wrong tactics'. The Chinese critique had consisted of two points:

> First, they told him, it was wrong to set the outside world against the Palestinians through hijacking of aircraft. Second [...] attacking regimes like Hussein's or King Faisal's [i.e. Saudi Arabia], solidly based as they seemed to be in Islamic conservatism, was a mistake as proven by the results of the Indonesian Communists' attacks on the Moslem religion – which led to the massacre of many thousands of Indonesian Communists and Chinese residents of Indonesia.[102]

Although events in Jordan entailed nothing like the human costs of the genocide in Indonesia of 1965–1966 during the euphemistically titled 'communist purge', it nonetheless points to the Chinese global perspective on events in Jordan and with it an element in the split between Habash and Haddad that would later occur in 1972.

The CIA-backed connection

The second case of a back-channel initiative involves Mustafa Zayn, described in British documents as 'a midlevel government official' in Lebanon who acted as an intermediary between the ICRC and the PFLP in the critical second half of September. On 15 September, following a call from the PFLP's Bassam Abu Sharif, Zayn was able to visit a group of hostages held in Ashrafiyeh, including his own administrative assistant Richard Dunn, who had been on the BOAC flight.[103] On 19 September Zayn met with ICRC representatives Pierre Boissier and Marcel Boisard in Beirut, and for the next six days acted as a conduit to the PFLP in Lebanon. The discussions, however, reportedly remained mired in mutual stubbornness and scepticism. The PFLP at the one end refused to release a precise list of its hostages, and Israel at the other refused to issue a formal acceptance of the principal of a hostage-for-prisoner exchange, the Berne Group in-between baulking at acting as a formal guarantor for Israeli participation.[104]

While Boissier had the impression that Zayn's PFLP contacts were 'very influential figures, among the most important of the organization', and that he was therefore in a 'position of authority to negotiate',[105] the British described the Beirut conduit as 'a somewhat Alice-in-Wonderland dialogue'.[106] Despite the reservations about the bona fides of whom exactly they were ultimately talking to, Zayn himself was nonetheless ultimately considered to be 'a man of standing in Beirut'[107] and the channel became the main preoccupation of the Berne Group up until 25 September, especially after midnight on 21 September when Zayn communicated a proposal that the majority of the non-Israeli and non-dual citizens (read optimistically to be fifty-one or fifty-two of the hostages) be taken to safety and released, the small remainder (by the same token two or three) to be moved to a secure place for as long as negotiations with Israel continued.[108]

After three protracted days of circular and agonized debate, on 24 September the parties in Berne – including Israel, which two days earlier had described accepting the PFLP's discriminatory proposal as 'a shameful subjugation to an abominable blackmail'[109] – finally agreed on the wording of a commitment to the exchange principle that Boissier so desperately wanted in order to further the negotiations.[110] The Berne Group's undertakings were written up in two letters. The one that was intended also for the PFLP, and was free to be made public, included the following formulation:

> The government of the United Kingdom, Germany and Switzerland consent to the release of the seven prisoners held in Europe, together with the body of Miss Khaled's companion, and the Government of Israel consents to the release of the two Algerian officials.

In the confidential letter, intended for Boissier's eyes only, the wording was slightly more ambiguous but potentially wider, stating that acceptance of the clause meant that 'the Israeli Government in effect accepts the principle of an exchange, as they had previously done on the occasion of the hijacking of a TWA aircraft to Damascus'.[111] All this wrangling came to naught. On 25 September Boissier left Beirut for Geneva, unaware of the freeing of the first European hostages in Amman. For its part the Berne Group, equally unaware that he had left, cabled Boissier now rescinding the content of the letters of guidance of 24 September, although any potential confusion was reportedly spared due to the fact that Boissier had anyway failed to speak to Zayn between the prior instructions and his departure.[112]

Although ultimately unfruitful, this channel between the PFLP and the Berne Group via Zayn and the ICRC is of greater significance than might appear at first glance. The figure referred to as 'Mustafa Zayn' in contemporary documents is Mustafa M. Zein, who was by no means a 'midlevel' Lebanese official but rather a special advisor to Sheikh Zayid bin Sultan al-Nahyan of Abu Dhabi, the British hostage Richard Dunn being a lawyer employed by Zein in the Emirate of Sharjah. Of more pertinence – and eloquent testimony to his credentials – is the fact that Zein was the man responsible in 1969 (as will be discussed below) for forging and facilitating the legendary contacts between Fatah's rising star and later BSO leader Ali Hassan Salameh and the CIA through Robert Ames, a case officer in the agency's Middle Eastern Directorate of Operations.[113]

According to Zein's own account, he took up his role as a negotiator with the ICRC at Robert Ames's explicit request, in other words on behalf of the CIA. Ames reached him by phone in Abu Dhabi with the solicitation that he come to Beirut and assist in establishing contacts with his 'friends' in the PFLP. These acquaintanceships originated from Zein's vice-presidency of the Organization of Arab Students in the United States and Canada in 1964.[114] As Zein explains, the organization had at the time been run by the Arab Nationalist Movement (ANM), with whom Zein was subsequently involved in Cairo.[115] The ANM in turn was, to put it in a truncated manner, the predecessor organization to the PFLP.[116] Zein describes that, using these contacts, 'the most important issue of my mission was to place the passengers in a very safe place during the fighting'.[117]

As to the mystery of whom he was talking to in the PFLP in Lebanon and Jordan, Zein explains that his first point of contact in Lebanon was Ghassan Kanafani, the PFLP's speaker and editor of its magazine *Al-Hadaf*. Kanafani in turn contacted Bassam Abu Sharif, the deputy editor of *Al-Hadaf* who was in Amman, on Zein's behalf, asking him, as Zein recalls, to 'clear my visit with Dr. Haddad as a negotiator'. Zein then travelled to Amman together with Kanafani, where he shared a room with Abu Sharif in the Intercontinental Hotel. According to Zein, Abu Sharif 'played a major role in keeping the hostages safe'. However, his ultimate discussion partner, via Abu Sharif, was Haddad himself. Parallel to this, in his efforts to secure comfort for the hostages he was also in contact with PLO chairman Arafat via Ali Hassan Salameh. Importantly, as Zein explains, 'the PFLP knew that I was in contact with high American officials and accepted to negotiate with me'.[118] Hard as it is to crystal-gaze the PFLP's hierarchy or chain of command, Zein also states that Abu Maher, the PFLP's point-man for so many other diplomatic petitioners in Jordan during the crisis, 'gave his full support to my efforts in Amman'.[119]

Considering the purported pedigree of Zein's assignment, that is, its initiation by the CIA, it is on the face of things strange that on 20 September the State Department cabled the US Embassy in Beirut stating that they believed that the 'time has now rpt [repeat] now come to break off contact with Zayn on matter of hostages'. The State Department feared that the direct contacts with the embassy were being taken by the PFLP as an indication of the US government's tacit acceptance of the PFLP's terms, and although the contacts with Zein had 'served a useful purpose during the period when movement of hostages in Amman was frozen because of civil war', in the meantime the situation was more stable, making the ICRC the proper 'forum' and Amman the proper 'place' for negotiations.[120] Whether or not the direct channel to Zein was indeed capped, or rather simply briefly suspended, the State Department expressed a renewed interest in the Beirut connection on 24 September, albeit with the caveat that they strongly doubted that 'PFLP interlocut[o]r with whom Boissier has been talking represents those elements actually holding the hostages'.[121]

Britain cuts a deal

Leaving aside the constellations in the PFLP-Zein-ICRC negotiations and the conundrums they raise, the reason for their abandonment and demise on 25 September would appear more evident: they were superseded by the imminent successful conclusion of manoeuvres via a different covert back channel. The country that managed to finally cut the Gordian knot of the hijacking crisis was Britain, sealing a three-way deal with the PFLP brokered with the assistance of President Nasser of Egypt.[122]

The idea apparently originated with the British prime minister Edward Heath and was first internally floated by Foreign Secretary Sir Alec Douglas-Home on 18 September, offering the prospect of 'the eventual solution of the problem' by approaching either President Nasser or the Arab League.[123] In the event it was Nasser whose good offices were called upon. As Heath recalled it, he and Nasser had met in 1969 and exchanged warm words, Nasser saying that were Heath ever to become prime minister he would like to visit Britain. In return he extended an open offer of assistance should it ever be needed. So it was that at the critical stage in the hostage crisis Heath decided to remind Nasser of his overture, writing to him on 23 September.[124] Heath's letter contained a concrete commitment to release all of the seven imprisoned Palestinians in Europe and the assurance that were Nasser able 'to arrange this exchange' it would greatly serve to enhance the relationship between Britain and Egypt.[125] 'We had absolutely nothing to lose by such an attempt', Heath later recalled.[126] The initiative was a unilateral one, and none of the other countries in Berne were appraised of it, Douglas-Home warning British diplomats: 'You should not, of course, reveal the existence of [the prime minister's] message to your colleagues.'[127]

At the same time as Heath's supplication, events in Jordan became more convoluted. On 25 September a group of fifteen hostages managed to flee to Jordanian army lines in Amman. Their two PFLP guards had simply unceremoniously departed, leaving the doors to the house unlocked as fighting in the Jebel Al-Hussein refugee camp had closed in.[128] Instead of prompting a sigh of relief, this turn of events caused apprehensions – particularly on the part of the British and the Swiss – that the PFLP might try to re-seize the freed hostages or undertake further hijackings to make good their lost bargaining chips.[129] This jitteriness was compounded by the fact that all of the remaining hostages were now Americans, leaving Britain, Switzerland and West Germany on the horns of a dilemma whether to go ahead with the release of the seven prisoners, thus leaving the United States and Israel in the lurch.[130]

On 26 September Egypt presented a way out of the predicament when the Egyptian Minister of Information, Muhammad Heikal, phoned the British ambassador to Egypt, Sir Richard Beaumont, informing Britain that the release of the remaining hostages could be secured in return for an 'undertaking' by Britain, also on behalf of Switzerland and West Germany, that the seven fedayeen would still be released. Roughly an hour later, and prior to any British response to Egypt, the PLO announced that the remaining thirty-eight American hostages were to be immediately and unconditionally freed and handed over to the Egyptian Embassy that very afternoon. As hostage David Raab comments, this pledge could not have been given without the concurrence of the PFLP who were physically holding them. British ambassador Phillips interpreted the move as a last-ditch attempt to salvage a vestige of credibility while in fact bowing to the pressure of the Jordanian onslaught:

> It looks as if the fedayeen, faced with the inevitable prospect of having all the hostages recovered by the army and thus losing their bargaining counters, are making it appear that they have already voluntarily decided to hand them back as a gesture in order to ensure the release of the fedayeen prisoners held in Europe.

At roughly the same time a man presenting himself as an adviser to the Egyptian Embassy in Amman delivered a note to journalists at the Intercontinental Hotel, purportedly from the PFLP, stating that the hostages would be delivered to the ICRC via the Egyptian Embassy within forty-eight hours in accordance with a decision taken by the PLO.[131] Sure enough, an hour later thirty-two American hostages held in the Ashrafieh district of Amman were voluntarily handed over to the care of the Egyptian diplomat, accompanied by a PFLP representative.[132] It was subsequent to this that British diplomats in Berne, Bonn and Washington were instructed to approach their host counterparts to obtain their agreement for an exchange supervised by Egypt, the FCO's instructions again stressing: 'You should not, repeat not, reveal that President Nasser has made this offer in response to a personal message from the Prime Minister.' On no account was Israel to be appraised of the arrangement: the priority was 'to clinch the deal quickly' to preclude Israel pressing for Leila Khaled's extradition.[133] Although the United States initially wavered, urging that proceedings be delayed in the hope that events would oblige a wholesale release 'without giving anything in exchange', the three European countries pressed ahead, the British cabinet judging that due to the Egyptian initiative they were collectively 'under a clear and moral obligation to carry out the terms of the bargain'.[134] There was some nail biting over the next three days, with the West Germans pressing that the United States expressly bless the deal and the Swiss expressing anxiety about adverse reactions from the PFLP to handing the seven prisoners over to Egypt.[135] Nonetheless, on 29 September Egypt, true to its word, finally delivered the remaining six 'star' hostages to safety in Irbid, again supervised by the same anonymous Egyptian diplomat. In response the seven European fedayeen prisoners were transported to Cairo, arriving on 1 October.

Who was Egypt's unsung troubleshooting 'diplomat' and how prominent was he in retrieving the hostages? Thanks to Raab's meticulous research we know that he was an Egyptian intelligence officer called Youssef Azziz el-Dien.[136] He was formally attached as a secretary to the Arab peace mission, headed by Sudanese president Jaffar Nimeiry, that had first arrived in Amman on 23 September. The delegation included the Egyptian army's Chief of Staff General Mohammed Ahmed Sadiq, and it would be fair to guess that he took Azziz el-Dien in tow with him.[137] Within this context it might also be usefully speculated whether Azziz el-Dien performed more than just one role in Jordan. Nimeiry and Sadiq not only managed to prize the Fatah leaders Abu Iyad (Salah Khalaf) and Farouk Kaddoumi out of the clutches of their Jordanian captors on 23 September but also spirited Yasser Arafat and Ali Hassan Salameh out of Amman to safety in Cairo after Arafat had announced his acceptance of a ceasefire on 24 September, thus paving the way to the Cairo Accord of 27 September.[138] In his recollections Abu Sharif describes that the perilous task of physically getting Arafat to the Arab delegation was arranged by an Egyptian intelligence officer 'whose name I never learned' at a meeting with Arafat at the PFLP's secret Amman headquarters, where it was agreed that the dash across the battle lines would be jointly organized by the Egyptian officer and Arafat's chief bodyguard Salameh.[139]

As to the significance of Azziz el-Dien's efforts in freeing the last hostages, despite some deprecating voices there can be little doubt that he – and thus Egypt on Britain's behalf – was the key player. On 26 September Ambassador Beaumont in Cairo had cabled that it was 'far from clear' whether Egypt had indeed 'played an influential part' or had not simply 'horned in on something that was already taking place', but this was not a view shared by his counterpart on the ground in Amman.[140] Two days later, Ambassador Phillips expressed the belief that Azziz el-Dien was 'the last, if not only, chance' of getting the last six hostages out, as he was the only person with real influence with the PFLP.[141] In his later post-mortem on events, Phillips's conclusion was equally clear, stating that the Egyptian Embassy had played a 'major part' in securing the release of the final thirty-eight hostages and that

> it was undoubtedly thanks to the efforts of an Egyptian Intelligence officer at the UAR [United Arab Republic] Embassy here that a group of 32 American-Israeli

hostages were freed on the 27th [sic], and the final group of six [...] on 29th September. Even the shock of Nasser's death did not delay the execution of his orders to secure the release of the hostages.[142]

Switzerland and the United States concurred, the former noting that 'the UAR obviously exerted their influence in freeing the hostages',[143] and the latter that Azziz el-Dien was to be given 'credit for qte [quote] bringing home the bacon unqte [unquote] on final hostage release'.[144]

Prime Minister Heath's verdict on the end of the crisis leaves no room for ambiguity that a bargain had been sealed:

> Despite [...] protests [from the *Daily Telegraph* and Conservative backbenchers] the Leila Khaled incident had reminded us all that a government's first duty is to negotiate, even with terrorists, rather than immediately sending in the Marines, with guns blazing. In this case, the hostages emerged unhurt and only token concessions were offered in return.[145]

On the face of things these 'token concessions' were limited to a promise of improved diplomatic relations with Egypt and the release of the seven prisoners, but rather than drawing a final line under the affair the PFLP considered that the deal encompassed further trade-offs that had yet to be fulfilled – demands that would continue to exercise the diplomats of various countries through to December.

Aftermaths

Deal or no deal? – The PFLP's post hoc demands

The sources demonstrate that the British government was always clear that it was the PFLP with whom they were ultimately bargaining and not Egypt as a proxy, and indeed wanted it to be so. Already on 26 September Ambassador Beaumont was instructed to inform Egyptian information minister Heikal that Britain, West Germany and Switzerland 'remain ready to consider an exchange for all hostages, but we must be clearer that we are dealing with those who have control over them and can deliver them. Present reports are confusing.'[146] In subsequent comments drawn up for Heath in preparation for a visit by Israeli prime minister Meir in early November, the FCO proposed that were he to be pressed on the matter he would 'probably wish to restate that there was an agreement *with the captors*, brought about largely as a result of the Prime Minister's own intervention in sending a message to President Nasser'.[147]

True, on 26 September Information Minister Heikal had assured the British ambassador that the proposed agreement was not conditional on any Israeli releases,[148] but already two days later the Egyptian Embassy, while reassuring that there were no strings attached to the release of the last six hostages, added the proviso that the PFLP expected Her Majesty's Government to apply pressure on Israel to release the two Algerians detained in Israel on 14 August (especially as they had been removed from a BOAC flight) and that the PFLP expected the release of twelve 'fedayeen' being held in Israel, a list of whom would be forthcoming.[149] The numbers involved would imply a garbled version of PFLP demands that Israel had already told the United States on 18 September they were in principle willing to meet, that is, to release the two Algerians and the ten Lebanese soldiers, a readiness that was repeated publicly on 27 September.[150] A further potential stumbling block was removed on 29 September when Israel also began with the phased release of the 450 Palestinians rounded up in mid-September.[151]

It therefore must have come as an unpleasant surprise to all concerned when the ante was upped on 30 September in a note hand-delivered by Azziz el-Dien to the American and British Embassies in Amman expressing the expectation that a total of fifty-six prisoners be released, corresponding to the number of hostages the PFLP had last held. In a sense this was the list that the Berne Group had been so vainly trying to coax out of the PFLP over the preceding three weeks, and in its now concrete form the fifty-six names consisted of the two Algerians, the ten Lebanese and the seven in Europe whose release was at this point imminent, leaving an added surplus of thirty-seven named prisoners held in Israel, including the Swiss Bruno Breguet (listed as '1 Swiss').[152] The 'interlocutor' who approached the American Embassy claimed to be speaking on behalf of 'the fedayeen central committee' (i.e. not simply the PFLP). Importantly, the enlarged list was accompanied by the considerable sweetener 'that if demands are met fedayeen will give word of honor that there will be no further hijackings'. However, the carrot came with a stick: 'Interlocutor stressed that if demands are i [sic] met, this would be a strong weapon to use in convincing fedayeen that goal can best be reached through negotiation. Frustration of this effort might have opposite effect – that is, that escalating violence is the only way to achieve result.' The US Embassy commented that they were 'skeptical about value of pledge re [regarding] no future hijackings', but that a 'public statement eschewing such activity would be of such obvious value that efforts to obtain it worth considerable risk'.[153] On being informed of the development, the State Department promptly tried to nip it in the bud. Instructions were issued that the embassy 'immediately' contact Azziz el-Dien to inform him that the US government refused to accept the list, to act as a channel for the PFLP or to have anything to do with the matter 'directly'.[154] The list given to the British Embassy was identical, likewise accompanied by the guarantee from Azziz el-Dien (referred to as 'Yousuf') 'that if these 56 were released the P.F.L.P. would cease any further hijackings'.[155] The FCO obligingly forwarded the list to the Israeli Embassy in London the next day, where the envelope was forensically opened, the contents photocopied, and then resealed and returned marked 'unopened'.[156] Four days later, on 5 October, Israel publicly rejected any demands to release the additional guerrillas.[157]

The Swiss consternation at also being approached by Azziz el-Dien must have been all the greater as they were apparently still unaware of the precise mechanics behind the deal.[158] The contacts were made via the ICRC's delegate in Amman and were worriedly discussed by Ernesto A. Thalmann, the Swiss observer at the UN, with the British ambassador to Berne, Eric Midgley, on 6 October. Thalmann described a repeat visit by a 'UAR embassy official', presumed by Midgley to have been 'Yousuf' (i.e. Azziz el-Dien), who 'had said that his "contacts" wanted Berne group to exert pressure on Israelis to release 49 detainees (i.e. 56 listed [...] less the seven flown to Cairo on 1 October)'. The Egyptian official had announced that he would return again in two days in the expectation of an Israeli response, repeating the 'same vague threats of what would happen if PFLP's demands were not met, but said that if they were all hijacking would cease'. Thalmann and Midgley agreed that the best response would be to block the approach by informing 'Yousuf' that the Berne Group had been disbanded and its mandate to the ICRC had fallen into abeyance, meaning that it could no longer serve as a channel.[159] If needed, the ICRC could offer to pass any subsequent messages to the relevant governments: moreover the Egyptian government was perfectly able to talk to the 'four governments concerned' (i.e. Britain, Switzerland, the United States and West Germany) itself, although admittedly the ICRC had the added advantage that it could pass communications from Egypt to Israel. In concluding, Midgley reported that he had agreed with Thalmann that he would recommend that the FCO instruct the British ambassador in Cairo to talk to Information Minister Heikal, 'pointing out that Yousuf's activities were condoning if not encouraging PFLP's threats of further hijackings and were contrary to spirit of bargain we had struck with Nasser'.[160] Thalmann also had an opportunity to take the matter up with an Egyptian diplomat on 14 October. The diplomat knew 'Youssof', but was apparently ignorant of his role, which did not stop Thalmann from airing his concerns:

> In response to my remark that we had fulfilled our part of the 'deal' and therefore considered the issue, as far as it concerned ourselves, as settled, he simply responded that the continuing threats against us and the other states was due to the fact that Israel had been incorporated into the Berne group.[161]

If and how these retroactive and seemingly opportunistic demands were defused, or whether they were simply ignored as bluster in the hope they would go away, is unclear. However, they would resurrect themselves two months later, albeit in a thoroughly scaled-down version. On 2 December Bruno Breguet was sentenced to fifteen years' imprisonment by an Israeli military court, prompting the PFLP to issue an internationally reported communiqué accusing the Berne Group of having reneged on a 'verbal agreement' to release not only the prisoners in Europe, but likewise the two Algerians, the Lebanese soldiers and Breguet, and threatening unspecified 'retaliation'.[162] The Swiss Eidgenössisches Politisches Departement (EPD, the Federal Political Department as the Swiss Foreign Ministry was called at the time) was duly alarmed, pointedly reminding its embassy in Beirut that such an 'agreement', verbal or otherwise, had never been given. Similar claims against the Berne Group had been made in the past, said the EPD, but Switzerland had met its 'obligations' at the time; the Berne Group had never had any discretionary power over the freeing of

Israeli prisoners and was anyway now long defunct. In view of the media excitement over the PFLP's claims, such fictions needed to be rigorously countered, while at the same time the EPD had to try to prophylactically ward off any such threats, 'even if vaguely formulated'.[163] Whereas the EPD's proposal was that the problem be best taken up with the Lebanese Foreign Ministry, albeit without creating any impression of nervousness about the communiqué, the Swiss ambassador to Israel reportedly urged a different, more direct and pandering plan of action. In the words of his British counterpart in Tel Aviv, the Swiss ambassador considered that the 'overt pressure' in the PFLP's threat to avenge Breguet's sentence 'would only succeed in hardening the Israeli attitude', and therefore his suggestion to the Swiss government was 'that they try and pass a message to the PFLP, telling them that such threats will not help Brejued [sic], and could easily prejudice Swiss efforts to do so'.[164]

The intensification of British and US contacts to the Palestinian guerrilla movement

In his postscript on the crisis, the British ambassador to Jordan J. F. S. Phillips ruminated on what lessons there were to be learned. Great Britain had been undoubtedly right to stick to the 'common position', but had been ultimately 'handicapped by our choice of negotiators'. The ICRC had in retrospect proven ineffective: the first main batch of hostages had been released due to the pressure of events and thanks to the PLO, and the release of the rest had been achieved by the Jordanian army and President Nasser. Intermediaries, wrote Phillips, had a tendency to hamper the pace of bargaining, 'distort the meaning of the other party' and in the worst case (referring explicitly to ICRC representative Rochat) 'superimpose their own ideas'. Therefore he was certain, despite what were unique circumstances that would probably not repeat themselves, that 'there would have been more chance of a real negotiation if the representatives of the countries concerned in Amman could have dealt directly with the PFLP, if necessary on behalf of the Israel "observers" in Berne as well'.[165]

None of this can have sounded in the least outlandish to the ears of the senior civil servants and government mandarins in the FCO, or by the same token the shadowy foreign policy combatants in the British Secret Intelligence Service (better known under the name MI6, short for Military Intelligence, Section 6),[166] as such direct contacts had in fact already been established prior to September 1970.

One example buried in FCO files is that of a 'quiet and informal dialogue' enacted over a period of months in the second half of 1969 by members of British Embassy staff in Amman with an 'informal contact at a fairly high level' from Fatah who had talked to them, with the knowledge of the Jordanian authorities, 'with increasing authority' and a 'professed unconcern that contact with British Embassy officials would do him any harm'. Not only was he 'a bigger fish' than had initially been thought but he was apparently talking to them, as the British Embassy excitedly reported in quotation marks, 'under instructions'.

> We think that this is a useful dialogue. It enables us to keep in touch with what is now virtually one of the pillars of the state, and, as the form of current

Palestinian Nationalism, a movement which may one day be a government. But, most important, this link has already enabled us to sort out tactfully and quickly the occasional dangerous misunderstanding between the fedayeen and individual British subjects and in this respect it may prove invaluable in the months ahead.

Significantly, the source said that despite Fatah's condemnation of its actions it 'had no intention of doing anything at all about the PFLP'.[167]

The contact person was later established by the embassy to be Ahmad Azhari, nominally the deputy director of Fatah's information office in Amman under Kamal Adwan. In October 1969 J. A. Shepherd from the embassy and Azhari both emphasized to each other that 'the contact was personal and in no way represented an official link between Al Fatah and the British Embassy'. Nonetheless, Azhari accepted that it was 'to the benefit of both parties that mutual understandings should be increased', agreeing to further conversations in the future. Revealingly, the two men not only talked openly about Fatah's military planning for forthcoming guerrilla operations against Israel and about the troubles caused by the PFLP's 'wanton terrorism', but Shepherd also expressed a hope to Whitehall that officers from Scotland Yard and Immigration and Customs might helpfully in the future distinguish between the PFLP and Fatah in dealing with airport arrivals to Britain. Once again British Embassy reasoning focused on the alignment of forces within the PLO, betraying a degree of wishful thinking and perhaps even gentle prodding. In the context of the PFLP's recent 'bomb outrages' in Western Europe, Azhari stated that Fatah needed 'friends' abroad, not 'enemies', with Shepherd inferring from his comments that 'while Fatah will not itself risk the odium of clobbering the PFLP, it would not intervene if the [Jordanian] régime had a go'.[168]

In December 1969 Shepherd had the opportunity to encounter another leading Fatah figure, this time PLO Executive Committee member Kamal Nasser – counted by commentators as having belonged to Fatah's 'centralists'.[169] During a long conversation with Shepherd, Kamal Nasser 'roundly denounced' terrorist attacks in Western Europe, which he stated only served to discredit the Palestinian movement 'and were entirely contrary to PLO policy'. Fatah's leadership was said to be incensed about the most recent attack in Athens, and Nasser 'expected them to put a stop to this kind of activity'.[170] Judging from the subtext of the report and those previously, this was precisely what the British were hoping to hear. Without being able to trace the precise pattern of these contacts, by early 1971 they had expanded to include Kamal Adwan as well, one of the founding members of Fatah and a key figure in the Central Committee of the Palestinian National Congress. In January 1971 Adwan discussed the current situation of the fedayeen in Jordan with a British Embassy official, informing him that they planned to go underground and continue their actions against Jordan.[171]

In terms of British ambassador Phillips's December 1970 thoughts on the possible future desirability of a direct channel to the PFLP, Great Britain's potentially most controversial contact was with Ghassan Kanafani, the PFLP's chief spokesman and editor of the PFLP paper *Al-Hadaf*.[172] When communications with Kanafani first began is unclear to date, but according to the sometimes vainglorious Leila Khaled, after being freed from captivity on 30 September 1970 Kanafani had told her that during the hijacking crisis 'the British ambassador came to the door of the PFLP headquarters with the embassy emblem, off the front door, and the flag, and told him, "take this as a hostage. Leila will be released"'.[173] Be it as it may, in late summer 1971 no lesser a figure than Sir Richard Allen, the recently retired FCO undersecretary of state for the Middle East and Africa, cordially met with Kanafani in Beirut,[174] and I. R. Callan of the British Embassy in Beirut reported on an in-depth discussion on internal fedayeen developments with Kanafani in late June 1972.[175] Mere days later, on 8 July 1972, Kanafani and his niece were killed in Beirut by a car bomb, generally thought to have been planted by the Israeli secret service Mossad.[176] Callan for one lamented his passing, writing that 'in the immediate future it will not be so easy for us to obtain PFLP views because, by Kanafani's assassination, we have lost a valuable contact whom I found personally agreeable and forthcoming'.[177]

As an aside to these contacts it is worth noting that it was not only Kanafani who met a violent end, but so too did the British Embassy's interlocutors Kamal Nasser and Kamal Adwan, gunned down along with Mohammed Yousef al-Najjar (Abu Yousef) during the Israeli 'Spring of Youth' commando operation mounted in Beirut on 9–10 April 1973. The raid was part of a string of assassinations – known popularly under the epithet 'Wrath of God' – that officially targeted the BSO's leadership in revenge for the attack on the Munich Olympics in September 1972. That Nasser and Adwan maintained contacts with the British Embassy in Beirut might be nothing more than a coincidence, and indeed there is nothing per se that precludes the people with whom the British were talking from also having been key BSO members. Nevertheless, the question of whether there was a correspondence merits some consideration, not least because there have always been murmurings that the Israeli assassination campaign of late 1972 to mid-1973 had also deliberately targeted influential Palestinian thinkers and moderates.[178] One such voice is the West German neo-Nazi and Fatah member Willi Pohl, who was recruited as a CIA source in the mid-1970s.[179] In his 1979 semi-fictional memoirs, Pohl wrote that the three men killed in the Beirut raid of April 1973 had been 'precisely those Palestinians […] who had spoken out against the actions of Black September'.[180]

This line of thought was given substance in a documentary series made by British journalist Peter Taylor and broadcast in 1993. One of the figures to appear before the camera was General Aharon Yariv, the former head of the Directorate of Israeli Military Intelligence AMAN. During the interview Yariv controversially admitted that the killings had targeted not only figures thought to be tied to the BSO and the Munich attack but also PLO and Fatah leaders in general who were not. Asked about the case of the PLO representative to France Dr Mahmoud Hamshari, who was killed in Paris on 16 December 1972, Yariv said that as far as he could remember Hamshari had had no direct involvement in Munich but had been a legitimate target by virtue of being 'directly involved in PLO activities'.

> Q. But that's very broad, PLO activities. He could have been a politician. He could have been a writer, a thinker, a supporter.
> A. That, yes, but he was in a leadership position.
> Q. And that justifies his murder?
> A. In order to make them stop, yes.[181]

That some of those caught in the crosshairs of Israeli operations were essentially targets of opportunity was recently likewise confirmed to Israeli journalist Ronen Bergmann by an anonymous AMAN officer, who said in more strident and unapologetic terms:

> We looked at the organization as one entity, and we never accepted the distinction between the people who dealt with politics and those who dealt with terror. Fatah was a terrorist organization that was murdering Jews. Anyone who was a member of such an organization had to know that he was a legitimate target.

As Bergmann comments, this thinking 'allowed the Mossad to kill the people it could, not necessarily those the agency believed it should'.[182]

A further case that gives grounds for speculation is that of Basil Raoud al-Kubasi, a PFLP representative shot down in Paris on 6 April 1973. An academic and an intellectual, al-Kubasi was described after his death as Habash's 'roving ambassador'.[183] Al-Kubasi had been a source to the British on the PFLP's predecessor organization the ANM in 1963 and had been targeted for recruitment by the CIA while studying in the United States in the mid- to late-1960s. Although his formal status with the CIA is unclear, it has been established that he acted as a sometime source to CIA case officer Robert Ames.[184] Therefore, if one of the designs of the Israeli assassination programme was indeed a psychological attrition, to inflict a feeling of demoralization within the Palestinian movement, it is worth asking whether there was not a further potential corollary, namely a stymieing of Western-PLO contacts. Outlandish as it might appear at first glance, it is nevertheless a scenario expressed by CIA case officer Graham Fuller to American journalist Kai Bird: 'I know [...] there was a lot of anger among officers that the Israelis seemed to be deliberately gunning down our assets who could provide influential info on the Middle East other than Mossad channels'.[185]

What the al-Kubasi case also illustrates is that if the British were breaking any unwritten rules of political decorum with their contacts to Palestinian leaders they were not alone – the Americans were doing likewise. Indeed, it might well be surmised that both countries were largely informed about each other's actions, FCO Deputy Undersecretary of State Peter Hayman writing in June 1970:

> We regularly exchange information with the Americans in London about the fedayeen, both informally with the US Embassy and through American (mostly

CIA) attendance at the weekly JIC [Joint Intelligence Committee] meetings, and through exchanges of intelligence assessments. I agree with you that there is probably very little information that has not been shared with the other and that our differences tend to be ones of interpretation.[186]

That the Americans, like the British, had already established links with the Palestinians by this point can be read from a State Department cable to Ambassador Dean Brown in Jordan of 20 November 1970, asking him to sound out King Hussein for his views on US interaction with Palestinian groups, including the question whether he believed the United States 'should begin to broaden our contacts with Palestinians in various capitals of the Arab world'. On 23 November Brown reported back that King Hussein had mentioned that he was aware that United States officials were meeting with various Palestinians (plural) in Amman and Beirut, that he had 'no objection' to such contacts, and indeed that he was interested to hear what their understanding of Palestinian thinking was.[187]

There are one or two further minor clues as to the scheme of these contacts. One of them concerns Brown's predecessor as ambassador to Jordan, Harrison Symmes, who was very unusually declared persona non grata by King Hussein in mid-April 1970. According to most accounts, his dismissal was due to his role in dissuading Assistant Secretary of State Sisco from visiting Jordan following the army's failure to prevent attacks on the American Embassy and cultural centre in Amman by Palestinian rioters on 15 April.[188] However, an alternative version of events is that Symmes was expelled for having established contacts with a number of fedayeen leaders, the liaison having reportedly been picked up through the bugging of Symmes's phone calls by the Jordanian secret services.[189] If these feelers indeed displeased the Jordanians, they were nevertheless in line with an emerging current in the State Department's thinking at the time. Following his return from the Middle East Sisco penned some first tentative proposals to factor the Palestinians into the peace equation, arguing that to date the United States had wrongly been treating the Palestinian question as a 'refugee problem' when they had in fact become a 'quasi-independent force in much of the area'.[190] Linked to this development is an inquiry by Secretary of State Rogers to thirteen embassies in the Middle East sent out at some point prior to April 1970 canvassing their views on direct contacts to the Palestinians, accompanied by the stricture that the embassies 'should take no action that might be construed as official recognition of the PLO or the fedayeen movement'. Six US missions replied that they considered the proposal a constructive one.[191] This in turn matches a message from the US ambassador to Lebanon Dwight Porter to the State Department in March that the embassy was deliberately initiating contacts to the fedayeen. Such a move, said Porter, 'could perhaps help assure against blatant misrepresentation of misunderstandings of our position, give Palestinians feeling we recognize they are legitimate party and in some measure moderate or diffuse opposition to our initiatives'.[192] With whom contacts had been established is unclear, but an electronic cable from the US Embassy in Beirut from May 1974 mentions that the PLO representative in

Lebanon, Shafiq al-Hout, had had 'sporadic contacts' with embassy staff over the preceding five or six years, that is, since around 1969.[193]

What the significance of the symmetry is unclear, but it is interesting to note that a similar opening to the PLO and Fatah was being duplicated by West Germany at around the same time, as shown in documents recently unearthed by the German historian Lutz Maeke. On 17 April 1970 the West Germany Auswärtige Amt (AA, Foreign Office) wrote to its representatives in Amman, Beirut, Cairo and Damascus asking them to submit detailed reports on the fedayeen movement, explaining that 'greater importance is being attached to the Palestinian organizations in the Western capitals, and they are being weighed as a factor in political deliberations'.[194] Although the AA's instructions contained no mention of exploring the feasibility or expediency of contacts, both Amman and Cairo answered in precisely these terms – presumably not of their own accord. The report from Amman shows that the embassy had apparently put out feelers to the main Palestinian organizations in one form or another, pointing out that unlike the PFLP or the DFLP (who by implication had rejected the idea), Fatah was 'certainly interested in contacts' with West Germany, a 'willingness to meet' helped by the fact that so many high-ranking Fatah and PLO cadre had studied in West Germany.[195] Nevertheless, warned the West German diplomat, Fatah would 'arrange their contacts to West European governments and institutions more cautiously' – in other words more so than previously had been the case – so as 'not to excite the suspicions of the others or to be branded as traitors to the common cause', adding that they would 'be obliged to keep their idea, discussed in the tightest leadership circles, of perhaps also initially agreeing to a negotiated solution, largely secret'.[196]

The West German diplomats in Cairo went a stage further and had already initiated contacts by the time they replied to Bonn, implying that they had received either prior instructions or the general latitude to do so:

> The establishment of contact with the PLO and Fatah representative offices produced a positive echo amongst all the Palestinians. The reception of my member of staff by Gamal Arafat [Yasser Arafat's brother] and Ahmed Abbas [the deputy PLO representative in Cairo under Gamal el Surany] was markedly friendly. Our initiative was considered by the perfectly self-confident PLO and Fatah members to be a sign of German interest in the resistance and as proof of the increasing political weight of the liberation movement.

Most importantly, 'the continuation of the contacts to the PLO and Fatah's interlocutors was agreed'.[197] That these Cairo contacts were indeed resumed is evident from a telegrammed report of November 1970, detailing the contents of 'lengthy conversation' between a member of the West German diplomatic staff and Ahmed Abbas. The frank discussion covered the ramifications of various international and domestic developments, including a direct threat by Abbas that were Jordan and Egypt to move towards a separate peace with Israel or to force the PLO to suspend their cross-border raids against Israel, the 'PLO would switch to targeting Western oil interest throughout the entire Middle East with commando operations' – a 'really major act' designed to ensure that 'the rights of the Palestinians could no longer be ignored'.[198] As in the British case, the lineage and intensity of these contacts still remain hazy, but the fact that the West German diplomats in Beirut had – like the Americans – also cultivated exchanges with Shafiq al-Hout from the late 1960s onwards presumably constitutes a further stone in the mosaic.[199]

As far as concerns the United States, the crucial contact, and for that matter the one now known in greatest detail, was that to Ali Hassan Salameh, aka 'The Red Prince'.[200] The stations of Salameh's career are laid out in detail in the literature, but the salient points are worth rehearsing here to give an indication of just how large a fish the CIA had landed in cultivating him as a clandestine source.[201] Born in 1942 as the son of Sheikh Hassan Salameh, he had spent some time in West Germany as a graduate engineer and joined Fatah in 1964. As a protégé of Arafat's, Salameh had spent two years in Kuwait on behalf of the PLO before being seconded to Fatah's intelligence and reconnaissance apparatus Jihaz al-Razd, joining a six-week training course given by the Egyptian Mukhabarat (secret service) to an elite group of Fatah members in Cairo from August to September 1968. Working under Abu Daoud (Mohammad Daoud Oudeh), Salameh's security remit included liaising with foreign sympathizers, leading, for instance, to encounters with members of the nascent West German Red Army Faction (RAF), including Andreas Baader and Ulrike Meinhof, in Jordan in summer 1970.[202] Following the Jordanian crisis of September 1970 Salameh was charged with forming a special internal Fatah security apparatus, a powerful body later known as Force 17. These numerous covert roles effectively predestined him for his next incarnation when between 1971 and 1973: he acted as an operational leader in the BSO, responsible for the planning and execution of a number of attacks in Western Europe.[203]

Salameh's induction as a CIA source – a role that he would play, with interruptions, until his death in a Mossad-orchestrated car bomb attack in Beirut on 22 January 1979 – came about in late 1969. The contact was mediated by Mustafa Zein, who had known Salameh since 1964 from Cairo, and the initial meetings were conducted by CIA officer Robert Ames – who himself would be killed in the bombing of the US Embassy in Beirut on 18 April 1983.[204] According to his biographer Kai Bird, Ames's pitch to Salameh through Zein was that he had been personally authorized by President Nixon to 'explore the possibility of contact between the USA and the PLO'. As exaggerated as this claim seemingly was – at their first meeting Ames this time said that his mandate to open a channel came from the National Security Council (NSC) – the bait worked, and the liaison between the two men became established to the extent that CIA director Richard Helms was apprised of the evolving conduit in late January 1970. Because of the potential blowback of maintaining contacts with what was considered a terrorist organization, Helms in turn informed President Nixon (and by surmise National Security Adviser Kissinger too) about the back channel sometime in the summer of the same year. By mid-1970, the relationship had evolved to the stage that Salameh was assigned a cryptonym, MJTRUST/2 – 'MJ' standing for Palestine, 'trust' perhaps indicating the quality of the contact, and '2', significantly, that he was the second such figure in the organization to have been identified as a contact.[205]

The relationship, according to Bird, was

> a two-way street in which Ames tried to influence Salameh to have the PLO act more like a political party – and less like a guerrilla organization – while Salameh tried to influence Washington, through Ames, to understand that it was unrealistic for U.S. policy makers to ignore the Palestinian cause.[206]

As Frank Anderson, a fellow CIA case officer and later chief of station in Beirut, explained it to Bird:

> Ali's ambition was to turn the back channel into a real diplomatic relationship. [...] He wanted the relationship to evolve into a de facto recognition of the PLO. But on our side, we had to cloak the relationship as an intelligence operation. At the same time, Ali had to make it seem to his own people that this was diplomacy, not intelligence. In the end, we committed more diplomacy, and he conveyed more intelligence.[207]

The information Salameh initially gave Ames was not without its critics. Based on Salameh's reading of developments, Ames argued that King Hussein's rule in Jordan was doomed to end and that the fedayeen could not only withstand any attempt to crush them but would ultimately prevail – a view shared by others within the intelligence and foreign policy establishments such as the ambassador to Jordan Symmes.[208] One of the dissenters was the CIA chief of station in Amman Jack O'Connell, who believed that Salameh was feeding Ames faulty intelligence that the fedayeen were winning the struggle for Amman when in fact the Jordanian army was chafing at the bit to crush them. O'Connell recounts: 'The U.S. government was deeply divided. State was pessimistic [i.e. about the viability of King Hussein's rule]. The agency was split between my views in Amman and the views of Bob Ames [...] stationed in Beirut and in liaison with Arafat's intelligence chief, Ali Hassan Salameh.'[209]

Senior CIA officials also became troubled by the ambiguous status of the channel and decided that the best solution was to formalize it by recruiting Salameh as a paid agent. Ames was against the idea, but dutifully played his part, telling Zein that it had been agreed in Washington that a dialogue was to be opened with the PLO. Zein set up and hosted the meeting, which took place with CIA officer Vernon Cassin, a former chief of station in Damascus and Amman, in the Cavalieri Hilton Hotel between 18 and 21 December 1970. A crude and tactless pitch was made to buy his loyalties, said to have left Salameh deeply insulted.[210] Whereas some accounts state that the contact between Ames and Salameh temporarily ceased as a result of the fiasco,[211] Bird states that Salameh and Ames continued to meet on sporadic occasions until May 1971, after which contacts between the two men did dry up, only to be resumed again in March 1973.[212]

The potential diplomatic opening

None of these British and American, or for that matter West German, contacts were rouge encounters, nor did they occur in a vacuum rather they took place in a clearly evolving political context. Clues as to the sea change taking place in Western attitudes towards the Palestinian problem had already been evident in the Rogers Initiative prior to September, but the Jordanian hijacking crisis, very much as the PFLP intended, threw the issue into sharp relief and helped focus the minds of Western policy makers.

The rumbles had already started during the September crisis itself. On 21 September French president Georges Pompidou had written to President Nixon about his alarm at the prospect of US intervention in Jordan, at the same time underscoring his belief that it had been false of the Great Powers to ignore the Palestinians and arguing that it was key that they be invited to participate in the resolution of the Arab–Israeli conflict. On 26 September the French referred to the Palestinians as being a 'political fact', and by October the French government had discussed the situation with the Soviet Union and had formulated a proposal that in the long term some form of Palestinian self-determination was desirable.[213] On 12 October National Security Advisor Kissinger and Assistant Secretary of State Sisco held a joint background press briefing on the situation in the Middle East after events in Jordan, during which Sisco cautiously sketched out a scenario for the next five years based on the assumption that the United States could 'stabilize' the region. This vision foresaw the Arabs adopting 'a live and let live attitude' vis-à-vis Israel, with Israel granting 'at least part of the Arab demands' regarding the occupied territories, and, pointedly, 'giving expression to the Palestinian movement and very likely in the form of some entity'.[214] Great Britain likewise followed suit. On 31 October, three days prior to the arrival of Israeli prime minister Meir in London, British foreign secretary Alec Douglas-Home delivered a major foreign policy statement in a speech in Harrogate, constituting the first official British expression of support for UN Security Council Resolution 242 and effectively calling for an Israeli withdrawal to the pre-1967 boundaries. Douglas-Home pleaded for a 'negotiated settlement' that 'included the Palestinians', noting the need to take their 'legitimate aspirations' into account, including 'their desire to be given a means of self-expression'.[215]

In fact, a major NSC policy review of the Palestinian question was underway behind the scenes in Washington, involving the Senior Review Group (SRG) and the Washington Special Actions Group (WSAG), with input from the State Department and intelligence agencies. Galvanized by the events in Jordan, it was acknowledged that the fedayeen movement represented a potent and potentially destabilizing force in the Middle East equation and that Palestinian political aims had to be addressed in one form or another within the ongoing efforts to revitalize the Middle East peace process. These discussions lasted through to the end of 1970 and beyond, grappling with various scenarios that might channel the objectives of the Palestinian nationalist movement, including the possible necessity of a Palestinian entity, perhaps even statehood.[216]

One of the key dilemmas was whether and if in what form to forge contacts with Palestinian leaders, and recently published documents – although still incomplete – now shed a new light on how the CIA's conduit to Fatah via Ali Hassan Salameh fed into thinking in Washington. At a meeting of the SRG and the WSAG on 15 October Kissinger instructed that the issues to be covered in the policy review should encompass the following questions: 'What does their identity as Palestinians entail? How should we establish contact with them? What would be the implications? Would this be seen as a way of scuttling [King] Hussein?' At the same meeting, the contents of two 'interesting intelligence reports' were discussed, based on information from a senior Fatah member. Fatah, said the reports, wanted to abandon the PLO and form a new front organization, analogous to the Algerian Liberation Front, capable of undertaking negotiations for the 'emergence of new Palestinian State' with concrete borders and apparently dropping calls for the outright elimination of Israel but nonetheless planning for its 'reduction in size'. U. Alexis Johnson of the State Department commented that were the reports to be valid 'it is the first time a Palestinian organization has been willing to accept the existence of the State of Israel and organize itself for negotiations'.[217] On 19 October the CIA met again with their 'clandestine contact'. His name is redacted, but he is described as a senior Fatah official, his status having been confirmed by 'other independent assets'. The contact

> advised that, with the approval of Fatah leader Arafat, Fatah proposed a 'confidential' meeting in the immediate future somewhere in Europe between senior Fatah officials and one or more senior U.S. Government officials. [Name redacted] listed six items which Fatah wished to discuss, and asked that the U.S. side limit itself to no more than ten principle policy or political matters which it wished on the agenda.

The six sounding points were requests for US government clarifications on various basic issues, including what its definitions were of 'the rights of the Palestinian people' and the term 'Palestinian entity', and what its stance was on the continued existence of Jordan as a country. CIA director Helms emphasized the need to give 'at least a tentative reply within the next few days', confident that Fatah's request was 'bona fide and that the Palestinians who would attend such a meeting would represent the Fatah leadership'.[218]

Likewise on 15 October, the State Department moved ahead and queried its embassies as to how best to incorporate the Palestinians into talks and to persuade moderate Arab states to temper fedayeen demands.[219] Although apparently out of the loop on the ongoing discussions between the CIA and Fatah via Salameh, in late October Assistant Secretary of State Sisco informed the SRG that there were signs that Fatah might be willing to reverse its positions and accept UN Security Council Resolution 242 and the Rogers Initiative. In response to a recent 'overture', an 'interim message' had been sent to Fatah to indicate that their ideas were 'being studied', and Sisco was urging that this be followed up by proposing a meeting between US and Fatah officials in Europe.[220] On 4 November, the SRG recorded that the United States had 'moved towards acknowledging Palestinian interests and concerns in high-level public statements by US officials and have expanded our contacts with a wide range of Palestinians, including members of the fedayeen organizations'. Despite agreeing that a way had to be found to tie the Palestinian leadership into the negotiations, the participants agreed that this should not involve recognition of particular Palestinian groups or an assurance of a separate Palestinian state 'at this stage'.[221]

Taken together these documents illustrate two facts. Firstly, the mechanism involved is an early example of Kissinger's famed practice of covert 'back-channel' politics whereby the State Department was sidelined, or for that matter usurped, in favour of direct conduit via the CIA to the NSC, as personified in the figure of Kissinger himself. In addition, while State Department suggestions of a direct contact to Fatah were apparently ignored, a number of for all intents and purposes direct meetings were nevertheless held, simply using the offices of the CIA instead. In this sense the CIA-Fatah conduit of late 1970 presages the famed PLO-US dialogue of 1973–1974, suggesting moreover that the latter was a previously rehearsed reiteration of the former.[222] Secondly, the initial bait given to Salameh by the CIA about an authorization from President Nixon or a mandate from the NSC may have been a calculated dissimulation, but the record now shows that the dialogue with the CIA not only involved considerably more substance than accounts to date would suggest, but also reveals that Fatah's messages were indeed being read and considered by National Security Advisor Kissinger in person, who was being exclusively briefed by CIA director Helms. These two aspects in turn raise the key question of whether this tentative opening to Fatah was not in fact a deliberate ruse in what has been described as Kissinger's evolving 'standstill diplomacy'.[223]

Despite Fatah's entreaties, Kissinger obviously baulked at the idea of an 'official' meeting. On 5 November Helms reported to Kissinger that although the other side was 'seriously disappointed' with the 'failure to send a representative', they could 'understand, and, in fact, obviously accept, our factual explanation that a variety of practical factors prevent a speedy response to Fatah's proposal to establish a dialogue, but many other Fatah leaders might not be able to do so'. Fatah, said the intermediary (name redacted), was 'extremely aware' of the risks it was running in its dialogue with the United States, as well as the concomitant 'imperative need, in the interest of its survival, to keep its contact with the U.S. Government absolutely secret'. Fatah's overriding wish was to hold 'policy talks' with the United States.

> Fatah's interest in honest, secret dialogue with the U.S. Government at this time is the product of many considerations, such as: (A) Its recognition that the United States is a key power factor in the area, especially vis-à-vis Israel; (B) Its sensing, from recent statements by senior U.S. Officials, that the U.S. Government has finally come to realize that no lasting peaceful settlement is possible without the consent and active participation of the Palestinian people and its leadership (and Fatah is confident that it alone can provide that leadership); (C) Fatah's present readiness to accept the establishment of a Palestine entity (and in fact to furnish

the government of such an entity) and the pragmatic necessity for this entity to live in peace with and indeed to enter into cooperative relations with Israel; and (D) Its realistic recognition that to become viable economically, a Palestine entity will require sizable foreign aid, especially from the United States.

The CIA's contact urged the US government to recognize 'the emotional imperative of the younger Palestinian generation to assert itself combatively, even at mortal cost', adding a thinly veiled warning that if Palestinian pride 'is not permitted to channel itself into constructive effort (e.g. within the context of a Palestine entity), it will vent itself violently and destructively against all foes, real or imagined'.[224]

On 24 November Helms reported personally to Kissinger again on the CIA's most recent meeting with their contact. Fatah was at repeated pains to demonstrate that it was acting as a responsible prospective partner. In a series of trips to Arab leaders Arafat had obtained their agreement for the decision to form a sovereign and independent 'State of Palestine', and the methods for doing so.[225] Presumably in an attempt to pre-empt and assuage potential American fears, Fatah importantly emphasized that the new state would not serve as an irredentist launching pad. Their point to the Arab leaders was that Israeli retaliations against them would cease 'once all displaced Palestinians were in one place', and that 'the Palestinians themselves would never venture attacks against Israel because Israel could easily destroy them since the Palestinians would possess no conventional military capability'. It was crucial that Fatah and the US government sit down together 'at a senior level' within the next seven to ten days to exchange ideas before the idea of the creation of a state became public. Fatah's proposal involved Jordanian territory, not only on the West Bank, but parts of the East Bank too, the CIA's contact warning ('dramatically but not threateningly') that were the United States to oppose these annexations, Fatah and the Arab states would, in his own words, 'respond harshly' and the two sides would 'look at each other through a wall of flames'.[226]

Despite the ostensibly broad-ranging nature of the NSC policy review and the consensus of the need to concretely include the Palestinians in the Middle East peace process, the tide of thinking inexorably turned and the opportunities on offer were ultimately never explored. In early December 1970 a telegram to the US Embassy in Jordan, approved by Kissinger, expressed the continued view that it was 'desirable that Palestinians at some appropriate stage become participants in the negotiating process as well as partners in any peace settlement if that peace settlement is to stick'. Disregarding the 'Palestinian factor', said Kissinger, 'would tend to dash hopes of those whom we believe hold moderate views'.[227] The issue of responding favourably to Fatah's continuing requests for a meeting was also addressed. The telegram indicated that although King Hussein would be consulted, he would not be given a 'veto' over any decision. Opinions, however, were shifting. Kissinger conceded that Arafat's moves to try and establish an independent state, and Arab support for such a state, had a certain 'logic', but he nonetheless viewed them with suspicion. According to Kissinger, the Palestinian leadership had failed to renounce their aims to reverse the Jewish character of Israel, meaning that the key to a solution lay with 'the established government in Jordan'.[228]

That a reversal was underway is also evident from the minutes of an SRG meeting on 17 December. There was a consensus that there could be no return to treating the 'Palestinian issue' simply as 'a refugee problem', but at the same time there was, as Assistant Secretary of State Sisco summarized it, 'no policy decision favoring a separate Palestinian entity'. The implication was, said Sisco, 'that we are keeping everything on ice. We will keep the door open without pushing ahead'. As far as contacts to Fatah were concerned, a response to the Palestinians themselves was now a fallback contingency should 'a new development occur'. Moreover, as CIA director Helms noted, the force of the Palestinian position was weakening, the 'disarray' among them having become 'even worse than when we talked about this earlier'. The policy review itself had come to the conclusion that 'the most feasible and reasonable objective' was 'some form of Palestinian entity focused primarily on the West Bank and Gaza, in association with the King, under the Hashemite umbrella and in the framework of the Jordanian state'. King Hussein was ultimately prepared to offer this entity 'very considerable autonomy', a prospect that it was judged Israel might also agree to.[229]

Salameh presumably also began to realize that he and Fatah were being kept dangling and that the balance was tilting against them – a recognition that perhaps contributed to his anger at the December meeting in Rome. On 7 January 1971 Helms reported to Kissinger that the CIA contact had refused to continue their meetings without a substantive clarification from the US government on their 'political attitude to the Palestinian movement' in the form of 'an official agenda of topics to be discussed at this next meeting'. Helms considered that the hardening of the source's attitude might be genuine: 'We shall endeavor, however, to induce him to continue to maintain at least occasional contact with us for "the informal exchange of views".'[230] In this sense, by the close of 1970 a crossroads had been passed: US policy makers decided to pass up the opportunity of a dialogue with Fatah, instead adopting a wait-and-see stance and thus by default barring a potential Palestinian entry into the peace process.

Fatah's ascendency and the PFLP's renunciation of hijackings

Despite the terrible bruising that the fedayeen movement had taken from the Jordanian army in the second half of September, it was widely considered that Fatah had acquitted themselves admirably and had come out of the conflict as the clear winner among the guerrilla organizations, and with them Arafat as the key leader – positions confirmed in the Cairo Accord of 27 September and further cemented in the subsequent Amman Agreement of 13 October.[231] The latter protocol, for instance, allowed Habash, as well as Nayef Hawatmeh of the splinter DFLP, to re-enter Jordan, but only if constrained within the straightjacket of the PLO Central Committee.[232] As the newly published American documents show, the crux of the matter is that Fatah undertook a concerted effort to exploit this newfound status as leverage to insert the Palestinian nationalist movement into the Middle East peace process. Considering Fatah's hostility towards the Rogers Initiative pre-September, this ambition represented a veritable volte-face.

Minus the content of the CIA's communications to Fatah via Salameh, or for that matter Kissinger's comments to Helms, it is impossible to know to what extent this about-turn might have been cued by US officials or whether Fatah's moves were based on a wishful reading of what it saw as US nods. Be it as it may, the stereo nature of developments from October onwards lends them a conspicuously synchronized appearance. Although ultimately fruitless, these moves also have a deeper historical significance: they are evidence of a current of pragmatism and realpolitik within the Palestinian movement, a speculative willingness to negotiate and make concessions with Israel, and a recognition that the key to the solution of the Palestinian–Israeli conflict lay in Washington. Of equal importance, however, is the date – these stances had already been formulated, however tenuously, in late 1970 and not first immediately prior to and following the Yom Kippur War of October 1973 as is commonly held.

The prospect of advancing to become a recognized negotiating party in the Middle East peace process entailed a pressing need to wield the disparate Palestinian forces into a common force and to consolidate them, both internally and externally. This perforce meant co-opting or reining in the recalcitrant PFLP. As early as 9 October the PFLP organ Al-Hadaf cited a PFLP spokesman as saying that the five major fedayeen organizations in Jordan (the Palestinian Liberation Army, Fatah, the Syrian-backed Saiqa, the PFLP and the DFLP) had agreed to a military merger and coordination under a five-man joint military committee set up by the PLO Central Committee.[233] On 13 October these moves took on an overtly political and public character when in Paris a figure calling himself General Abu Sameeh Touqan and describing himself as one of the leaders of the 'Palestinian Revolutionary Council' publicly announced moves to form a Palestinian 'provisional revolutionary government' in exile in order to enter into negotiations with Israel. The prospective government was said to have fifteen members (ten civilians and five generals), including Arafat and Habash. The revolutionary government would call for the unification of all resistance organizations under a unified command, and Touqan added that 'Habash has agreed to join with us on condition that the struggle for the liberation of Palestine should be independent of other Arab governments'.[234] Touqan's claims were perhaps a trial balloon, but a day later Radio Tunis reported that Habash had sent a message to Arafat expressing approval for Arafat's actions and stressing that the current situation demanded new forms of cooperation and greater solidarity within the PLO Central Committee.[235]

These intentions were regurgitated a month later, on paper at least, in an article in the Fatah newspaper *Fath*, which on 15 November described intentions to form a 'Palestinian Liberation Front' along Vietnamese lines. Each organization was to be permitted to continue its own internal political and organizational activities, but the 'Front' would be responsible for overall political and military direction, the prelude to the dissolving of all the separate groups into one central military command comprising the 'unified Palestinian revolutionary forces', politically subject to the decisions of the PNC and the PLO Central Committee. A week later it was said that Habash had accepted the formula, expressing the PFLP's willingness 'to take far-reaching steps towards unity, with the exception of a full merger, since the present conditions are not suitable for complete unity'.²³⁶ For the CIA, were it to be carried out, this 'formal merger' of the fedayeen groups' military and political structures would represent 'a success for Fatah in its efforts to form a united front totally dominated by itself'. As a corollary it would point to 'the extreme weakness of the smaller groups', although were they to accede it would 'probably reflect only an effort on their part to buy time until they could rebuild their organizations'.²³⁷

Although Fatah's vaunted vision of a 'Front' organization proved stillborn in terms of a political negotiating body, as far as a guerrilla umbrella was concerned it met with some limited success.²³⁸ For one Issam Sartawi's Iraqi-backed Action Organization for the Liberation of Palestine (AOLP) was confronted by Fatah with a merge-or-perish ultimatum in late 1970, whereupon it ceased to exist as an autonomous terrorist group and was subsumed into Fatah.²³⁹ As far as the unruly PFLP was concerned, Fatah efforts would appear to have also had some traction, at least outwardly. On 5 November 1970 British Cabinet Secretary Burke Trend wrote to Prime Minister Heath on the subject of airport security, saying that the secret service to date saw no reason to justify relaxing the measures in place, despite mitigating items of intelligence. The first was that 'Jordanian questioning of PFLP prisoners suggests that the PFLP may now be less preoccupied with hijacking'; the second was that Arafat had personally 'recently told Mr. Anthony Nutting that he had a written undertaking from George Habash that the PFLP would not engage in further hijackings'.²⁴⁰ This ambivalence was still evident in December when the British Embassy in Beirut commented in relation to PFLP threats over Breguet's imprisonment in Israel that an airline hijacking was potentially 'always on the cards, although you will have seen reports indicating that PFLP have been firmly told by the PLO not to hi-jack any more aircraft', adding in parenthesis that 'alleged PFLP plans to attack shipping do not appear to have met with the same degree of disapproval'.²⁴¹ By February 1971, the British FCO reported that although Arafat was 'fully aware of the need to curb' the 'uncontrolled activities of maverick groups like the PFLP', unity was still a distant prospect: 'There is still no sign that Habash intends to work with the PLO or the Palestinian Congress. Indeed there are signs that to many fedayeen the extreme attitudes of the PFLP are more attractive than those of Arafat.'²⁴²

The PFLP itself was anyway badly mauled and marginalized following the September crisis, begging the question how much arm-twisting was required to make it fall into line. The real ramifications of what the defeat in Jordan meant were yet to fully play themselves out, and a general hubris meant that internal recriminations initially remained muffled.²⁴³ Nonetheless, one of the first targets was Habash in person, his vanishing act to the Far East during the momentous standoff with the Jordanian regime being too conspicuous to be blithely overlooked.²⁴⁴ From 5 to 13 November 1970 the PFLP held a weeklong expanded Central Committee meeting that exposed its internal rifts. Even as the plenum opened, inside sources were quoted as saying that a decision had been made to remove Habash as general secretary, to be replaced by a triumvirate of Haddad, Abu Maher and Leila Khalid. Quickly denied as 'sheer fantasy', the proceedings still evinced a deep criticism of Habash, reportedly not only for his absence during September but also for a recent letter addressed to Arafat expressing his willingness to place himself at the PLO Central Committee's disposal and to alter the PFLP's basic strategy.[245] In essence the meeting was a showdown between the disparate old and new guards within the PFLP, Habash playing his well-practised role as a mediator and so securing his re-election as general secretary. Haddad tried to defend his actions in triggering the September crisis, but in the end the younger 'leftists' won out, forcing through a formal and publicly issued commitment to suspend all so-called external operations[246] – a decision that Habash would tirelessly point to over the coming years, albeit not without an intrinsic ambiguity.[247]

Leaving aside the imponderables of to what extent Fatah's cajoling was effective and how substantial the PFLP's repeated statements forswearing hijackings were, the crucial point is that the PFLP did indeed cease international hijackings for a period of almost one and a half years. This hiatus finally ended on 22–23 February 1972 with the hijacking of a Lufthansa flight en route from New Delhi to Athens. In terms of the prior late-1970 moratorium, the circumstances of the incident are telling. Commandeered to Aden, the capital of South Yemen, the hijackers resorted to a flag of convenience intended to mask their true affiliation by identifying themselves as belonging to the 'Organization for Victims of Zionist Occupation'. Moreover, instead of demanding the release of any political prisoners the hijackers extracted a $5-million (DM 15.5 million) ransom from Lufthansa and the West German government, handed over in a cloak-and-dagger operation in Beirut. The hijacking led to angry recriminations within the PFLP, and ultimately a major split in March 1972 amidst accusations that the terrorist die-hards around Haddad had reneged on the agreed no-hijacking codex.[248] The split was further fuelled by claims that the Haddad faction had siphoned off most of the $5-million ransom for themselves.[249] The general agreement is that the ransom served as seed money to finance a renewal of Haddad's now rogue 'outside operations',[250] and together with the BSO his so-called PFLP Special Command would open a new and decidedly more deadly chapter in the history of Palestinian terrorism.

Notes

1 Dedicated in memory of John C. Schmeidel (1957–2013). The author would like to express his warmest appreciation to Kai Bird, Marcel Gyr, Lutz Maeke, James R. Stocker and Mustafa M. Zein for their generous assistance in supplying documents and information. A note of deep thanks also goes to Adrian Hänni for his expertise and his editorial solicitude and generosity.
2 Edward Heath, *The Course of My Life: My Autobiography* (London: Hodder & Stoughton, 1998), 323.
3 Memorandum from the Director of Central Intelligence Helms to the President's Assistant for National Security Affairs (Kissinger), 5 November 1970, in: Steven Galpern (ed.), *Foreign Relations of the United States 1969–1976*, XXIII, *Arab-Israeli Dispute, 1969–1972* (Washington: U.S. Government Printing Office, 2015), Doc. 180, https://history.state.gov/historicaldocuments/frus1969-97v23 (henceforth *FRUS 1969–1976*, XXIII).

4 In the British case, papers have in the best event often been withheld and retained by the ministries concerned and in the worst gutted from the files at source. See, for instance, the files PREM 15/124, 15/125, 15/201, 15/202 and 15/203 at The National Archives, Kew, London (henceforth TNA), in which a total of forty-three British cabinet documents pertaining to the September 1970 hostage crisis are listed as 'removed and destroyed'. Whereas in the British case the contents of the documents concerned are largely impossible to reconstruct, American archival practice offers a modicum of transparency by recording the subject taglines of withheld material. See, for instance, in our context, the message attributes on the withdrawal notifications for Electronic Telegram, US Embassy Beirut to Secretary of State, 26 September 1974, which read 'PFLP quits PLO with blasts as Arafat's alleged secret contacts with USG[overnment]'. This and all other US Department of State electronic cables cited below are from the Central Foreign Policy Files released by The National Archives, Washington DC, currently covering the years 1973–79 and accessible online in annual sections under https://aad.archives.gov/aad/series-list.jsp?cat=WR43 (henceforth simply Electronic Telegram).

5 In the specific case of Palestinian terrorism, this no-parlance edict was embodied in the so-called Kissinger Ban on either recognizing or even negotiating with the PLO and written up in a secret memorandum to Israel in the Sinai II Disengagement Agreement of September 1975. See Steve Posner, *Israel Undercover: Secret Warfare and Hidden Diplomacy in the Middle East* (Syracuse, NY: Syracuse University Press, 1987), 265–74.

6 Miles Copeland, *The Game of Nations: The Amorality of Power Politics* (New York: Simon and Schuster, 1969).

7 Marcel Gyr, *Schweizer Terrorjahre: Das geheime Abkommen mit der PLO* (Zurich: Verlag Neue Zürcher Zeitung, 2016).

8 Interdepartementale Arbeitsgruppe '1970', *Schlussbericht* (3 May 2016), 5. Emphasis in the original. The short body of the report has pagination, whereas the appendixes do not. The report, containing numerous important documents on the September hijackings, is available under https://www.eda.admin.ch/content/dam/eda/de/documents/publications/Geschichte/interdepartementale-arbeitsgruppe-1970_de.pdf (accessed 1 January 2020, henceforth *Schlussbericht*).

9 The earliest gesture identified by this author that can be construed as such dates from late 1973, that is, at the same time as the ongoing 'dialogue' between the U.S. government and PLO representatives. Shortly prior to Secretary of State Kissinger's visit to Lebanon in December 1973, both Fatah and the Egyptian authorities expressed concern that the PFLP might attempt an attack on him. The Egyptians reportedly pressurized Fatah to prevent any such incident, in response to which Fatah was said to have 'placed certain PFLP officials under restraint and PFLP terrorist leader Wadi Haddad under surveillance'. See Electronic Telegram, US Embassy Beirut (Buffum) to US Embassy Amman for Secretary of State, 15 December 1973.

10 The case best documented to date involving such a diplomatic pact with the PLO concerns West Germany in late 1977. See Matthias Dahlke, Das Wischnewski-Protokoll: Zur Zusammenarbeit zwischen westeuropäischen Regierungen und transnationalen Terroristen 1977, *Vierteljahresheft für Zeitgeschichte* 2 (2009), 201–15.

11 Rumours and accusations of similarly framed agreements occasionally surfaced in the press in the later 1970s. Some of them were speculative, for instance, in January 1974 when the Beirut-based *An-Nahar* reported (citing what were described as

anonymous well-informed sources) that the Greek government was preparing to release the two Palestinian perpetrators of the deadly Athens Airport attack of 5 August 1973 (in which three were killed and fifty-five wounded) in return for a pledge by the PLO to cease activities in Greece in a deal negotiated between the fedayeen and the Greek Embassy in Beirut, mediated by 'Lebanese and Arab personalities'. See Electronic Telegram, US Embassy Beirut (Houghton) to Secretary of State, 28 January 1974. Others were more detailed and concrete, for instance, reports of an anti-terrorism agreement between West German interior minister Gerhart Baum and Libyan leader Colonel Muammar Qaddafi in late November 1978. See Ware gegen Ware, *Der Spiegel*, 27 November 1978, 25–6.

12 Marc Tribelhorn, Es gab keine Berührungsängste, *Neue Zürcher Zeitung*, 12 April 2016, 15. The author also ventured the opinion that any deal was more likely to have taken place subsequent to the events of September 1970 and not immediately during them, a point also discussed by Gyr in this volume.

13 The figures for the number of hostages taken on each flight and in total vary marginally from source to source. The ones used here are from David Raab, *Terror in Black September: The First Eyewitness Account of the Infamous 1970 Hijackings* (New York: Palgrave Macmillan, 2008).

14 There is considerable confusion in the literature as to how the hijackers were allowed to board the Pan Am flight after arousing the suspicions of El Al staff, but all accounts put it down to a simple security glitch of one sort or another. They include West German journalist Jörg Andrees Elten, who singularly claims that the hijackers had come to the attention of the Israeli foreign secret service Mossad in their attempts to buy flight tickets in late August and that efforts had been made to shadow them. See Jörg Andrees Elten, *Flugzeug entführt: Der aufsehenerregende Report über die vier Flugzeugentführungen der palästinensischen Befreiungsfront* (Munich: Wilhelm Goldmann Verlag, n.d. [1973]), 22–4. Other Western agencies would appear to have likewise had prior intelligence of a forthcoming operation. Edward F. Mickolus, *Transnational Terrorism: A Chronology of Events, 1968–1979* (Greenwood Press: Westport, Connecticut, 1980), 208, mentions an Interpol warning regarding Palestinians travelling from Beirut to Europe that was intercepted by ham radio operators and was reported by the Belgian newspaper *Le Soir* on 5 September. Neil C. Livingstone, *The Cult of Counterterrorism: The Weird World of Spooks, Counterterrorists, Adventurers and the Not-Quite Professionals* (Lexington, MA: Lexington Books, 1990), 366, claims a case officer from the US Navy's Task Force 157 (otherwise known as the Navy Field Operations Support Group) learned of the PFLP's hijacking plans on 1 September. Livingstone comments: 'Why warnings from 157 were not heeded remains a mystery to this day.'

15 See J. F. S. Phillips (British ambassador to Jordan), Foreign and Commonwealth Office (FCO) Diplomatic Report No. 567/70, The Dawson's Field Hijackings, 22 December 1970, 9 pp., here 4, in: TNA, FCO 17/1374 (henceforth Phillips/FCO, Dawson's Field Hijacking).

16 PFLP speaker Abu Sharif later claimed that the BOAC hijacking was in fact unplanned and therefore completely unexpected, having been undertaken on the spontaneous initiative of a Palestinian admirer of Leila Khaled in Bahrain. See Bassam Abu Sharif and Uzi Mahnaimi, *Best of Enemies* (Boston: Little, Brown, 1995), 84–5. At least one aspect of this account is to be doubted, namely that the hijacker was resident in Bahrain. According to investigations by Dubai Special Branch, the suspected hijacker had entered the country illegally from Iraq on 6 September and

has spent three days preparing the operation. See Telegram No. 188, Dubai (Coles) to FCO, 9 September 1970, in: TNA, FCO 14/778.
17 Abu Sharif and Mahnaimi, *Best of Enemies*, 61.
18 The precise dates of Habash's trip are hazy. For the most reliable dates, putting his arrival in Pyongyang to 2 September, see *Middle East Record* 5 (1969–1970), 272 (henceforth *MER: 1969–1970*).
19 See Oriana Fallaci, A Leader of the Fedayeen: 'We want a war like the Vietnam war', *Life*, 22 June 1970, 20–4, here 21, where Habash patiently expounded: 'Let me explain: the attacks of the Popular Front are based on quality, not quantity. We believe that to kill a Jew far from the battleground has more of an effect than killing 100 of them in battle; it attracts more attention. And when we set fire to a store in London, those few flames are worth the burning down of two kibbutzim. Because we force people to ask what is going on, and so they get to know our tragic situation. You have to be constantly reminded of our existence.'
20 There are many versions of this famous quote. Here from John K. Cooley, *Green March, Black September: The Story of the Palestinian Arabs* (London: Frank Cass, 1973), 1.
21 From the perspective of this current essay, see, in particular, James Stocker, Diplomacy as Counter-Revolution? The 'Moderate States,' the Fedayeen and State Department Initiatives towards the Arab–Israeli Conflict, 1969–1970, *Cold War History* 12/3 (2012), 407–28.
22 See William B. Quandt, *Peace Process: American Diplomacy and the Arab-Israeli Conflict Since 1967* (Washington, DC: Brookings Institution Press, 2001), 72–4.
23 Yitzhak Rabin, *The Rabin Memoirs*, 2nd ed. (Bnei Brak: Steimatzky, 1994), 130–45, here 145. See further Quandt, *Peace Process*, 69; Robert Dallek, *Nixon and Kissinger: Partners in Power* (New York: HarperCollins, 2007), 219–23.
24 Cited in Paul Thomas Chamberlin, *The Global Offensive: The United States, the Palestine Liberation Organization, and the Making of the Post-Cold War Order* (Oxford: Oxford University Press, 2012), 112 and fn. 23, 285.
25 Ibid., 113 and fn. 27, 285. Quote as in the original.
26 Ibid., 113 and fn. 28, 286. Syntax corrected.
27 Saïd K. Aburish, *Arafat: From Defender to Dictator* (New York: Bloomsbury, 1998), 108.
28 *MER: 1969–1970*, 270.
29 See Andrew Gowers and Tony Walker, *Behind the Myth: Yasser Arafat and the Palestinian Revolution* (London: W. H. Allen, 1990), 83; Amnon Kapeliuk, *Yassir Arafat: Die Biographie* (Heidelberg: Palmyra, 2005), 125–6. For first-hand accounts of the meeting between Nasser and Arafat, see Mohamed Heikal, *The Road to Ramadan* (London: Collins, 1975), 96–7; Shafiq al-Hout, *My Life in the PLO: The Inside Story of the Palestinian Struggle* (London: Pluto Press, 2011), 84–5. Contemporary claims that Nasser had in fact given King Hussein a green light to crush the Palestinian movement in Jordan were apparently part of a Jordanian secret service disinformation campaign. See Abu Ijad, *Heimat oder Tod: Der Freiheitskampf der Palästinenser* (Düsseldorf: Econ Verlag, 1979), 118–20.
30 *Die Internationale Politik 1970*, supplementary vol. II, *Zeittafel/Register* (1971), Z 188.
31 Kapeliuk, *Arafat*, 126.
32 See J. P. Tripp (FCO Near Eastern Department) to Sir P. Adams, Hijacking, 15 September 1970, 5 pp., here 2, in: TNA, PREM 15/202. Although his accounts need to be taken with a liberal pinch of salt, see also Bassam Abu Sharif, *Arafat and the*

Dream of Palestine: An Insider's Account (New York: Palgrave Macmillan, 2009), 27: 'Contrary to the wishes of my colleagues, I decided to release all the women and children and anyone else who had nationalities and/or positions that would not have been of use to us in negotiating a prisoner exchange', in other words all hostages 'deemed liabilities to us'.

33 See Seymour H. Hersh, *The Price of Power: Kissinger in the Nixon White House* (New York: Summit Books, 1983), 235–6.
34 Henry Kissinger, *White House Years* (Boston: Little, Brown and Company, 1979), 601. Strictly speaking Israel had conceded to hijacking demands prior to this point. On 23 July 1968 the PFLP hijacked an El Al flight to Algiers, releasing the remaining twelve Israeli hostages on 31 August, with Israel in return freeing sixteen Arab prisoners on 3 September in what was described as a humanitarian gesture. On 29 August 1969 the PFLP successfully hijacked a TWA flight to Damascus, retaining two Israeli hostages who were held until 5 December and released in exchange for some seventy Arabs imprisoned in Israel.
35 For initial ICRC reluctance to become involved and the ambiguity of its mandate, see Raab, *Terror*, 44–5 and 50–1.
36 The British FCO speculated that the demands made on West Germany were a further makeshift element in the operation: no attempts had been made to hijack a Lufthansa flight, no mention of the Munich prisoners was made in the first PFLP conference announcing their demands, and the three prisoners belonged to a rival group, Issam Sartawi's short-lived AOLP. See Phillips/FCO, Dawson's Field Hijacking, 4.
37 Despite continuous exhortations by the ICRC, the PFLP failed to deliver a definitive list of the prisoners held in Israel it wanted released. This refusal to be pinned down was viewed by the FCO as a deliberate manoeuvre: 'The PFLP is not an organisation of the kind which would necessarily draw up an authoritative list of names and then stick to it in a negotiation if a better "target of opportunity" offered.' See J. P. Tripp (FCO Near Eastern Department) to Sir P. Adams, Hijacking, 15 September 1970, 3, in: TNA, PREM 15/202.
38 See also Timothy Naftali, *Blind Spot: A Secret History of American Counterterrorism* (New York: Basic Books, 2005), 42 and fn. 67, 342–3, stating that the White House was relieved that the hijackers made no demand for the release of Sirhan Bishara Sirhan, the Palestinian killer of Democratic senator and presidential candidate Robert Kennedy, as it allowed them the luxury, despite US hostages, of shifting the onus for a resolution onto Britain, Switzerland and West Germany. It was initially reported in the media that the PFLP's demands did include the release of Sirhan Sirhan. See WP, Women, Children Freed; Men Kept, *International Herald Tribune*, 8 September 1970, 1. On 8 September Sirhan Sirhan's mother, accompanied by his lawyers Luke McKissack and Mike McCowan, tried to board a TWA flight to Jordan, only for officials of the Immigration and Naturalization Service to cancel the lawyers' passports without explanation, reportedly acting on instructions from the State Department and thus blocking their journey. By this point the PFLP had denied that they were seeking Sirhan Sirhan's release. See Sirhan Lawyers Charge U.S. Thwarts Their Flight to Jordan, *The New York Times*, 9 September 1970, 16. For the PFLP's fascination with Sirhan Sirhan, not only for his action but also for the fact that he was, like many exponents in the PFLP (most prominently Habash and Haddad), a Christian, not a Muslim, and thus a cause célèbre with which to counter clichés about the Palestinian cause, see the idiosyncratic Walid Amin Ruwayha, *Terrorism and Hostage-Taking in the Middle East* (n.p., 1990), 311–17.

39 For the precise wording of the PLO Central Committee's decisions, issued on 11 September, see Telegram No. 520, Amman (Phillips) to FCO, 11 September 1970, in: TNA, FCO 14/779.
40 See Cooley, *Green March*, 112; Kamal Salibi, *The Modern History of Jordan* (London: I. B. Taurus, 1993), 236.
41 Kissinger, *White House Years*, 607. Kissinger's account also details ineffectual contingency planning by the Oval Office, the Cabinet Room and the WSAG to intervene directly in the hostage situation, including 'wild ideas' to use a nerve gas to immobilize the hijackers and hostages alike. This planning merged with the later concrete military mobilizations designed to intimidate the Soviet Union and its perceived proxies, Syria and Iraq, to stop them intervening in the crisis. See ibid., 602–7. Naftali, *Blind Spot*, 48, partly adopts Kissinger's interpretation but argues that the PLO's hostage release was undertaken to maintain a tactical leeway by trying to ward off the eventuality of a rumoured US or indeed Israeli armed intervention, which would have thwarted all hopes of potentially being able to topple King Hussein.
42 Abu Sharif and Mahnaimi, *Best of Enemies*, 87–8. In a subsequent recital of events Abu Sharif again mentioned the general nervousness about a military response, albeit by Israel, but stated that the blowing up of the planes had been undertaken in the belief that Jordanian forces might mount an attack on Dawson's Field. See Abu Sharif, *Arafat*, 28.
43 CIA Directorate of Intelligence, Intelligence Report, Fedayeen – 'Men of Sacrifice', December 1970, 46 pp., here 25, https://cryptome.org/cia-pulp/cia-esau-47.pdf (accessed 1 January 2020, henceforth CIA Intelligence Report, 'Fedayeen').
44 Telegram From the Department of State to Certain Diplomatic Posts, 13 September 1970, in: Linda W. Qaimmaqami and Adam M. Howard (eds.), *Foreign Relations of the United States, 1969–1976*, XXIV, *Middle East Region and Arabian Peninsula, 1969–1972; Jordan, September 1970* (Washington: U.S. Government Printing Office, 2008), Doc. 238, https://history.state.gov/historicaldocuments/frus1969-76v24/ch6 (henceforth *FRUS, 1969–1976*, XXIV).
45 *Schlussbericht*, appendix B-1, entry under 12 September 1970.
46 Ibid., appendix D-1, "Sitzung des Bundesrates von 13. September 1970 / 0115 Uhr." This view was not shared by the FCO: 'The hijackings have been planned by a small and determined group whose planning has been realistic even in the face of unforeseen setbacks, and whose control over its executives – presumably also a small band – has been admirable. There is no sign of dissension among the PFLP organisers themselves.' J. P. Tripp (FCO Near Eastern Department) to Sir P. Adams, Hijacking, 15 September 1970, 3, in: TNA, PREM 15/202.
47 See *MER: 1969–1970*, 250.
48 J. R. A. Bottomley to Gallagher (no departmental markings), 9 September 1970, in: TNA, FCO 14/778. See also the same information in Telegram No. 262, FCO (Douglas-Home) to Amman, 9 September 1970, ibid. Neither document expresses any incredulity about Hammarskjöld's claim or any suggestion that he was a fabulist.
49 The only element that can be added to this equation is the repeated suggestion throughout the 1970s that various airline companies (at the time national or quasi-national concerns) paid protection money to insure themselves against Palestinian hijackings. Here are two from numerous examples. In March 1974 the US Embassy in Beirut reported a 'local rumor' (which it itself was disinclined to believe) that the British Airways predecessors BOAC and BEA had been 'paying monthly protection

money' to the PFLP and that the PFLP's 'income' from the 'racket' had been halved when the two companies merged. Calls for the 'tribute' to be paid in full had been rebuffed, leading to the British Airways hijacking of 3 March 1974. See Electronic Telegram, US Embassy Beirut (Godley) to Secretary of State, 4 March 1974. More bizarrely, perhaps lost in translation, see, for instance, a third-hand and anonymous report to the West German Bundeskriminalamt (BKA, the Federal Criminal Police Office) in January 1976, stating that the Kuwaiti oil minister had related that during the OPEC attack in Vienna in December 1975 the peculiarly garrulous PFLP operative Ilich Ramírez Sànchez (aka Carlos, 'the Jackal') had claimed that West Germany paid the 'Baader-Meinhof successor organization' DM 2.5 million a year to abstain from attacks against Lufthansa and West German airports. See Electronic Telegram, US Mission Berlin (George) to Secretary of State, 23 January 1976. (For further claims of Lufthansa having paid financial indemnities see fn. 249 below.) This excludes the numerous publically recorded occasions when airlines, or for that matter governments, paid on-the-spot ransoms during hostage incidents.

50 Phillips/FCO, Dawson's Field Hijacking, 3. The months March to July 1970 indeed saw a 'lull' in airline hijackings, in fact an absence, although El Al and Pan Am offices were bombed on 24 April in Istanbul and Izmir in Turkey. The 21 February 1970 attacks are uniformly attributed to Ahmed Jibril's PFLP splinter group, the PFLP-GC (General Command). For new evidence on the 21 February 1970 attacks discovered by the author, see Marcel Gyr, Neue Hinweise im Fall 'Würenlingen', *Neue Zürcher Zeitung*, 15 September 2016, 17; Marcel Gyr, Terrorakt von 1970 wird überprüft, *Neue Zürcher Zeitung*, 5 July 2017, 13. Note that it has also been claimed that in March 1970 a Swissair representative approached François Genoud – a Swiss dyed-in-the-wool Nazi, banker to the Algerian National Liberation Front, an *éminence grise* in PFLP operations, later companion and mentor to terrorist Illich Ramírez Sànchez (aka Carlos), CIA subject of interest and chatting partner to the Swiss Bundespolizei (BUPO, the Swiss Federal Police) – to negotiate an end to the attacks against the airline. See Willi Winkler, *Der Schattenmann: Von Goebbles zu Carlos – Das mysteriöse Leben des François Genoud* (Berlin: Rowohlt, 2011), 186.

51 The seven fedayeen consisted of two PFLP members from an attack on an El Al flight on the tarmac at Athens Airport on 26 December 1968; two PSF members were involved in a hand grenade attack on an El Al office in Athens on 27 November 1969, in which one person had been killed and fifteen wounded; and three PFLP members were arrested at Athens Airport during an attempt to hijack a TWA flight on 21 December 1969.

52 A. M. Goodenough (British Embassy Athens) to A. E. Palmer (FCO Southern European Department), 18 August 1970, in: TNA, FCO 17/1011.

53 Stewart Steven, *The Spy-Masters of Israel* (New York: Macmillan Publishing Co., 1980), 245.

54 See, for instance, James A. Arey, *The Sky Pirates* (London: Ian Allen, 1973), 90–1; Mickolus, *Transnational Terrorism*, 195.

55 Albert G. Fischer, 'Die kriminelle Bedrohung der SWISSAIR von 1967 bis 1973', handwritten and typed manuscript, n.d. (mid-1970s), *c.* 300 pp., in private Fischer family possession, made available to Marcel Gyr 6 October 2017, who kindly extended extracts to author.

56 Ibid., 26–31. According to Fischer's account, Rochat confirmed that the 22 July hijacking had been a collaboration between the PSF and the PFLP, detailing that their original intention had been to fly the plane on to Switzerland to also force the release

of the Kloten Airport attackers. Rochat added that because of the criticisms of his role in Athens he would in future only act as a mediator at the express request of the Swiss Federal Council.

57 *Schlussbericht*, appendix B-1, entries under 13, 14 and 19 August.
58 Ibid., entry under 16 August.
59 Ibid., entry under 21 August 1970.
60 AP, 'Bonn agrees to release 3 Arabs seized in Munich' and UPI, Swiss Will Free 3 Arabs to Ransom 155 Victims, *International Herald Tribune*, 8 September 1970, 2.
61 Relations between Israel and the Red Cross reached a new nadir in May 1972 amidst accusations that the Israeli authorities had knowingly abused the ICRC's willingness to conduct negotiations, and eventually its vehicle livery too, to enable the storming of a Sabena aircraft commandeered to Lod airport by the BSO on 8–9 May.
62 Telegram No. 818, Tel Aviv (Barnes) to FCO, 11 September 1970, in: TNA, FCO 14/779.
63 Telegram from the Embassy in Switzerland to the Department of State, 11 September 1970. *FRUS, 1969–1976*, XXIV, Doc. 224.
64 Cited in Raab, *Terror*, 114.
65 "Israelis Round up 450 Arabs as Counter-hostages to PFLP," *International Herald Tribune*, 14 September 1970, 1–2. See also Abu Sharif and Mahnaimi, *Best of Enemies*, 87: 'We were sent a message to say that if we harmed any of our hostages, the Israelis would do the same to the people they were holding. It was exactly the kind of reaction we expected from them, and we ignored it.' On 22 September the PFLP, in a note to the ICRC, expressed its conviction that Israel had been 'incited' to its actions by the other four powers in Berne. See Walter Jost, *Rufzeichen Haifa: Tatsachenbericht einer Fedayin-Geisel* (Zurich: Schweizer Verlagshaus, 1972), 241–2, putting the number of people detained at 3,500 (perhaps a typographical slip).
66 Michael Bar-Zohar and Eitan Haber, *The Quest for the Red Prince* (London: Weidenfeld and Nicolson, 1983), 105.
67 Telegram No. 573, Amman (Phillips) to FCO, 15 September 1970, in: TNA, PREM 15/202. Although this version of Israel's notification was third-hand (coming from British activist Michael Adams, who had picked it up at the PFLP's headquarters from 'a friend' whose brother, Hatim Anabtawi of Nablus, was one of the coerced emissaries), Phillips was inclined to give credit to it.
68 The British, for instance, noted that despite West German blandishments, Wischnewski 'represented an important element of the Social Democratic Party' and had been accompanied to Amman by SPD general secretary Hans-Eberhard Dingels. See Emergency Unit (R. Hanbury-Tension) to Private Secretary, 14 September 1970, in: TNA, FCO 14/781. Suspicions about the true nature of Wischnewski's mission were also publicly reported. See, for instance, UPI, Wischnewski bei Ministerpräsident Rifai, *Neue Zürcher Zeitung*, 15 September 1970.
69 Raab, *Terror*, 98.
70 Elten, *Flugzeug entführt*, 50.
71 Hans-Jürgen Wischnewski, *Mit Leidenschaft und Augenmaß: Im Mogadischu und anderswo* (Munich: C. Bertelsmann, 1989), 127–33. The second meeting with Abu Maher apparently consisted of an offer of money to provide for the hostages, which was rejected. In his memoirs, the gist of Wischnewski's narrative would date his second meeting with Abu Maher to 12 September. While giving the same sequence, 'Die Grenate war ein Irrtum', *Der Spiegel*, 5 October 1970, 142, dates his meetings

with Abu Maher to 12 and 15 September, his meeting with Arafat having taken place on 14 September.
72 Telegram No. 165, FCO (Douglas-Home) to Berne, 13 September 1970, in: TNA, FCO 14/780.
73 Wischnewski, *Leidenschaft und Augenmaß*, 131. Wischnewski's contacts apparently ceased with the outbreak of fighting in Jordan when he became effectively trapped in the West German Embassy. The most bizarre aspect of his mission was that on leaving Jordan on 25 September he took what he described as two 'odd fellow countrymen' with him who had been handed over by the Jordanian army. Apparently unwittingly, Wischnewski thereby facilitated the exfiltration of the West German neo-Nazis Udo Albrecht and Willi Pohl who had joined the fedayeen. See Ibid., 135–6; Stefan Aust, *Mauss: Ein deutsche Agent* (Hamburg: Hoffmann und Campe, 1988), 271–3. Both men would go on to have colourful international terrorist careers in West Germany and with Palestinian groups through to the 1980s, as well as taking up extracurricular employment – Albrecht with the West German Bundesnachrichtendienst (BND, the Federal Intelligence Service) and the East German Ministerium für Staatssicherheit (MfS, Ministry for State Security), Pohl with the CIA.
74 Emergency Unit (R. Hanbury-Tension) to Private Secretary, 14 September 1970, in: TNA, FCO 14/781. The document outlines that a response was to be given to Bonn saying 'the activities of British journalists could be safely ignored'.
75 Cooley, *Green March*, 187.
76 Elten, *Flugzeug entführt*, 164–6. That Adams was acting as a conduit is also evident from the fact that early in the hijacking PFLP speaker Abu Sharif had given an authorized statement to him setting a new deadline for their demands to be met. See Telegram No. 484, Amman (Phillips) to FCO, 9 September 1970, in: TNA, FCO 14/778.
77 *Schlussbericht*, appendix B-1, entry under 25 September 1970, giving his name as 'von Krayen'.
78 An unpublished memoir by von Crayen, written in October 1986 and based on entries in a lost diary, describes the delegation as having arrived prior to the blowing up of the planes (i.e. on 12 September). He subsequently became trapped in his Amman hotel with the outbreak of fighting (i.e. on 17 September), recording that 'towards the close it was just myself and the Swiss Ambassador Dubois in Amman'. According to the recollections of von Crayen's daughter, Beatrix von Crayen, her father was absent in Jordan for a total of two to three weeks, and the dates of his time in Jordan are given elsewhere as 7 to 23 September. The memoir was generously made available to Marcel Gyr by Beatrix von Crayen in June 2017. Extracts and details were supplied to the author by Gyr in email correspondence, 28 June 2017. See also Marcel Gyr, Für die Swissair auf heikler Mission, *Neue Zürcher Zeitung*, 28 July 2017, 15.
79 'Protokoll der Vorsprache einer Swissair-Delegation bei den Herrn Bundesräten Graber und Bonvin am 25. September 1970 um 10.10 h', 25 September 1970, in: Schweizerisches Bundesarchiv (henceforth BAR), E2001#1980/83#231*. Courtesy of Marcel Gyr. References from the document are given in a truncated form in *Schlussbericht*, appendix B-1, entry under 25 September 1970.
80 Cited in Raab, *Terror*, 117. The *Schlussbericht*, appendix B-1, entries under 13 September 1970 records that the proposal had been given to Dubois via the ICRC's federation member the Red Crescent and otherwise contains no reference to any

direct contacts nor for that matter records any communications from Dubois to Berne surrounding von Crayen's mission whatsoever.
81 *Schlussbericht*, appendix B-1, entry under 14 September 1970.
82 'Protokoll der Vorsprache einer Swissair-Delegation bei den Herrn Bundesräten Graber und Bonvin am 25. September 1970 um 10.10 h', 25 September 1970, in: BAR E2001#1980/83#231*.
83 Ibid. It might be speculated that 'Bassam' was PFLP deputy speaker Bassam Abu Sharif, or perhaps also Leila Khaled's later husband Bassam Zayed. Abu Maher's name also appears as one of his interlocutors in Alexander von Crayen's unpublished memoir. The ellipses in the protocol of von Crayen's meeting with Councillor Graber on 25 September given in the *Schlussbericht* are such that the names Abu Maher and Bassam are omitted.
84 Ibid.
85 *Schlussbericht*, appendix B-1, entry under 25 September 1970.
86 Situation memo, n.a., 'The Hi-jacking Crisis', 18 September 1970, in: TNA, PREM 15/203.
87 'Report of a telephone conversation between Sir Dennis Greenhill, Dr. Henry Kissinger and Mr. Joe Sisco held on September 17, at approx. 1.00 p.m.', in: TNA, PREM 15/203. Also cited and discussed in Miriam Joyce, *Anglo-American Support for Jordan: The Career of King Hussein* (New York: Palgrave Macmillan, 2008), 55.
88 Situation memo, n.a., 'The Hi-jacking Crisis', 18 September 1970, in: TNA, PREM 15/203.
89 Joyce, *Anglo-American Support*, 55 and fn. 31, 169.
90 Telegram from the Department of State to Certain Diplomatic Posts, 13 September 1970, in: *FRUS, 1969–1976*, XXIV, Doc. 236.
91 That Israel's obstinacy against taking part in a 'global solution' to the hostage crisis was perhaps based on something more than simple political obtuseness was alluded to during a meeting of the Swiss Federal Council on 21 September where the head of the Eidgenössisches Politisches Departement (EPD, the Federal Political Department as the Swiss Foreign Ministry was called at the time) was cited as reporting that the Israeli ambassador Arieh Levavi had hitherto refused to make any sort of concessions 'based on the argument that he knew from a reliable source that there was no risk to the hostages'. See *Schlussbericht*, appendix D-1, 'Sitzung des Bundesrates vom 21. September 1970/9 Uhr', 1–2. That Israel had inside information might also be read into a telegram from the British Embassy in Tel Aviv: 'Israeli military intelligence have told us that they have information from a highly confidential source (presumably an agent with the PFLP) that Habbash has threatened to kill all the hostages unless the Jordan Army stops firing.' Telegram No. 861, Tel Aviv (Barnes) to FCO, 17 September 1970, in: TNA, FCO 14/782.
92 Telegram from the Department of State to Embassies in Jordan, Switzerland, the Federal Republic of Germany, the United Kingdom, and Israel, 19 September 1970, in: Susan K. Holly and William B. McAllister (eds.), *Foreign Relations of the United States, 1969–1976*, E-1, *Documents on Global Issues, 1969–1972* (Washington: US Government Printing Office, 2005), Doc. 73, https://history.state.gov/historica ldocuments/frus1969–76ve01/ch1sub3 (henceforth *FRUS 1969–1976*, E-1). On 16 September British officials reported that the PFLP had issued a demand for 'an official statement by the Israeli government agreeing in principle to free two Algerians arrested in Tel Aviv, one Swiss boy at Haifa, the ten Lebanese captured in exchange for Rosenwasser, in addition to an understanding to exchange commandos

against hostages'. See SITREP, 0800 16 September 1970, in: TNA, PREM 15/124. Rosenwasser refers to the Israeli watchman Schmuel Rosenwasser, seized by Fatah guerrillas in northern Israel on 1 January 1970, in response to which the Israeli Defense Forces had launched a raid into Lebanon the following day and seized ten Lebanese soldiers. Rosenwasser was finally released in February 1971 in exchange for Mahmoud Hijazi, who on 1 January 1965 had been the first Fatah infiltrator to be caught in Israel, later sentenced to thirty years' imprisonment. See Zeev Schiff and Raphael Rothstein, *Fedayeen: The Story of the Palestinian Guerrillas* (London: Vallentine, Mitchell, 1972), 90 and 185. For the obscure case of the detention of the two Algerian intelligence officers, see Yaacov Caroz, *The Arab Secret Services* (London: Corgi Books, 1978), 408–9.
93 SITREP, 0700 20 September 1970, in: TNA, PREM 15/124.
94 Telegram from the Department of State to the Embassy in Switzerland, 19 September 1970, in: *FRUS, 1969–1976*, XXIV, Doc. 268.
95 Joyce, *Anglo-American Support*, 55 and fn. 32, 169.
96 *Schlussbericht*, appendix D-1, "Sitzung des Bundesrates vom 13. September 1970/0115 Uhr," 2. The other floated candidate was India.
97 *MER: 1969–1970*, 272, citing a report from the Lebanese PFLP organ *Al-Hadaf*, and also citing a Radio Pyongyang broadcast of 20 September stating that the PFLP delegation that had arrived in North Korea was still in the country 'studying the revolutionary strategy of PM Kim Il-sung', and adding (as given in *An-Nahar* on 21 September) that the date of Habash's departure 'had not yet been decided'.
98 Telegram No. 591, Peking (Denson) to FCO, 17 September 1970, in: TNA, FCO 14/782. The message cites information imparted to the British head of chancery by the Swiss chargé d'affaires 'in confidence' a day earlier and likewise places Habash in Peking at the time. See also SITREP, 0700 18 September 1970, in: TNA, PREM 15/124, stating that the Swiss had asked the Chinese to mediate on their behalf with Habash.
99 Telegram No. 324, Berne (Midgley) to FCO, 25 September 1970, in: TNA, FCO 14/785.
100 Telegram No. 659, Peking (Denson) to FCO, 12 October 1970, in: TNA, FCO 14/786. See also the statement by Pierre Micheli, the general secretary of the EPD: 'They [the Chinese government] have informed Habash of our wishes and additionally told him that they condemn plane hijackings.' (*Schlussbericht*, appendix D-2, '21. Sitzung des Koordinationsauschusses von Donnerstag, den 24. September 1970, 21.00 – 01.00 Uhr', 4).
101 *MER: 1969–1970*, 272. See also Luftpiraten: Anschlag auf den Frieden, *Der Spiegel*, 24 December 1973, 56–8, here 57, stating that the September hijackings marked the "official end" of PFLP air piracy, per se: 'The Soviets and the Chinese, the principal financiers of the Marxist doctor, threatened him with an ultimatum that they would discontinue their financial and armed assistance if Habash did not immediately cease endangering international air traffic.'
102 Cooley, *Green March*, 143.
103 Raab, *Terror*, 134.
104 Ibid., 169–70 and 172.
105 Cited in ibid., 178. See also *Schlussbericht*, appendix D-1, 'Sitzung des Bundesrates vom 21. September 1970 / 9 Uhr', 1: 'Herr Boissier considers his dialogue partners in Beirut to be very important people, although there are at least grounds to be doubtful about their influence in Amman.'

106 Phillips/FCO, Dawson's Field Hijacking, 7.
107 Draft letter to Boissier as given in *Schlussbericht*, appendix D-2, '21. Sitzung des Koordinationsauschusses von Donnerstag, den 24. September 1970, 21.00 – 01.00 Uhr', 2.
108 Raab, *Terror*, 189; *Schlussbericht*, appendix D-2, '19. Sitzung des Koordinationsauschusses von Dienestag, den 22. September 1970, 16.15 – 17.15 Uhr und von 20.00 – 21.15 Uhr'.
109 *Schlussbericht*, appendix D-2, '20. Sitzung des Koordinationsauschusses von Mittwoch, den 22. September 1970, 20.00 – 22.05 Uhr', 3. Raab, *Terror*, 205, states that the Israeli U-turn came after pressure from US secretary of state Rogers.
110 In fact the Berne Group had already agreed on 17 September to issue Boissier with a statement in the name of the governments of West Germany, the United States, Britain and Switzerland that read: 'Mr. Boissier could point out to PFLP that previously Israel has in effect already agreed to "principle" of such exchange of prisoners for Israelis held by Syria in connection with previous TWA hijacking and by its evident willingness (as indicated privately to ICRC) to release two Algerians as part of agreement in present case.' See *Schlussbericht*, appendix D-2, '15. Sitzung des Krisenstabes von Donnerstag, den 17. September 1970, 16.25 Uhr', 6. For some unexplained reason the ICRC had failed to pass this communication on to Boissier, and more inexplicably this blunder was apparently not noticed in Berne until 24 September. US deputy chief of mission Richard David Vine stated that 'if this is were to be the case it would be a very grievous situation'. See ibid., '21. Sitzung des Koordinationsauschusses von Donnerstag, den 24. September 1970, 21.00 – 01.00 Uhr', 2. See also Raab, *Terror*, 205, who details that the mislaid 17 September communication had stated that Zayn could be informed more starkly that Israel 'obviously' accepted the principle of an exchange.
111 *Schlussbericht*, appendix D-2, '21. Sitzung des Koordinationsauschusses von Donnerstag, den 24. September 1970, 21.00 – 01.00 Uhr', 4–5. The TWA hijacking by the PFLP referred to was that of 29 August 1969 when all of the hostages were released save for two Israeli men, ultimately exchanged in December the same year, not for fedayeen but Syrian and Egyptian prisoners (usually numbered, respectively, at 13 and 58).
112 Raab, *Terror*, 209. Although the majority of the protocols of the Berne Group's meetings are reproduced in facsimile in appendix D-2 of the *Schlussbericht*, some are not, including the sittings numbered 22, 23 and 24. Sitting 21 was on 24 September and sitting 25 took place on 1 October 1970. This leaves a critical lacuna in the published record.
113 For Zein's biography, see Kai Bird, *The Good Spy: The Life and Death of Robert Ames* (New York: Crown Publishers, 2014), 75–82. That Zein and 'Zayn' are one and the same person has been confirmed in detail in correspondence between the author and Mustafa M. Zein, generously mediated by Kai Bird on 2 July 2017.
114 Mustafa M. Zein, email to Kai Bird, 2 July 2017, forwarded to the author; Mustafa M. Zein, email to the author, 17 July 2017.
115 Mustafa M. Zein, email to the author, 17 July 2017. See also Bird, *Good Spy*, 77–9.
116 For the history of the ANM, see Walid Kazziha, *Revolutionary Transformation in the Arab World: Habash and His Comrades from Nationalism to Marxism* (London: Charles Knight & Company, 1975); Helga Baumgarten, *Palästina: Befreiung in den Staat – Die palästinensische Nationalbewegung seit 1948* (Frankfurt am Main: Suhrkamp, 1992).

117 Mustafa M. Zein, email to Kai Bird, 2 July 2017.
118 Mustafa M. Zein, email to the author, 17 July 2017.
119 Ibid.
120 Telegram from the Department of State to the Embassy in Lebanon, 20 September 1970, in: *FRUS, 1969–1976*, XXIV, Doc. 277.
121 Telegram from the Department of State to certain diplomatic posts, 24 September 1970, ibid., Doc. 324. The cable states that the same doubts were shared by Boissier, adding that Boissier's strategy was to 'smoke out [a] valid negotiator on PFLP side'. See also ibid, fn. 2, outlining the embassy's response a day later, reporting that it was no longer acting as a conduit and stating that Zein had been informed that the US government would not accept the submission of any more PFLP proposals, which should instead be handed to the ICRC. Significantly or not, at roughly the same juncture, the Swiss Federal Political Department (EPD) issued instructions to its embassies in Beirut on 22 September and in Bagdad on 24 September telling them to abstain from any face-to-face initiatives with the PFLP to avoid the danger of 'duplications' of the ongoing ICRC discussions and 'that might be exploited by the PFLP to our disadvantage'. See *Schlussbericht*, appendix B-1, entries under 22 and 24 September 1970, here the message to Beirut. The cable to Bagdad uses an almost identical wording, but refers to 'the opposite party', the message having been prompted by the Bagdad Embassy's own suggestion that it try and contact the PFLP.
122 According to Zein, Egypt 'took over the negotiations from me'. (Mustafa M. Zein, email to Kai Bird, 2 July 2017).
123 Phillips/FCO, Dawson's Field Hijacking, 7. Heath, *My Life*, 323, dates the germination of the idea to 25 September.
124 Raab, *Terror*, 195. The avenue had not only occurred to the British. As coincidence would have it, a day later, on 24 September, the Israeli ambassador Arie Levavi proposed to the Berne Group that Sudanese president Jaffar Nimeiry be approached in an attempt to have the hostages released in an appeal to 'the Arab sense of honor', with a similar overture to be addressed to Cairo. EPD general secretary Micheli declined to act with the explanation that Swiss–Sudanese relations were tense, instead deferring to the British, but saying that Switzerland was nevertheless willing to extend the necessary feelers to Egypt and the Arab League. See *Schlussbericht*, appendix D-2, '21. Sitzung des Koordinationsauschusses von Donnerstag, den 24. September 1970, 21.00 – 01.00 Uhr', 3–4.
125 Cited in Raab, *Terror*, 195.
126 Heath, *My Life*, 323, adding 'I should have been delighted to fulfil my side of the bargain and invite Nasser to Britain, but on 28 September, two days after I received his message, he died'.
127 Cited in Raab, *Terror*, 195.
128 Teleprinter conference with Amman, 1600 25 September 1970, in: TNA, PREM 15/125. See also Michel Garin, Rescued Praise Their Captors, *The Times*, 26 September 1970, 1; Raab, *Terror*, 207–8.
129 See Arthur Reed, Renewed threat to British airlines feared, *The Times*, 26 September 1970, 1; 'Swiss troops to reinforce airport guards', ibid., 4.
130 Raab, *Terror*, 210.
131 Ibid., 213–14.
132 Ibid., 214–17. See also Jost, *Rufzeichen: Haifa*, 303, describing the diplomat as walking using a crutch, his name unknown.
133 Cited in Raab, *Terror*, 215–16.

134 Ibid., 215–16 and 221. On 28 September Swiss Federal Councillor Graber released a press communiqué stating: 'The Federal Council has determined that – even although the planes were destroyed – the conditions set for the release of the perpetrators of the Kloten attack will be considered as having been met as soon as the last group of remaining hostages in Jordan has been evacuated.' See *Schlussbericht*, appendix D-2, 'Sitzung des Bundesrates vom 28. September 1970 / 0830 Uhr', 4.

135 SITREP, 0700 28 September 1970, in: TNA, PREM 15/125. In response to Bonn, the British obtained a confirmation from the Americans. Were West Germany to require greater reassurances, they were notified they should obtain them themselves, with the British government internally deciding that it would, if need be, proceed without West German participation. In response to Berne, the British assured Switzerland that Egypt had acted as the main mediator in resolving the crisis.

136 Raab, *Terror*, 214.

137 Abu Sharif, *Arafat*, 28, states that King Hussein and President Nasser had earlier discussed the potential ramifications of the hostage crisis, most importantly the worry that it might trigger an Israeli intervention. From the structure of his account, these discussions took place around 11–12 September, resulting in Nasser's agreement that Jordan undertake a limited military operation, flanked by 'Egyptian political efforts to negotiate with the PFLP'. This might suggest a previously established channel between Egypt and the PFLP. General Sadiq had already arrived in Amman on 17 or 18 September in an attempt to broker an immediate end to the Jordanian-Palestinian fighting as soon as it had broken out. See Cooley, *Green March*, 117; Edgar O'Ballance, *Arab Guerilla Power: 1967–1972* (London: Faber and Faber, 1974), 147; Heikal, *Road to Ramadan*, 98.

138 Abu Ijad, *Heimat oder Tod*, 129–31; Bird, *Good Spy*, 101.

139 Abu Sharif, *Arafat*, 31–3.

140 Cited in Raab, *Terror*, 216.

141 Ibid., 224.

142 Phillips/FCO, Dawson's Field Hijacking, 2 and 8.

143 Swiss EPD general secretary Micheli, *Schlussbericht*, appendix D-2, '25. Sitzung des Koordinationsauschusses von Donnerstag, den 1. Oktober 1970, 16.00 – 16.45 Uhr', 2.

144 Telegram 5465 from the Embassy in Jordan to the Department of State, 30 September 1970, in: *FRUS 1969–1976*, E-1, Doc. 77.

145 Heath, *My Life*, 323.

146 Raab, *Terror*, 216.

147 Foreign and Commonwealth Office, 'Defensive Speaking Note', 2 November 1970, in: TNA, PREM 15/105. Emphasis added. This interpretation is also underlined by the later Prime Minister Margaret Thatcher, who wrote in her memoirs 'Ted … was certain that we were right to negotiate with the PFLP'. Cited in Joyce, *Anglo-American Support*, 57.

148 Telegram [No. missed in author's transcription], Cairo (Beaumont) to FCO, 26 September 1970, in: TNA, PREM 15/125. Also cited in Raab, *Terror*, 213. This matches FCO instructions the same day that 'further consultation with [Israel] is unnecessary' due to the fact that no new demands were being made on them and that Israel's hostages 'have always been treated primarily as a U.S. concern'. Cited in ibid., 215.

149 Telegram [No. missed in author's transcription], Amman (Phillips) to FCO, 28 September 1970, in: TNA, PREM 15/125. Also cited in Raab, *Terror*, 224.

150 AP, Israelische Bereitschaft zu Gefangenfreilassung, *Neue Zürcher Zeitung*, 28 September 1970. The two Algerians were subsequently released on 14 October. See Cooley, *Green March*, 156, fn. 8.
151 Teresa Fava Thomas, *American Arabists in the Cold War, 1946-75: From Orientalism to Professionalism* (London: Anthem Press, 2016), 153.
152 Telegram No. 723, Amman (Phillips) to FCO, 30 September 1970, in: TNA, FCO 14/786.
153 Telegram 5465 from the Embassy in Jordan to the Department of State, 30 September 1970, in: *FRUS 1969-1976*, E-1, Doc. 77. See also Raab, *Terror*, 231, stating that it was the PLO who gave its 'word of honour' that in return hijackings would cease, adding that Israeli intelligence described the people whose release was wanted as 'star performers'.
154 Raab, *Terror*, 231.
155 Telegram No. 723, Amman (Phillips) to FCO, 30 September 1970, in: TNA, FCO 14/786. For the offered quid pro quo see also SITREP, 0700 1 October 1970, in: TNA, PREM 15/125.
156 Raab, *Terror*, 231.
157 O'Ballance, *Arab Guerilla Power*, 159.
158 See the EPD message to the Swiss ambassador in Tel Aviv of 30 September 1970: 'Even when it has not yet been entirely established by whom and based on which intercession and commitments hostages were released, Federal Council will not retrospectively revoke its given pledge.' *Schlussbericht*, appendix B-1, entry under 30 September 1970.
159 Telegram No. 364, Berne (Midgley) to FCO, 6 October 1970, in: TNA, FCO 14/786. According to Raab, *Terror*, 221, the last meeting of the Berne Group had taken place on 27 September. Israel, surprisingly, had for the first time requested that a further session be held on 28 September to review events and float ideas for the future but had then cancelled the meeting without explanation. The *Schlussbericht*, on the other hand, contains the record of a final sitting of all the members of the Berne Group from 1 October. See *Schlussbericht*, appendix D-2, '25. Sitzung des Koordinationsauschusses von Donnerstag, den 1. Oktober 1970, 16.00 – 16.45 Uhr'.
160 Telegram No. 364, Berne (Midgley) to FCO, 6 October 1970, in: TNA, FCO 14/786.
161 *Schlussbericht*, appendix B-1, entry under 14 October 1970.
162 PFLP communiqué, issued on 5 December, as reported by the SDA and the AFP, in ibid., 21. The number of Lebanese soldiers was put at eleven, not ten: this matches variations in other sources, which range between ten and twelve.
163 *Schlussbericht*, appendix B-1, entry under 8 December 1970.
164 P. M. Forster (Tel Aviv) to M. E. Pike (FCO Near Eastern Department), 16 December 1970, in: TNA, FCO 17/1289.
165 Phillips/FCO, Dawson's Field Hijacking, 8.
166 Although the original British National Archive files on the Palestinian guerrilla movement once contained documents from MI6 and its domestic counterpart MI5 (referred to euphemistically as 'the Box'), as well as from the Cabinet Office's Joint Intelligence Committee (JIC), almost without exception these are no longer in the archived files.
167 C. D. Lush (British Embassy Amman) to R. E. Evans (FCO Near Eastern Department), 'Embassy contacts with Al-Fatah', 3 October 1969, in: TNA, FCO 17/691. In response to questions on Fatah's position on contacts to foreign governments, the source had said, inter alia, that 'it might be worth contacting the

West Germans and talking to them', but on no account would he communicate with the United States. The embassy for its part informed the contact that they recognized that 'recent outrages' had been the work of the PFLP and not Fatah.
168 J. A. Shepherd (British Embassy Amman) to L. V. Appleyard (FCO Near Eastern Department), 'Conversation with 'Ahmad' of Al Fatah', 10 October 1969, in: TNA, FCO 17/691. Kamal Adwan's name is spelt 'Adwani' in the document. For a report on a further meeting with Azhari on the situation in Lebanon, see also J. A. Shepherd (British Embassy Amman) to C. W. Long (FCO Near Eastern Department), 'A Fatah view on the Lebanon crisis', 28 November 1969, in: TNA, FCO 17/683. The British contacts to Azhari are also referred to in Barry Rubin and Judith Colp Rubin, *Yasir Arafat: A Political Biography* (London: Continuum, 2003), 44–5.
169 John W. Amos II, *Palestinian Resistance: Organization of a Nationalist Movement* (New York: Pergamon Press, 1980), 61.
170 J. A. Shepherd (British Embassy Amman) to C. W. Long (FCO Near Eastern Department), 16 December 1969, in: TNA, FCO 17/980.
171 Joyce, *Anglo-American Support*, 68.
172 Kanafani had originally joined the ANM in 1954, and along with Habash and Haddad had founded the PFLP in 1967. Following the 1969 departure of Nayef Hawatmeh and the formation of the breakaway DFLP, he had remained the PFLP's most articulate and intellectual spokesman, also acting as the contact point to a wide range of international groups from South America, Western Europe, the Arabian Peninsula and the Gulf. See Amos, *Palestinian Resistance*, 238.
173 Cited in Sarah Irving, *Leila Khaled: Icon of Palestinian Liberation* (London: Pluto Press, 2012), 59.
174 D. A. Gore-Booth (FCO Near Eastern Department) to C. P. Carter (British Embassy Amman), 2 September 1971, in: TNA, FCO 17/1374. Following his retirement, Allen became the director of the Middle East Association business group, and his contact with Kanafani roughly coincides with a visit to Beirut by the Ariel-sponsored Conservative Group in early September 1971, during which meetings were held with Kanafani and the PLO's Lebanon representative Shafiq al-Hout. See Peter Joy, 'The Palestinians & the Jedda Conference' (handwritten report), 9 September 1971, in: TNA, FCO 17/1375.
175 I. R. Callan (British Embassy Beirut) to E. V. Beckett (FCO Near East and North Africa Department), 1 July 1972, in: TNA, FCO 17/1708.
176 The attack is interpreted as retaliation for Kanafani's public justification of the notorious massacre of twenty-six people and wounding of over eighty others at Lod Airport on 30 May 1972, perpetrated by recruits to the PFLP from the Rengo Sekigun, the Japanese Red Army, and claimed in the name of a "Commando Patrick Arguello."
177 I. R. Callan (British Embassy Beirut) to E. V. Beckett (FCO Near East and North Africa Department), 10 July 1972, in: TNA, FCO 17/1708.
178 Palestinian economist Dr Fadle Naqib, for instance, conjectured that 'Mossad was not after the muscle of the Palestinian revolution, but its soul'. Cited in Bird, *Good Spy*, 144.
179 For the recruitment of Pohl, aka Willi Voss, to spy for the CIA within the PLO, see Duan R. Clarridge and Digby Diehl, *A Spy for All Seasons: My Life in the CIA* (New York: Scribner, 1997), 157–8, where Pohl was as yet unnamed. For fuller details, see Karin Assmann et al., Ein Mann, drei Leben, *Der Spiegel*, 31 December 2013, 34–6.

180 E. W. Pless (pseud.), *Geblendet: Aus den authentischen Papieren eines Terroristen* (Zurich: Schweizer Verlagshaus, 1979), 149. See also Ami Pedahzur, *The Israeli Secret Services and the Struggle Against Terrorism*, paperback ed. (New York: Columbia University Press, 2010), 45, who surmises that Nasser 'was not even directly involved in terrorist activities against Israel'; that despite being the number two in Fatah's hierarchy, al-Najjar had been 'primarily a political figure whose involvement in the direct planning of attacks against Israel was minor'; and that although Adwan had indeed been in charge of Fatah's West Bank structures that had also launched terrorist attacks, such attacks from the West Bank had declined at the time.

181 Peter Taylor, *States of Terror: Democracy and Political Violence* (London: BBC Books, 1993), 14–20, here 20.

182 Ronen Bergman, *Rise and Kill First: The Secret History of Israel's Targeted Assassinations* (Random House: New York, 2018), 161. Emphasis in the original.

183 Bird, *Good Spy*, 142–3. Al-Kubasi was in Paris at the behest of the PFLP, apparently charged with forging contacts with European Leftists, although a Palestinian news agency claimed that he had been 'on a mission' to meet with a French government official.

184 Ibid., 67–8 and 140–5. Bird also cites Duane R. Clarridge (the CIA's chief of operations for the Near East Division, 1973–1975, and deputy chief of the Near East Division for Arab Operations, 1975–1978) as saying 'Mr. K was a chattering contact not a spy'. Bird's own assessment is that 'Mossad was probably unaware that they'd assassinated someone who might have still been an active source'. Ibid., 143 and 144.

185 Ibid., 145. This has also been claimed to have been part of the criteria of the 1979 killing of Ali Hassan Salameh, an unnamed senior Mossad officer who was involved in the operation, for instance, informing Bergman that 'cutting this channel [between the CIA and the PLO] was very important, to show that no one was immune – and also to give the Americans a hint that this was no way to behave toward friends'. See Bergman, *Rise and Kill First*, 219.

186 Peter T. Hayman (FCO Near Eastern Department) to Philip Adams (British Embassy Amman), 3 June 1970, in: TNA, FCO 17/1059. The words 'mostly CIA' have been diligently redacted from the typed copy of the letter, but the censor overlooked them in the accompanying handwritten draft. Hayman may well have been even better informed than his formal position suggests. During revelations in 2014 and 2015 concerning a government cover-up of Hayman's paedophile tendencies it was widely claimed – but remains unproven – that at some point in his career he had served as the deputy chief of MI6.

187 Telegram from the Department of State to the Embassy in Jordan, 20 November 1970, in: *FRUS 1969–1976*, XXIII, Doc. 185, including fn. 6. Emphasis added.

188 For Symmes's own account on the events behind his dismissal, see Association for Diplomatic Studies and Training, Moments in U.S. Diplomatic History, 'Jordan, 1970 – An Attack on the Embassy and a Dispute with the King', http://adst.org/2015/03/jordan-1970-an-attack-on-the-embassy-and-a-dispute-with-the-king (accessed 1 January 2020).

189 Avi Shlaim, *Lion of Jordan: The Life of King Hussein in War and Peace* (New York: Alfred A. Knopf, 2008), 326–7. The same explanation for Symmes's dismissal is given in Kai Bird, *Crossing Mandelbaum Gate: Coming of Age between the Arab and Israelis, 1956–1978* (New York: Scribner, 2010), 271. Ambassador Symmes had at some point authored a State Department paper with the title 'Some Unthinkable Thoughts: A Jordan Without Hussein', arguing that the United States should, in his words, 'cut its

losses' and that assistance to King Hussein was 'obstructing a possible solution to the problem of Palestine'. See Thomas, *American Arabists*, 151. This aspect of Western diplomatic thinking falls outside the purview of this article, but the possibility of potentially abandoning the Hashemite Monarchy in Jordan to the Palestinians was a contingency widely discussed in the FCO and State Department documents throughout the second half of 1970, the British being more amenable to the idea than the Americans.

190 Stocker, Diplomacy as Counter-Revolution? 418. Sisco's reflections were passed all the way up the administrative hierarchy to President Nixon and resulted in the first steps towards a review of US attitudes on the possibility of a 'Palestine Option'. See Simen Zernichow and Hilde Henriksen Waage, The Palestine Option: Nixon, the National Security Council, and the Search for a New Policy, 1970, *Diplomatic History* 38/1 (2014), 182–209, here 190–1.

191 Zernichow and Waage, Palestine Option, 189. This stricture was based on instructions issued by Rogers's predecessor Dean Rusk in March 1965, determining that the US government considered that the PLO had 'no official status whatsoever'. Rogers attached Rusk's statement to his query, undated by the authors, and repeated his non-recognition warning again on 9 April and 18 July 1970. See Ibid., 186, 189 and 191.

192 Stocker, Diplomacy as Counter-Revolution? 418.

193 Electronic Telegram, US Embassy Beirut (Godley) to US Consul Jerusalem for Secretary of State, 17 May 1974. Supporting evidence is also given in Rubin and Rubin, *Arafat*, fn. 49, 281, citing a telegram from the American Embassy to the State Department of 11 April 1969 recounting information from Shafiq al-Hout under the heading 'PLO view of Hussein's visit to US'. Hout leaves these contacts unmentioned in his autobiography, but twice escaped being killed in this period, the first incident involving a rocket attack on the PLO office in Beirut on 15 October 1969 and the second a letter bomb in late July 1972. See Al-Hout, *My Life*, 75–6 and 107.

194 Cited in Lutz Maeke, *DDR und PLO: Die Palästinapolitik des SED-Staates* (Berlin: De Gruyter, 2017), 87.

195 Ibid., 90–1.

196 Embassy Amman to Auswärtiges Amt (AA), 'Palästinensiche Widerstandsorganisationen', 21 May 1970, in: Politisches Archiv des Auswärtigen Amts (PA-AA), record group B 36 ('Bundesrepublik Deutschland, Zentrale, Länderreferate Naher und Mittlerer Osten'), file 402, sheets 311–45, here 318. Also partly cited in Maeke, *DDR und PLO*, 90. Interestingly, the report also records under 'Financing' that 'the donors [to the PLO] include large West European corporations; donations already offered by U.S. big businesses have seemingly been rejected'. See Ibid., sheet 316. Copies of this and other PA-AA documents, including those cited below, were generously provided to the author by Lutz Maeke.

197 Representation Cairo to AA, 'Palästinensiche Widerstandsorganisationen', 22 May 1970, in: PA-AA, record group B 36, file 402, sheets 354–65, here 364. The report also expressed satisfaction that Abu Issa, the deputy head of the PLO's radio department, had indicated an interest in West Germany's denials concerning weapons deliveries to Israel and claims that West Germany was training Israeli pilots.

198 Telegram No. 775, Representation Cairo, '[P]alaestina-[B]efreiungsorganisation', 11 November 1970, in: PA-AA, record group B 36, file 402, sheets 451–3, here 451.

199 See Maeke, *DDR und PLO*, 148, fn. 144.

200 The links between Salameh and the CIA were first sensationally revealed by the journalist David Ignatius in an article in the *Wall Street Journal* in February 1983, later fleshed out in his 1987 *Agents of Innocence*, a *roman à clef*. The records on Salameh's relationship with the CIA are said to fill a total of fifteen volumes. See Bird, *Good Spy*, 103.
201 For Salameh's general biography, see Bar-Zohar and Haber, *Red Prince*; Bird, *Good Spy*.
202 See Stefan Aust, *Der Baader Meinhof Komplex* (Hamburg: Hoffmann und Campe, 1986), 109-10.
203 An independent confirmation of sorts of Salameh's role in Western Europe is contained in the autobiography of the Red Army Faction (RAF) member Margrit Schiller. According to Schiller, in summer 1973 part of the RAF group she joined (commonly referred to as the 'Gruppe 4.2', after the date of their subsequent collective arrests on 4 February 1974) was active in the Netherlands helping to prepare a hijacking of an El Al flight. The attack had been planned by 'the Al-Fatah headquarters in Lebanon' and was to have been carried out by a joint Palestinian-West German commando, the Palestinian contingent having already arrived in the Netherlands. After weeks of delay, a message was received from 'Abu Hassan', i.e. Salameh, that the attack had been postponed. Schiller further describes Salameh as the RAF group's 'crucial Palestinian friend': 'Abu Hassan […] represented the radical faction within Al Fatah that promoted a cooperation with the RAF. Arafat himself was always opposed to it.' Margrit Schiller, '*Es war ein harter Kampf um meine Erinnerung*': *Ein Lebensbericht aus der RAF* (Hamburg: Konkret Literatur Verlag, 1999), 121-3.
204 Based on Bird, *Good Spy*, the stations of Ames's career are as follows. Ames joined the CIA in 1960, serving as a Directorate of Operations case officer in Saudi Arabia (1962-1966), South Yemen (1967-1969) and Lebanon (1970-1971). In 1972 he temporarily served as a replacement chief of station in North Yemen. After serving in Tehran in 1973, Ames was promoted to chief of station in Kuwait, a post he held until 1975 when he became chief of the Near East/Arabian Peninsula Branch at the Directorate of Operations, serving stints in Beirut in 1977 and 1978, the year he became a national intelligence officer in the Near East and South Asia (NESA) Division of the National Intelligence Council. His position at the time of his death was the NESA director in the Directorate of Intelligence, a post he received in 1981.
205 Ibid., 83-5, 91-5 and 103.
206 Ibid., 105.
207 Ibid.
208 Ibid., 95 and 98.
209 Jack O'Connell and Vernon Loeb, *King's Council: A Memoir of War, Espionage, and Diplomacy in the Middle East* (New York: W. W. Norton & Company, 2011), 99-100. Also cited and discussed in Bird, *Good Spy*, 95-7.
210 Salameh was reportedly crudely offered a monthly retainer of $300,000 to coordinate activities between the PLO and the CIA. Cassin subsequently claimed that Salameh had angrily refused to cooperate with the CIA in combating terrorism. However, according to Zein it had been Cassin who had abandoned the pitch after being informed by him, Zein, that Salameh had told him that Cassin was offering that the CIA fund the PLO to the tune of $35 million a year as well as extending official recognition. Zein also claims to have mischievously informed Cassin that a pleased Arafat had been duly informed. See Bird, *Good Spy*, 104-8.

211 Wilhelm Dietl, *Die Agenten des Mossad: Operation Roter Prinz* (Düsseldorf: ECON Verlag, 1992), 215–16; Simon Reeve, *One Day in September: The Story of the Munich Olympics Massacre* (London: Faber and Faber, 2000), 156. Journalist Peter Taylor was given similar details of the Rome meeting by one of Salameh's later CIA case officers. According to this version of events, the mishap was smoothed over the very next day, accompanied, in Taylor's words, by 'talk of dialogue between the US Administration and Chairman Arafat's office'. See Taylor, *States of Terror*, 43. A further – likewise angrily rebuffed – attempt to recruit Salameh as an agent was apparently made following the Munich Olympics massacre of September 1972. See ibid., 43–4; Bird, *Good Spy*, 135–6.
212 Bird, *Good Spy*, 108 and 138.
213 Chamberlin, *Global Offensive*, 125 and 127. Chamberlain also claims that following the September crisis France was not only one of the first Western countries to express support for a Palestinian state but also 'to open contacts with the fedayeen'.
214 Cited in Quandt, *Peace Process*, fn. 87, 419.
215 Alec Douglas-Home, *The Way the Wind Blows: An Autobiography by Lord Home* (London: Collins, 1976), 259–60 and 300–1.
216 The review was passed over in silence in Kissinger's memoirs and long went unregistered by historians. See, for instance, Quandt, *Peace Process*, who despite being a high-level State Department insider not only leaves it unmentioned but identifies a major pro-Israeli tilt in US foreign policy in the months following September 1970. The substance of the review was first outlined in 2004 in Derick L. Hulme, Jr., *Palestinian Terrorism and U.S. Foreign Policy, 1969–1977: Dynamics of Response* (Lewiston: The Edwin Mellen Press, 2004), 54–6. It was treated in some detail in 2012 in Chamberlin, *Global Offensive*, 128–9 and 131–6, and was discussed in full in 2014 in Zernichow and Waage, Palestine Option.
217 Minutes of a Combined Senior Review Group and Washington Special Actions Group Meeting, 15 October 1970, in: *FRUS 1969–1976*, XXIII, Doc. 172. The State Department's Office of the Historian was unable to locate either of the intelligence reports referred to, but see reference to the detail of it, including the proposed boundaries of this prospective state, in Memorandum from the Director of Central Intelligence Helms to the President's Assistant for National Security Affairs Kissinger, 24 November 1970, in: Ibid., Doc. 186. The minutes of the meeting are also cited in Zernichow and Waage, Palestine Option, 196–7.
218 Memorandum from the Director of Central Intelligence Helms to the President's Assistant for National Security Affairs Kissinger, 23 October 1970, in: *FRUS 1969–1976*, XXIII, Doc. 174. The apparatus to the document cites a CIA Intelligence Information Report of 20 October 1970, likewise reporting on a meeting of 19 October with a Palestinian source with access to senior Fatah officials. The CIA were informed that a State Department announcement on the possible creation of a Palestinian state as part of a wider Middle East settlement, given on 15 October and reported on the title page of *The New York Times* a day later, had been 'well received' by Fatah leaders, including Arafat. These officials, according to the source, had 'noted that the Soviet Union has never mentioned the possibility of creating a Palestinian state, and, in fact, has been against the establishment of such a state'. See Ibid., fn. 2.
219 Zernichow and Waage, Palestine Option, 197–8.
220 Ibid., 198–9. The authors surmise that Sisco's proposal was ignored by the SRG.
221 Stocker, Diplomacy as Counter-Revolution? 422.

222 See James R. Stocker, A Historical Inevitability? Kissinger and US Contacts with the Palestinians (1973–76), *The International History Review* 39/2 (2017), 316–37. Article courtesy of James R. Stocker.
223 See Quandt, *Peace Process*, here in particular 86.
224 Memorandum from the Director of Central Intelligence Helms to the President's Assistant for National Security Affairs (Kissinger), 5 November 1970, in: *FRUS 1969–1976*, XXIII, Doc. 180. The historians of the FRUS series noted that they had been unable to find a prior memorandum of 29 October 1970 referred to by Helms concerning Fatah's approaches. See ibid., fn. 2. On 9 November Arafat held a widely reported press conference in Cairo charging that US troops had directly fought in Jordan in September and claimed that the September conflict had been the result of a CIA plan to liquidate the guerrilla movement. See UPI, Arafat: U.S. Troops Fought in Jordan, *International Herald Tribune*, 10 November 1970, 1–2. Given the ongoing CIA-Fatah contacts, the accusations assume a potentially different meaning – either a posturing intended to stave off suspicions from more radical Palestinian factions and/or a cryptic bluster addressed to those in the know in Washington expressing impatience at US foot-dragging.
225 Arafat indeed undertook a flurry of trips at the time, meeting with heads of state in Lebanon (23–24 October), Egypt (3–10 November), Libya (11–12 November), Algeria (12–14 November), Morocco (14–15 November), Tunisia (16–19 November), Libya again (20–22 November) and Syria (25 November). Further Fatah-Arab talks took place in December, including with Saudi Arabia. See *MER: 1969–1970*, 329.
226 Memorandum from the Director of Central Intelligence Helms to the President's Assistant for National Security Affairs (Kissinger), 24 November 1970, in: *FRUS 1969–1976*, XXIII, Doc. 186. The State Department was also apprised of the contacts, as shown in the previously mentioned communication to the Amman Embassy of 20 November, asking that King Hussein sanction a widening of contacts to the Palestinians. The telegram contains an outline of the 'channel' and Fatah's request to meet with 'one or more senior U.S. officials', noting that although no such meeting had been held the channel was being kept open. See Telegram from the Department of State to the Embassy in Jordan, 20 November 1970, in: Ibid., Doc. 185.
227 Cited in Hulme, *Palestinian Terrorism*, 55. Likewise in December Kissinger informed President Nixon that 'the September crisis in Jordan brought to the fore the issue of how the Palestinians can be dealt with in a peace settlement'. Although the United States was 'not rushing to support the Palestinians', said Kissinger, 'we like everyone else recognize the need to find some way to bring them into the settlement process'. (Ibid.).
228 Ibid. For the context of King Hussein's veto, see Zernichow and Waage, Palestine Option, 201–2, detailing that in early December US ambassador Brown in Jordan had apprised King Hussein of the possibility of such a meeting, offering him the prerogative to block it should he so wish.
229 Minutes of a Senior Review Group Meeting, 17 December 1970, in: *FRUS 1969–1976*, XXIII, Doc. 192. Also cited in Zernichow and Waage, Palestine Option, 204–5.
230 Memorandum from the Director of Central Intelligence Helms to the President's Assistant for National Security Affairs (Kissinger), 24 November 1970, in: *FRUS 1969–1976*, XXIII, Doc. 186, fn. 2.
231 'Of the guerilla movements, Al Fatah emerged best from the conflict. Its organisations and military training sustained the brunt of the army assaults and Yasir Arafat was acknowledged at the Cairo Conference and in the Amman Agreement

of 13 October to be the undisputed head of the whole fedayeen movement'. FCO Research Department, Middle East Section, 'The Effects of the September Crisis in Jordan on the Fedayeen Movement', 2nd draft, 23 February 1971, 9 pp., here 3, in: TNA, FCO 17/1375. According to the CIA's more subdued assessment, during the civil war 'the PLO Central Committee was recognized as the only legitimate fedayeen bargaining body, and Arafat clearly emerged as its spokesman'. Furthermore, events had shown 'that the more radical groups had suffered the most and that Fatah emerged relatively stronger'. See CIA Intelligence Report, 'Fedayeen', 25.

232 Salibi, *Modern History of Jordan*, 240.
233 *MER: 1969–1970*, 317. According to the spokesman, the committee would have full authority to make decisions for the fedayeen forces in the Amman area, with the intention of extending coordination to northern Jordan. At the same time, a special committee was to be set up to study plans for a broader and more permanent form of joint organization. The PFLP announcement was not confirmed by representatives of any of the other organizations, but a report in the *New York Times* of 10 October cited political observers in Beirut as saying that there was no reason to doubt the move. On 17 October Arafat, in his capacity as 'commander in chief of the Palestinian revolution', issued an order stating that all future military communiqués concerning attacks on Israel would be made in the name of the entire fedayeen movement and would be announced by the official spokesman of the 'Palestinian revolutionary forces'.
234 Reuters, Palestinian Government in Exile Planned, *The Times*, 14 October 1970, 1. Heightening the drama of the announcement, Touqan further claimed that the presidents of the United States, France, Great Britain and the Soviet Union, as well as the UN Security Council and all Arab leaders, had been informed of his proposals.
235 *MER: 1969–1970*, 317. The report was echoed a day later by the BBC, apparently earning Habash's criticism from within the wider PFLP leadership. Note that likewise on 14 October the Tunisian government urged Washington to take up contacts with Arafat and Fatah. See Joyce, *Anglo-American Support*, 60 and fn. 66, 170. This was followed less than a week later by similar calls from Algeria. See Chamberlin, *Global Offensive*, 127 and fn. 86, 288. For the Tunisian role, see further Zernichow and Waage, Palestine Option, 198, fn. 50.
236 *MER: 1969–1970*, 317–19.
237 CIA Intelligence Report, 'Fedayeen', 25.
238 For the further vicissitudes and ultimate withering of the proposed 'Palestinian Liberation Front' between November 1970 and early 1971, see *MER: 1969–1970*, 317–19. According to historian Yezid Sayigh, the initiatives for a merger had come from the reverse direction. The PFLP, in efforts to 'regain its composure', had repeatedly raised the issue of Palestinian national unity, culminating in a memorandum to the PLO Central Committee in late December urging the formation of a new national front, followed by a formal proposal for such at the Eighth Palestinian National Council in March 1971. The PFLP's incentive was to 'circumvent the Fateh-dominated PLO by establishing a new body in which all guerrilla groups would enjoy equal representation and freedom of action'. See Yezid Sayigh, *Armed Struggle and the Search for a State: The Palestinian Movement, 1949–1993*, paperback ed. (Oxford: Oxford University Press, 1999), 272–4, here 272.
239 Tessa Szyszkowitz, *Der Friedenskämpfer: Arafats geheimer Gesandter Issam Sartawi* (Vienna: Picus Verlag, 2011), 32, dating the ultimatum to December 1970 and the AOLP's disappearance as effective by mid-1971. See also CIA Intelligence Report,

'Fedayeen', 26, dating reports of the AOLP's dissolution within Fatah to November 1970.

240 Burke Trend, Memorandum to the Prime Minister, 'Airport Security: Policing at Airports if Civil Police Forces are withdrawn', 5 November 1970, in: TNA, PREM 15/203. Despite this, MI6 cautioned that the PFLP was 'not a tight-knit organisation', and that even minus a 'safe haven' such as Dawson's Field they were still able to conduct their 'blackmail tactics' from 'a grounded aircraft on a "friendly" airfield'. Anthony Nutting is presumably Conservative Party MP Sir Harold Anthony Nutting, the former Joint Parliamentary Undersecretary of State for Foreign Affairs from 1951–1954 and Minister of State for Foreign Affairs from 1954–1956, who resigned his post over what he saw as British duplicity over the Suez invasion of 1956. A prominent supporter of Michael Adams's CAABU, Nutting was banned from entering Israel to visit the West Bank in November 1969, reportedly for having told students in Beirut days earlier that, as paraphrased by the Jewish Telegraph Agency, 'the Palestinian question can be solved only by force and that it was up to the Palestinian guerrillas to impose such a solution'. See Foreign Ministry Confirms It Has Barred Entry of Anthony Nutting, Now a Journalist, *JTA Daily News Bulletin*, 13 November 1969, 2, http://archive.jta.org/article/1969/11/13/2951345/foreign-mi nistry-confirms-it-has-barred-entry-of-anthony-nutting-now-a-journalist (accessed 1 January 2020).

241 A. J. Sindall (British Embassy Beirut) to C. W. Long (FCO Near Eastern Department), 12 December 1970, in: TNA, FCO 17/1107.

242 FCO Research Department, Middle East Section, 'The Effects of the September Crisis in Jordan on the Fedayeen Movement', 2nd draft, 23 February 1971, 5, in: TNA, FCO 17/1375. On 17 January 1971 Fatah spokesman Kamal Adwan heavily criticized the PFLP, accusing its members of having fled the 'Battle of Karameh' without fighting in March 1968 and Habash of having hidden in North Korea during the civil war in Jordan in September 1970. Adwan added that Fatah would use all necessary force against the PFLP to protect the Palestinian resistance movement. See O'Ballance, *Arab Guerilla Power*, 169.

243 On 15 December Farouk Kaddoumi was quoted in the Egyptian *Al-Ahram* as saying that the PFLP plane hijackings had been 'no more than a publicity stunt that almost cost us the backing and support of world opinion'. See *MER: 1969–1970*, 338. Also cited in Sayigh, *Armed Struggle*, 270.

244 On 17 October *Al-Hadaf* published an official explanation for Habash's absence, reporting that he had gone abroad in response to a long-standing invitation and had broken off his visit on learning of the outbreak of hostilities on 17 September. In reality he had remained away until after the conflict had long blown over. See Sayigh, *Armed Conflict*, 272.

245 *MER: 1969–1970*, 226.

246 Cooley, *Green March*, 152; O'Ballance, *Arab Guerilla Power*, 168; Sayigh, *Armed Struggle*, 272.

247 For instance, in March 1972, Habash told a PFLP conference 'because the friendly socialist countries did not manifest an understanding of the hijacking of aircraft, the Popular Front had decided to suspend the practice forthwith'. In August 1973 he was cited as saying: 'We discovered that our friends in the world did not understand us, and did not understand our right to make use of such methods in view of the special conditions and the special struggle of the Palestinian people, and eventually we ceased to do it.' For these and other statements repeating the PFLP's rejection

of hijacking stretching down to 1979, see Ariel Merari and Shlomi Elad, *The International Dimensions of Palestinian Terrorism* (Boulder, CO: Westview, 1986), 31–4.

248 For the contradictory descriptions of the PFLP split of March 1972, see Thomas Skelton-Robinson, Im Netz verheddert: Die Beziehungen des bundesdeutschen Linksterrorismus zur Volksfront für die Befreiung Palästinas (1969–1980), in: Wolfgang Kraushaar (ed.), *Die RAF und der linke Terrorismus*, Vol. 2 (Hamburg: Hamburger Edition, 2006), 828–904, here 851–2.

249 See Benoît Faucon, *West Bankers: From Arafat to Hamas – How Money Made and Ruined the PLO and How It Can Bounce Back* (London: Masreq Editions Ltd., 2010), 35–6.

250 The PFLP enjoyed none of the financial largess given to other mainstream Palestinian fedayeen organizations by countries such as Saudi Arabia and had to financially fend for themselves. Throughout the subsequent 1970s ransom demands became an almost exclusively defining hallmark of operations by Haddad and his group's later offshoots and affiliates, giving them much of their pirate image. See Electronic Telegram, US Embassy Beirut (Buffum) to Secretary of State, 25 July 1973, reporting that the joint hijacking of an JAL Amsterdam–Tokyo flight to Libya by the Japanese Red Army and the PFLP on 20–24 July 1973 had all the traits of a Haddad operation, most importantly the payment of a ransom, judged to have been prompted by the fact that 'PFLP treasury again depleted' and based on the fact that the tactics 'so closely resemble that used by PFLP to obtain money from FRG [Federal Republic of Germany]' in the Lufthansa ransom hijacking of February 1972 'when treasury similarly depleted'. According to media reports at the time, the West German authorities had initially tried to keep details of the ransom covered up, the *Spiegel* referring to a 'world-wide secrecy pact'. The ransom was allegedly paid to indemnify Lufthansa against such attacks in the future, but when word of it leaked the hijackers told *Bild am Sonntag* that they no longer felt obliged to keep their side of the bargain. See Winkler, *Schattenmann*, 196–7. See also Neil C. Livingstone and David Halevy, *Inside the PLO: Covert Units, Secret Funds and the War against Israel and the United States* (New York: William Morrow, 1990), 187 and 206, claiming that following the hijacking Lufthansa made annual payments of $5–10 million to 'elements within the PLO' and/or the PFLP in return for immunity against further attacks, a 'system' that remained in place until the Lufthansa hijacking of October 1977 to Mogadishu, Somalia.

Chapter 6

THE LODO MORO

ITALY AND THE PALESTINE LIBERATION ORGANIZATION

Tobias Hof

Introduction

Francesco Cossiga, long-time member of the Christian Democratic Party (DC), Minister of the Interior (1976–8), prime minister (1979–80) and president of the Italian Republic (1985–92), was known for his controversial interviews. In 2008, he spoke to a journalist for the Israeli newspaper *Yedioth Ahronoth* and claimed that in 1979 the Italian Servizio per le Informazioni e la Sicurezza Militare (SISMI) had informed him about a secret agreement between the Italian government and the Palestine Liberation Organization (PLO) known as Lodo Moro. This pact granted the Palestinians the right to roam freely in and operate out of Italy as long as they did not carry out an attack on Italian soil. Jews, however, were not protected by this agreement. Cossiga was shocked when his interview did not cause a big outcry in Italy or anywhere else.[1]

Seven years later an apparently newly discovered telegram from 18 February 1978 about a meeting between SISMI Colonel Stefano Giovannone – the Italian 'Lawrence of Arabia' – and George Habash, founder and leader of the Popular Front for the Liberation of Palestine (PFLP), changed everything: Habash warned Giovannone about an imminent terrorist attack that would be carried out by European terrorists and might also affect Italy. Even though he was not able to provide further information, he assured Giovannone that the PFLP still adhered to a policy of non-belligerence towards Italy. The telegram supposedly revealed a close connection between the PFLP and the Italian secret service as well as the existence of the Lodo Moro.[2] The dispatch led to controversial debates: Was there a connection between the Aldo Moro kidnapping in 1978 and the agreement between Italy and the Palestinians? What was the exact content of the Lodo Moro and how long did it last? Can it shed new light on the bombing in Bologna in August 1980? And is there a similar agreement between Rome and terrorist groups such as Hezbollah or even the Islamic State today?[3] Whereas some scholars, politicians and state officials dismiss the significance – or even existence – of the Lodo Moro, others such as former magistrate Rosario Priore regard it as the key to understanding the major terrorist attacks that have struck Italy since the late 1970s. In his recent book *I segreti di Bologna* (*The Secrets of Bologna*) he claims that the Lodo Moro offers a common explanation for the kidnapping and subsequent murder of Moro in 1978 as well as the Bologna incident.[4]

In this chapter I want to clarify what we know so far about the Lodo Moro, its genesis and potential implications for Italy. Historians, however, are faced with a dilemma when trying to examine these issues: While there are many rumours and half-truths circulating in the public, political and academic discourses, relevant documents related to the Lodo Moro are scarce. Many records are still classified and not accessible.[5] As a result my findings will be preliminary and are the product of a critical analysis of the facts and available documents. The following study is based primarily on parliamentary debates, newspapers and the hearings and reports of the Parliamentary Commission to Inquire into the Kidnapping and Murder of Aldo Moro, which met between 23 May 1980 and 19 April 1983;[6] the Parliamentary Commission to Inquire into Italian terrorism, which gathered from May 1988 to July 2001;[7] the controversial Mitrokhin Commission, which began its work in 2002 and was shut down in 2006 without publishing a final report;[8] and finally, the second Parliamentary Commission to Inquire into the Kidnapping and Death of Aldo Moro, created in May 2014. Additionally, biannual parliamentary reports from the Italian intelligence community will be used.

Three central topics will be addressed: first, I want to examine the genesis of the Lodo Moro within an international context. In doing so, I would like to highlight several factors that might have contributed to an agreement between Rome and the PLO, such as economic and foreign policy interests. However, in this regard historians are faced with another obstacle: a concise history of Italian foreign policy since the 1950s has yet to be written.[9] Based on these results, I am going to analyse in a second step possible links between the Lodo Moro and the kidnapping and subsequent murder of Aldo Moro. I will also briefly address the question of why conspiracy theories still dominate the memory of many Italians when it comes to the Moro murder case, despite the fact that the events surrounding the case have been more or less correctly constructed. I will not join in the controversial discussion between believers and non-believers of conspiracy theories and attempt to 'discern between "real" conspiracies and purported ones',[10] which is almost impossible, because a conspiracy theory by definition cannot be countered, as it is able to integrate and neutralize any invalidation in an alleged master plan. Finally, I will focus on the connection between the Lodo Moro and the terrorist attacks in Italy in the early 1980s by analysing Italian foreign policy in general, Italian–Palestinian relations in particular and the disputes within the PLO. By looking at these issues I want to contribute to the ongoing debate about the Lodo Moro and hopefully shed new light on the genesis and impact of the Italian–Palestinian connection.

The genesis of the Lodo Moro

On 22 July 1968, members of the PFLP hijacked an Israeli El Al plane on its way from Rome to Tel Aviv. It was the first time a Palestinian organization committed a terrorist attack on European soil to publicize the plight of its people.[11] George Habash justified this action two years later: 'When we hijack a plane it has more effect than if we killed a hundred Israelis in battle. [...] For decades world opinion has been neither for nor against the Palestinians. [...] It simply ignored us. At least the world is talking about us now.'[12]

In the following years Palestinian terrorists would continue to strike European countries, among them Italy. In the summer of 1972 the group Black September carried out an attack in Trieste and attempted to strike at the Leonardo da Vinci-Fiumicino Airport in Rome.[13] Italian authorities were aware that their country was not only a potential target but also a major route for the terrorists. Members of Black September acquired their weapons in the Italian capital before committing the massacre during the 1972 Olympic Games in Munich. One year later, Rome became the centre of Palestinian terrorism in Europe: in April and September, Italian security forces arrested seven suspected terrorists before they carried out an attack.[14] However, on 17 December 1973, a group of Palestinians who had links to the Black September group invaded Fiumicino Airport, took several hostages and set fire to a Pan American Boeing 707. Shortly after, they hijacked a Lufthansa plane and forced its crew to fly them to Kuwait. There the terrorists surrendered to the Kuwait authorities and after negotiations between Kuwait, Egypt and the PLO, they were handed over to the PLO. These attacks resulted in the deaths of thirty-four people.[15] One day after the Fiumicino incident a heated debate took place in the Italian Chamber of Representatives. Several politicians not only were concerned about the security of Italy but also linked the assaults to the broader context of the Israeli–Palestinian conflict. Flaminio Piccoli (DC) reminded the audience of how important a stable peace in the Middle East was for Italian interests. He called for economic help for the Palestinian people and stressed their legitimate right to land. Europe, he argued, must support these claims, because it would be the only way to stop international terrorism. He insisted that the attacks were carried out by a radical group that wanted to jeopardize the peace talks in Geneva. Piccoli concluded that it would be the duty of the government to support any form of negotiations that would promote Palestinian interests and consequently establish long-lasting peace in the region.[16] All of a sudden, Palestinian terrorist attacks ceased on Italian soil. The terrorist scene became dominated by right-wing and left-wing terrorism, culminating in the kidnapping and subsequent killing of Moro by the Red Brigades (BR) in the spring of 1978.[17]

What were the reasons for this abrupt cessation? According to Rosario Priore, the Fiumicino incident persuaded the then Minister of Foreign Affairs, Aldo Moro, to seek a closer relationship with the PLO. Several meetings between the Palestinians and Moro's envoy, Colonel Stefano Giovannone, resulted in a non-belligerent period for Palestinian terrorist organizations in Italy.[18] Until today, however, we do not have any records of these meetings. Abu Anzeh Saleh, a key figure in the Lodo Moro and representative of the PFLP in Italy, stated that the agreement was based only on mutual trust and the word of honour between Giovannone and Habash.[19] Priore, too, confessed that he has yet to find written proof but he insisted that multiple high-ranking Palestinians and Italians testified to the existence of the Lodo Moro.[20] However, the lack of written records poses a serious problem that has until now been buried under a multitude of sometimes far-reaching conspiracy theories. As long as these documents are missing and as long as we have to rely on the testimonies of individuals who often pursue their own agenda, the exact wording and implication of the Lodo Moro remain shrouded in mystery. Were, for instance, Jews really excluded from the Lodo Moro as Cossiga claimed in 2008? What were the exact terms and time frame of the agreement and who knew about it on the Palestinian and the Italian sides, respectively? Was only the PFLP or the entire PLO part of the agreement? Were the connections between the PLO and Italian left-wing extremist groups part of the conversations? Answers to those questions, however difficult to find, are essential to evaluating and assessing the Lodo Moro and countering the often more exciting conspiracy theories. Clues to these issues can be found by historically contextualizing the events of the early 1970s within Italian foreign policy and the history of the PLO.

Since the 1950s Italy has 'sought to construct for itself a role as a medium-sized regional power able to exercise serious influence in both Europe and the Mediterranean'.[21] After the Suez Crisis and the consequent decline of French and British influence, Rome saw an opportunity to expand its own standing in the region. This new strategy entailed a re-evaluation of previous relations with the Arab world and is often associated with the name of Enrico Mattei, a member of the DC and president of the state-run petroleum company Ente Nazionale Idrocarburi (ENI). His plan was essentially based on economic considerations: due to the constant shortage of natural resources in Italy, he wanted to expand Italian influence in Arab countries to secure better and cheaper access to local oil fields. During his presidency at ENI, Mattei was able to secure low-cost petroleum from the Arab world, which massively contributed to the Italian economic miracle. He was backed and supported by influential members of the DC such as Giuseppe Pella and Amintore Fanfani.[22]

Even though Mattei attempted to maintain a close relationship with the United States, the political establishment in Washington became suspicious of Italian intentions. Rome's foreign policy came into conflict with US companies and interests in the region and also harmed the position of America's closest ally in the region: Israel. Well-respected American journalist Cyrus Sulzberger accused the Italian government of pursuing a dangerous path. He alleged that Mattei wanted to leave NATO and become a neutral country in order to play a more important role in the Mediterranean and acquire cheaper petroleum rights in the Arab world.[23] The divergent interests of Italy and the United States became apparent in the Six-Day War in June 1967. Whereas Washington sympathized with Israel, Italy reacted cautiously so as not to jeopardize its relationship with the Arab countries and its access to Middle Eastern petroleum. Then Prime Minister Aldo Moro, speaking at the General Assembly of the United Nations (UN) on 21 June 1967, referred to the situation as a humanitarian, social and political problem.[24]

The Italian economy's dependence on imports of cheap foreign petroleum became apparent after the Yom Kippur War and the subsequent oil crisis in 1973. The price Italy had to pay for oil increased massively and damaged the country's economy. It put an end to the economic miracle and caused the first drop in the GDP after the Second World War.[25] The Italian government was well aware of the vulnerability of the country's economy. Thus, as early as the late 1960s, Rome was looking for different ways to decrease this dependency. Two plans were widely circulated among politicians and industrialists: on the one hand, Italy stepped up its efforts to replace oil with natural gas. This led to closer contact with the Soviet Union, as well as North African countries such as Libya.[26] However, the relationship with Muammar Gaddafi's Libya was never smooth. In 1970, the Libyan government confiscated the possessions of 17,000 Italians who lived in the country. Despite these and other tensions, the Italians still pursued diplomatic negotiations with Gaddafi. In 1976, for example, the two countries signed economic deals.[27] The continuing relations with Libya received a lot of criticism in Italy, Europe and the United States. The Italian government was accused of indirectly sponsoring terrorism.[28] On the other hand, Moro still wanted to secure cheap oil by strengthening and expanding the dialogue with Arab countries. Rome, for instance, denied Americans the right to use Italian airports to support Israel during the Yom Kippur War in order to maintain their good relations with Arab countries.[29] Furthermore, on 8 November 1973, Moro urged the European Economic Community to issue a statement regarding the 'need for Israel to end the territorial occupation' and recognizing the 'legitimate rights of the Palestinians'.[30] Italy also welcomed Yasser Arafat's speech at the General Assembly of the UN on 14 October 1974 and supported Arafat's diplomatic strategy by allowing the PLO to establish a liaison office in Rome. Thus, while not ignoring moral concerns, Rome's attempt to be the voice of the Palestinian people in the West was massively influenced by Italy's dependency on Arab petroleum.[31]

Considering these long-term goals of Italian foreign policy regarding the Israeli–Palestinian conflict, it is debatable whether the Fiumicino Airport attack was the real trigger for the rapprochement between Rome and the PLO. Rosario Priore mentioned that PLO representatives offered Italian Foreign Ministry officials a secret deal for the first time in October 1973. He was not, however, able to give convincing proof for his thesis; the document he cited originated a month before the supposed meeting took place.[32] General Armando Sportelli, a former member of SISMI, stated that the Lodo Moro began in 1971. According to Sportelli, it was a deal between Moro and Arafat in which the latter promised not to carry out attacks in Italy or against Italians in return for Rome's diplomatic support.[33] Vito Miceli, the Arabophile head of the Servizio Informazioni Difesa until 1974, confirmed that in 1971 all members of the Italian cabinet knew about this deal.[34] Furthermore, we have a couple of examples that indicate the existence of an agreement between the PLO and Rome before 1974: in February 1973, the Italian authorities released two PLO members who were involved in the hijacking of the El Al plane in July 1968. In September of the same year law enforcement arrested five Palestinians who were in possession of a surface-to-air missile (Strela). Prime Minister Mariano Rumor, anxious about a possible reprisal by the PLO, pushed for their release. Only fifty days before the Fiumicino Airport attack they were set free, despite being sentenced to five years and two months of imprisonment.[35] However, if Italian contacts with the PLO leadership already existed – and the Italians apparently kept their part of the bargain – why did the Fiumicino attack happen?

To find answers to this question, we must look briefly at the history of the PLO. When Yasser Arafat became its chairman in early 1969, the very heterogeneous PLO consisted of six different groups, of which Arafat's Fatah and Habash's PFLP were the most prominent.[36] Under Arafat's leadership the PLO tried to establish contact with Western countries, which culminated in Arafat's speech at the UN in 1974.[37] Secret agreements with Western governments were also part of this strategy. Journalist Marcel Gyr, for instance, has uncovered contacts between the Swiss government and Farouk Kaddoumi, who was responsible for the PLO's foreign relations and since 1973 headed the political department of the PLO in Beirut. The meetings took place after PFLP terrorists hijacked a Swiss airplane in September 1970. A deal was struck that the PLO would not carry out further attacks in Switzerland and Berne would support the PLO on a diplomatic level. Over time, however, the Palestinians increased their demands and put more pressure on the Swiss government.[38] In an official report, however, the Swiss government denied that such an agreement had ever existed.[39] Other deals apparently existed between the Palestinians and the French and Spanish governments.[40] In 1974 Arafat officially declared a 'terrorist armistice' for Western Europe.[41]

This tactic, however, did not go unchallenged within the PLO: in particular Habash's PFLP, founded in 1967 with the help of Syria, wanted to achieve a Palestinian state through class struggle and revolution against Israel and other Arab countries the organization considered to be reactionary, such as Jordan, Saudi Arabia and Egypt.[42] Moreover, Habash accused Arafat's Fatah of reconciliation with Israel. In September 1974, the PFLP seceded from the PLO Executive Committee and the Palestine Central Council and formed the Palestinian Rejection Front within the PLO. They were joined by other influential groups such as Ahmed Jibril's Popular Front for the Liberation of Palestine-General Command (PFLP-GC) and the Abu Nidal Organization (ANO). The Black September group also consisted mostly of members who were critical of Arafat and challenged his leadership.[43]

Thus, the Palestinians who committed terrorist attacks in Italy in the early 1970s belonged to groups that openly criticized Arafat's more moderate attitude towards Western countries. Attacks like the one in Fiumicino in December 1973 illustrated the internal power struggle within the PLO. They were meant to jeopardize closer cooperation between Italy and the PLO and therefore undermine Arafat's legitimacy as the leader of the Palestinian people. Contemporaries such as Piccoli described the attacks as an attempt to sabotage Arafat's strategy. What we do not know for certain, however, is if Arafat and the mainstream PLO knew about these attacks. Some scholars argue that Arafat was personally responsible for the creation of Black September in 1971 and deliberately used terrorism to force the West towards a more conciliatory view of Palestinian demands, while at the same time pretending to be a peaceful leader.[44] Nonetheless, there is no doubt that Arafat and the mainstream PLO tried to cover up any attack against the West that was carried out by Palestinians. Because, by violating the official restrictions, these

Palestinian terrorists only disclosed Arafat's weakness as a leader and the deep division within the PLO.[45]

This internal power struggle in the early 1970s exemplifies the dilemma PLO leaders would face in the coming years: by propagating a political settlement based on compromises, regarded as treason by more radical fringes in the PLO, they jeopardized Palestinian unity.[46] To safeguard PLO unity its leadership condemned the armed struggle in Europe, but did little to eradicate it. Furthermore, they advocated a short-term political settlement that was never considered final – a strategy that helped to minimize tensions between the mainstream PLO and the Rejection Front for the most part of the 1970s.[47] Moreover, the civil war in Lebanon, which broke out in the mid-1970s, and Arafat's speech at the UN in 1974 – proof of the success of his diplomatic strategy – weakened his opponents. Once Arafat had marginalized his critics, the ideas behind the Lodo Moro could finally prevail.

Even though it seems that many Western European countries adopted a similar strategy to the Lodo Moro, the existence of such a symbiotic relation between the PLO – regarded as a terrorist organization by many countries in the early 1970s – and a Western democracy is unsettling. It poses several complex diplomatic and security questions: as early as 1968 it was well known that the PFLP in particular had contacts with left-wing extremist groups in Europe and was supplying left-wing terrorist groups such as the German Red Army Faction (RAF) with weapons and offering them training facilities in Lebanon.[48] Were Italian law enforcement and politicians aware of a similar clandestine cooperation? And if so, how did it influence the relationship with the PLO leadership? Furthermore, the internal power struggle within the PLO turned any deal into an agreement whose effectiveness and stability correlated with Arafat's standing. And last but not least, the Swiss case illustrates the complexity and unpredictability of a deal with the PLO: governments could never be certain that the Palestinians would not press for further concessions.

The Lodo Moro and the Moro kidnapping

Rome, 16 March 1978, shortly after 9.00 a.m.: the president of the DC, Aldo Moro, is on his way to the Chamber of Deputies, where a vote of confidence in the second minority government of Giulio Andreotti is about to occur. He is accompanied by his five bodyguards. Suddenly a Fiat blocks the way. The passengers of the car, members of the BR, open fire. More terrorists, dressed in the uniform of the Italian airline Alitalia, appear and attack the convoy. A short time later the shooting is over: four security guards are dead, the fifth will die later in hospital. An unharmed Moro is dragged into a waiting car. He would be held hostage for fifty-five days, during which time the police was unable to rescue him. On 9 May, Moro's body was found in the trunk of a red Renault in the Via Caetani in Rome. Today a memorial plaque can be found at the spot where the grisly discovery was made.[49]

Shortly after the ambush numerous conspiracy theories began to spread. At the core of many of these theories was the belief that the BR was controlled by a foreign power. The list of potential masterminds reads like a who's who of secret services, states and clandestine organizations: from the CIA to the German BND to the KGB; from the NATO clandestine organization Gladio to an international network of Masonic lodges, from the Czechoslovakian to the British government – the headquarters of Italian terrorism was anywhere but not at home. It did not take long for this notion to gain popularity: only 10.1 per cent of Italians surveyed in January 1982 believed that Italian left-wing terrorism was a domestic phenomenon. A total of 58.2 per cent, however, believed the terrorists were controlled by a foreign power.[50]

A controversial, sometimes polemic, debate quickly developed between adherents and opponents of these theories. Sergio Flamigni, a former senator for the Italian Communist Party and a member of the first Moro Commission, has written several books in which he argues that Moro fell victim to a sinister plot involving several secret agencies from around the world.[51] This inspired journalists and political commentators inside and outside Italy to spin their own theories, which were often more bizarre than the original ones.[52] The American historian Richard Drake – who published one of the first document-based, historical studies on the Moro case and its aftermath[53] – argued that instead of shining light into dark corners the various parliamentary commissions and the publications of their reports helped spread these theories. The debates often degenerated into party political quarrels, only intended to legitimize the position of the commissioners' own party during the kidnapping. The published findings of the commissions 'reinforced the public's confusion about Moro's abduction and death. As usual in such a climate of uncertainty, conspiracy theories gained the upper hand.'[54]

The Lodo Moro was never explicitly mentioned during the interrogations or in the published documents of the first Moro Commission. At most, Palestinian groups featured as organizations that logistically supported left-wing extremism and terrorism in Italy and Europe or as a possible mediator between the BR and the Italian state.[55] Only Aldo Moro himself alluded indirectly to the Lodo Moro in a couple of letters he sent to his colleagues during the kidnapping: he urged them to abandon the 'policy of toughness' and to start negotiations with the terrorists. Moro argued that the government had successfully talked to terrorists before – the Palestinians – and should continue this policy.[56] The Lodo Moro, however, became a central aspect of the second Moro Commission. In December 2014 Rosario Priore testified before the commission and argued that the telegram of 18 February 1978 foretold the kidnapping and subsequent murder of Moro. What else could Habash have meant by a serious terrorist attack that would be carried out by European terrorists? However, if the Italian secret service knew about a possible threat against Moro why was he not better protected?[57] Furthermore, Priore stated that the order to kill Moro was not given by Mario Moretti, then head of the BR. Without being able to provide more details, he claimed that the order must have come from a higher level outside Italy. However, by extensively outlining the Lodo Moro he suggested that the reasons for Moro's kidnapping and killing were to be found in Moro's foreign policy.⁵⁸ Gero Grassi, a member of the commission, was not as cautious as Priore. According to him, Moro was working tirelessly for peace in the Middle East and had proposed the idea of national self-determination and promoted the two-state solution. Grassi argued that this policy was the reason for Moro's kidnapping and subsequent murder. He claimed that the Israeli secret service Mossad gave weapons to the BR to carry out the attack and thus destabilize Italy. A country in turmoil would not have been able to continue its support for the PLO – a theory that was put forward by the PLO in 1978 and reached prominence for the first time in 1999.⁵⁹

How plausible are these theories? Was the telegram referring to the Moro kidnapping and if so, why did Habash know about it? Was the abduction really an attempt to undermine Italy's foreign policy and a reaction to the Lodo Moro? Let us take a closer look at the telegram that has caused such a public outcry since 2014:

> Deputy Director informed STOP I have met my usual contact from 'PFLP' Habash this morning who strongly recommended me not to leave Beirut, considering he might have to urgently contact me for information regarding terrorist operation of considerable scope allegedly planned by European terrorists that could involve our country, carried out as a joint project recently discussed by representatives of extremist organizations in Europe STOP At my repeated requests for more details he assured me that 'PFLP' will operate in honoring the confirmed commitments that are aimed at excluding our country from plans of a terrorist nature, adding that he will only provide me with necessary elements so that our authorities can adopt appropriate measures STOP End. Do not inform services connected to PLO Rome.⁶⁰

The information Habash gave to Giovannone was very vague. He basically urged him to stay in Beirut, based on rumours about a possible, future terrorist attack in Europe. However, he did not provide any details about the nature or location of the potential threat. Therefore, historian Marco Clementi declared that Habash did not refer to the kidnapping, but, rather, to a potential bomb attack somewhere in Europe.⁶¹ Rumours about possible terrorist attacks were definitely not scarce at a time when Italian and West German left-wing had terrorism reached its peak.

I would like to add two more thoughts: first, the telegram's content was often only superficially interpreted. In contrast to many commentaries, the telegram did not mention any far-reaching secret pact between Rome, the PFLP or the PLO. Habash merely stated that his organization would continue to exclude Italy from any terrorist attacks and thus confirmed Arafat's non-belligerent strategy for Europe. However, the fact that a group known for its opposition to Arafat's moderate tactics, a group that had seceded from the mainstream PLO in 1974, was honouring Arafat's policy has often been overlooked. In addition, the last sentence of the text – 'Do not inform services connected to PLO Rome' – has often been ignored. Apparently, the Italian secret service had a connection to the PFLP and tried to keep this line of communication separate from the connection with the mainstream PLO. Consequently, we must differentiate between two different Lodo Moros: one, more official, with Arafat's PLO; another, more secret, with the radical PFLP.[62] From this reading the telegram proves the internal split of the Palestinian organization.

And second – something that has also been neglected in recent discussions – the existence of the telegram was already known to members of the first Moro Commission. The SISMI report, which was submitted to the commission in 1980, referenced Giovannone's cable, yet concluded that no more information was available and further investigations seemed to support this.[63] Pressed by commission member Paolo Cabras, General Giuseppe Santovito denied the importance of the telegram.[64] However, the second part of the telegram – the reference to the Palestinian non-belligerent policy – was mentioned neither in the report nor by Santovito. Why was it left out? Why did only Cabras bother to ask about the February warning? All conspiracies aside, one thing is certain: the fact that SISMI had contact with Habash's PFLP was already public knowledge by 1980. Moreover, the mutual information sharing between the PFLP and SISMI indicates good relations between the two organizations. However, this information did not spark any controversy in parliament, the commission or in public.

The Lodo Moro might have been triggered by Aldo Moro – at least according to the information we possess today – but it was not Moro's decision alone nor was he the only person representing a policy that sought a rapprochement with the Palestinians. As shown, Italian politicians – especially from the DC – had reached out numerous times to the Arab world since the 1950s. While this strategy was at first based predominantly on economic considerations, the fear of future terrorist attacks also led the Italian government to strengthen contact with the PLO. To assume that killing Moro, who neither held a government position nor had exceptional influence on the course of Italian foreign policy in 1978, would change this policy contradicts any logical assessment of foreign policymaking.

Furthermore, there is no proof to suggest that Mossad – or any other foreign secret service – wanted to sabotage the Italian pro-Arab foreign policy by murdering Moro. Vladimiro Satta has convincingly and extensively shown that there is no evidence for any external intervention in the kidnapping and murder of Moro and has pointed out substantial flaws in these theories.[65] Yes, there is no doubt that Moro supported the Palestinian cause and that Arafat declared that the 'Moro kidnapping is also an attack on the Palestinians'.[66] This could explain why the PLO was involved in several efforts to contact the BR in March and April of 1978.[67] These attempts were supported by the Italian secret services, which were aware that the Palestinians – especially the PFLP – possessed contacts in the left-wing extremist scene dating back to the early 1970s.[68] Conspiracy theories and the idea of a 'puppet master' who jeopardized all these attempts are handy explanations for why all rescue and negotiation attempts failed. However, the complexity of the situation and the unwillingness of both the BR and the Italian government to negotiate in the first place are often ignored. Priore, for example, dismissed the hard-line stance of the Communist Party and the fact that it was hard to communicate with a terrorist group that had gradually lost contact with the left-wing extremist scene after 1976.[69]

However, why are these conspiracy theories surrounding the Moro murder case still so prominent? Francesco Cossiga has expressed his astonishment that the left and the right continually try to blame external forces and cannot accept the fact that the kidnapping and murder were carried out by Italian terrorists.[70] Besides the desire to explain the inexplicable and to rationalize the irrational, it is obvious that many of these theories – including the ones connecting the kidnapping with the Lodo Moro – are attempts to blame an external power for events that occurred in Italy. These theories serve to deflect self-criticism and domestic cause analysis.[71]

The Lodo Moro and the Bologna massacre

Bologna, 2 August 1980, shortly after 10.20 a.m.: a bomb explodes in the Central Train Station, killing eighty-five people and injuring over 200. In 1995, after years of investigation, trials and false leads, Francesca Mambro and Giuseppe Fioravanti, members of the right-wing terrorist organization Nuclei Armati Rivoluzionari, were sentenced to life imprisonment for committing the attack. Both, however, have always maintained their innocence.

In July 2016 Rosario Priore, who has investigated right-wing terrorism in Italy for years, propagated another theory: the Bologna attack was an act of retaliation by the Palestinians, because Rome had violated the Lodo Moro.[72] He dismissed the right-wing terrorism theory as an attempt by SISMI to cover up the Lodo Moro. According to him, everything began in November 1979 when the Carabinieri arrested left-wing extremists Daniele Pifano, Giuseppe Nieri and Giorgio Baumgartner in Ortona as well as the Palestinian Abu Anzeh Saleh for the possession of two Strela missiles.[73] All four were sentenced to seven years' imprisonment for arms smuggling on 25 January 1980.[74] During the trial, George Habash officially requested the return of the weapons. Priore argued that, by denying his demands, the Italian authorities had violated the Lodo Moro. Despite warnings from SISMI, Cossiga was little concerned about potential retaliatory acts by the PFLP. Instead, he was angered by the discovery of weapons deals between the BR and the Palestinians and wanted to show strength in the face of public criticism. At this point the story becomes even more complicated: the PFLP supposedly contacted the Libyan leader Muammar Gaddafi, who also held a grudge against the Italians at that time. Gaddafi then approached the Organization of International Revolutionaries, a group founded by well-known terrorist Ilich Ramírez Sánchez, known as Carlos. Then, on 2 August 1980, Thomas Kram, a member of Carlos's group, carried out the bombing in Bologna.[75] Can we really draw this direct line between the arrests in November 1979 and the Bologna massacre? Were the arrests the end of the Lodo Moro?

To begin with we need to critically examine Priore's main arguments, which are predominately based on circumstantial evidence, newspaper articles and oral testimonies. First, he fell short of providing convincing evidence and addressing contradictory statements.[76] For instance, Bassam Abu Sharif, one of the main leaders of the PFLP, also demanded the return of the confiscated weapons. However, he promised that there would be no retaliation if the Italian state did not comply.[77] Moreover, neither he nor Habash actually demanded the release of Saleh.[78] Second, Priore seemed to exaggerate the importance of the first conviction in January 1980. Due to the complicated Italian justice system the sentence was not yet finalized. Already in February 1981, State Attorney Domenico Sica travelled to Lebanon to assure Fatah and the PFLP that Saleh's release would occur very soon – sure enough, he was released six months later.[79] Was Sica's pledge only a reaction to the bombing in Bologna? In light of Sica's travel, the Italian justice system, the aforementioned examples from the early 1970s and given the contacts between Rome and the Palestinians, it seems much more probable that the Palestinians and the Italian officials were in constant contact to find a solution to the problem. Thus, the entire conception of the attack as an act of retaliation appears questionable. Why would the PFLP go through all this trouble when there was really nothing to gain?

Third, Priore presented the neo-fascist theory from a narrow and one-sided perspective. He argued that SISMI favoured the far-right explanation to avoid drawing attention to the Lodo Moro and the fact that Rome had violated the agreement, and thus could be judged indirectly responsible for the Bologna attack.[80] However, he ignored the Servizio per le Informazioni e la Sicurezza Democratica (SISDE), the Italian civil secret service, which was also responsible for combatting international terrorist organizations operating in Italy. It was SISDE that dealt with the situation in Ortona and provided evidence that the Bologna attack was carried out by neo-fascists.[81] Moreover – without neglecting the fact that Italian law enforcement agencies were informed about Thomas Kram travelling to Italy and staying in Bologna the day the bombing happened – we should not ignore the fact that the attack showed many similarities to far-right bombings during the 'strategy of tension'.[82] In particular, the fact that nobody claimed responsibility for the attack fits into the pattern of Italian and European right-wing terrorism in the 1970s and 1980s.[83] Priore's arguments as to why the Palestinians did not claim responsibility for Bologna are not convincing for two reasons: first, bombings were not the first weapon of choice for Palestinian terrorists, who preferred using kidnappings and hostage-taking to draw attention to their demands. Second, Palestinians usually claimed responsibility for terrorist attacks committed by them. Even Carlos, who worked for the PFLP until 1975, often claimed responsibility for his actions. [84]

Last but not least, let us examine Priore's argument that the Italian state – and Cossiga in particular – violated the Lodo Moro as evidence emerged that Palestinian groups supported left-wing terrorist groups in Italy.[85] Was this discovery really new and problematic? Could it have undermined the Lodo Moro and led to a retaliatory act? Italy – as well as many other European states – knew that far-left groups within the PLO had contacts with left-wing terrorist organizations in Europe.[86] Compared to the RAF, the cooperation between the BR and the Palestinians seemed less substantial. The Italian secret services were aware of these connections, but made it clear that the mainstream PLO under

Arafat stopped any dealings with Italian left-wing extremists in the early 1970s – approximately at the same time that Rome opened discussions with the PLO.[87] In 1979 the BR contacted the PFLP to request weapons and logistic support. The exact extent of this cooperation has yet to be uncovered.[88] Considering that the Italian authorities were aware of the links between left-wing terrorist groups and parts of the PLO, Cossiga's outrage appears more like a symbolic act intended to calm the Italian public, especially after he was accused during the Ortona trial of having known everything about the dealings between the BR and the Palestinians.[89] Cossiga's defence strategy also became apparent in his 2008 interview, where he made Moro responsible for the Lodo Moro and claimed that the secret service did not tell him any details about the agreement between Rome and the Palestinians.[90] Considering, however, that he was the Minister of the Interior between 1976 and 1978 and thus also responsible for Italian anti-terrorism measures, his allegations should be critically scrutinized.[91] Overall, Cossiga used the interview to present himself in a favourable light to the newspaper's Israeli readership by rejecting any blame for the pact between Rome and the PLO.

Let us now contextualize the arrests in November 1979 and the Bologna attack and integrate them into the larger sphere of domestic and international politics in the late 1970s and early 1980s. After Aldo Moro's murder and the Iranian hostage crisis in 1979, the Italian government continued to negotiate with, rather than confront, the Arab countries and continued to support the Palestinian cause in the international arena. Given the vulnerability of the Italian economy, Rome tried to maintain the role of an honest broker between the Arab countries and the West by keeping communications open with the PLO. Neither the increasing tensions after the Soviet invasion in Afghanistan nor Cossiga's presumedly hostile attitude towards the Arab countries changed this strategy. On 13 June 1980, the European Council under Italian leadership issued a statement in favour of further negotiations with the PLO that sparked criticism in Israel and the United States. In March 1981, Farouk Kaddoumi visited Rome to meet with Italian foreign minister Emilio Colombo. In September of the following year, Arafat met Giulio Andreotti and Colombo in Rome and discussed an official recognition of the PLO. Even Italy's relations to states like Libya were maintained despite highly controversial issues such as the status of Malta and the murdering of Libyan dissidents in Italy.[92] However, economic considerations as well as the belief that international isolation would only strengthen radical fringes within Libya convinced policymakers in Rome to continue negotiations with Tripoli. In December 1980, the Libyan Foreign Secretary's visit to Rome was followed by an announcement that Gaddafi would come to Italy the following spring. Even though this move was widely criticized, it was another example that Italy still planned to keep its partnership with Libya. Six years later, tensions arose again when Libya was accused of supporting the ANO – still, Italy was against military actions.[93] To summarize, in the late 1970s and early 1980s Italy was an important supporter of the Palestinian cause in the Western world. Endangering this support by carrying out a terrorist attack intended to spread fear, suspicion and chaos, and to undermine the stability of Italy seems to be a self-destructive idea and runs contrary to the strategy of the

PLO and the PFLP. Considering all these points, it seems unlikely that the Bologna attack was an act of retaliation against Italy orchestrated by the PFLP. While the role of Carlos's group as well as the Libyan government might tell a different story, only further investigation and de-classification of documents will clarify the case.[94]

It must have been a huge shock when Palestinian terrorists once again officially took credit for attacks in Italy. On 9 October 1982, a member of the ANO attacked the Great Synagogue in Rome. A baby was killed and thirty-seven people were injured. Osama Abdel al-Zomar, while in Greek custody, was convicted by an Italian court for his part in the attacks. The authorities in Athens, however, did not extradite him to Italy, but deported him to Libya in 1989. On 7 October 1985, four members of the PLF hijacked the Italian cruise ship MS Achille Lauro. They killed the passenger Leon Klinghoffer, a 69-year-old Jewish American in a wheelchair and threw him overboard. On 27 December 1985, four terrorists of the ANO attacked the Leonardo da Vinci-Fiumicino Airport. They killed sixteen people and injured ninety-nine. Three of the attackers were killed, while one was wounded and taken into custody.[95]

Do these attacks symbolize the breakdown of the Lodo Moro? Again, we are not able to provide a definite answer. However, the available information points to a slightly different answer. The first argument might sound cynical but should also be considered: most victims of these attacks were Jewish. Thus, if Cossiga's 2008 statement about the Lodo Moro was true, these attacks did not violate the pact between Rome and the Palestinians per se. Second, these assaults were carried out by groups that opposed Arafat's two-state policy and his more moderate approach towards Western Europe, highlighting Arafat's weaker position within the Palestinian orbit rather than an end of the Lodo Moro. A look at the history of the PLO once again supports this theory.

As early as 1979 – even before the arrests in Ortona – the Italian secret services were worried about possible terrorist attacks carried out by Arab groups and informed the Italian parliament accordingly.[96] Although the mainstream PLO still honoured the Lodo Moro, the Iranian hostage crisis and the emergence of religious terrorism made the Palestinian terrorist scene more complex. Arafat, whose leadership had been continually challenged since the late 1970s, tried to regain control by distancing himself from the Camp David Agreement as well as the 1980 European Council statement, as both were categorically rejected by the radical fringes within the PLO.[97] But, it was not until the summer of 1982 that Arafat ran into serious problems: on 6 June Israel invaded Lebanon and forced over 11,000 members of the PLO to seek refuge in different Arab states by late August 1982. The invasion symbolized a huge setback for Arafat and led to a decrease in the influence of Fatah. Consequently, it also undermined Arafat's idea of a two-state solution, which was proposed by his close associates as early as 1978 and which he himself again proclaimed in July 1982. Arafat's weakness was further emphasized by a revolt in May 1983 and the subsequent split of the PLO in 1985.[98] Therefore, the attack on the synagogue in 1982 and the *Achille Lauro* hijacking in 1985 corresponded – once again – to a time when Arafat's leadership was challenged.

Consequently, these events should not be interpreted as the end of the agreement between the mainstream PLO and Rome that had existed since the early 1970s. Despite Arafat's decline, he maintained a good relationship with Italy, a fact that was emphasized by the way the political elite reacted to the attacks of the early 1980s. The attack against the synagogue and the *Achille Lauro* hijacking were interpreted as 'criminal acts' against the moderates within the PLO and the peace process in the Middle East.[99] The government in Rome accepted the PLO's – and also the PFLP's – denial of any involvement and blamed the *Achille Lauro* affair on a radical fringe of the PLF that was not following Arafat's policy.[100] Moreover, during the *Achille Lauro* hijacking, the Italians denied American arrest warrants for the hijackers and even protected the head of the PLF, Abu Abbas, from US special forces – a move that led to a serious conflict with the Americans while the Israelis accused Rome of having a special arrangement with the PLO. In contrast, Arafat called on the Italian prime minister Benito Craxi to remind him about the deal between Rome and the PLO and Abu Abbas told the hijackers that 'Italy is our friend'. The *Achille Lauro* episode emphasizes the fact that both Rome and the mainstream PLO wanted to honour their good relationship.[101]

Conclusion

Since the early 1970s an agreement has existed between the Italian government and the PLO under Yasser Arafat. This assessment should not be too surprising considering Rome's foreign policy and the strategy and tactics of Arafat's mainstream PLO. For decades, Italy sought a middle ground of non-involvement in the Palestinian–Israeli conflict due to economic, strategic and security considerations. Earlier than many other West European countries, the Italian parliament has given de facto recognition to the PLO and Italian political leaders have categorically criticized Israel's presence in the occupied territories as illegal.[102] The relationship between the PLO and Italy might have resulted in dangerous compromises, 'but they are different from the international support for terrorism and do not reflect Italian cabinets and the PLO going to bed together'.[103] For Arafat an agreement with Rome was a logical step within his larger diplomatic strategy after he recognized the negative consequences of the armed struggle in Europe. Therefore, any pact with Italy fit Arafat's broader policy and is mirrored by several agreements that existed between the PLO and other West European states.

Considering the motivations and reasons for an agreement, the Lodo Moro was not exceptional and its significance should not be exaggerated. Utilizing the Lodo Moro – and the suspected end of it – as a means of understanding the wave of unsolved terrorist attacks and tragic incidents that struck Italy since the late 1970s cannot at present be supported by convincing evidence. In this chapter I have argued that the reasons for the attacks carried out by Palestinian terrorists in Italy since 1973 should be found in the international context and especially in the internal power struggle within the PLO. However, due to a lack of written records many important questions are still shrouded in mystery. As long as no such documents are accessible – and not only for politicians in the parliamentary commissions but also for historians and academics alike – the Libyan connection to the 1980 Bologna bombing or the exact content of the Lodo Moro cannot be fully understood or explained. Moreover, it is not known how many agreements existed and who knew about them – an important question that has not so far been asked. The much-cited telegram from 18 February 1978 suggests the existence of at least two separate deals.

Despite all these uncertainties, theories and assumptions have dominated the political and public discourse for the last decade. Why did Cossiga's statement in 2008 and, especially, the 'discovery' of the February telegram spark such a controversy? One possible answer can be found by looking at the historical context of these revelations. Since 2004, attacks carried out by Islamic terrorists have swept Europe. London, Madrid, Paris, Nice, Istanbul, Berlin – all major European powers fell victim to indiscriminate terrorist attacks with one exception: Italy. Despite the fact that the Vatican or Rome as the 'cradle of Western Civilization' would be a prestigious target for Islamic terrorist organizations, no attack has been carried out in the country as of yet. Italians are wondering why Al-Qaeda as well as the Islamic State in Iraq and Syria (ISIS) have spared their nation. Could it really be that the law enforcement authorities have learned their lesson on how to counter terrorist activities, as the *Süddeutsche Zeitung* recently suggested?[104] Many Italians and scholars seem suspicious: a lack of trust towards state authorities in general and law enforcement in particular, as well as the stereotypical image of Italy as a weak, inefficient and corrupt country still dominate the public discourse. With this in mind, scholars and the public turn to secret pacts and dubious dealings to explain the inexplicable: using every vague indication about the original Lodo Moro, they argue that a secret agreement, a Lodo Moro Due, currently exists between Rome and contemporary Islamic terrorist groups such as Hezbollah, Al-Qaeda and ISIS.[105] Even though this interpretation ignores the differences between the terrorist groups of the 1970s and 1980s and current organizations, for many it is more convincing than assuming that Italian law enforcement agencies have so far been successful in preventing terrorist attacks in their country.

Notes

1 Flaminia Sabatello, Il Lodo Moro e le rivelazioni del magistrato Priore sulla strage di Fiumicino, *L'informale*, 16 December 2015, www.linformale.eu/il-lodo-moro-e-le-rivelazioni-del-magistrato-priore-sulla-strage-di-fiumicino (accessed 1 January 2020); Enthüllungen rund um Aldo Moro: Italiens Geheimabkommen, *Neue Zürcher Zeitung*, 13 May 2016; A 30 anni dall'attacco alla Sinagoga di Roma: che cos'è stato il Lodo Moro, *Mosaico*, 10 October 2012, http://www.mosaico-cem.it/articoli/a-30-anni-dallattacco-alla-sinagoga-di-roma-che-cose-stato-il-lodo-moro (accessed 1 January 2020).

2 Hearing Marco Clementi, 17 June 2015, Commissione Parlamentare di Inchiesta sul rapimento e sulla morte di Aldo Moro, in Atti Parlamentari, Camera dei Deputati,

Senato della Repubblica, XVII Legislatura (henceforth Commissione Moro 2), Resoconto Stenografico, 9; Gilbero Dondi, Patto anti-attentati con i palestinesi: Ecco la prova dell'accordo segreto, *Quotidiano.net*, 8 October 2015, www.quotidiano.net/cronaca/lodo-moro-palestinesi-1.1374442 (accessed 1 January 2020).
3 L'ipotesi di Lucia Annunziata: Un 'Lodo Moro' bis con i terroristi islamici, *L'informale*, 26 August 2016, www.linformale.eu/3681-2 (accessed 1 January 2020).
4 Valerio Cutonilli and Rosario Priore, *I segreti di Bologna: La verità sull'atto terroristico più grave della storia italiana* (Milan: Chiarelettere, 2016).
5 Enthüllungen rund um Aldo Moro: Italiens Geheimabkommen; Alessandro Fulloni, Togliere il segreto al dossier del Lawrence d'Arabia italiano, *La Stampa*, 22 October 2016; L'ultimo segreto nelle carte di Moro: 'La Libia dietro Ustica e Bologna', *La Stampa*, 26 October 2016.
6 Commissione parlamentare d'inchiesta sulla strage di via Fani e sul sequestro e l'assassinio di Aldo Moro e sul terrorismo in Italia, in Atti Parlamentari, Camera dei Deputati, Senato della Repubblica, VIII Legislatura, Doc. XXIII, n. 5 (henceforth Commissione Moro).
7 Commissione parlamentare d'inchiesta sul terrorismo in Italia e sulle cause della mancata individuazione dei responsabili delle stragi, in Atti Parlamentari, Senato della Repubblica, Camera dei Deputati, XIII Legislatura, Doc. XXIII, n. 64 (henceforth Commissione Stragi).
8 Commissione parlamentare d'inchiesta concernente il dossier Mitrokhin e l'attività d'intelligence italiana, in Atti Parlamentari: Senato della Repubblica, Camera dei Deputati, XIV Legislatura (henceforth Commissione Mitrokhin). The commission was set up by the government of Silvio Berlusconi with the clear intention of discrediting leading opposition figures by tying them to the KGB – without providing any clear evidence.
9 Antonio Varsori, The Foreign Policy of the First Republic: New Approaches, *Journal of Modern Italian Studies* 20/3 (2015), 292–7, here 292 and 294.
10 Beatrice De Graaf and Cornel Zwierlein, Historicizing Security – Entering the Conspiracy Dispositive, *Historical Social Research* 38/1 (2013), 46–64, here 56.
11 Bruce Hoffman, *Inside Terrorism* (New York: Columbia University Press, 2006), 63–4.
12 Cited in ibid., 66.
13 Cutonilli and Priore, *I segreti di Bologna*, 45–6.
14 Mark Ensalaco, *Middle Eastern Terrorism: From Black September to September 11* (Philadelphia: University of Philadelphia Press, 2008), 55 and 66.
15 Alfredo Mantica and Vincenzo Fragalà, Il Contesto delle Stragi: Una Cronologia 1968–1975, in Commissione Stragi, Vol. I, Tomo III, 229; Hearing of Rosario Priore, 11 November 1999, in Commissione Stragi, Vol. II, Tomo IV, 516.
16 Atti Parlamentari, Camera dei Deputati, Discussioni, Resoconto Stenografico (henceforth Camera, Discussioni), VI Legislatura, 18 December 1973, 11943; see also Ensalaco, *Middle Eastern Terrorism*, 66–7.
17 Tobias Hof, *Staat und Terrorismus 1969–1982* (Munich: Oldenbourg, 2011), 44–66.
18 Contulli and Priore, *I segreti di Bologna*, 52–6.
19 Gabriele Paradisi, La strage? Figlia del tradimento del 'lodo Moro', *Il Tempo*, 11 October 2013. Since August 1972 the Italian police has known that Saleh was a member of the PFLP. See Questore Iaselli, Telegramma al Ministero dell'Interno, Perugia, 10 August 1972, in Commissione Mithrokin, Document 249.6.
20 Hearing of Rosario Priore, 17 December 2014, in Commissione Moro 2, Resoconto Stenografico, 14–15; Cutonilli and Priore, *I segreti di Bologna*, 56–60.

21 Varsori, The Foreign Policy of the First Republic, 294.
22 Luigi Vittorio Ferraris, *Manuale della politica estera italiana: 1947–1993* (Rome: Laterza, 1996), 206–8; Christopher Duggan, *The Forces of Destiny: A History of Italy since 1796* (London: Penguin Books, 2008), 555.
23 Cyrus Sulzberger, Foreign Affairs: The Panga-Wielders and NATO, *New York Times*, 26 November 1958; Cyrus Sulzberger, Foreign Affairs: Summarizing an Italian Inquiry, *New York Times*, 1 December 1958; Cyrus Sulzberger, Foreign Affairs: How Italy Hopes to Help the Arabs, *New York Times*, 25 July 1959.
24 Ferraris, *Manuale della politica estera*, 166–71.
25 Pier Angelo Toninelli, Energy and the Puzzle of Italy's Economic Growth, *Journal of Modern Italian Studies* 15/1 (2010), 107–27, here 123; Paolo Malanima and Vera Zanagni, Introduction: 150 Years of Italian Economy, 1861–2010, *Journal of Modern Italian Studies* 15/1 (2010), 1–20, here 8 and 10; Raymond Lubitz, *The Italian Economic Crises of the 1970s*, International Finance Discussion Papers, No. 120, June 1978, 32.
26 Ferraris, *Manuale della politica estera*, 266.
27 Ibid., 235. Some journalists describe the continuing deals between Rome and Gaddafi as the first Lodo Moro. See Italia, il primo Lodo Moro fu con la Libia di Gheddafi, *La Stampa*, 24 May 2016; Così nel '71 bloccammo un golpe Gheddafi, *La Stampa*, 26 August 2016.
28 Mantica and Fragalà, Il Contesto delle Stragi, 160 and 236.
29 Contulli and Priore, *I segreti di Bologna*, 92.
30 Ferraris, *Manuale della politica estera*, 270.
31 Paola Gaspardis, *Lo status dell'OLP nella diplomazia italiana* (Siena: Prospettiva Editrice, 2009), 26.
32 Cutonilli and Priore, *I segreti di Bologna*, 52 and 56.
33 Lodo Moro, la verità dello 007 che lo negoziò, http://www.pierolaporta.it/lodo-moro-la-verita-dello-007-che-lo-negozio (accessed 1 January 2020).
34 Il nostro agente è svelto come un missile, *L'Espresso*, 27 January 1980, 8.
35 Ibid., 8 and 10; Cutonilli and Priore, *I segreti di Bologna*, 51; Mantica and Fragalà, Il Contesto delle Stragi, 222 and 228.
36 Hoffman, *Inside Terrorism*, 63 and 79.
37 Barry Rubin and Judith Colp Rubin, *Yasir Arafat: A Political Biography* (Oxford: Oxford University Press, 2003), 38.
38 Jean Zieglers geheime Mission, *Neue Zürcher Zeitung*, 20 January 2016.
39 Zwei Namen mit Sprengkraft, *Neue Zürcher Zeitung*, 29 December 2016; Interdepartementale Arbeitsgruppe '1970' (IDA 1970), *Schlussbericht*, Eidgenössisches Departement für auswärtige Angelegenheiten (EDA), Berne, 3 May 2016, https://www.eda.admin.ch/content/dam/eda/de/documents/publications/Geschichte/interdepartementale-arbeitsgruppe-1970_de.pdf (accessed 1 January 2020).
40 Hearing of Rosario Priore, 15 December 2014, in Commissione Moro 2, Resoconto Stenografico, 15–16; Cutonilli and Priore, *I segreti di Bologna*, 43–4.
41 Hoffman, *Inside Terrorism*, 79–80.
42 Ibid., 72; Cutonilli and Priore, *I segreti di Bologna*, 33; Shaul Mishal, *The PLO under Arafat: Between Gun and Olive Branch* (New Haven: Yale University Press, 1986), 42.
43 Ibid., 43–4; Hearing of Paolo Emilio Taviani, 1 July 1997, in Commissione Stragi, 385.
44 Rubin and Rubin, *Yasir Arafat*, 60–1.
45 Hoffman, *Inside Terrorism*, 80.

46 Il nostro agente è svelto come un missile, 10; Mishal, *The PLO under Arafat,* 21-3 and 43.
47 Ibid., 51.
48 Thomas Skelton-Robinson, Im Netz verheddert: Die Beziehungen des bundesdeutschen Linksterrorismus zur Volksfront für die Befreiung Palästinas (1969-1980), in Wolfgang Kraushaar (ed.), *Die RAF und der linke Terrorismus* (Hamburg: Hamburger Edition, 2006), 828-904; Tom Parker and Nick Sitter, The Four Horsemen of Terrorism: It's Not Waves, It's Strains, *Terrorism and Political Violence* 28/2 (2016), 197-216, here 201.
49 Agostino Giovagnoli, *Il caso Moro: Una tragedia italiana* (Bologna: Il Mulino, 2005), 25-38; Pino Casamassima, *Il libro nero delle Brigate Rosse: Gli episodi e le azioni della più nota organizzazione armata dagli 'anni di piombo' fino ai nostri giorni* (Rome: Newton Compton, 2007), 146-202.
50 Le Br. Io e le vedo cosi, *L'Espresso*, 10 January 1982, 8.
51 Sergio Flamigni, *La tela del ragno: il delitto Moro* (Milano: Kaos, 1988); Sergio Flamigni, *Il covo di Stato* (Milano: Kaos, 1999); Sergio Flamigni, *La sfinge delle Brigate rosse* (Milano: Kaos, 2004); Sergio Flamigni, *Le idi di marzo: Il delitto Moro secondo Mino Pecorelli* (Milano: Kaos, 2006).
52 See Regine Igel, *Terrorjahre: Die dunkle Seite der CIA in Italien* (Munich: Herbig, 2006); Regine Igel, Linksterrorismus fremdgesteuert? Die Kooperation von RAF, Roten Brigaden, CIA und KGB, *Blätter für deutsche und internationale Politik* 10 (2007), 1221-35; Daniele Ganser, *NATO's Secret Armies: Operation Gladio and Terrorism in Western Europe* (London: Routledge, 2005).
53 Richard Drake, *The Aldo Moro Murder Case* (Cambridge: Harvard University Press, 1995).
54 Ibid., 82-3; Richard Drake, The Aldo Moro Murder Case as Politics, in George Kassimeris (ed.), *Playing Politics with Terrorism: A User's Guide* (New York: Columbia University Press, 2007), 36-61, here 45.
55 Hearing of Giulio Grassini, 1 July 1980, in Commissione Moro, Vol. IV, 205; Sequestro Moro, le rivelazioni sul ruolo dei leader palestinesi, *Corriere della Sera*, 22 December 2016.
56 Paradisi, La strage? Figlia del tradimento del 'lodo Moro', *Il Tempo*, 11 October 2013.
57 Cutonilli and Priore, *I segreti di Bologna*, 70; Giuseppe Fioroni, Relazione sull'attività svolta, 10 December 2015, in Commissione Moro 2, Doc. XXIII, n. 10, 130-1.
58 Hearing of Rosario Priore, in Commissione Moro 2, 6-9.
59 Gero Grassi, Aldo Moro, l'Europa e il Mare Mediterraneo, 31 August 2016, http://www.gerograssi.it/cms2/index.php?option=com_content&task=view&id=6203&Itemid=149 (accessed 1 January 2020); Robert Katz, *Days of Wrath: The Ordeal of Aldo Moro, the Kidnapping, the Execution, the Aftermath* (Garden City: Doubleday, 1980), 264.
60 Translation from Italian by the author. The telegram can be found in Fioroni, Relazione sull'attività svolta, 130-1; Cutonilli and Priore, *I segreti di Bologna*, 263.
61 Hearing of Marco Clementi, 9.
62 In 1980 the Italian ambassador in Lebanon, Stefano D'Andrea – always considered to be an adversary of Giovannone – admitted to an agreement with the PLO. However, he denied any cooperation with the PFLP (Cutonilli and Priore, *I segreti di Bologna*, 103). D'Andrea's statement also seems to prove the existence of two different channels to the heterogeneous PLO.

63 Servizio per le Informazioni e la Sicurezza Militare, Rapporto per l'inchiesta parlamentare sulla strage di Via Fani sul sequestro e l'assassinio di Aldo Moro, in Commissione Moro, Vol. CVI (henceforth Rapporto SISMI), 9.
64 Hearing of Giuseppe Santovito, 1 July 1980, in Commissione Moro, Vol. IV, 183.
65 Vladimiro Satta, *Il caso Moro e I suoi falsi misteri* (Saverio Mannelli: Rubbettino, 2006), 440–9; see also Hearing of Marco Clementi, 10–11.
66 Cited in Katz, *Days of Wrath*, 264.
67 Hearing of Giuseppe Santovito, 1 July 1980, in Commissione Moro, Vol. IV, 182–3; Rapporto SIMSI, 57–8 and 65; Documentazione pervenuta alla Commissione del SISDE, in Commissione Moro, Vol. XXVIII, 27; Katz, *Days of Wrath*, 263.
68 Cutonilli and Priore, *I segreti di Bologna*, 74–7.
69 Hof, *Staat und Terrorismus*, 211–20 and 319–21.
70 Hearing of Francesco Cossiga, 26 February 2004, in Commissione Mitrokhin, Resoconto Stenografico, 14.
71 For conspiracy theories and the Moro kidnapping, see Tobias Hof, The Moro Affair – Left-Wing Terrorism and Conspiracy in Italy in the Late 1970s, *Historical Social Research* 38/1 (2013), 232–57; Vittorio Coco, Conspiracy Theories in Republican Italy: The Pellegrino Report to the Parliamentary Commission on Terrorism, *Journal of Modern Italian Studies* 20/3 (2015), 361–76.
72 Abu Iyad propagated this theory for the first time in an interview in the *Corriere del Ticino* on 19 September 1980. See Commissione Stragi, XI. Legislatura, Doc. XXIII, n. 13, 76.
73 Cutonilli and Priore, *I segreti di Bologna*, 13–15 and 25–6. The incident was briefly mentioned in Relazione sulla politica informativa e della sicurezza e sui risultati ottenuti, in Atti Parlamentari, Camera dei Deputati, VIII Legislatura, Doc. LI, n. 3, 11.
74 Salvatore Sechi, Strage di Bologna, chi ha sottovalutato la pista palestinese e perché, in Commissione Moro 2, Doc. 547/1, 6.
75 Ibid., 6, 10 and 13; Cutonilli and Priore, *I segreti di Bologna*, 100, 150–1 and 235.
76 For example, he based his argument predominantly on a document that is undated. Even though he acknowledged that problem, he used the telegram nonetheless to prove his thesis. See Cutonilli and Priore, *I segreti di Bologna*, 105, 159 and 266. Incorrect information, which undermines Priore's credibility, can be found in the footnotes of Cutonilli and Priore, *I segreti di Bologna*, 52, 56 and 100.
77 Ibid., 101.
78 Il nostro agente è svelto come un missile, 7.
79 Cutonilli and Priore, *I segreti di Bologna*, 216–17.
80 Ibid., 171 and 184.
81 Relazione sulla politica informativa e della sicurezza e sui risultati ottenuti, in Atti Parlamentari, Camera dei Deputati, VIII Legislatura, Doc. LI, n. 5, 22 May 1981, 23.
82 Hof, *Staat und Terrorismus*, 48–54.
83 To support his argument, however, Priore claimed that the Oktoberfest bombing in Munich (1980) was also committed by Libya without providing any convincing evidence for his far-reaching thesis. See Cutonilli and Priore, *I segreti di Bologna*, 197 and 214.
84 For his arguments, see Ibid., 123–4.
85 Ferraris, *Manuale della politica estera*, 378, also claimed that this discovery strained the relations between Rome and the PLO.

86 See Relazione sulla politica informativa e della sicurezza e sui risultati ottenuti, in Atti Parlamentari, Camera dei Deputati, VIII Legislatura, Doc. LI, n. 1, 22 May 1979, 12; Ibid., n. 2, 22 November 1979, 9.
87 Hearing of Giuseppe Santovito, 166–7, 170 and 187; Hearing of Giulio Grassini, 211.
88 Commissione Moro, Vol LIV, 292–3.
89 Il nostro agente è svelto come un missile, 7.
90 A 30 anni dall'attacco alla Sinagoga di Roma: che cos'è stato il Lodo Moro, *Mosaico*, 10 October 2012, www.mosaico-cem.it/articoli/a-30-anni-dallattacco-alla-sinagoga-di-roma-che-cose-stato-il-lodo-moro (accessed 1 January 2020).
91 During Moro's kidnapping Cossiga was approached by the PLO. Therefore, it is possible that he knew about the contacts between the PLO and the far left or even about the contacts between the Italian secret service and the PLO already in 1978. See Sequestro Moro, le rivelazioni sul ruolo dei leader palestinesi, *Corriere della Sera*, 22 December 2016.
92 Priore argued that the Italians gave the names of the dissidents to Gaddafi to improve the relations with Libya in a time of crisis. However, he did not provide substantial evidence for his claims (Cutonilli and Priore, *I segreti di Bologna*, 119). It is certain, though, that the Italian secret services were concerned about the killings of Libyan dissidents and indirectly blamed Gaddafi for the murders. See Relazione sulla politica informativa e della sicurezza e sui risultati ottenuti, in Atti Parlamentari, Camera dei Deputati, VIII Legislatura, Doc. LI, n. 3, 22 May 1980, 11; Ibid., n. 4, 22 November 1980, 8 and 15.
93 On the relations between Italy and the Arab countries, see Ferraris, *Manuale della politica estera*, 377–95.
94 Even Priore speculated that Bologna might have been Gaddafi's personal retaliation act against Italy (Cutonilli and Priore, *I segreti di Bologna*, 143).
95 Ensalaco, *Middle Eastern Terrorism*, 164–8.
96 Relazione sulla politica informativa e della sicurezza e sui risultati ottenuti, in Atti Parlamentari, Camera dei Deputati, VIII Legislatura, Doc. LI, n. 1, 22 May 1979, 13 and 15; Ibid., n. 2, 22 November 1979, 9.
97 Milash, *The PLO under Arafat*, 86.
98 Ibid., 65–70 and 165.
99 Camera, Discussioni, VIII Legislature, 11 October 1982, 52715–16.
100 Camera, Discussioni, IX Legislature, 8 October 1985, 31850–1.
101 Michael K. Bohn, *The Achille Lauro Hijacking: Lessons in the Politics and Prejudice of Terrorism* (Washington, DC: Potomac Books, 2004), 12, 21, 34, 39 and 42.
102 Francesco Sidoti, Terrorism Supporters in the West: The Italian Case, in Noemi Gal Or (ed.), *Tolerating Terrorism in the West: An International Survey* (London: Routledge, 1991), 105–43, here 129.
103 Ibid., 128.
104 Grazie mille, Signori, *Süddeutsche Zeitung*, 24, 25 and 26 December 2016, 3.
105 Riccardo Ghezzi, L'ipotesi di Lucia Annunziata: Un 'Lodo Moro' bis con i terroristi islamici, *L'informale*, 26 August 2016, www.linformale.eu/3681-2 (accessed 1 January 2020).

Chapter 7

PACT WITH THE (UN)WANTED?

THE WISCHNEWSKI PROTOCOL AS A SPOTLIGHT
FOR AUSTRO-GERMAN 'AGREEMENTS' WITH
TRANSNATIONAL TERRORISTS IN THE LATE 1970S

Matthias Dahlke

A substantial part of the 1970s anti-terrorism diplomacy took place in secret and informal settings. Traces of such activities are thus rarely found in the archives. In 2008, a remarkable document was rather accidentally found in the archives of the Friedrich Ebert Foundation in Bonn where the records of the Social Democratic Party of Germany (SPD)'s secret diplomat and state minister for special tasks Hans-Jürgen Wischnewski are collected. This rare discovery, the extensive 'Wischnewski Protocol', provides hard evidence concerning agreements between the Austrian government and terrorists, with an additional involvement of German representatives.[1]

This chapter will thus introduce a very special episode in German–Austrian counterterrorism activities in the late 1970s, gliding along the outstanding source of the Wischnewski Protocol. This protocol was written as a record of a secret top-level 'trilateral' meeting in Vienna in November 1977. Since the protocol is very condensed and hard to understand without a certain framing, this chapter will first provide some background information on the events and protagonists, and then move on to an in-depth analysis of motivations, interests and results.

The source itself is an extensive protocol of a secret meeting between Palestinian terrorists and Western government representatives on 24 November 1977 in Vienna. One day before the meeting, Minister Wischnewski received a confidential phone call from the Austrian capital and learned that a secret meeting was about to take place. He sent a very close staff member to attend the meeting as his envoy and to subsequently write a protocol report for Federal chancellor Helmut Schmidt. Wischnewski obviously kept a private copy of this protocol, which made its way to the archives of the Friedrich Ebert Foundation.

The Wischnewski Protocol is a spotlight – no more, no less. There have been a number of public conjectures pertaining to the existence of cooperation with terrorists, but solid evidence remained yet to be found. As a result, scholars felt compelled to rely either on oral sources from intelligence circles (not always beyond all doubts) or statements by high-ranking politicians. One example might be a remark made by the certainly well-informed Saudi oil minister Ahmed Zaki Yamani: 'There is some sort of agreement or gentlemen's agreement, if you will, that terrorists will not operate inside Austria.'[2] Speculations on a kind of 'state sanctioned anarchism'[3] as a determining factor for the outcome of events date back to as far as the extorted release of the terrorists who perpetrated the Munich massacre in 1972 by means of an airplane hijacking to Zagreb. Not only do the Palestinian terrorists confirm speculations about collusion between terrorists and West European governments in the Wischnewski Protocol, but it also becomes clear that the Austrian government did not object: 'Cooperation with Austria was already agreed upon.'[4]

Why precisely did such a 'pact with the devil' come to pass in 1977? What interests did the Austrian chancellor Bruno Kreisky pursue? What role did Germany play? And how does the Wischnewski Protocol blend in with the development of the anti-terrorism policies of the 1970s in Western Europe?

The year 1977 – at the peak of terrorism

The year 1977 was the climax and turning point of terrorist violence in Germany as well as in a number of other countries. More than fifty attacks on people and objects were documented by the 'official calendar of terrorist events'[5] in Germany alone. The 'German Autumn', which, contrary to the popular belief at the time, was neither particularly German nor seasonally bound, has become a constituent part of German collective memory. The tragic course of events is still well known to the broad public thirty years later: Attorney General Siegfried Buback was shot in his car in April; in July, the CEO of the Dresdner Bank, Jürgen Ponto, died during an attempted abduction and though a 'rocket' launch attack on the Attorney General's Office in Karlsruhe in August ultimately failed, it amplified a lasting impression of escalating violence in Germany. In September, the events culminated in the abduction of Hanns Martin Schleyer, who served as president of the Confederation of German Employers' Associations and the Federation of German Industries. The action had one goal: forcing the German government to release leading imprisoned Red Army Faction (RAF) members. A Palestinian group of terrorists hijacked the Lufthansa aircraft 'Landshut' to further substantiate that demand.

While German decision-makers had chosen to make concessions almost unconditionally[6] during the 1972 Summer Olympics attacks and the 1975 kidnapping of conservative CDU politician Peter Lorenz, they now pursued an agenda of not giving in. Discussions on counterterrorism strategies included options such as retaliatory measures towards the RAF detainees that may even have stretched the limits of the legal system and the rule of law too far.[7] In the case of the attack on the German Embassy in Stockholm in 1975, Chancellor Schmidt had left the responsibility of solving the problem with the Swedish government and therefore dared to take a first step in the direction of not negotiating with terrorists. Even the disastrous outcome of his decision (with several dead and severely wounded hostages and terrorists)[8] did not make the German government change its new approach, as can clearly be seen in 1977: the German government was adamant in maintaining its chosen course of action during the kidnapping of the 'Landshut' aircraft, and after a spectacular rescue mission by the GSG 9 in the Somali capital of Mogadishu they managed to free the passengers in October 1977. Minister Wischnewski played a significant role as a direct observer and special negotiator on the scene. The RAF prisoners in Stuttgart Stammheim then committed suicide under dubious circumstances, and manhunts of unprecedented size and effort[9] were carried out in the whole of Germany. In retrospect it becomes clear that this took the sting out of the steadily swelling wound of left-wing terrorism.

As events escalated, fundamental questions regarding counterterrorism measures arose as well. For instance, the question was raised whether the setting up of databases by the *Bundeskriminalamt* (Federal Criminal Police Office) would turn out to be a threat to civil rights rather than an opportunity to strengthen investigation efforts: allegedly, excessively harsh measures 'eroded the legitimacy of state leadership, or rather the state's capacity to solve societal problems',[10] and new ways of government action had to be found.[11]

Although the drastic events of 1977 in Germany are outstanding, it is important to broaden perspectives instead of focusing solely on Germany and left-wing terrorism. The transnational range of action and interdependences of the wide variety of terrorist actors is visible in many more cases than just the odyssey of the 'Landshut' plane from Majorca to Mogadishu. The picture is similar in the kidnapping of Schleyer, who was taken from Cologne to The Hague and Brussels only to be found murdered in the French city of Mulhouse.[12] Neither was German terrorism in 1977 a singularity. Several other countries faced serious terrorist threats in 1977 as well, for example, the Netherlands: 1977 was not the only year in which German RAF terrorists shot and killed Dutch police officers. RAF terrorists also hid their prominent hostage Schleyer there, and in the very same year South Moluccan terrorists invaded a school and a train and took 150 people hostage in the eastern parts of the kingdom. Spain was faced with the atrocities of the 1977 Massacre of Atocha, in which transnational right-wing terrorists murdered communist trade unionists. In Austria, the industrial magnate Walter Palmers was kidnapped by the 2 June Movement. In Paris, a bomb detonated at the gourmet food supermarket Fauchon, and even in Moscow three bombs that can allegedly be traced back to Armenian terrorists exploded in the metro.

How did European governments deal with these differently perceived threats? Almost all European countries were affected by terrorist acts to a greater or lesser extent since the early 1970s. Facing these challenges, they developed and implemented different anti-terrorism measures according to the demands of their national history paths.[13] Given the post-Second World War security architecture, Germany chose the decentralized approach of *Innere Sicherheit* ('inner security'), primarily implemented by the German *Länder* (federal states).

Despite very different national approaches to countering terrorism in practice, and after several years of experience with terrorist attacks, an international consensus took shape around the year 1976 that terrorist attacks were no singular events and that this 'recent' phenomenon would not disappear of its own accord. From around 1975-6, European countries enhanced international anti-terrorism collaboration,[14] thus bringing together their respective approaches. This consequently led to the emergence of the now globally prevailing dictum of not negotiating with terrorists.[15]

The 'honest broker' Kreisky and his guests

Other than the fact that it was Kreisky who would act as host when the diverse group met on 24 November 1977 in Vienna, nothing seemed to be set in stone. All participants kept their cards close to their chests, and everyone had a different motive. But who took the initiative? Which underlying interdependences became apparent in this meeting?

For Wischnewski, the encounter seemed to have a spontaneous and rather informal tone. In the accompanying letter to Helmut Schmidt, which included the protocol, he commented that Kreisky, over the telephone, had informed him only the day before, in a rather 'cautious manner' that 'he was hosting guests from a region he and I are very familiar with and that they plan on disclosing a message most crucial for the government'. Under the condition of 'absolute secrecy', Wischnewski was advised to send a personal representative to Vienna.[16] Wischnewski sent his closest staff member, Peter Kiewitt.

According to the protocol, this international gathering between the representatives of Austria, Germany and the PLO was merely one of several meetings. However, as it seems, Wischnewski was not involved in the manifold preparatory work and exploratory talks. A few weeks prior to these negotiations, a meeting took place between PLO representatives and Willy Brandt, the leader of the ruling SPD, which subsequently led 'the PLO leadership to the conclusion that Germany might be willing to cooperate with the PLO in one way or another'.[17] Brandt as well as Germany's federal government and the SPD 'have hitherto adopted a constructive attitude'.[18] The SPD chairman had wished for a political 'gesture',[19] and PLO leader Yasser Arafat had every intention of fulfilling such a wish with the meeting in Vienna.

Therefore, it seems eminently reasonable to believe that the German representative was not only an observer but also the political target during the talk mediated by Kreisky. The fact that the Austrian Federal Chancellor had addressed the previously uninvolved Wischnewski, who, in turn, sent the protocol to Schmidt rather than to Brandt points to a less than ideal coordination between the SPD leadership and the federal government.

Kreisky, of course, was not solely motivated by his function as an 'honest broker'. He also pursued vested interests in the planning and success of the negotiations. These interests were closely connected to the ongoing threat of terrorist attacks

Austria was exposed to – a series of events, which subsequently paved the way for a comprehensive Austrian counterterrorism policy. Two attacks in particular forced the Austrian government to adopt a strategic position: in 1973, a number of Jewish transit passengers from the Eastern bloc were taken hostage at the train station at the border town of Marchegg. In this instance, Kreisky decided to meet the terrorists' demands with the counterproposal of closing a transit facility in Schönau Castle set up by the Austrian government for Jewish emigrants. Despite protests throughout the world, the transit of Jews through Austria was, in fact, never stopped. The transit centre was set up in a different location a few months later, but this time without public attention or media coverage. By implication, Kreisky had managed to de-medialize and de-symbolize the Jewish transit. This ultimately reduced security dangers not only to the transit passengers but also for Austria itself.

The second prominent event was the attack on the OPEC Ministerial Conference in Vienna in December 1975. More than sixty hostages were taken, among them eleven oil ministers. The perpetrators were a multinational terrorist group led by the infamous Carlos, a Venezuelan terrorist working for Waddie Haddad's Popular Front for the Liberation of Palestine-Special Operations Group (PFLP-SOG). The decision on how to eventually deal with the OPEC attack was highly influenced by the events of Marchegg of 1973, and an already failed and amateurish attempt to free the hostages taken by Carlos. The government, initially without, and finally with, Kreisky's involvement, complied with the demands of the terrorists. Among others, they demanded a public broadcast of a reading of their proclamation, which happened to be written in French. During this incident, too, it could clearly be seen that Kreisky was more interested in ensuring a smooth handling of the hostage-taking and a dispersion of responsibility than in a confrontation with the terrorists. His amicable contacts with Algeria in particular made a relatively mild outcome possible; it is highly likely a ransom was paid by Saudi Arabia or Iran (presumably the main targets of the attack) and all hostages were released.

It did, however, require the 'German Autumn' and the Palmers kidnapping in 1977 before the special unit 'Cobra', a counterpart of the German special unit GSG9, was founded as a successor to its preceding task forces. Kreisky's previous anti-terrorism diplomacy, which was characterized by a willingness for broad concessions in 1973 and 1975, proved to be less haphazard and reactive than is often perceived. On the contrary, there are clear indications that, hidden from the public sphere, Kreisky was actively working on anti-terrorism policies. In the aftermath of Marchegg, he increasingly invited Arabic heads of state or government to Vienna – acts always understood as an integral part of his security policy.[20] His seemingly lenient, but ultimately resolute, stance towards transnational terrorists provided him with attention and influence within the Arab world in particular. After Marchegg 1973, Kreisky proposed *Fact-Finding-Missions* to be set up by the Socialist International (SI).[21] Under this umbrella, he was more and more able to be involved in the developments in the Middle East as a renowned European Middle East expert – which last but not least was also an advantage for Austria's economic policy and security.

Given this background, at least one consultation took place between Kreisky and the PLO representative Issam Sartawi before the Wischnewski Protocol meeting in Vienna. This prior meeting resulted 'in the agreement that the PLO should assist Europe in the fight against terrorism. The Central Committee of the PLO accordingly decided to provide the Austrian public security institutions with information and aid in countering terrorist acts.' Moreover, 'Austrian Chancellor Kreisky wanted to extend this cooperation to the Federal Republic of Germany'. 'The PLO leadership', said Sartawi, 'did not mention any substantial contradictions to this suggestion.'[22]

Kreisky apparently arranged this meeting as part of a long-term counterterrorism policy, which was dominated by a foreign policy approach – bearing in mind that his political success largely depended on broad international acceptance of the PLO, including the recognition by Germany. As a prerequisite for this, the PLO had to reconsider some of its positions; at that time it had not only started to revise its political terrorism strategies but also considered setting up 'a sort of headquarters on neutral ground. Vienna seemed suitable based on the positive attitude of Chancellor Kreisky'.[23] Kreisky's 'internationalization strategy',[24] which generally meant to make neutral Austria as internationally interconnected as possible, could hence profit from the transformation within the new PLO.

Kreisky also made sure to avoid potential surprises. To that end, he pointed out to Israeli representatives that a meeting with wanted terrorists would take place under his watch and responsibility in Vienna. The protocol states: 'Upon notification of Chancellor Kreisky, Israeli intelligence is aware of their stay in Vienna; the Israelis did, however, discontinue their investigations on his request.'[25]

For the German side, cooperation with the PLO was not quite as self-evident. For Bonn, the relations with Israel were more 'important' for historical reasons – despite their being less privileged than previously conceived, as could be seen by the example of the Olympic Games massacre of 1972 and the following rift with Israel. With the prohibition of the General Union of Palestinian Students/Workers, the first established, albeit unofficial, PLO office in Bonn was closed down after the attack during the 1972 Olympics, and the PLO representative Abdallah Frangi was expelled from the country despite significant protests.[26] Also, in Western Germany there were no prominent advocates (like Kreisky in Austria) devoted to furthering Arab interests – merely a few well-informed and interested politicians, such as Hans-Jürgen Wischnewski or Hans-Eberhard Dingels from the SPD party headquarters, who, rather, played a (albeit important) background role. On the part of the CDU, Gerhard Schröder, who spontaneously met Arafat in 1974 when he was head of the Foreign Affairs Committee, has to be mentioned.[27] Even Willy Brandt participated only in significant Middle East activities when he was head of the SI. Once he did, however, his involvement was all the more dedicated – not least because he was clearly influenced by Kreisky. As chancellor (1969–74), Brandt had made official visits to Israel, and mediated between Golda Meïr and Kreisky at the 1973 meeting of the SI in London, which was crucial for European Middle East politics. Constantly striving for international reconciliation and being a fervent fighter against National Socialism, Brandt said in his memoirs that 'hardly any topic [...] was burdening more than the fraught and tense relationship between Israel and its Arabic neighbors'.[28] Despite searching for compromise, his heart obviously belonged more to the Israeli side.

Unlike Austria, the German willingness to enter into dialogue with the PLO terrorists did not have its roots in a lengthy prehistory of strong links and close contacts to the Arafat organization, but, rather, in the emergency situation that was the 'German Autumn'. It was these circumstances that caused Wischnewski not to hesitate when Kreisky approached him with his invitation.

Finally, the Austrian Chancellor Kreisky, his Minister for the Interior, three employees of the Federal Ministry of the Interior, the German envoy sent by Wischnewski and two high-ranking PLO representatives (who were wanted terrorists) attended the secret meeting in November 1977. On the PLO side, the first to be mentioned is Ali Hassan Salameh,[29] 'crown prince' of Yasser Arafat, security chief and 'Minister for the Interior' of the PLO. He was also responsible for the personal safety and the legendary bodyguards of Arafat. In the press he was nicknamed 'Red Prince' or 'Abu Hassan' and presumed to be the co-organizer pulling the strings behind numerous attacks – among them the Munich massacre during the 1972 Summer Olympics, which caught him in the crosshairs of Israeli countermeasures: in 1973, Israeli operatives 'accidentally' killed a Moroccan waiter they mistook for Ali Hassan Salameh in Norwegian Lillehammer.[30] It was not until 1979 that the Mossad succeeded in assassinating the heavily guarded PLO security chief in Beirut with a car bomb, which left eight people dead and at least twice that number wounded.[31] The current co-editor of the *Washington Post*, David Ignatius, who worked as a Middle East correspondent for the *Wall Street Journal* in the 1970s, reported that Ali Hassan Salameh maintained contact with the United States going as far back as 1970. This thesis was verified and expanded through written primary sources in 2014: the first contact between the CIA and Salameh was made as early as 1969.[32] In 1974, this contact was extended to a 'mutual non-aggression pact'[33] on the occasion of Arafat's United Nations address. These findings seem to confirm that Salameh was not only experienced at PLO-related secret diplomacy but also had excellent relations with Western governments.

The second Palestinian at the table was the physician Dr Issam al-Sartawi, a close consultant of Arafat for Western Europe and the United States. By his own account, he was 'authorized by the PLO leadership'[34] to attend the meetings. He had represented the PLO at the SI and 'never hid the fact that for some time, he believed, only violence and terror could lead to a satisfactory outcome for the Palestinians'.[35] In 1979, together with the Israeli Lova Eliav, Kreisky proposed him as a nominee for the first Bruno Kreisky Prize for Services to Human Rights. Over time, Sartawi turned his back on the terrorist strategy. This presumably led to his assassination by the ANO[36] during a SI conference in the Portuguese city of Albufeira in 1983.

PLO proposals to Western Germany

According to the wording of the protocol, the meeting aimed primarily at a more substantial cooperation between the PLO and Germany. It remains open whether this impression is altered by the perspective of the protocol's author or by the simple fact that there was a lesser need to talk about Kreisky's concerns as the PLO and Austria had already entered into intense talks. At any rate, the PLO representatives declared outright that Germany, in its function 'as the strongest nation in Western Europe',[37] played a pivotal key role in their urge to gain international recognition.

> The PLO considers a generally positive attitude by Germany to be crucial regarding the positioning of the other Western European countries. Should the EC [European Communities] member states – e.g. within the scope of the EPC [European Political Cooperation] – reveal an intention to recognize the PLO, it would, according to the PLO's opinion greatly encourage the American administration to take steps accordingly.[38]

So far, US President Jimmy Carter had been most accommodating towards the Palestinian cause, but he still did not speak out in favour of recognizing the State of Palestine, the Palestinian envoys explained. The position adopted by the United States was 'ambivalent', said Sartawi; this could clearly be seen when considering 'that the American government holds talks [with the PLO] but prefers to do so in Paris rather than Washington'.[39] A recognition of the PLO by Western Europe, triggered by German advocacy, would have a positive impact on the United States as well.

The offer made by the PLO, in case cooperation could be agreed on, was unambiguous:

> The PLO [would] change its previous policies, and instead of [only] distancing itself from terrorist acts, they would, on the basis of its intimate knowledge – notably of the European terrorist scene, actively participate in the fight against terrorism.[40]

Moreover, 'the PLO security forces have all the necessary documents to make it largely impossible to carry out terrorist acts in the future'.[41] Salameh also alluded to internal knowledge he had regarding the kidnapping of Schleyer, which he described as 'a big mistake': 'A new operation could be possible following thorough preparations in approximately 3 months.'[42] 'The most prominent terrorists', however, were now on the run and required 'logistical assistance (flats, documents, etc.)'. The PLO seemed to be very familiar with the West German terrorist scene. This made cooperation, according to Salameh, immensely valuable to the Germans. The author of the protocol wrote:

> This resulted from the immediate personal knowledge the PLO has about all terrorists. He [Salameh] himself lived in Düsseldorf for about a year, and later trained a few of the German terrorists in Palestinian camps. He was aware of the whereabouts of all wanted terrorists connected to the kidnapping of Schleyer.[43]

The German envoy noted on the further remarks concerning the whereabouts of wanted terrorists: 'Italy is apparently of particular importance as a base for international terrorism.'[44] The PLO representatives suggested contacting German security authorities immediately: 'In order to defeat international terrorism effectively, other affected countries have to be included in multilateral covert actions.'[45] Salameh showed an effective understanding of equipping his proposals with a threatening posture:

> After the defeats, suffered in particular because of the German government, individual terrorist groups strive to establish a Terrorist International in order to counteract international efforts in combating terrorism.[46]

According to Salameh, however, there were limitations to the PLO's willingness to cooperate. An extradition of terrorists 'over whom they are currently exercising control'[47] or a change in the position towards Israel was out of the question. Moreover, an extradition of 'German terrorists, who have to be regarded as misguided children,'[48] could not occur. In any case, it would be more effective to work towards a 'changing of minds'.[49] On the other hand Salameh held out the prospect of 'draining terrorism for the upcoming 10 years'[50] by forwarding obtained information to Western European governments and by exerting influence on terrorists. The prerequisite was an 'international approach [...] as terrorists have their bases everywhere'[51] and would support each other logistically.

Simultaneously, the PLO representatives did not hold back on criticism regarding the course of action chosen by German authorities. The German envoy noted:

> The strong security measures and the discussion on strengthening penal law is evaluated as a success by German terrorists. They believe to have disclosed the fascist character of our state. [...] To be successful, we would have to focus to a greater extent on the mindset of the terrorists, who feel like heroes hunted by the entire establishment, and who are, as such, willing to die. The 'Black September' for example, was never an organization; rather, it was a particular mental attitude.[52]

The sole consideration PLO representatives expected in return was 'a certain degree of recognition'[53] and the political backing of Arafat. The point in time was chosen wisely by the PLO. Germany had just emerged from the 'German Autumn' and no one could be sure whether terrorism had reached and surpassed its peak or not. Simultaneously, the Palmers kidnapping in Austria had just ended,[54] and as a result of both these circumstances, the PLO could count on a great willingness of Austrian and West German politicians to tread even the unconventional path of accepting 'pacified' terrorists as allies in the fight against terrorism.

A new PLO

To give sufficient credibility to the proposals made by the PLO representatives, the Palestinians had to make it very clear as to why they, as long-time terrorists, would be worth being considered as a partner by West European governments. Sartawi emphasized that during the last meeting of the 'PLO council in Cairo' a different attitude towards terrorism was adopted.[55] Unlike '4-5 years' ago, when the PLO was 'in a kind of state of war with all other countries outside of the Arab world',[56] their targets now included only military ones and those on Israeli-occupied territories. These early stages were a necessity rather than a mistake. As Salameh emphasized, 'he fully acknowledged all actions he contributed to during the PLO's phase of war'.[57] But now, at a point where the PLO 'has found broad recognition and where they have gotten closer to the goal of establishing their own state',[58] they were pursuing a substantially new course. Terrorist groups in Europe with solely 'nihilistic views' focused on 'the destruction of any kind of order' as opposed to the PLO, which aimed to establish 'state order' and was therefore 'opposed to the terrorists'.[59] Consequently, a fundamental change had to be implemented: 'As yet, the PLO was content to simply observe all terrorist groups without actively engaging in the fight against terror.'[60] This was evidently about to change. However, the PLO envoys restrained themselves immediately and claimed that there was a limit to the PLO's assertiveness:

> The diversity of players makes it difficult to curb terrorist acts; where they can, however, the PLO has exercised its control to prevent a number of [terrorist] acts. [...] Only Palestinian fringe groups and terrorist groups in Germany, France, Japan and Latin America contest this [new] attitude [of the PLO].[61]

Also, 'the PLO has a limited influence'[62] on the terrorist acts committed by Libya and Iraq. Admittedly, the transformation of the revolutionary PLO to a tamed 'representative of legitimate rights of Palestinian citizens'[63] was accompanied by considerable image problems. During the meeting, Arafat's envoy Sartawi emphasized that the PLO's change of course to a 'state-like entity'[64] went hand in hand with the danger of a loss of influence over radicalized groups. In the past, the PLO had helped terrorists and was still deemed 'leader of the revolution'.[65] The PLO was still the organization where all information came together. While the PLO, of course, intended to 'cooperate closely with West European governments in ending the terror',[66] they had to 'uphold the revolutionary image of the PLO in order to utilize this position in combating terrorism'.[67] Arafat and his closest confidants in particular 'endorse a moderate approach. If they cannot assert themselves, extremists who support terror would take over the PLO leadership'.[68]

Interestingly, the PLO representatives did not disguise their legally (and ethically) highly problematic behaviour: 'As proof of the [new] attitude of the PLO' they brought up killing the wire-pullers of the Rome and Athens attacks:[69] 'At the time, Abu Mahmud, a Palestinian who operated in the service of Libya, committed a terror attack for personal reasons and contrary to the interests of the PLO. In order to prevent Abu Mahmud from committing further acts of terror, he was neutralized.'[70]

Considering these statements, Austria's interior minister Erwin Lanc was rather sceptical and wondered whether it was appropriate to recognize the PLO publicly.

Although one is 'in need [of the PLO] [...] to fight terrorism effectively [...] such recognition is a question of domestic rather than foreign policy [...], in particular at a time of elections'.[71] Sartawi countered skilfully that 'progressive European governments [...] could be endangered and even overthrown by acts of terror, but not by recognizing the PLO'.[72] Furthermore, PLO cooperation with Western countries was politically useful for both parties: the state reacts 'harshly' to attacks and 'as a whole, with the support of its population' it moves 'to the political right'[73] – which would be a serious detriment not only to plans made by the PLO but also to the interests of left-wing parties in Europe overall.

In this manner, the PLO tried to show Western governments that their balancing act between revolutionary image and international acceptability could be beneficial for both sides. In return for the political support for Arafat they promised to engage in strategies to actively combat terrorism by utilizing their privileged access. This alleged change from Saul to Paul might not appear convincing nowadays, but at the time, after the circumstances surrounding the 'German Autumn' and the kidnapping of Palmers, they hit the nerve of the West German and Austrian governments and caused a resolution to tread unconventional paths in anti-terrorism policies.

In the aftermath of Vienna

Whether any agreements were reached between Austria, Western Germany and the PLO in Vienna is not on record. The PLO's request for political support was answered, however. In October 1978, the Palestinian observer at the UN Industrial Development Organization in Vienna was given the same rights as all other diplomats in Vienna. The 'information center Palestine' was unofficially authorized as contact office in Germany starting in 1978. In July 1979, Kreisky attracted strong media attention when he invited Arafat and Brandt to Vienna and thus punctuated the fact that the PLO was socially and politically acceptable. It is likely that Kreisky invited the chairman of the SI and Nobel Peace Prize Laureate primarily for reasons of public legitimacy: that Kreisky 'would receive [Arafat] almost like a guest of honor was not agreed upon with Brandt and probably not to his liking'.[74] Thereafter, both countries went their separate ways. In October 1979, Kreisky spoke out in front of the General Assembly of the United Nations and emphasized that Austria now recognized the PLO as the official representative of Palestine. In addition, he provided the 'peculiar explanation'[75] that Austria did not have an international advocate for Austrian independence at the time of National Socialism. In December 1979, Arafat appointed a representative of the PLO to the Austrian government, a move which Kreisky officially took 'note of' in March 1980. The act of recognition was thus finalized. In Germany, however, the PLO was not recognized as the diplomatic representation of Palestine until 1993, just after Israel had formally accepted the PLO as a dialogue partner.

The PLO has, to a certain degree, also fulfilled its part of the deal and did, in fact, help Austrian and German counterterrorism. Sartawi acted as a go-between to link the PLO's security service and Austrian authorities. On several occasions, he relayed information on suspicious movements – often directly to interior minister Erwin Lanc or to the chief of criminal police at Vienna airport. In 1981, Sartawi even provided a questionnaire to assist the interrogation of captured members of the ANO. This passing on of information might have been a significant factor in Sartawi's violent death at the hands of an ANO gunman in 1983. In West Germany on the other hand, the BKA remained in contact with its Palestinian counterparts during the 1980s. Thus, according to Abdallah Frangi, long-time PLO representative in Bonn, it was possible to keep terrorism away from West Germany.[76]

In the long-run evaluation, the Vienna meeting on 24 November 1977 may have had only a mild effect on the fight against transnational terrorism, although it may have prevented a number of attacks. Kreisky had already predicted the things to come at the press conference dealing with the OPEC attack in 1975: 'When terrorist movements begin a process of legalization, new terrorist organizations always emerge in their place.'[77] The vastly more radical ANO gained strength in the shadow of the tamed PLO and carried out attacks primarily against allegedly apostate countrymen. In the year 1981, Vienna was the scene of two attacks of the group: one on Heinz Nittel, president of the Austrian–Israeli Friendship League, and another one on the main synagogue of Vienna, in which two people were killed. Abu Nidal's breakaway organization struck Austria three times between 1981 and 1985, leaving scores dead and wounded. So, in the end, the Palestinians could uphold their side of the bargain only to a certain degree. Austria's security especially was not particularly enhanced, since Arafat never attempted to exercise direct control over the numerous groups his organization was composed of.

Conclusion and evaluation of the Wischnewski Protocol

The Wischnewski Protocol is a spotlight on secret diplomacy in the late 1970s, which alone, of course, cannot answer the many questions pertaining to the dimension of the cooperation between West European governments and terrorists. Other meetings and contact channels, which most probably existed, would have to be taken into consideration to see the bigger picture. At the very least, the Wischnewski Protocol proves that a gathering took place between Western government officials and delegates sent by the PLO who were internationally wanted terrorists. This illustrates that the cooperation between Western governments and transnational terrorists went further than often suspected. The basis for this cooperation consisted of three different 'national' interests overlapping in this agreement. While the PLO, in its efforts to transform its image, hoped to achieve international recognition by mediation through Kreisky, Kreisky, in a second step through Germany, tried to use the same circumstances for a twofold purpose: to enhance his international reputation and to further strengthen his *Internationalisierungspolitik* (internationalization politics), which he considered most crucial for Austrian security.

On the West German side, there was great demand for information from the PLO after the 'German Autumn' – for example, regarding the whereabouts of fugitive RAF terrorists. It must remain open whether there was an opposition between the Federal Chancellery and the SPD leadership. It is without doubt, however, that Willy Brandt with his public meeting with Arafat and Kreisky in Vienna in 1979, and Kreisky with his strategy of gradually recognizing the PLO's mission in Vienna, fulfilled their parts in a 'pact' – whatever the specifications of such a 'pact' might have been. The Palestinians on their side fulfilled their part of the 'pact' as well and helped – to a certain degree – German and Austrian counterterrorism at least in some aspects and for a limited period of time, until more radical Palestinian groups took over the lead in violent actions.

The Wischnewski Protocol reflects clearly the ethical dilemma of dealing with terrorists. From a short-term perspective, the Palestinian insider information most likely did help a lot to counter-terrorism effectively and, eventually, save lives. In the long run, the negative aspects of such a 'deal with the devil' prevail. Such secret deals always bear a certain risk of political blackmail as no political leader wants to be publicly affiliated with terrorists. Also, over time, agreed terms decrease in attractiveness as both sides get used to them. So the trade-off balances keep shifting and ultimately require new negotiations. Kreisky, however, being in the very unenviable position of having to make strategic decisions between bad and worse, literally dared to come to terms with the '(un)wanted' and rendered his country a service, at least for a certain period of time.

Notes

1 See letter of Wischnewski to Schmidt, 25 November 1977, to which a tripartite protocol of the meeting on the day before is attached, in HWAK 863, Archive of Social Democracy at the Friedrich Ebert Foundation, Bonn (henceforth: Wischnewski Protocol). This document was first presented to the public in Matthias Dahlke, *Das Wischnewski-Protokoll: Zur Zusammenarbeit zwischen westeuropäischen Regierungen und transnationalen Terroristen 1977*, Vierteljahrshefte für Zeitgeschichte *(VfZ)* 57/2 (2009), 201–15, and analysed in a broader context in Matthias Dahlke, *Demokratischer Staat und Transnationaler Terrorismus: Drei Wege zur Unnachgiebigkeit in Westeuropa 1972–1975*, PhD thesis, Humboldt University Berlin (Munich: Oldenbourg, 2011). This article is a revised and translated version of the first-mentioned article. Special thanks go to Julia Schulz, Svetozar Dimitrov and Thomas Riegler for their help. Almost all quotes that are presented here in English are, of course, originally in German. The originals can be found in the VfZ article of 2009 mentioned earlier, which is also accessible online. The overarching project was part of a research project at the Institut für Zeitgeschichte (Institute of Contemporary History) Munich-Berlin on counterterrorism policy in Western Europe in the 1970s and 1980s, www.ifz-muenchen.de/forschung/demokratien/projektuebersicht/demokratischer-staat/#c3817 (accessed 5 January 2017), and was generously funded by the Gerda Henkel Foundation in Dusseldorf.
2 Jeffrey Robinson, *Yamani: The Inside Story* (London: Simon & Schuster, 1989), 255.

3 Günter Gaus, Schlapper Staat? *Der Spiegel*, 6 November 1972, 25.
4 Wischnewski Protocol, part I, 1.
5 Official calendar of terrorist events 1967–1980, published by the Federal Ministry of the Interior, printed in Axel Jeschke, Wolfgang Malanowski, *Der Minister und der Terrorist: Gespräche zwischen Gerhart Baum und Horst Mahler* (Reinbek bei Hamburg: Rowohlt, 1980), 155–222.
6 Matthias Dahlke, *Der Anschlag auf Olympia '72: Die politischen Reaktionen auf den internationalen Terrorismus in Deutschland* (Munich: Meidenbauer, 2006); Matthias Dahlke, 'Nur eingeschränkte Krisenbereitschaft': Die staatliche Reaktion auf die Entführung des CDU-Politikers Peter Lorenz 1975, *VfZ* 55/4 (2007), 641–78.
7 Many documents from these days are still classified. The minutes of telephone calls between Helmut Schmidt and the president of the German parliament Karl Carstens give an idea which directions the hard-liners were discussing. Georg Bönisch and Klaus Wiegrefe, Massive Gegendrohung, *Der Spiegel*, 8 September 2008, 48–53.
8 On 24 April 1975, RAF's *Kommando Holger Meins* occupied the West German embassy in Stockholm, Sweden, took twelve hostages, and successively executed two German diplomats when their demands were not met. Since the German government categorically refused to negotiate with the terrorists, the Swedish government had no other choice but to begin preparations for a storming of the building. Before this could happen, TNT explosives inside the building detonated. Eventually, this ended the occupation, leaving several severely wounded hostages and terrorists. For all details, see Michael März, *Die Machtprobe 1975: Wie RAF und Bewegung 2. Juni den Staat erpressten* (Leipzig: Forum Verlag Leipzig, 2007).
9 Klaus Weinhauer, Staatsmacht ohne Grenzen? Innere Sicherheit, 'Terrorismus' – Bekämpfung und die bundesdeutsche Gesellschaft der 1970er Jahre, in Susanne Krasmann and Jürgen Martschukat (eds.), *Rationalitäten der Gewalt: Staatliche Neuordnungen vom 19. bis zum 21. Jahrhundert* (Bielefeld: Transcript Verlag, 2007), 215–38, here 224.
10 Ibid., 230; Klaus Weinhauer, Terrorismus in der Bundesrepublik der Siebzigerjahre: Aspekte einer Sozial- und Kulturgeschichte der Inneren Sicherheit, *Archiv für Sozialgeschichte* 44 (2004), 219–42.
11 Stephan Scheiper, Der Wandel staatlicher Herrschaft in den 1960er/70er Jahren, in Klaus Weinhauer, Jörg Requate and Heinz-Gerhard Haupt (eds.), *Terrorismus in der Bundesrepublik: Medien, Staat und Subkulturen in den 1970er Jahren* (Frankfurt: Campus Verlag, 2006), 188–216.
12 Jakko Pekelder, *Sympathie voor de RAF: De Rote Armee Fraktion in Nederland, 1970–1980* (Amsterdam: Mets & Schilt, 2007), 12–13.
13 On the concept of path dependence, see especially Paul Pierson, *Politics in Time: History, Institutions, and Social Analysis* (Princeton, NJ: Princeton University Press, 2004). See also Paul Pierson and Theda Skocpol, Historical Institutionalism in Contemporary Political Science, in Ira Katznelson and Helen V. Milner (eds.), *Political Science: State of the Discipline* (New York: W.W. Norton, 2002), 693–721.
14 A comprehensive and document-based analysis of the international cooperation in combatting terrorism in Western Europe in the early 1970s remains a desideratum. Evidence of cooperation on a technical level can be found since 1970. See Note regarding a conference of the European Security Services on 18 September 1970 in Paris, in B 106/102148, Bundesarchiv Koblenz. In the following years, in particular after the 1972 Munich massacre, international expert groups, set up largely under the leadership of the Netherlands, emerged and met at regular intervals. An example

is the Groep Fonteijn, which was transformed into the intergovernmental TREVI network by the Council of the EC in December 1975. See, among others, the documents in the Archief Ministerie van Buitenlandse Zaken, Code 9, 1965–1974, 5539. Starting in 1976, the question of terrorism appeared in the agendas of bi- and multilateral summits. Additionally, a conference involving European Interior Ministers debating measures of deepened cooperation that had been promised since 1972 finally took place in 1976.

15 It is an open secret that governments pay ransom in abduction cases time and again – no matter whether they are of a criminal or terrorist nature.
16 All quotations appear in the letter Wischnewski addressed to Schmidt on 25 November 1977, see Wischnewski Protocol.
17 Wischnewski Protocol, part I, 1.
18 Ibid., part II, 3.
19 Ibid.
20 See Kreisky at the Council of Ministers, record 131, 10 September 1974, 4, in Minutes of the Council of Ministers, Box 375, BKA, Archive of the Republic – Austrian State Archives.
21 See the verbatim report for this – in terms of Middle East policy – highly meaningful conference, in Internationaal Instituut voor Sociale Geschiedenis, Amsterdam, Archief SI, 347.
22 For all quotations, see Wischnewski Protocol, part II, 1.
23 Ibid., 4.
24 Oliver Rathkolb, *Internationalisierung Österreichs seit 1945* (Innsbruck: Studien Verlag, 2006), 62–78; Oliver Rathkolb, 'Europa mit der Seele suchen...': Bruno Kreiskys andere Europa-Visionen, in Foundation Bruno Kreisky Archive et al. (eds.), *Bruno Kreisky: Seine Zeit und mehr, Era and Aftermath* (Vienna: Studien Verlag, 2000), 87–103.
25 See letter of Wischnewski to Schmidt, 25 November 1977, in Wischnewski Protocol.
26 See history of the General Delegation of Palestine in Germany, www.palaestina.org/index.php?id=10 (accessed 1 January 2020).
27 Schröder did not inform his colleagues in advance and thus provoked a strong controversy. See Franz Eibl, *Politik der Bewegung: Gerhard Schröder als Außenminister 1961–1966* (Munich: Oldenbourg, 2001), 26; For the rather limited impact of this meeting, see Dietrich Strothmann, Gespräch mit Arafat: Gerhard Schröders Damaskus-Erlebnis, *Die Zeit*, 27 December 1974, 1.
28 Willy Brandt, *Erinnerungen* (Hamburg: SPIEGEL-Verlag, 2006), 457.
29 The Wischnewski Protocol identifies the Palestinian as 'Ali Salami'; however, in light of the described responsibilities, there can be no doubt that this must have been Ali Hassan Salameh. See the not entirely unambiguous portrayal in (published under various titles) Michael Bar-Zohar and Eitan Haber, *The Quest for the Red Prince: Israel's Relentless Manhunt for One of the World's Deadliest and Most Wanted Arab Terrorists* (Pequena, CT: The Lyons Press, 2002).
30 N. N., Terrorism, Fatal Error, *Time Magazine*, 6 August 1973, content.time.com/time/magazine/article/0,9171,903989,00.html (accessed 1 January 2020).
31 N. N., Death of a Terrorist, *Time Magazine*, 5 February 1979, content.time.com/time/magazine/article/0,9171,946209,00.html (accessed 1 January 2020).
32 Kai Bird, *The Good Spy* (New York: Broadway Books, 2014).
33 David Ignatius, In the end, CIA-PLO links weren't helpful, *The San Diego Union Tribune*, 12 November 2004, legacy.sandiegouniontribune.com/uniontrib/20041112/news_lz1e12ignatiu.html (accessed 7 January 2017).

34 Wischnewski Protocol, part II, 3.
35 Hans-Jürgen Wischnewski, *Mit Leidenschaft und Augenmaß: In Mogadischu und anderswo* (München: Bertelsmann, 1989), 162. Wischnewski mentions he met al-Sartawi 'through Bruno Kreisky'.
36 For information on the ANO, see information compiled by the Federal Ministry of the Interior under the title 'Tod in Bagdad' in its journal *Öffentliche Sicherheit* 11/12 (2002).
37 Wischnewski Protocol, part II, 2.
38 Ibid., part I, 1.
39 Ibid., part II, 4.
40 Ibid., part I, 1.
41 Ibid., part II, 3.
42 Ibid., part III, 1.
43 Ibid., 2. Based on these hints, the German author of the protocol drew the conclusion that all wanted persons, in particular the lawyer Jörg Lang, must be located in Beirut.
44 Ibid.
45 Ibid., part I, 2.
46 Ibid., part III, 1.
47 Ibid., part II, 5.
48 Ibid., part III, 2.
49 Ibid.
50 Ibid., 3.
51 Ibid.
52 Ibid.
53 Ibid., part II, 2.
54 See the separate remarks by Minister of the Interior Lanc concerning the Palmers kidnapping, in Ibid., part III, 4. The Austrian textile manufacturer Walter Palmers was kidnapped by the 2 June Movement in 1977. The kidnapping was a money-raising measure, and Palmers was quickly set free after a ransom was paid. The terrorists were arrested at the Swiss border.
55 Although the writer of the protocol quotes Sartawi speaking of the PLO Council, it is highly likely that he is speaking of the Palestine National Council, the highest authority in the PLO, which met in Cairo in March 1977. See Wischnewski Protocol, part II, 1.
56 Both quotations in Ibid.
57 Ibid., part III, 1.
58 Ibid.
59 All quotations in Ibid.
60 Ibid., part II, 3.
61 Ibid., 1.
62 Ibid., 4.
63 Ibid., part III, 1.
64 Ibid., part II, 2.
65 Ibid.
66 Ibid.
67 Ibid.
68 Ibid., 3.
69 It is unclear which attacks are exactly referred to. Perhaps the airport attacks from August and December 1973. On the other hand, it seems more plausible that PLO

representatives, as a proof of their transformation, referred to rather 'small-scale' incidents that cannot be found in the literature.

70 Wischnewski Protocol, part II, 4.
71 All quotations in Ibid., 5.
72 Ibid.
73 Both quotations in Ibid., 2.
74 Peter Merseburger, *Willy Brandt 1913–1992: Visionär und Realist* (Munich: DVA, 2004), 756.
75 John Bunzl, *Gewalt ohne Grenzen: Nahost-Terror und Österreich* (Vienna: Braumüller, 1991), 60.
76 For Palestinian and German–Austrian cooperation in the late 1970s / early 1980s, see several publications by Thomas Riegler, for example, Diplomatie und Terror: Die Operationen des PLO-Geheimdienstes 1979 in der BRD und in Österreich, *Journal for Intelligence, Propaganda and Security Studies (JIPSS)* 8/1 (2014), 30–58; Ein österreichischer Weg, *JIPSS* 6/1 (2012), 149; *Tage des Schreckens: Die OPEC-Geiselnahme 1975 und der modern Terrorismus* (E-Book, 2015), 272–6; *Im Fadenkreuz: Österreich und der Nahostterrorismus 1973 bis 1985* (Vienna: V&R unipress, 2010), 397–402. For Germany, see Dieter Schenk, *Der Chef: Horst Herold und das BKA* (Hamburg: Hoffmann und Campe, 1998), 341; See also Abdullah Frangi, *Der Gesandte: Mein Leben für Palästina. Hinter den Kulissen der Nahost-Politik* (Munich: Heyne, 2011), 273.
77 Press conference by Bruno Kreisky, presumably 22 December 1975, approx. 1 o'clock, ORF recording, transcription by the author, in Austrian Media Library, 9-03922_001.

Chapter 8

HEZBOLLAH AS AN IRANIAN PROXY IN THE AGE OF THE COLD WAR

Ryszard M. Machnikowski

The emergence of Iran's revolutionary proxy force in Lebanon

Hezbollah is probably the best example of a 'terrorist entity' exploited by the Middle Eastern states (in this case Iran and Syria) as a tool to reduce the regional influence of Western powers (and Israel) within the context of the Cold War. In this case that tool proved itself to be quite effective. Though we can't be absolutely sure about the exact nature of the links between this organization and the governments of Iran and Syria, it seems obvious that without external assistance, particularly from Iran, the impact of this 'Shia militia' would have been less visible and intensive. According to Eitan Azani,

> Iran helped, and is still helping, Hezbollah build its global terrorist network. Iran also helps the organization operate its network with agents from its security forces and the Iranian Revolutionary Guards, which operate from Iranian embassies worldwide. During Hafez Al-Assad's reign, Hezbollah was a Syrian proxy terrorist organization. Syria was the reigning power in Lebanon and it controlled the activities of the various elements in Lebanon, including those of Hezbollah. Hezbollah did not completely submit to Syria's authority and from time to time there were even differences of opinion between the two.[1]

This foreign assistance included the delivery of money and weapons, the participation of Iranian instructors in training and the providing of intelligence and logistical support.[2] The primary institution responsible for supervision and contacts with Hezbollah was the Iranian Revolutionary Guard Corps' *Al Quds Force* (Brigades):

> The Quds Force, a paramilitary arm of the Revolutionary Guard with ten thousand to fifteen thousand personnel, emerged as the de facto external affairs branch during the corps' expansion. Its mandate was to conduct foreign policy missions – beginning in Iraq's Kurdish region – and forge relationships with Shiite and Kurdish groups. The Quds Force has since supported terrorist

activities and armed pro-Iranian militant groups across the Middle East and beyond, including in Lebanon, the Palestinian territories, Iraq, Afghanistan, the Gulf states, and several others, according to the U.S. State Department.[3]

Hezbollah, widely labelled as a 'terrorist organization' in the Western world, has been recognized as a 'resistance movement' in its region and gained legitimacy not only through terrorist action and military fight but also through social care and assistance provided to local Shia population as well as joining Lebanon's political life.[4] Today, it is not only a 'Shia resistance militia' but also a dominant political force playing a major role in the Lebanese power play.

Western powers claim that Hezbollah is responsible for the April 1983 US Embassy bombing, the October 1983 Beirut barracks bombing, the December 1983 Kuwait City bombings (aimed at Western as well as local targets), the September 1984 bombing of the US Embassy annex in East Beirut, hijackings of Air France planes in August 1983 and July 1984, of TWA Flight 847 in June 1985 and an Air Afrique plane in July 1987, as well as the Lebanon 'hostage crisis', lasting more than ten years and resulting in several deaths of Western, mostly American, hostages. Moreover, Hezbollah's operatives conducted numerous terrorist operations in France between 1986 and 1987. Hezbollah's actions against Israel include suicide attacks against the Israel Defense Forces (IDF) facilities in Tyre, Lebanon, in November 1982 and November 1983 (in both actions more than 100 Israeli servicemen and approximately sixty Lebanese and Palestinian prisoners were killed), waging a bloody guerrilla campaign against IDF forces occupying South Lebanon and the South Lebanon Army (SLA) Christian militia supported by the Israelis, and a terrorist campaign against Israeli civilians.

These 'terrorist attacks' (according to Western sources) are deemed by Hezbollah supporters to be a 'legitimate military response' to Israeli invasions and Western interference in the Middle Eastern conflict and the civil war in Lebanon. Regardless of the kind of analytical category one may apply to Hezbollah's actions it should be noted that the application of political violence in any form (suicide bombings, hijackings of planes, kidnappings, guerrilla warfare) by this group was meticulously planned and perfectly executed:

> Already in the 1980's, Hezbollah attacks were characterized by innovation, professionalism and a high level of daring that was new to the Lebanese arena. This was due largely to the implementation of the principle of sacrifice by the organization's activists, who blew themselves up against multinational forces and IDF targets in Lebanon. Moreover, the organization's activity in Lebanon had the professional fingerprints of the Iranian Revolutionary guard who trained Hezbollah for their attacks and supplied them with explosives, weapons and technological equipment. Analysis of the organization's operational characteristics from its inception to the present indicates a continuous improvement in the organization's activists' level of operational capabilities and the technological means they use in order to circumvent the defensive measures the IDF used in Lebanon and security apparatuses used around the world.[5]

This 'operational prowess' impressed both its enemies and allies.[6]

Seemingly, the sudden emergence of a new Shia 'militia' in Lebanon had been perceived as a surprise but today it looks almost inevitable. It seems that four factors contributed to Hezbollah's foundation, and influenced its structure and the logic of action: (1) the long-standing civil war in Lebanon (which started in 1975); (2) the successful Islamic Revolution in Iran (1979), which brought to power and influence militant Shia factions in the region; (3) Israeli and Western intervention in this country (1982); and, *last but not least*, (4) the sustained Syrian–Israeli conflict. Taken together, these factors resulted in the emergence of this Lebanese Shia Islamist militia/resistance force/terrorist organization, which ultimately managed to transform itself into a powerful political force in Lebanon.[7]

First of all, it was the Lebanon conflict that generated the social and political conditions for the establishment of the new Islamic Shia force in this country. Internal tensions and rifts within the Amal organization, then the primary Shia powerbroker in Lebanon, provided the necessary human resources to be used by external actors, mainly Iran. It was the emergence of a Shia Islamic revolutionary force in the region and afterwards the successful Islamic Revolution in Iran, which provided some Shia factions in neighbouring Lebanon with an example and a pattern to follow. As Eitan Azani rightfully claims:

> The success of the Iranian Islamic revolution became a source of inspiration and stimulation for the revolutionary movements, particularly the Shiite movements, which sprang up in the 1980s. They were led by religious militants, under the leadership of Khomeini, who promoted the vision of an Islamic nation. The Hezbollah movement in Lebanon is one of the torch-bearers of this goal.[8]

The authorities of the newborn Islamic Republic of Iran were more than prone to carry the torch of the 'Islamic revolution' around the region and mobilize and exploit vast human resources there.[9] Azani notes:

> As a revolutionary Shiite organization with a universal Islamic outlook, Hezbollah has adopted three central objectives that derive from Khomeini's teachings and principles and has been striving to implement them since its inception: 1. Implementation of Islamic law in Lebanon as part of a universal Islamic revolution – this objective has always been part of Hezbollah's agenda, though the organization's leaders attempted to blur this point since the 1990s in order to promote current objectives in Lebanon. […] 2. Expulsion of the foreign forces in Lebanon – this was one of Hezbollah's primary goals and it took much pride in the fact that it was the cause for the expulsion of the multinational forces from Lebanon in the 1980s and the expulsion of Israel from Lebanon in 2000. Hezbollah claims its mission is not complete as long as the Shebba farms are in Israeli hands and, therefore, there is a need for the continuation of the 'resistance' in its current form. […] 3. The destruction of Israel and the liberation of Jerusalem – one of the pillars of Hezbollah's ideology is the struggle against the state of Israel (the 'Little Satan') until its destruction and the liberation of

Jerusalem. Due to this principle and in order to achieve this objective, Hezbollah feels committed, ideologically and in practice, to strive for an ongoing conflict with Israel with all means possible on all fronts. In light of this, Hezbollah constantly stresses its basic approach to Israel and its goal to destroy it. As a result of Hezbollah's aforementioned attitude towards Israel, it rejects the possibility of any future accords with Israel, any possibility of recognizing its existence as a national entity in the region or of any co-existence with Israel.[10]

Iran with its powerful Revolutionary Guard Corps and skilful intelligence apparatus did not hesitate to form and support a Shia 'revolutionary vanguard' in Lebanon. Certainly, this could not have been realized without Syrian consent. The loss of the Golan Heights to Israel influenced Syrian policies towards Israel. President Assad's regime was seeking another proxy force that could militarily engage Israel in South Lebanon,[11] and supersede vanishing Palestinian organizations, which were being forced into exile by the Israeli 'Operation Peace for Galilee' in 1982 (ultimately the Syrians even fought its former allies, the remnants of the Palestine Liberation Organization in Lebanon). Syria could not afford to get involved in an open armed conflict against Israel for the obvious reason that it would have been totally defeated by the IDF. Hence, the Syrian regime was more than willing to accept the foundation of the disciplined and well-equipped armed 'guerrilla force', guided by the Iranian 'instructors'. The task of a military engagement of the IDF forces occupying southern Lebanon (which were supported by the so-called SLA) was passed to Hezbollah militants. Ultimately, they proved to be much more effective than their Palestinian predecessors.

Moreover, the arrival of Western military 'peacekeeping' contingents under the blue flag of the UN in 1982 was perceived in Tehran and Damascus as yet another forcible interference by the West into this region's internal affairs. Hezbollah forces had been used to deter this Western military involvement and derail Western policies towards the Middle East, as it was widely perceived that the West (primarily the United States and France) had been supporting Israel and Lebanese Christian militias (and Iraq) as tools to limit Iranian and Syrian influence in the region. It should come as no surprise that the combination of the aforementioned factors – socially, the existence of a large Shia population ready to resist any foreign enemy; politically, the will of the rulers of the newborn 'revolutionary' Iran to utilize Shia populations in the region to get a grip there along with Syrian acceptance for this Iranian action within its domain, and the physical presence of foreign armies on Lebanese soil – resulted in the foundation of the powerful Shia military 'militia' ready for necessary sacrifices in its fight against multiple enemies.

Application of political violence

As a result, the Beirut and Kuwait bombings of 1983–4 (the US Embassy as well as US Marines and the French paratroopers barracks were attacked) could clearly be understood both as an attempt to get rid of the American and French military presence in Lebanon and the region and as a revenge for the plentiful US, French (and Kuwaiti) actions against Iran, including financial and military assistance to Iraq in its war against Iran (1980–8).[12] The 'Islamic Jihad Organization', which took responsibility for the bombings, was commonly regarded as a 'cover' for Hezbollah militants (or even the Iranian Al Quds Force), who were perceived as a 'front' for this Iranian involvement. These terrorist actions brought a new quality to the tradecraft of international terrorism and proved that terrorist methods could bring huge political outcomes and benefits through forcing the enemy to military retreat and abandon its previous policies. The US Embassy bombing in Beirut on 18 April 1983 was so powerful that it killed sixty-three people, including seventeen Americans – among them eight CIA operatives including top officials such as Near East director Robert Ames, who was visiting Beirut that day, and the Chief of the CIA station in Beirut, Kenneth Haas. This could not be considered as a mere coincidence and shows the quality and accuracy of information available to the plotters of this attack. The US and French barracks bombing on 23 October 1983 was the ultimate proof of the deadly skills of the perpetrators. In almost simultaneous truck attacks on two separate targets, the US Marine Corps barracks at the international airport in Beirut and the 'Drakkar' barracks of the French Para regiments in a distant part of the city, 241 American and fifty-eight French servicemen were ultimately killed. This was the largest single day death toll of American soldiers since the Vietnam War and of French soldiers since the Algerian War. The explosions were so powerful that they managed to raze large parts of both buildings.

The next round of Hezbollah's attacks against Western targets took place in Kuwait City on 12 December 1983. A truck filled with gas cylinders entered the gates of the US Embassy in Kuwait and exploded inside, destroying almost completely one of the buildings there. Miraculously, only five people were killed in this attack. An hour later a car bomb went off outside the French Embassy killing no one and wounding only five people. Another car bomb exploded at the living quarters for the American employees of Raytheon Corporation in Kuwait City. Only one person was killed in this attack. Approximately at the same time, the Shuaiba Petrochemical Plant, the Electricity Control Center, and the Kuwait International Airport were attacked with car bombs, fortunately causing no fatalities.

The political result of these attacks was the prompt withdrawal of all American, French (and Italian) 'peacekeeping' forces from Lebanon by 31 March 1984. Both US and French armed forces responded with some retaliatory attacks against Hezbollah as well as Iranian and Syrian [sic!] targets in Lebanon, though the scale of this reprisal was rather limited. Western military presence on Lebanese soil was violently ended and American and French policies towards this country were almost utterly compromised. As an addition to this application of violence, a suicide car bomber attacked an annex of the US Embassy located in East Beirut on 20 September 1984, killing twenty-three people, including two Americans at the US Defense Attaché's Office. The US and British ambassadors were slightly wounded as they were having a meeting in this building at the moment of the attack.

Hezbollah also used another successful tactic to harass and intimidate Western governments – the abductions of mostly American and French hostages in Lebanon. The very first Westerner kidnapped in Lebanon within this context was David Dodge, the president of the American University of Beirut (AUB). This happened on 21 July 1982 and he was released almost exactly a year later. In 1984, Frank Regier, an engineering professor at the AUB and Frenchman Christian Joubert were abducted, followed by Jeremy Lewin, a journalist working for CNN, and William Buckley, the CIA station chief in Lebanon (the captors ultimately killed him, after he had been interrogated and tortured). The next American citizen abducted in Beirut was Benjamin Weir, followed by Peter Kilburn (who was killed on 17 April 1986). In 1985, Hezbollah abducted Father Lawrence Jenco, Terry Anderson, David Jacobsen, Thomas Sutherland, French journalist Jean-Paul Kaufman, the scientist Michel Seurat and three employees of the French Embassy. A year later three Americans followed suit: Frank Reed, Joseph Cicippio, Edward Tracy and a number of Frenchmen had been captured by groups connected to Hezbollah. In 1987, kidnappings included those of three American employees of the Beirut University College in West Beirut: Alann Steen, Jesse Turner, Robert Polhill, American television correspondent Charles Glass and French journalist (and Israeli spy) Roger Auque. On 17 February 1988, the last American hostage, Col. William Higgins, was abducted in Lebanon. He was hanged probably in 1989. The 'Lebanon hostage crisis' lingered on for years. The last American hostage, Terry Anderson, was released only on 4 December 1991 and the last Western hostages, the Germans Thomas Kemptner and Heinrich Struebig, were released on 17 June 1992. Moreover, a number of British, Irish, Saudi, Swiss and West German nationals were also kidnapped but ultimately released. Abductions of Americans in Lebanon led the Reagan administration to be involved in negotiations with Iran over the fate of the hostages, which eventually ended in the huge 'Iran–Contra scandal'.[13]

In addition to the kidnapping campaign, some Western citizens were killed during this period. On 18 January 1984, Malcolm H. Kerr, the president of the AUB, was shot in the back of the head as he approached his office. On 18 September 1986, Christian Gouttière, the French military attaché in Lebanon was murdered by Hezbollah. Terrorists fired three shots into Colonel Gouttière's head after he had parked his car outside the French Embassy compound in eastern Beirut.

As a part of this vast terrorist campaign against the West, Hezbollah further managed to hijack planes to use them as bargaining chips for the release of Hezbollah operatives. On 26 August 1983, an Air France plane was hijacked after departure from Austria, apparently by Hezbollah operatives. They demanded the release of Lebanese prisoners held in France and the cessation of French military aid to Iraq, Lebanon and Chad. On 31 July 1984, another Air France plane was hijacked while flying from Frankfurt to France. It was forced to land in Iran, where it was blown up by the hijackers. An organization calling itself the Islamic Organization for the Liberation of Jerusalem claimed responsibility for the hijacking. Moreover, on 14 June 1985, TWA flight 847, a Boeing 727 flying from Athens to Rome, was hijacked by Hezbollah operatives. During the second stop in

Beirut, the Hezbollah operatives murdered Robert Dean Stethem, a United States Navy diver, and dumped his body from the plane. The hijackers demanded the release of seventeen terrorists held in Kuwaiti jails for their involvement in the December 1983 bombing of Western targets as well as the release of 766 Lebanese Shiites kept in Israeli prisons. (One month after the hijacking, Israel released more than 700 Lebanese detainees). On 24 July 1987, an Air Afrique plane flying to the Congo was hijacked over Milan. The hijacker appeared to be Hezbollah operative Hossein Ali Mohammed Hariri, who demanded the release of his two brothers, terrorists being held in West Germany (one of them on charges of involvement in the June 1985 hijacking of the TWA plane). Moreover, he demanded the release of terrorists held in France at that time, including Hezbollah operatives. During a refuelling stop at Geneva Airport the hijacker killed one French national and wounded a stewardess. Ultimately, Swiss police managed to take control of the plane and arrest him.

Hezbollah terrorist activity was not limited to Lebanon but struck European soil as well. As a study by the Meir Amit Intelligence and Terrorism Information Center reports:

In 1986 [...] three series of mass murder attacks were carried out in Paris by detonating explosive devices in crowded places. The terrorist attacks, which nearly paralyzed the city, took place in February, March and September [1986], hitting commercial centers, intercity trains, the Paris Metro, the Champs Elysees, the Eiffel Tower and other public sites. Eleven people were killed and over 220 injured in the attacks. Responsibility was claimed by an unknown network calling itself the Committee for Solidarity with Near Eastern Political Prisoners (CSPPA). [...] In early 1987 French security forces exposed a Shi'ite network headquartered in a Muslim school in a Parisian suburb, directed by Fouad Ben Ali Saleh [...]. The members of the Hezbollah-affiliated network were detained in March 1987 as they were about to complete preparations for a new wave of terrorist attacks. [...] According to the French prosecution, the network worked for Hezbollah to force France to stop its assistance to Iraq during the Iran-Iraq War and free detained terrorists. [...] A second network was exposed in Paris in March-April 1987. Its operatives were affiliated with one of Hezbollah's terrorist groups in Europe. It was exposed after the arrest of Hezbollah operatives in Italy and Germany in January 1987. The network's operatives were involved in preparations for terrorist attacks and maintained contact with the Iranian embassy in Paris. In 1987 approximately sixty people were arrested on suspicion of involvement or membership in the terrorist network.[14]

Extensive investigations led the French police to another suspect:

Wahid Gordigi [or Gordiji, as it is usual Western spelling – note by the author], who worked as an interpreter at the Iranian embassy in Paris. Gordigi was suspected of coordinating many of the terrorist operations carried out in 1986. [...] Wahid Gordigi escaped to the Iranian embassy and was able to avoid being arrested. Iran, which argued that he had diplomatic immunity (even though he was not officially listed as a diplomat) gave him asylum and refused to extradite him [...]. French police forces then surrounded the Iranian embassy in Paris. In response, the Iranian police laid a siege to the French embassy in Tehran.[15]

As a result Franco–Iranian diplomatic relations deteriorated significantly: 'On July 16, 1987, Iran said it was reducing the staff of its Paris embassy and threatened to break off relations within 72 hours unless France stopped blockading the embassy and punished a policeman who had beaten an Iranian representative [...]. Hezbollah reacted by taking several French citizens hostage in Lebanon.'[16]

The net result of these 'terrorist campaigns' (or 'military pressure' in the parlance of Hezbollah supporters) on American and French military servicemen and civilians is pretty impressive. Through these actions of Hezbollah, its Iranian and Syrian masters ultimately managed to derail Western policies towards Lebanon and limit US and French military and diplomatic capabilities in the region, reducing the influence of these states to a significant degree. Hezbollah actions persuaded Lebanese factions, particularly Christians, that their Western allies were powerless, and the determination of Western powers to forward their political goals there was hugely limited by the ability of Hezbollah 'resistance' to inflict heavy casualties on its enemies. Moreover, the 'hostage crisis' ultimately drew President Reagan's administration into the 'Iran–Contra affair', which ended in a prolonged and embarrassing investigation, congressional hearings and prosecution of its top officials. The 'Iran–Contra' scandal caused huge internal political turmoil seriously endangering the president. Only loyalty and numerous unlawful actions of his close accomplices (and the death of CIA Director William Casey) saved him from further embarrassing procedures. Public support for the beleaguered US president plummeted rapidly over the period of the investigation.[17]

In all these ways Iranian leaders, through the actions of Hezbollah militants, were able to influence internal politics in the United States and ultimately brought about dismissals and, later, indictments of many prominent members of the US government, including Secretary of Defense Caspar Weinberger, the National Security Advisors John Poindexter and Robert McFarlane and Assistant Secretary of State Elliott Abrams, to mention only the most influential.[18] Moreover, as Magnus Ranstorp neatly notes: 'U.S. willingness to engage in concessions with Iran and the Hezbollah not only signaled to its adversaries that hostage-taking was an extremely useful instrument in extracting political and financial concessions from the West but also undermined any credibility of U.S. criticism of other states' deviation from the principles of non-negotiation and no concession to terrorists and their demands.'[19] French policies were also affected to a significant degree by Iran's proxy. Iranian- (and Syrian-) supported terrorism against France in the Middle East and on French soil, campaigns in which Hezbollah was, of course, a central actor, led to a remarkable turn in French foreign policy towards an accommodation of Syria and Iran between September 1986 and spring 1988. The French government repaid a US$1 billion loan from the Shah era to the Iranians, even extradited some members of the Iranian resistance to the Iranian regime and restarted full diplomatic relations with the Islamic Republic, which had been broken off in 1981. With the Syrian regime, the French cut a deal in 1986 that traded French arms, economic aid and diplomatic support in return for the Syrian pledge to cease support for terrorism in France, secure the release of French hostages in Lebanon and provide intelligence on Lebanese terrorists.[20] Hence, the ability of France to exert influence on its former 'Mandatory territories' was significantly lowered and the relations between Iran and France deteriorated for a long time.

Hezbollah against Israel

Hezbollah actions against Israel can be seen as a similar success. The Tyre suicide bombings against the IDF's headquarters in November 1982 could be perceived as a major rehearsal before the subsequent attacks on Western targets in Lebanon. In November 1982, a car filled with explosives struck a building in the city of Tyre used by the Israeli military and secret services. As a result, ninety-one Israeli soldiers, border guards and Shin Bet operatives were killed, fifty-five people including twenty-seven Israelis were wounded. This kind of attack was repeated on 4 November 1983 when a suicide bomber in a car entered a building in Tyre used by the IDF, the Israeli Security Agency, and the Israel Border Police and destroyed it, killing sixty people, including twenty-eight Israeli security personnel, and wounding twenty-three people. Since then, Hezbollah fighters waged a guerrilla campaign against IDF and SLA forces, attacking military patrols and bases as well as waging a campaign of psychological warfare. Increased harassment by Hezbollah forces influenced the Israeli decision to withdraw to the 'Security Zone' in South Lebanon in February–April 1985. As the Meir Amit Center study suggests:

> The collapse of the May 17 Agreement, coupled with the wave of attacks against IDF troops in Lebanon, eventually led to Israel's unilateral withdrawal from Lebanon without a political agreement (1985). Furthermore, the political and military vacuum left by the IDF's withdrawal and the collapse of the power of the pro-American and pro-Israeli Lebanese factions was filled by Syria and Iran. Thus, in the mid-1980s a new era began in the internal Lebanese arena, marked by a significant decline in the political influence of the United States, Israel, and the West. On the other hand, Syrian and Iranian influence grew while Hezbollah gradually became the leading military and political power in Lebanon.[21]

This 'hit-and-run' guerrilla-type of conflict was backed by Katyusza rocket attacks on civilian targets in northern Israel and, according to the Meir Amit Center study, supplemented with

> kidnapping and abducting Jews: after the IDF withdrew from Lebanon in 1985, Hezbollah carried out a wave of abductions of Lebanese Jews from families that had lived in Lebanon for generations. About half of the captives were over the age of fifty. They were executed several months after being abducted. As usual,

Hezbollah did not claim responsibility but hid behind a pseudonym of the Organization of the Oppressed on Earth. The abductions began in late March 1985 in Wadi Abu Jamil, the Jewish quarter of western Beirut. Eight Jews were abducted simultaneously in a carefully planned operation, including Isaac Sasson, leader of the Jewish community, and Dr. Elie Hallaq, the community physician. The captors demanded the release of hundreds of Lebanese detainees held in Israel and in the South Lebanese Army's Al-Khiyam detention facility. When their demands were not met the hostages were executed one by one. Some were buried at the Jewish cemetery in eastern Beirut; the other bodies were never found.[22]

Hezbollah continued to carry out armed attacks on Israeli targets after the end of the Cold War and neither the 1989 Taif Agreement designed to end the civil war in Lebanon nor even the final withdrawal of all Israeli troops from Lebanese soil in May 2000 managed to stop them. At the same time, in the 1990s, Hezbollah has successfully transformed itself from a 'resistance movement' into a key political player in Lebanon.[23]

The story of Hezbollah – the story of political success

Regardless of which factors exactly led to the emergence of Hezbollah in Lebanon in the early 1980s, the bloody record of this organization is a story of remarkable success. Hezbollah's militant activities, including its wide array of terrorist tactics – suicide attacks, murders, hijackings of planes, and kidnappings of foreign hostages – proved to be effective politically. Political violence in the form of terrorism applied by Hezbollah resulted in a tremendous political outcome benefitting its foreign promotors, Iran and Syria. As a 1985 'Hezbollah manifesto' openly stated:

> Let us put it truthfully: the sons of Hezbollah know who are their major enemies in the Middle East – the Phalanges, Israel, France and the US. The sons of our umma are now in a state of growing confrontation with them, and will remain so until the realization of the following three objectives: (a) to expel the Americans, the French and their allies definitely from Lebanon, putting an end to any colonialist entity on our land; [...] These are Lebanon's objectives; those are its enemies. As for our friends, they are all the world's oppressed peoples. [...] We see in Israel the vanguard of the United States in our Islamic world. It is the hated enemy that must be fought until the hated ones get what they deserve. [...] Our primary assumption in our fight against Israel states that the Zionist entity is aggressive from its inception, and built on lands wrested from their owners, at the expense of the rights of the Muslim people. Therefore our struggle will end only when this entity is obliterated. We recognize no treaty with it, no cease fire [*sic*], and no peace agreements, whether separate or consolidated. We vigorously condemn all plans for negotiation with Israel, and regard all negotiators as enemies, for the reason that such negotiation is nothing but the recognition of the legitimacy of the Zionist occupation of Palestine.[24]

The objectives mentioned in this earliest 'official' statement by Hezbollah, apart from the 'liberation of Jerusalem', have been largely achieved through its militant activity, including numerous acts of terrorism. Hezbollah's actions managed to expel the Americans and the French out of Lebanon and contributed to the Israeli withdrawal first to the Security Zone and finally out of the country altogether. Definitely, all of these developments were fully in tune with the political goals of Iran and Syria – regimes that had a long history of both open and clandestine hostilities towards the West and Israel. The end of the Cold War and the end of the civil war in Lebanon has not stopped Hezbollah's terrorist activity against Israel, as it has still been used as a proxy in a fight against Israelis and Westerners. According to the Meir Amit Center report:

> Hezbollah's terrorist campaign led to proxies' being used by Iran for terrorist activities. It allowed the Iranians to initiate terrorist attacks while denying any involvement in them and to avoid a head-on clash with the United States. The Lebanese Hezbollah, Iran's leading proxy, also did not claim responsibility for its terrorist attacks and used pseudonyms. Categorical denial of any involvement in terrorist attacks has since become a trademark of both Iran and Hezbollah, even when the evidence for their involvement is solid (such as the AMIA bombing in Argentina). Politically, it can be said in retrospect that Iran's terrorist campaign in the 1980s, which focused on the United States and France, had significant achievements: in the short term, the terrorist attacks led to the withdrawal of the multi-national force from Lebanon (February 1984), which had been deployed in Beirut in the summer of 1982 to supervise the withdrawal of the Palestinian forces and maintain peace. The withdrawal of the multi-national force was perceived as an American loss of interest in the developments in Lebanon, and considerably weakened its political influence in the Lebanese arena and the Middle East in general.[25]

The group also expanded its terrorist activities far beyond the Middle Eastern area of operations. Further terrorist attacks against Israelis for which Hezbollah has been blamed include the bombing of the Israeli Embassy in Buenos Aires in 1992, the 1994 bombing of a Jewish cultural centre in Buenos Aires, the 1994 Israeli Embassy bombing in London, and, most recently, a bus bombing in the Bulgarian city of Burgas in 2012. Hezbollah attacks from Lebanon on Jewish civilian targets have also continued in northern Israel. Hezbollah has never left this bloody path of terrorist attacks against civilians and it is highly probable that it will continue terrorist activities in the future, as they definitely can be perceived as providing vast political benefits for both Hezbollah leaders and their Iranian masters.

Notes

1 Eitan Azani, *Hezbollah: A Global Terrorist Organization, Hearing of the House Committee on International Relations, Subcommittee on International Terrorism and Nonproliferation*, September 2006, in *Hezbollah's Global Reach, Joint Hearing*

(Washington, DC: U.S. Government Printing Office, 2006), 49–50, https://www.gpo.gov/fdsys/pkg/CHRG-109hhrg30143/pdf/CHRG-109hhrg30143.pdf (accessed 1 January 2020).

2 'Hezbollah's operational infrastructure was developed, almost entirely, with extensive Iranian backing. This aid included financial support, transportation of weapons, and training the organization's activists. Iran views Hezbollah's consolidation in Lebanon as a great success in the "export of the Islamic revolution". Even after Israel's withdrawal from Lebanon, Iran continues to see Lebanon as its front line against Israel and Hezbollah as a key factor in leading the struggle. For this reason, Iran continued to strengthen Hezbollah's military capabilities and consistently supported the continuation of Hezbollah's terror operations along the Israeli–Lebanese border. The Iranian Revolutionary Guards' "Quds Brigades" (Jerusalem Brigades), which are deployed in Lebanon, direct Iranian operations in the area and Iranian assistance to Hezbollah. The force provides guidance and military support for terror attacks against Israel. This support includes funding and varied military support expressed in the following ways: 1. Training and instructing Hezbollah activists in military and operational subjects, including advanced courses in Iran. 2. Transfer of military aid by air, via Damascus international airport, and through the "Quds Brigades" to Lebanon. Since Israel's withdrawal from Lebanon, the Iranians meticulously built up Hezbollah's military and operational capabilities. Over the years, large quantities of top-quality weapons have been transferred to the organization, including: advanced anti-tank missiles, katyusha rockets, cannons and various anti-aircraft missiles, SA-14 and SA-7 shoulder missiles, small-scale naval warfare equipment, ultralights, UAVs, and advanced weapons systems such as ground-to-ground long range rockets. It would appear that there is no terror organization worldwide that benefits from such a massive ongoing and regular supply of top-quality arms. Iran helped, and is still helping, Hezbollah build its global terrorist network. Iran also helps the organization operate its network with agents from its security forces and the Iranian Revolutionary Guards, which operate from Iranian embassies worldwide.' See Azani, *Hezbollah*, 49.

3 Greg Bruno, Jayshree Bajoria and Jonathan Masters, *Iran's Revolutionary Guard*, Council on Foreign Relations Backgrounder, 14 June 2013, https://www.cfr.org/backgrounder/irans-revolutionary-guards (accessed 3 June 2017).

4 Judith Palmer Harik, *Hezbollah: The Changing Face of Terrorism* (New York: Palgrave Macmillan, 2005).

5 Azani, *Hezbollah*, 51.

6 Matthew Levitt, *Hezbollah: The Global Footprint of Lebanon's Party of God* (Washington, DC: Georgetown University Press, 2015).

7 Palmer Harik, *Hezbollah*.

8 Eitan Azani, *From Revolutionary and Pan-Islamism to Pragmatism and Lebanonization*, International Institute for Counter-Terrorism (ICT) Publication, 27 April 2006, https://www.ict.org.il/Article/941/From%20Revolutionary%20and%20Pan-Islamism%20to%20Pragmatism%20and%20Lebanonization (accessed 1 January 2020).

9 'Shiite ideology and the principles according to which Hezbollah operates were shaped by Ayatollah Khomeini and they constitute the basis for the organization's activity to this day. The following are key principles that were handed down by Khomeini: 1. Obtaining legitimacy for Shiite activism – Until the time of Khomeini's rule, the Shiites were passive and oppressed due to their being a minority within the Muslim world (90% of which are Sunni Muslims). Under Khomeini, the Shiites

underwent a change and became an active group that strives to achieve political goals, including the use of violent measures. Khomeini called for action by the "oppressed" (Shiites) against the "oppressors". 2. Delegitimization of corrupt Muslim regimes – Khomeini classified the regimes that do not follow Sharia law as corrupt and illegitimate, thus sanctioning the means to overthrow them. 3. Joining the Jihad against corrupt Arab rulers and the West as a means to promote the idea of the Islamic nation. 4. Defining the enemy – Khomeini coined two phrases that defined the enemies of Islam: the "Great Satan" – the US, and the "Little Satan" – Israel. 5. The principle of sacrifice – Khomeini reformulated the principle of sacrifice. He advocated a transition from the state of sacrifice to the state of self-sacrifice through Jihad against the enemies of Islam. As such, Khomeini founded the basis on which the phenomenon of suicide attacks as a strategic means for terrorism to achieve its goals developed. Hezbollah adopted the idea early on and carried out suicide attacks against foreigners in Lebanon between 1983–85. This method of operation was later adopted by other terrorist organizations. 6. The principle of "the rule of the jurisprudence" – According to Khomeini's approach, religious scholars need to run the Islamic state since they are the only ones that can interpret God's laws. This principle is unique to the radical Shiite thought and is strictly followed by Hezbollah as well.' See Azani, *Hezbollah*, 43.

10 Ibid., 43–4.
11 Palmer Harik, *Hezbollah*, 31.
12 James G. Blight et al., *Becoming Enemies: U.S.-Iran Relations and the Iran-Iraq War, 1979–1988* (Lanham: Rowman & Littlefield, 2012); William Echikson, French-Made Jets May Escalate Iran-Iraq War, *The Christian Science Monitor*, 8 September 1983; Bryan R. Gibson, *Covert Relationship: American Foreign Policy, Intelligence and the Iran-Iraq War, 1980–1988* (Santa Barbara: Praeger, 2010); Helen Chapin Metz, Arms from France, in Helen Chapin Metz (ed.), *Iraq: A Country Study* (Washington, DC: Government Printing Office, 1988); Judith Yaphe, Changing American Perspectives on the Iran-Iraq War, in Nigel Ashton and Bryan Gibson (eds.), *The Iran-Iraq War: New International Perspectives* (London: Routledge, 2013).
13 Bob Woodward, *Veil: The Secret Wars of the CIA 1981–1987* (New York: Simon and Schuster, 1987); David M. Abshire, *Saving the Reagan Presidency: Trust Is the Coin of the Realm* (College Station: Texas A&M University Press, 2005); Malcolm Byrne, *Iran-Contra: Reagan's Scandal and the Unchecked Abuse of Presidential Power* (Lawrence, KS: University Press of Kansas, 2014).
14 Hezbollah's Terrorist Activities during the 1980s, in *Hezbollah: Portrait of a Terrorist Organization*, The Meir Amit Intelligence and Terrorism Information Centre, 18 December 2012, 123–4, http://www.terrorism-info.org.il/Data/articles/Art_20436/E_1 58_12_1231723028.pdf (accessed 1 January 2020).
15 Ibid.
16 Ibid.
17 Jane Mayer and Doyle McManus, *Landslide: The Unmaking of the President, 1984–1988* (Boston: Houghton Mifflin, 1989), 292, 437.
18 Report of the Congressional Committees Investigating the Iran-Contra Affair, with Supplemental, Minority, and Additional Views (Washington, DC: Government Printing Office, 1987).
19 Magnus Ranstorp, *Hizballah in Lebanon: The Politics of the Western Hostage Crisis* (New York: St. Martins Press, 1997), 203.

20 Jeremy Shapiro and Bénédicte Suzan, The French Experience of Counter-terrorism, *Survival: Global Politics and Strategy* 45/1 (2003), 67–98; Michel Wieviorka, French Politics and Strategy on Terrorism, in Barry Rubin (ed.), *The Politics of Counterterrorism: The Ordeal of Democratic States* (Washington, DC: Paul H. Nitze School of Advanced International Studies, 1990), 61–90; Luc Chauvin, French Diplomacy and the Hostage Crisis, in: ibid., 61–90. I would like to thank Adrian Hänni for bringing these events to my attention.
21 Hezbollah's Terrorist Activities during the 1980s, 104.
22 Ibid.
23 Azani, *From Revolutionary and Pan-Islamism to Pragmatism and Lebanonization*.
24 An Open Letter: The Hizballah Program, 16 February 1985, available at http://www.cfr.org/terrorist-organizations-and-networks/open-letter-hizballah-program/p30967 (accessed 31 March 2017).
25 Hezbollah's Terrorist Activities during the 1980s, 103–4.

Chapter 9

THE PROPAGANDA CAMPAIGN FOR THE PFLP IN SWITZERLAND 1969-70

Daniel Rickenbacher

Introduction

Recently, the events of 1969–70, when Switzerland was the target of Middle Eastern terrorist groups, have become the focus of intensive public interest. A book by a Swiss journalist claimed that Switzerland had concluded a secret deal with the PLO in the wake of the hijacking of five airplanes, including one from Swissair, in September 1970.[1] However, a special governmental commission, which was set up after the book's publication to investigate these claims, disputes this.[2] While this chapter does not address the issue directly, it provides a background to these events, which is currently missing from the discussion. The terror campaign, which first struck Switzerland in February 1969, had been engineered by Wadie Haddad, a leader of the paramilitary group Palestinian Front for the Liberation of Palestine (PFLP) and a Lebanese Christian of Palestinian origin. Haddad was convinced that Israel was unbeatable through conventional military means. From the beginning, the campaign had a dual purpose. On the one hand, he sought to attack Israel's soft underbelly, which he identified as Israel's line of communications to Western Europe and the United States. On the other hand, the staging of sophisticated and effect-seeking terrorist attacks was meant to capture the attention of the Western public with the purpose of raising awareness for the Palestinian cause. In many ways, Haddad's approach recalled the propaganda of the deed, a strategy that had been pioneered by anarchist movements in the nineteenth and early twentieth centuries. However, the PFLP's propaganda of the deed was complemented to a significant degree by traditional, non-violent propaganda of the word.

Terrorist organizations' endurance is shaped by three external factors: the strength of their supporter base, the effectiveness of the counterterrorism response and outside sponsorship.[3] Since the late 1960s, activists from the European New Left provided essential support to the PFLP. Propaganda of the deed and of the word was important to gain this support. As I will show, the trial against three PFLP terrorists, which was held in late 1969 in the Swiss city of Winterthur, is exemplary in this regard. A public support campaign was organized by the Arab League and Fatah, which was active in Switzerland and abroad. It sought to raise sympathy for the indicted PFLP terrorists and their cause while also building up pressure against Switzerland to release the terrorists. The campaign co-opted anti-Zionist actors and groups from within Switzerland, many of them from the New Left. The establishment of these organizations was the result of a concerted strategy to engage the European public and in particular the New Left.

While the literature on state support for terrorist groups pays some attention to diplomatic support,[4] the issue of propaganda is seldom addressed. However, states can play a critical role in raising support for guerrilla and terrorist organizations via propaganda – as they did in the case of the PFLP. This was not a new phenomenon, especially not in the context of the Middle East. Already during the Arab Revolt in Palestine (1936–9), pro-insurgency propaganda was carried out by the Arab National Bureau in Damascus, which answered to the Syrian Foreign Office.[5] In our case, the Arab League office, which was attached to the Yemeni diplomatic mission in Geneva, funded and organized the campaign to a large degree. Single Arab states, like Algeria or Libya, further involved themselves in the campaign, hoping to gain prestige from their support for the Palestinian cause. The events of 1969–70 in Switzerland thus offer an interesting case of studying the interaction between states, terrorist organizations and propaganda networks during this critical period in Switzerland's confrontation with modern terrorism. The present chapter also sheds light on the unexplored history of Fatah and Arab League networks in Switzerland.

The 1969 attack in Zurich-Kloten

The PFLP, which was responsible for the terror wave against Switzerland in 1969–70, was a product and agent of the militarization of Palestinian politics after the Arab defeat in the Six-Day War. In December 1967, the Palestine Liberation Front merged with two offshoots of the Arab Nationalist Movement to form the PFLP. The new organization was chaired by George Habash, an Orthodox Christian Palestinian.[6] The PFLP opposed the takeover of the PLO by Fatah in late 1968 and moved from Nasserism to socialism. The ideological and political confrontation with Fatah contributed to the PFLP's radicalization in those years.[7] In 1968, Wadie Haddad established the commando branch of the PFLP and assumed its leadership. Unlike the PLO, which organized an abortive military insurgency in the West Bank in 1968, the strategy focused on Israeli soft targets abroad. In line with the propaganda of the deed approach, these attacks would advertise the Palestinian cause to the world public.[8] In a meeting of the PFLP leadership in December 1967, Haddad had set out the details of his strategy:

> What do I mean by that? I mean spectacular singular actions. These will direct the attention of the world towards the Palestine question. The world will ask: 'What's the Problem in Palestine? Who are the Palestinians? Why are they doing this?' At the same time, these operations will be very painful for the Israelis. With prominent, sensational actions [...] – that is how we need to hit the neuralgic

points. In the end, the world will be fed up with the problem. She will end up with the conclusion that something must happen with Palestine. She will need to give us justice.[9]

Barely half a year after this statement, on 23 July, the PFLP launched an unprecedented campaign against Israeli civilian targets abroad, when three members of the PFLP hijacked an El Al Boeing 707 airplane on its route from Rome to Tel Aviv. They forced the crew to fly to Algiers, where they and the passengers were held hostage. Israel was compelled to free Palestinian prisoners in exchange for their release – a first big success for Haddad's strategy.[10] Only five months later, on 26 December 1968, two PFLP terrorists arriving from Beirut conducted another operation at Athens Airport. They attacked an El Al airplane parked at the tarmac, killing one passenger. Before their arrest, they distributed PFLP leaflets.[11]

A similar attack was planned for February 1969 in Zurich. A team of four, three men and a woman, Mohammed Abu El-Heiga, Ibrahim Yousef, Amena Dahbor and Abdel Mehsen, was preparing for the attack scenario during a three-week course in a PFLP military camp in the Nablus region in mid-January 1969. They learned the use of rifles and explosives, training the exact sequence of the operation. The first group, Abu El-Heiga and Ibrahim Yousef, arrived in Zurich on 8 February after a complex itinerary by plane from Damascus via Beirut, Rome and Paris. They carried grenades, petards and 9.3 kilograms of explosives. The second group, Abdel Mehsen and Amena Dhabor, arrived from Amman via Vienna on the same day. Their suitcases held two Soviet-produced Kalashnikovs, ammunition as well as a stack of PFLP flyers. The next days were spent in preparing for the attack and reconnoitring the airport. They were assisted by a certain Fuad Saad Zhaglul, possibly a fifth PFLP operative, who provided the group with a rental car. On 18 February, they decided to attack El Al flight LY432 from the parking lot. Two members of the team of four opened fire on the El Al airplane before take-off, wounding the co-pilot fatally. Another one threw a grenade in front of the plane to bring it to a halt. The next step betrayed Haddad's handwriting. They planned to blow up the airplane after its evacuation. However, since the first attack in July, Israeli airplanes had been accompanied by air marshals. The air marshal on this particular flight, a young Israeli named Mordehai Rahamim, descended from the airplane and pursued the attackers, killing Abdel Mehsen.[12] The three surviving PFLP attackers and Rahamim were subsequently tried in the city of Winterthur, north of Zurich.

The Arab League and the Fatah support network in Switzerland

Judicial scandals and an atmosphere of intimidation marked the second half of 1969. This climate was the product of a concerted campaign, which was coordinated by Fatah, the Arab League and several Swiss anti-Zionist organizations. The groundwork for the campaign had been laid in the years before the terror attack, when networks of Fatah, the leading Palestinian nationalist organization, penetrated Western Europe, including Switzerland. Since 1963, Fatah dominated the major Arab student association in Germany, the *Generalunion Palästinensischer Studenten* (GUPS). The German GUPS served as a model of the expansion of Fatah networks in Europe.[13] Although there was no official GUPS chapter in Switzerland, Fatah established an active presence in Switzerland in the late 1960s. In 1968, Fuad al-Shamali, a Lebanese Maronite, settled in Geneva as its representative, revealing his function to the public two years later. Shamali was a former student leader of the Syrian Social Nationalist Party, a far-right party, and was married to the daughter of the party's founder, Antun Saadeh. After a failed coup attempt and his subsequent flight from Lebanon, he became close to the Palestinian cause in his exile in Paris.[14] Shamali could count on the services of other Arab activists who made Switzerland their home in the late 1960s.[15] The main partners for this network were the Arab League, the nascent New Left and a selection of anti-Semitic and pro-Nazi activists, like the notorious Nazi publisher François Genoud. Genoud had become infatuated with the Arabs, when he met the Mufti during a trip through the Middle East in the 1930s and became a lifelong supporter of nationalistic Arab movements, first of the FLN, and later of the PFLP. He also remained a committed national socialist. With his financial wealth, which partly stemmed from his copyright on Nazi literature and partly from unclear sources, he also provided these groups with significant amounts of money.[16] His role in the campaign shall be discussed later.

The Fatah network in Switzerland was also actively supported by the infrastructure of the Arab League in Switzerland. The nature of the relations between the Arab League, the PLO and Fatah necessitates some explanation. The Arab League had opened an office in Switzerland in 1957 in the city of Geneva. As Switzerland did not grant diplomatic status to the Arab League and its representatives, they were attached to the Yemeni diplomatic mission.[17] In 1964, the PLO was founded under the auspices of Egypt, which was then the leader of Arab nationalism and largely controlled the Arab League. The destinies of both organizations were therefore strongly entwined and their cooperation explicitly stipulated in the 1964 Palestinian national covenant.[18] After the PLO's founding, the Arab League sought in vain to gain approval for a PLO representative in Switzerland from the Swiss authorities, which opposed that step. After its defeat against Israel in 1967, Egyptian dominance of Arab nationalism was significantly weakened. This forms the background of Fatah's takeover of the PLO in 1968. The PLO that settled in Switzerland in the late 1960s was therefore much different from the earlier PLO. Still, it maintained its close cooperation with the Arab League.

While the Fatah network in Europe at first directed the bulk of its activities towards the Arab diaspora, after 1967 it sought to reach out to the nascent student movement and the New Left. The latter's attitude towards Israel was much more hostile than that of the moderate, social democratic Left, a fact that facilitated the rapprochement.[19] This development was also reflected in Switzerland, where Fatah officials and the office of the Arab League in Geneva collaborated with the scene of Swiss anti-Zionist organizations. The most active organization in the campaign was the *Comité de Soutien au Peuple Palestinien* (Eng. Committee for the Support of the Palestinian People), which had been established in early 1969 in Geneva, right after the attack on the El Al plane in Kloten. It was headed by Pierre Louis Claude (b. 1937), a functionary of the Communist Party of Labor,[20] a party that received financial support from Moscow during the Cold War.[21] Fatah representative Fuad al-Shamali became active in the committee in a leading role in September 1969 before the start of the trial in Winterthur.[22] Shamali and the Arab League office in Geneva counselled the *Comité* in its propaganda strategy, with the office also organizing public events as well as printing and editing its propaganda. The secretary at the office, who was of Syrian nationality, proved responsible for these activities.[23] It is no overstatement to conclude that the *Comité de Soutien au Peuple Palestinien* was as much a project of the Arab League office and of Fatah as it was one of its New Left members.

Fatah propaganda and militant networks in Europe were overlapping. During the Six-Day War, the GUPS had recruited Arab students in Germany to partake in guerrilla warfare against Israel.[24] Most members of the New Left were young and fascinated by the adventurism associated with guerrilla warfare. Fatah peddled this feeling by inviting young leftists to its military training camps in Jordan. In mid-July 1969, New Left activists from all over Europe travelled to Jordan to receive military training and attend a congress of the General Union of the Palestinian Students. The GUPS was by then under control of Fatah and had effectively turned into the youth branch of the PLO.[25] The approximately 200 European volunteers were joined by a Swiss contingent of several *Comité de Soutien au Peuple Palestinien* members, including its leader, Pierre Claude,[26] who had been selected by Fuad al-Shamali. Meanwhile, Shamali, who used the pseudonym Abu Said, was suspected of being involved in terrorism in Europe. A confidential source alleged that he was, inter alia, responsible for a bomb attack on the El Al office in Brussels on 8 September 1969.[27] Furthermore, after his death in 1972, it was widely reported in European and Arab media that he had played a major role in planning the terror attacks of Black September, including the Munich massacre, underscoring Swiss suspicions.[28] Shamali's case illustrates the blurred boundaries between propaganda and militancy in Fatah's European network strategy.

Besides the *Comité de Soutien au Peuple Palestinien* in Geneva, the Arab League also supported other anti-Zionist groups, which did not fall into the camp of the New Left. Among those was the Lausanne branch of the *Comité de Soutien au Peuple Palestinien*, which eventually split from the movement. It was headed by the Frenchman and known anti-Semite Roger Henry. Henry was a colourful figure, who had volunteered to help the German occupied forces in France during the Second World War and had later been active for the Organisation Armée Secrète, an underground paramilitary organization opposing Algerian independence.[29] Another such group was the more moderate *Swiss–Arab Society*, which was established in May 1969 and chaired by Hans Ellenberger. It was entirely dependent on the Arab League, which paid its secretary's wages. Moreover, its offices were housed in the building of the Arab Commercial Bank.[30] One of its directors was François Genoud, who had co-founded the bank in 1958 with funds provided by wealthy Arabs, in particular from Saudi Arabia.³¹ The bank was involved in the so-called Khider affair. In 1962, FLN treasurer Mohammed Khider deposited the FLN's funds amounting to about 42 million Swiss Francs in Genoud's bank.³² After Khider fell out with the Algerian regime and went into exile in Switzerland in 1963, control of the money was contested between him and the Algerian regime. In 1964, Genoud spent four months in an Algerian prison as a result of the affair. Khider was eventually killed by the Algerian secret service in 1967.³³

Why did the Arabs proceed to establish and finance anti-Zionist front groups with Swiss leadership? Certainly, the Swiss leadership provided them greater credibility with their Swiss audience. Perhaps more importantly, Swiss law prohibited political activity by foreigners. The Arab League office in Geneva had run into problems with Swiss authorities several times in the past because of their propaganda activities against Western powers and Israel. Setting up Swiss front groups alleviated this problem. State support for propaganda networks offered similar gains to those received from supporting terror networks: 'Plausible deniability, the possibility to project power despite little geopolitical significance, and the enhancement of their image as fighters for the cause of the "oppressed".'³⁴

Défense de Rupture

The investigation of the PFLP's February attack in Kloten and the subsequent trial took almost a year, lasting until December 1969. It pitted the Arab states, the Palestinian national movement and their sympathizers against Israel, the Jewish community and the majority of the Swiss population. Both sides invested significant prestige and energy in the trial, underlining its character as a proxy battle for the larger Arab–Israeli conflict. Georges Brunshvig, the head of the Swiss Jewish community and a famous lawyer, defended the Israeli security officer Mordehai Rahamim, who was accused of manslaughter. Brunshvig had gained prominence through the Berne Trial by proving that the Protocols of the Elders of Zion were a forgery.³⁵ He was assisted by Gabriel Bach, Israel's state attorney and former prosecutor in the Eichmann trial. On 22 December, the three Arabs were sentenced to twelve years in prison, while the Israeli was acquitted. After the delivery of the judgement, Gabriel Bach expressed his hope that the sentence would set a precedent for future trials against terrorists. The team of Arab lawyers that consulted the defence lawyer, however, warned that 'the Swiss–Arab relations were at the beginning of a long winter'.³⁶ The second statement would prove more accurate in the coming years.

The investigation and the subsequent trial were overshadowed by a campaign against the Swiss judiciary, which started in June 1969. It sought to disrupt the investigation and subvert the credibility of the Swiss judiciary by insinuating that it had a pro-Israeli bias.³⁷ According to Peter Woog, the head of JUNA, the intelligence service that the Swiss Jewish community had set up in the 1940s during the Nazi threat, the first phase of the campaign was deliberated at a meeting of Roger Henry's Palestine committee on 11 June. The disturbances were meant to prepare

9. The Propaganda Campaign for the PFLP in Switzerland 1969-70

the ground for a second phase of the campaign, in which the Arab states would step in to pressure Switzerland.[38] At a press conference on 14 June 1969, Roger Henry made serious allegations against the investigating authorities. Henry presented the journalists with parts of the investigation file against Mordehai Rahamim, claiming that the documents had been sold to a Palestinian organization for 5,000 dollars by someone inside the office of the principal investigator. The Swiss defence lawyers also lodged a complaint against the principal investigator, asking him to abandon the case.[39] As a result of these charges, the director of justice (Attorney General) of the Canton of Zurich opened an investigation into the charges against the principal investigator, but speculated that Henry had probably gained access to the documents through the Arabs' defence lawyers.[40] The latter, however, claimed to have had no connection with the campaign, but admitted to have been in touch with the Arab Lawyers Union (ALU).[41] In a phone call between Henry and Shamali, which was tapped by Geneva police, it was revealed that part of the documents had been photocopied by Shamali himself.[42] Obviously, the alleged spy within the principal investigator's office was the Arab Lawyers' Union itself, which had passed on the documents to Shamali. This was not the only effort to disrupt the investigation. The Arab interpreter, a Syrian refugee, was the repeated target of insinuations and accusations of pro-Israeli bias by the Arab side. In September 1969, the Syrian embassy demanded his removal from the trial.[43] This call was joined a few days later by the pro-Arab organizations *Comité de Soutien et d'Aide au Peuple Palestinien* and *Centrale Suisse d'Assistance à la Palestine* in a public letter, wherein they also demanded the release of the PFLP terrorists.[44] The Egyptian newspaper *Al-Ahram* meanwhile incited its readers by telling them that the interpreter was an Israeli.[45]

After the resignation of the two Swiss defence lawyers, the ALU agreed to convene a meeting in Cairo at the end of September to discuss the defence of Palestinian terrorists in Switzerland, Belgium, the Netherlands and Greece with representatives from Algeria, Lebanon, Jordan and the PLO.[46] It is likely that not only the trial in Switzerland was discussed in this context but also the larger strategy for the defence of Palestinian terrorists in Europe. The strategy, which shaped the defence in Switzerland and other defences organized by the ALU, was characterized by public campaigning and the disruption of the regular trial process. Swiss authorities thus observed the use of the same tactic in a trial against PFLP terrorists in Greece in October 1969.[47] This tactic is generally known by its French expression as '*défense de rupture*', a term coined by Jacques Vergès in 1968 in his book 'De la stratégie judiciaire'.[48] Vergès was a Franco–Algerian lawyer and a member of the ALU, who popularized the tactic in a trial against FLN operative Djamila Bouhired in 1957. Besides disruption, the tactic seeks to invert the role of prosecutor and defendant. The courtroom is turned into a public stage, where the state stands accused for its alleged crimes. After the Cairo meeting, Vergès was made a member of the defence team for the PFLP operatives in Switzerland, which also included the Moroccan lawyer Abderrahmane Youssoufi, a friend of François Genoud.[49] However, to the disappointment of his supporters, he was only allowed to attend the trial as an observer and not as a regular defence lawyer.[50] The Swiss

Nazi and pro-Arab activist François Genoud might had a role in bringing Vergès to Switzerland, whom he had known since the 1960s, when his Arab Commercial Bank managed the funds of the National Liberation Front (FLN).[51] Genoud's role in the campaign is murky. After speaking with the defendants and the president of courts, he explained to the press that he is simply an 'uninterested, voluntary aide to the defense of the Palestinians'.[52] Unsurprisingly for such a mysterious figure, this seems to have been an understatement. Rather, he worked as an intermediary between different Middle Eastern actors. According to his biographer, Genoud was maintaining regular contact with PFLP external operations chief Wadie Haddad in Beirut, with the director of the Libyan secret service and with al-Shamali in Geneva. He travelled to the Middle East at least four times during the period, probably to coordinate with his contacts in the region. Haddad, whom Genoud considered to be a genius, was unconcerned with Genoud's national socialist convictions. They had a common cause in their fight against Israel. However, Genoud's presence at the trial was a strategic mistake. It exposed the PFLP to accusations of harbouring national socialist and anti-Semitic sympathies. In his defence, Genoud awkwardly claimed to be only an anti-Zionist, not an anti-Semite.[53]

Some Arab states, in particular Libya and Algeria, directly interfered in the trial. Libya sent two delegations in late November and early December to speak with the defendants.[54] The court expressed concerns, noting that the defendants became less cooperative after the first Libyan visit. However, the stance of the Swiss Department of Foreign Affairs prevailed, which hoped that the Libyans would act in 'a calming manner on the Arab countries'.[55] At the same period of time, Algeria also intervened. On 28 November, the Algerian foreign minister Abdelaziz Bouteflika criticized the trial harshly and asked the UN Secretary General U Thant to have the UN intervene on behalf of the defendants.[56] Three days later, on 1 December, a prominent Algerian delegation met with U Thant to re-emphasize their demands.[57] As mentioned earlier, Algeria was also strongly represented in the ALU defence team with Jacques Vergès and Amar Bentoumi, then the president of the bar in Algeria. What was the reason for Algeria's and Libya's involvement? After Egypt's defeat in the Six-Day War, its claim to leadership of the pan-Arab movement was significantly weakened and other Arab states vied for this position, among them Algeria. Besides authentic feelings, solidarity with the Palestinians also had the useful effect of increasing one's prestige in the Arab public opinion. Algeria had exploited this effect since the mid-1960s, when it played a pioneering role in supporting the PLO diplomatically and militarily.[58] Libya did not count among the most radical Arab regimes before 1969. In September of this year, however, the monarchy was overthrown. The military junta under Colonel Muammar Gaddafi, which succeeded it, was one of the most radical Arab nationalist and anti-Western regimes in the Middle East. Like Algeria, it co-opted Palestinian nationalism to increase its standing vis-à-vis its Arab competitors.[59] The Arab League summit in Rabat on 20 December 1969 gave further impetus to Algeria and Libya to style themselves as the defenders of the Palestinians, something the Swiss ambassador in Algiers was very aware of. He therefore advised the Swiss authorities not to call out the Algerians publicly and increase the tensions, but to collaborate with them,

9. The Propaganda Campaign for the PFLP in Switzerland 1969–70   215

as 'we have an interest [...] to play the game, although we know, that sometimes a false card slips in'.[60] Rather than fighting the interference of Arab states into domestic matters, the Swiss authorities did their best to accommodate their demands in order to cushion the blow of the campaign.

The external campaign

Both the internal and the external campaigns were meant to discredit the Swiss investigative authorities in the public and paint the picture of a Swiss judiciary biased in favour of the Israelis. Arabic media contributed to this acerbic climate. Many had sent special correspondents to cover the trial in Winterthur. One of them, a journalist for the Syrian newspaper *Al Baath*, designed a conspiracy theory obviously inspired by the Protocols of the Elders of Zion to explain the alleged Swiss discrimination against the Arab defendants: 'Following the June War 1967 [Six-Day War], when a congress of about 70 international billionaires took place in Jerusalem to examine the possibilities to finance the new "Israeli Empire" and when talk was there of about 1,500 billions of old French francs, the Swiss delegations came as 5th among the 14 capitalist countries represented at the congress.'[61] The Iraqi newspaper *Al-Jumhuriya* called for reprisals against Switzerland to 'make them understand that the Arab nation cannot be despised'.[62] Swiss pro-Arab activists, acting in the role of 'native informants', helped stoke this deleterious climate. On 2 October 1969, Hans Ellenberger and Roger Du Pasquier of the *Swiss–Arab Society* travelled to Egypt to meet with senior figures. Among others, they spoke to the editor-in-chief of the Egyptian newspaper *Al-Ahram*, to whom they gave advice on the Swiss mentality and how to best convince the Swiss public. Writing about this encounter one day later, the editor-in-chief reported that the Swiss asked for their support, complaining that 'the influence of Zionism is efficient in the Swiss sphere of information, which, while concealing the Arab point of view, supports forcefully the Israeli point of view'.[63] These newspaper articles were registered by the Swiss authorities and added to the feeling of being under siege.

The local and the external actors worked together to increase the pressure on Switzerland and prevent the normal course of the investigation. One of the external actors was the PFLP, which continued to intimidate Switzerland to secure the release of the terrorists. A letter sent on 24 August, whose content revealed that the organization had intimate knowledge of the events in Switzerland and was closely monitoring the situation, made exactly this demand and accused the Swiss authorities of being involved in a 'Zionist complot'.[64] It is likely that Haddad was informed through François Genoud on the developments in Switzerland.[65] Since mid-September 1969, there were increasing signs that the PFLP was preparing a new round of violence against Switzerland. The authorities first received a credible warning of an imminent hijacking of a Swissair machine.[66] Then, on 19 September, the PFLP in Amman issued a communiqué calling for an improvement of prisoner conditions in Switzerland and warning of possible revenge.[67] In early

October, PFLP spokesman Ghassan Kanafani proclaimed to the press that the group was considering the abduction of a Swiss ambassador to create a 'climate of understanding' with the Swiss authorities.[68] However, the next PFLP terror attacks, which took place on 27 November, did not target Switzerland but Athens. In early December, the authorities received another warning of a terror attack, this time on Swiss soil,[69] possibly on the trial in Winterthur. Then, on 21 December 1969, hardly by coincidence just one day before the passing of judgement, an attempt to hijack a TWA plane in Athens failed.[70] This was just a small foretaste of what was to come for Switzerland in 1970. Unknown to the public, Switzerland was already preparing for the next emergency.

Zarqa and the release of the PFLP Terrorists

To the general observer, the campaign had failed to achieve its objective. Instead of caving to the pressure, Switzerland condemned the three PFLP operatives to long prison sentences, exposing the country to further threats from the Arab world and to possible sanctions.[71] However, the internal communication of the Swiss government reveals that the campaign did not miss its target. In mid-December 1969, the Federal Office of Police wrote a legal opinion, which investigated the legality of evicting the three Palestinian terrorists after the trial without punishment. Cautiously, the legal order affirmed the legality of such a procedure.[72] In the meantime, Switzerland was again confronted with a terrorist attack in February 1970, when a bomb exploded aboard a Swissair machine and caused its crash close to Zurich, killing all forty-seven passengers and crew members. The Swiss investigations concluded in December 1970 that the perpetrators were Sufian Kaddoumi and Mousa Badawi Jawher of the PFLP-General Command.[73] Although the bomb was meant to explode on an El Al airplane, it showed the vulnerability of Switzerland to Middle Eastern terrorism.[74] Up to now, the legal opinion on the legality of the terrorists' release had not been followed by actions. However, on 22 July, a commando hijacked the airplane Olympus Airways B727 and successfully negotiated the release of PFLP terrorists imprisoned in Athens.[75] The Greek authorities thus set a precedent. These events and the internal debates were the background for the Swiss decision-making. Eventually, in August, the Federal Council and the authorities of the Canton of Zurich, where the PFLP prisoners were held, agreed to realize the scenario for which they had prepared since December 1969. In case of a life-threatening hostage situation, the Zurich authorities would immediately release the PFLP terrorists.[76]

On 6 September 1970, the crisis the Swiss were expecting eventually arrived. Palestinian terrorists hijacked three airplanes in mid-air. Two airplanes, a Swissair on its way to New York and a TWA flight, were flown to the abandoned British airstrip Dawson's Field near the Jordanian city of Zarqa. The third hijacked airplane, a Pan Am flight, was landed in Cairo and blown up one day later after the release of the passengers. A fourth attempt to hijack an El Al airplane on its way to New York failed: one of the two terrorists was killed and the other, the notorious Leila Khaled, was subdued and incarcerated after the plane was landed at Heathrow Airport. An ultimatum on September 7 demanded the freeing of the three PFLP convicts in Switzerland, three terrorists who stood behind an attack targeting El Al passengers in Munich in February 1970, and Leila Khaled in return for the non-Jewish hostages. The fate of the Jewish American hostages, however, would depend on the release of prisoners incarcerated in Israel.[77]

The Swiss authorities immediately set the mechanism into motion that had been agreed on beforehand to release the terrorists. The head of the Middle East section of the Swiss Foreign Ministry (EPD) Michael Gelzer informed the authorities in Zurich, where the terrorists were incarcerated, in this vein and the decision was communicated to the media. However, the United States opposed separate negotiations and urged a comprehensive deal to free all hostages – a notion to which the Swiss agreed. An abduction of a British BOAC airplane to Dawson's Field on 9 September further escalated the crisis. The PFLP obviously sought a negotiation chip for the release of Leila Khaled. The number of hostages had now risen to 416.[78] After a preliminary meeting in Washington, the four affected states – Switzerland, the United Kingdom, Germany and the United States – agreed to deal with the crisis from the Swiss capital Berne. The committee therefore came to be known as the Berne Group. The International Committee of the Red Cross (ICRC) acted as a mediator between the Berne Group and the PFLP while the Americans had to strike a balancing act between forestalling the Europeans' tendency to give and pressure Israel and overcoming Israel's principal opposition to a deal.[79]

On 12 September, the PFLP evacuated the airplanes at Dawson's Field and blew them up – a memorable moment in the history of terrorism, which was captured by cameras and later put on display all over the world. Most hostages were released. However, a group with nationals from each of the negotiating countries was kept at a secret location to preserve the leverage. The Berne Group was under considerable strain, as the Europeans were pushing for separate deals.[80] Israel partly relented and agreed to release two kidnapped Algerian intelligence officers, but the British felt this was not enough and urged the Americans to exert greater pressure on the Israelis.[81]

Finally, it was the Egyptian dictator Gamal Nasser, who, on British stipulation, was able to pull off a deal that would end the hostage crisis. Around 1 October, the PFLP set the remaining hostages free. In exchange, the European countries subsequently released their Palestinian prisoners.[82] The three convicted PFLP terrorists in Switzerland were picked up at a prison in a suburb of Zurich on 30 September 1970. Shortly before their departure at 11.50 p.m., the police presented them with an envelope, containing one thousand Swiss Francs. The money was donated by François Genoud and distributed among the three convicts.[83] The same day, François Genoud flew to Beirut and subsequently to Cairo, where he stayed until 10 October.[84] Unlike the British and the Germans, the Swiss government had not been ready to directly negotiate with the PFLP or the PLO during the Zarqa Crisis. Nevertheless, they broke with their legal and constitutional principles by freeing the convicted terrorists. As a result of the crisis, the Swiss wished to continue operating the Berne Group to coordinate anti-terrorist activities.[85]

Epilogue

The propaganda campaign outlined in this chapter made Switzerland realize its vulnerability to Arab sanctions and terror. As a result, Swiss authorities were preparing themselves to release the Palestinian terrorists, even 'contra constitutionem'.[86] The changes in Swiss policy and public opinion towards the Arab–Israeli conflict had more lasting effects. In the aftermath of the crisis, Switzerland sought to gain distance from Israel and improve its relations to the Arab world. One element of this strategy was the opening of negotiations with the PLO representative Daoud Barakat in early 1971 on the establishment of an official PLO mission in Geneva. The negotiations were aborted after a terrorist attack against the Jordanian mission in Geneva in December 1971, but the contacts were maintained. The left-wing press, in particular the Zurich *Tages-Anzeiger*, began to publish articles overtly critical of Israel.[87] Moreover, opinion polls conducted in February 1970 and summer 1975 on the Arab–Israeli conflict, which were commissioned by the Swiss Federation of Jewish Communities, suggested that public opinion in Switzerland had significantly shifted in favour of the Arabs. The seemingly paradox results were that the Swiss thought better of the Arabs after their country had been hit by Palestinian terrorism than before the attacks. While 37 per cent of the Swiss had blamed the Arabs for the conflict in 1970, the number had diminished to 14 per cent in 1975. That same year, 16 per cent stated that their opinion of the Arabs had changed in a positive direction in the last three years in contrast to just 5 per cent five years earlier.[88] Hence, the possibility that the propaganda campaign contributed to this shift of opinion should not be dismissed.

The 1969 campaign also marked a change in Arab strategy in the Arab–Israeli conflict. From a symmetric conflict, where Israel was fought with conventional weapons by the Arab states, to an asymmetric conflict, where Israel was fought by the means of propaganda, terrorism and guerrilla warfare but also by diplomacy, through non-governmental and semi-governmental organizations. This strategy would prove successful for the Palestinians, with the PLO gaining sympathy and diplomatic recognition in a remarkably short period of time. The campaign was also an important moment in the history of the Swiss New Left, which subsequently embraced the Arab nationalist narrative of the conflict. Under the impression that the trial was a farce of justice, some were radicalized. For instance, a nineteen-year-old Swiss high school student Bruno Bréguet, in the aftermath of the trial, joined the PFLP, trying to blow up an office building in Tel Aviv in June 1970.[89] Almost fifty years after these events, Switzerland has only now started grasping their importance for Swiss and international history.

Notes

1 Marcel Gyr, *Schweizer Terrorjahre: Das geheime Abkommen mit der PLO* (Zürich: NZZ Libro, 2016), 133.

2 Interdepartementale Arbeitsgruppe '1970': Schlussbericht, Schweizerische Eidgenossenschaft, 3 May 2016, 25, https://www.eda.admin.ch/content/dam/eda/de/documents/publications/Geschichte/interdepartementale-arbeitsgruppe-1970_de.pdf (accessed 1 January 2020).
3 Kevin Siqueira and Todd Sandler, Terrorists versus the Government: Strategic Interaction, Support, and Sponsorship, *Journal of Conflict Resolution* 50/6 (2006), 878.
4 Daniel Byman, *Deadly Connections: States that Sponsor Terrorism* (Cambridge: Cambridge University Press, 2005), 61.
5 Bashir Saadawi, Letter to Shakib Arslan, 31 January 1938, in Schweizerisches Bundesarchiv (Swiss Federal Archives), Berne (henceforth BAR), Dossier E2001D#1000/1552#8771*; Virginia Vacca, L'ufficio Nazionale Arabo Di Stampa E Propaganda Di Damasco E Le Sue Pubblicazioni, *Oriente Moderno* 18/12 (1938), 683–9.
6 Aaron Mannes, *Profiles in Terror: A Guide to Middle East Terrorist Organizations* (Lanham, MD: Rowman & Littlefield, 2004), 310.
7 Helena Cobban, *The Palestinian Liberation Organisation: People, Power and Politics* (Cambridge University Press, 1984), 144.
8 Wolfgang Kraushaar, *'Wann endlich beginnt bei Euch der Kampf gegen die heilige Kuh Israel?': München 1970: über die antisemitischen Wurzeln des deutschen Terrorismus* (Hamburg: Rowohlt, 2013), 27–8.
9 Bassam Abu Sharif and Uzi Mahnaimi, *Mein Feind – mein Freund: Ein Araber und ein Israeli kämpfen für eine gemeinsame Zukunft* (München: Droemer Knaur, 1996), 84–5; cited in Kraushaar, *'Wann endlich beginnt bei Euch der Kampf gegen die heilige Kuh Israel?'* 28.
10 Kraushaar, *'Wann endlich beginnt bei Euch der Kampf gegen die heilige Kuh Israel?'* 30.
11 'הנותאב לע לא סוטמ ופקת םילבחמ ינש', *Maariv*, 27 December 1968.
12 Bill of Indictment, Office of the District Attorney, 12 August 1969, BAR#E4320-05C#1995/234*137*.
13 Abdallah Frangi, *Der Gesandte: Mein Leben für Palästina. Hinter den Kulissen der Nahost-Politik* (München: Heyne, 2012), 98–102.
14 Pierre Pean, *L'Extremiste: Francois Genoud – De Hitler À Carlos* (Paris: Fayard, 1996), 337–8; Ilyich Ramirez Sánchez, Comment et pourquoi j'ai pris en otage les ministres de l'OPEP, 18 July 2006, http://www.alterinfo.net/Carlos-comment-et-pourquoi-j-ai-pris-en-otage-les-ministres-de-l-OPEP_a2451.html (accessed 1 January 2020).
15 'Union des Etudiants arabes', 10 May 1968, BAR#E4320C#1994/120#782*; 'Contrôle téléphonique de El-Shamali, 17.07.1969-31.10.1969', Service Politique du Corps de Police Genève, 26 November 1969, BAR#E4320-05C#1995/234*137*.
16 For more information on François Genoud, see Pean, *L'Extremiste*; Karl Laske, *Ein Leben zwischen Hitler und Carlos: François Genoud* (Zürich: Limmat Verlag, 1996); Willi Winkler, *Der Schattenmann: Von Goebbels Zu Carlos: Das Mysteriöse Leben Des François Genoud* (Berlin: Rowohlt, 2011).
17 Letter by Zoher Kabbani to Federal Councillor Max Petitpierre, 25 June 1957, BAR#E2001E#1970/217#2388*.
18 Harold M. Cubert, *The PFLP's Changing Role in the Middle East* (London: Psychology Press, 1997), 53.
19 For Germany's New Left, see Jeffrey Herf, *Undeclared Wars with Israel: East Germany and the West German Far Left, 1967–1989* (Cambridge: Cambridge University Press, 2016), 79–84.

20 Bericht 'Schweizerische Vereinigungen für die Unterstützung arabischer Palästinenser', Office of the Attorney General, 1969, BAR#E2005A#1978/137#2078*.
21 Aus dem Innenleben der PDA, *Neue Zürcher Zeitung*, 25 May 2003, https://www.nzz.ch/article8U945-1.257391 (accessed 1 January 2020).
22 'Contrôle téléphonique de El-Shamali, 17.07.1969–31.10.1969'.
23 'Contrôle téléphonique de la Délégation Permanente de la Ligue des Etats arabes, avenue Krieg 7, 12.01.1970 – 26.07.1970', Service Politique du Corps de Police Genève, 31 July 1970, BAR#E4320C#1995/390#1218*.
24 Ido Zelkovitz, *Students and Resistance in Palestine: Books, Guns and Politics* (London: Routledge, 2014), 47.
25 Ibid., 51; Herf, *Undeclared Wars with Israel*, 98–9.
26 'Note sur le stage de militants révolutionnaires en Jordanie', 11 August 1969, BAR#E4320C#1995/390#1209*.
27 'Rapport Sur Fouad-Assad El-Shamali', Swiss Federal Police, 10 September 1969, BAR#E4320C#1995/390#1209*.
28 Serge Groussard, *La Médaille de Sang* (Paris: Denoël, 1973), 153–5.
29 Bericht 'Schweizerische Vereinigungen für die Unterstützung arabischer Palästinenser'; Memo on Roger Henry, Swiss Federal Police, 31 July 1970, BAR#E4320-05C#1995/390#1211*.
30 Bericht 'Schweizerische Vereinigungen für die Unterstützung arabischer Palästinenser'; 'Contrôle téléphonique de la Délégation Permanente de la Ligue des Etats Arabes, avenue Krieg 7, 01.05.1969 –30.06.1969', Service Politique du Corps de Police Genève, 21 June 1969, BAR#E4320C#1995/390#1214*.
31 Pean, *L'Extremiste*, 228–9.
32 Ibid., 266.
33 Winkler, *Der Schattenmann*, 160–7.
34 Thomas Riegler, Quid pro Quo: State Sponsorship of Terrorism in the Cold War, in Bernhard Blumenau and Jussi M. Hanhimäki (eds.), *An International History of Terrorism: Western and Non-Western Experiences* (London: Routledge, 2013), 119.
35 On the trial see Hadassa Ben-Itto, *The Lie that Wouldn't Die: The Protocols of the Elders of Zion* (Elstree: Vallentine Mitchell, 2005), 269–349.
36 So ging der El-Al-Prozess in Winterthur zu Ende, *Tages-Anzeiger*, 22 December 1969.
37 Attentäter machen der Schweiz Sorgen, *Frankfurter Allgemeine Zeitung*, 16 July 1969.
38 Peter Woog, Arabische Propaganda, *Der Bund*, 11 July 1969.
39 Attentäter machen der Schweiz Sorgen.
40 Strafuntersuchung gegen Bezirksanwaltschaft Bülach, *Volksrecht*, 15 July 1969.
41 Die angegriffenen Anwälte schiessen zurück, *Tages-Anzeiger*, 16 July 1969.
42 'Rapport Sur Fouad-Assad El-Shamali'.
43 Letter by the General Consulate of Syria to the Swiss Department of Foreign Affairs, 9 September 1969, BAR# E4320-05C#1995/234*136*.
44 Letter by the Comité Suisse de Soutien et d'Aide Au Peuple Palestinien to Federal Councillor Willy Spühler, 13 September 1969, BAR#E4320-05C#1995/234*136*.
45 Les commandos de Zurich font la grève de la faim depuis 17 jours, *Al-Ahram*, 13 September 1969.
46 Appel lancé à la croix rouge pour sauver les commandos qui font la grève de la faim depuis vingt jours, *Al Baath*, 16 September 1969.
47 Letter by Swiss Chargé D'affaires in Athens to Swiss Foreign Office on the Attack of an El Al Airplane in Hellenikon, 7 October 1969, BAR#E4320-05C#1995/234*136*.

9. The Propaganda Campaign for the PFLP in Switzerland 1969–70   221

48 Saint-Pierre François, Non, Jacques Vergès n'a pas inventé la défense de rupture, *Le Monde.fr*, 20 August 2013, http://www.lemonde.fr/idees/article/2013/08/20/non-jacques-verges-n-a-pas-invente-la-defense-de-rupture_3463953_3232.html (accessed 1 January 2020).
49 Bernard Violet, *Vergès: Le maître de l'ombre (L'épreuve des faits)* (Paris: Seuil, 2000), 167–9.
50 Interrogation of Vergès, Memo, 16 December 1969, BAR#E4320-05C#1995/234*137*; Vergès Receives Safe Conduct, Telex, 16 December 1969, BAR#E4320-05C#1995/234*137*.
51 Laske, *Ein Leben zwischen Hitler und Carlos*, 171.
52 Ibid., 228–9.
53 Pean, *L'Extremiste*, 321; Winkler, *Der Schattenmann*, 170–9.
54 Note for the Federal Prosecutor's Office, 1 December 1969, BAR#E4320-05C#1995/234*137*.
55 Letter from Attorney General Hans Walder to Court President Hans Gut, 9 December 1969, BAR#E4320-05C#1995/234*137*.
56 Note for the Federal Prosecutor's Office.
57 ONU: Déclaration du représentant d'Algérie, *Algérie Presse Service*, 2 December 1969.
58 Cobban, *The Palestinian Liberation Organisation*, 31–2.
59 Jacob Abadi, Pragmatism and Rhetoric in Libya's Policy Toward Israel, *Journal of Conflict Studies* 20/2 (2000).
60 'Rapports algéro-suisses dans le contexte de la politique algérienne', 8 December 1969, BAR#E2001E#1980/83#921*.
61 L'interdiction de toute manifestation oratoire n'atteint pas les Sionistes, *Al Baath*, 1 December 1969, BAR#E4320C#1995/390#1214*.
62 Switzerland… Persistence on Wrong, *Al-Jumhuriya*, 15 September 1969.
63 A.H. El-Gammal, Editorial, *Al-Ahram*, 8 October 1969.
64 Letter by the PFLP to the Swiss Honorary Consul in Kuwait, 24 July 1969, BAR#E4320-05C#1995/234*136*; Letter from Michel Gelzer (Swiss Department of Foreign Affairs) to Attorney General Hans Walder, 4 December 1969, BAR#E4320-05C#1995/234*137*.
65 Pean, *L'Extremiste*, 321.
66 Memo for the Federal Office of Police on Planned Airplane Hijackings, 16 September 1969, BAR# E4320-05C#1995/234*136*.
67 Warning from the Popular Front to the Swiss Authorities, *Al Nour*, 20 September 1969.
68 Memo on Possible Plans of the PFLP to Kidnap a Swiss Ambassador, 7 October 1969, BAR#E4320-05C#1995/234*136*.
69 Memo by the Swiss Federal Police, 9 December 1969, BAR#E4320-05C#1995/234*137*; Memo by the Swiss Federal Police, 11 December 1969, BAR#E4320-05C#1995/234*137*.
70 Les trois libanais appréhendés dimanche à l'aéroport d'Athènes risquent au moins 20 ans de prison, *Le Progrès Egyptien*, 23 December 1969.
71 Arab Preparations to Adopt Measures against Switzerland after the Trial of the Commandos, *Al Thawra*, 28 December 1969.
72 'Kloten Attack, Eviction of the Terrorists Based on Art. 70 of the Federal Constitution', Memo, Swiss Federal Police, 19 December 1969, BAR# E4320-05C#1995/234*137*.
73 Kraushaar, '*Wann endlich beginnt bei Euch der Kampf gegen die heilige Kuh Israel?*' 443–5.

74 Ibid., 450.
75 Edward F. Mickolus and Susan L. Simmons, *The Terrorist List* (Westport: Praeger Security International, 2011), 39.
76 Aviva Guttmann, Une Coalition Antiterroriste Sous L'égide D'un Pays Neutre: La Réponse Suisse Au Terrorisme Palestinien, 1969–1970, *Relations Internationales* 3 (2015), col. 12.
77 David Carlton, *The West's Road to 9/11: Resisting, Appeasing and Encouraging Terrorism since 1970* (London: Palgrave Macmillan, 2005), 18. On the Zarqa crisis of September 1970 see also the detailed account of Thomas Skelton-Robinson in this publication.
78 Guttmann, Coalition Antiterroriste, cols. 18–26.
79 Carlton, *The West's Road to 9/11*, 18–20.
80 Guttmann, Coalition Antiterroriste, cols. 27–29.
81 Carlton, *The West's Road to 9/11*, 26–33.
82 Ibid., 34.
83 Memo on the donation of François Genoud to Mohammed Abu El-Heiga, Kantonspolizei Zürich, 1 October 1970, BAR#E4320-05C#1995/234*137*.
84 Travel Itinerary of François Genoud, Police de Sureté Vaud, 12 January 1971, BAR#E4320-05C#1995/234*137*.
85 Guttmann, Coalition Antiterroriste, cols. 35–38.
86 'Kloten Attack, Eviction of the Terrorists Based on Art. 70 of the Federal Constitution', Memo, Office of the Attorney General, 30 December 1969, BAR#E4320-05C#1995/234*137*.
87 Jonathan Kreutner, *Die Schweiz und Israel: auf dem Weg zu einem differenzierten historischen Bewusstsein* (Zürich: Chronos, 2013), 102.
88 Ibid., 124.
89 Gyr, *Schweizer Terrorjahre*, 51.

Chapter 10

THE UNITED STATES AND NICARAGUA

STATE TERRORISM DURING THE LATE COLD WAR

Philip W. Travis

On 6 November 1985, militants from the 19th of April Movement, sometimes called M-19, stormed the Colombian Supreme Court with assault rifles. The attackers were associated with the insurgent conflict raging in the country at the time. The militants seized the building and took a score of hostages in an aggressive attempt to gain concessions from the Colombian government. Just over a day later, the hostage crisis turned into a bloodbath as Colombia's armed forces stormed the building and an intense shootout unfolded thereafter. The tragic results included the death of eighty-nine people, including seven of Colombia's justices. It was a brutal act of terrorism linked to the gritty insurgent war waged in the country.[1]

After the events in Colombia, the United States, which under the Reagan administration redeveloped its policy on state terrorism, suggested that the act was facilitated, in part, by the government of Nicaragua. The United States insisted that the terror attack provided further evidence of the complicity of the Nicaraguan government in terrorism. Throughout the 1980s, the Reagan administration insisted that Nicaragua was a legitimate state terror threat. However, with respect to the Colombia attack, the Reagan administration appeared to possess scant evidence to suggest the Sandinista-led Nicaraguan government was directly involved in this act of terrorism. The primary evidence was intelligence suggesting that several of the weapons used were of Nicaraguan origin.[2] However, the allegation of complicity in the attack was only the latest of a series of developments that the United States insisted verified the wider assertion that Nicaragua was a state sponsor of international terrorism.

At the time of the Colombia attack the United States was waging a proxy war against the Nicaraguan government. Throughout the 1980s, it advised and supplied several insurgent groups that waged war, often brutally, on the government and the people of Nicaragua. The guerrillas were known as the Contras, and the Reagan administration fought a continual political battle with Congress and the American people over the funding of these guerrillas, which operated in violation of the sovereignty of Honduras, Costa Rica and Nicaragua. Because of the controversy swirling around the Contra War, the administration used any link to the M-19 attack in Colombia to build up its argument that Nicaragua was a state terror threat, and thereby justify its support for the war on that government.³

The September 11 attack is, with respect to American foreign policy, perhaps the most significant event of the twenty-first century. This event and its aftermath continue to shape the foreign and domestic policies of the United States today. The centrepiece of the Bush administration's War on Terror was the invasion of Iraq. In 2002 and 2003, the United States used the threat of terrorism to justify a unilateral war of regime change against Iraq, a country that the United States implied posed a potential threat due to its alleged Weapons of Mass Destruction (WMD) programme – which it suggested could fall into the hands of terrorists. Brian Glyn Williams, author of the 2017 book *Counter Jihad*, demonstrated that the Bush administration was obsessed over Iraq and that it consistently looked away from the real terrorist hotspots because of the geopolitical importance that Iraq represented to cabinet members influenced by neoconservatism.⁴ Eventually, after failing to gain support from the UN Security Council, the Bush administration went ahead with the invasion of Iraq despite strong, widespread international opposition. The decision carried significant ramifications for the region.⁵

In the intense atmosphere of debate following the invasion of Iraq, many historians like Lloyd Ambrosius, John Lewis Gaddis and Melvin Leffler debated whether this was the beginning of a new era in US foreign policy.⁶ In many respects, it was indeed a new era; however, the United States' interventionist policy against state sponsors of terrorism emerged first during the late Cold War. Today, more and more scholars are demonstrating a continuity between the Cold War and the War on Terror.⁷ This chapter contributes to this discussion by examining the case of Sandinista-led Nicaragua, a country labelled a terror state by the Reagan administration. This small Central American country was the focus of the United States' efforts to shape the state terror problem in the 1980s in such a way as to bring greater recognition to the use of offensive interventionist policies.

During the 1960s and 1970s, in the wake of Fidel Castro and Che Guevara's stunning success in the 1959 Cuban Revolution, leftist revolutionary movements appeared across Latin America. Almost no country in South or Central America was free of leftist insurgency. The majority of the groups rationalized the fight as against unrepresentative and repressive governments that were often identified as somehow caused by the imperialism of the powerful North American neighbour: the United States. The Cuban Revolution brought inspiration and aide to many groups like the Frente Sandinista de Liberacion Nacional (FSLN) in Nicaragua, the Farabundo Marti National Liberation Front (FMLN) in El Salvador and the Revolutionary Armed Forces of Colombia (FARC), which are just a few examples of insurgencies that derived inspiration from Latin Americanized versions of Marxism, Leninism and, in some cases, Maoism.

The revolutions, which spread like wildfire across the region during the late Cold War, caused a state terror response. This widespread and coordinated state terror campaign was neither Islamic, nor Middle Eastern, nor leftist. Rather, it was rightist, Latin American and, by the accounts of some in the State Department,

Christian. In South America, coups in Chile and Argentina during the 1970s resulted in hard-line regimes, aligned with the United States, which waged aggressive terror wars against leftists, both domestically and internationally. In 1976, the new Argentine leadership began a period of persecution known by historians as the Dirty War. Out of a paranoid concern with leftist insurgents, the Argentine government engaged in widespread kidnappings and executions. Under Pinochet's rule in Chile, of course, similar events occurred and, as in Argentina, on a massive scale.[8]

The state terror campaign among the Southern Cone[9] states during the late 1970s was not simply domestic but also an internationally coordinated operation. Operation Condor was the name used to refer to an international assassination plan that included several South American states. Argentina and Chile spearheaded the operation, which was intended to carry out coordinated attacks within foreign sovereign territory on radical leftist groups and enemies. Assistant Secretary of State Harry W. Schauldemen reported that Argentina defined the action as a global and Christian 'third world war'.[10]

The most publicized death connected to Condor took place only a matter of blocks from the White House and the United States Capitol. The assassination of Orlando Letelier in 1976 at Sheridan Circle in Washington, DC in a car bomb remains the most visible action of the Condor operation, but these operations also included planning for attacks in Europe on terrorist and leftist groups that fled the region following the rise of rightist governments across South America.[11] The Condor operation utilized US communication facilities in the Panama Canal Zone, and while the Kissinger-led State Department sought to discourage the action, Kissinger, possibly out of concern for alienating an ally, hesitated to intervene in order to prevent widespread human rights atrocities in 1976.[12]

During the 1970s, Central America also faced a situation all too common in the wider region of Latin America. Increasingly, anti-leftist dictatorships friendly to the United States faced violence from leftist insurgents that possessed connections to Cuba. In Nicaragua, the FSLN or Sandinistas grew in strength amidst a brutal repression by the dictator Anastasio Somoza Debayle and, in 1979, the insurgents overthrew the long-time US-supported government of Nicaragua. After his ouster from power, the Nicaraguan dictator was cut off from US aid or asylum. Fleeing for life, Somoza and his entourage ultimately took refuge in Paraguay. The leader in Paraguay was Alfredo Stroessner, a hard-right dictator whose cruelty was rivalled by few. While living near the capital of Asunción, Somoza was under personal guard, but hardly in a low profile. He travelled in a yellow Mercedes, lived in a large compound and attended lavish parties. Somoza's playboy lifestyle made it easy for his enemies to locate him. On 17 September 1980, the militants that killed Somoza riddled his Mercedes in a hail of machine gunfire and a violent blast from a rocket-propelled grenade.[13]

The Jimmy Carter administration seemed largely convinced that the new revolutionary government of Nicaragua was responsible for Somoza's death. Further, it considered the attack a case of international terrorism.[14] However, while there was apparently a consensus among Carter's closest advisors that the attack was connected to the Sandinistas, some, like the ambassador to Nicaragua Lawrence Pezzullo, seemed to believe that it did not represent any larger terrorist connection or anyway represent a fundamental tendency of Nicaraguan foreign policy towards the use of terrorism. Pezzullo believed the United States could work with the new Nicaraguan government.[15] The killing was an a revenge for decades of Somoza's repression. It was the capstone on a successful revolution, and was more connected to an insurgent war than to a case of state sponsorship of international terrorism. Lacking direct evidence connecting the government to the attack, the Carter administration decided to not enact its legal powers to use economic sanctions against state sponsors of terrorism in the case of Nicaragua.[16]

With the inauguration of Ronald Reagan, the United States reversed its policy relating to Nicaragua and state terrorism. Beginning in 1981, it suspended aid deliveries to Nicaragua and instituted a policy of supplying and advising a group of guerrillas, remnants of the Somoza regime that continued a military struggle across border regions in the north and south of the country.[17] Over time, this evolved into a policy designed to use economic sanctions to cripple the government and then military force applied through proxies to oust it from power. This was a Cold War case of pre-emptive regime change against an alleged state sponsor of terrorism.[18] But what evidence did the Reagan administration have on the Sandinistas to warrant such an aggressive policy?

First and foremost, the Reagan administration believed that the new Nicaragua was complicit in seeking to extend military violence throughout Central America, and starting in 1981 it imposed an ultimatum on the government demanding that it cease support for other revolutionaries and allow the guerrillas (the Contras) it was fighting to join the government. The Reagan administration did cite the case of the Somoza assassination as cause for its initial measures in 1981. However, the centrepiece of the Reagan administration's claim, and the justification for sanctions and war against Nicaragua, was the government's support of the guerrilla insurgency in the small Central American country of El Salvador: the FMLN.[19]

The FMLN had much in common with the FSLN in Nicaragua and insurgencies throughout the Americas. The group waged a guerrilla war, and this meant a wide variety of hostilities and activities that ranged from sabotage, kidnapping, small battles and ambushes, weapons trafficking, drug smuggling and assassination. Such activities were commonplace of insurgencies throughout the region, but during Reagan's first term the State Department identified the FMLN as a terrorist group and Sandinista-led Nicaragua as a state sponsor. This claim was a central component of the Reagan administration's policy in the region. Reagan's policy centred on aiding the Salvadoran government while simultaneously promoting clandestine operations and support for insurgents that waged war on the government of Nicaragua. Over the next several years, US intelligence organizations, the State Department, the Defense Department and the National Security council (NSC) developed a policy that merged anti-leftist foreign policy in Central America with its counterterrorism strategy. Perhaps one of the most interesting documents that demonstrate this change in US foreign policy came from a State Department report, circulated in 1984, that drew a formal distinction between terrorist groups and insurgencies.[20]

As terrorist incidents surged in the 1980s alongside violent conflicts in Central America, the Reagan administration took steps to redefine terrorism and through it state sponsors. In support for this development, the State Department circulated a report that provided a clear set of requirements for the categorization of a group as insurgent or terrorist. The report broadened the catalogue of terrorist acts while shrinking the definition of legitimate insurgencies. According to George Shultz's State Department, legitimate insurgencies referred to any organization whose 'members wear a uniform [and which] operates in the open [...] Its [insurgency] methods are military [and] its targets are military, both tactical and strategic, and its legitimate operations are governed by the international rules of armed conflict'. Finally, 'its primary interests [must] relate to one country'.[21] This document was part of an effort by the Reagan administration to create a paradigm whereby any insurgency opposed by the United States might fall into the category of terrorist and so too its supporters as state sponsors. Such a reclassification provided a powerful legal claim that aggressive pre-emptive actions were necessary in the case of Nicaragua.

Following the State Department report, the FMLN was no longer regarded by the United States as a legitimate insurgency, but rather a terrorist group – and a big one at that, as it numbered approximately 7,500.[22] Shortly thereafter, the FMLN appeared in State Department publications like *Terrorist Group Profiles*, which was an in-depth sourcebook on international terrorist groups complete with an eloquent opening message from Vice President George H. W. Bush.[23] Likewise, because of its support of the FMLN, Nicaragua was listed among the official state sponsors of terrorism in the top secret 1985 CIA report 'State Support for International Terrorism'.[24] These characterizations created the legal framework of the administration's policy of regime change against Nicaragua, which it implemented with growing ferocity in the mid-1980s.

The Reagan administration's redefining of insurgency and state terrorism was applied against the backdrop of several attacks on US servicemen and personnel deployed in areas of intense civil unrest and insurgent warfare. In 1983, Lt. Col. Albert Schaufelberger was killed as he waited for a companion outside of the Central American University in San Salvador, El Salvador. Schaufelberger was the head of the US military advisor programme with the Salvadoran government. He was gunned down in a hail of machine gunfire. That same year, an even more grave series of events occurred during the Lebanese Civil War as the United States experienced a catastrophic attack on a Marine barracks and on the Beirut embassy, resulting in the death of several hundreds. These events brought a heightened sense of concern to the issue of terrorism.[25]

Over the next two years, the conflict in Central America escalated, and in June 1985, the United States suffered the worst attack since its decision to take an advisory role in the Salvadoran conflict. At an outdoor café in San Salvador, guerrillas with ties to the FMLN killed four off-duty Marines along with several bystanders. The attack was the central catalyst for the Reagan administration to make a public declaration of its classification of Nicaragua as a state sponsor of international terrorism, which Ronald Reagan announced in his 8 July 'outlaw states' speech. The attacks on US personnel in El Salvador, he insisted, were carried out because of Nicaragua's support of the FMLN, and this was evidence of Nicaragua's role as a state sponsor of international terrorism.[26]

Despite the arguments of the Reagan administration regarding Nicaragua's support for the FMLN, not all believed that this necessarily amounted to support for international terrorism. Among those most vocally opposed to the administration's argument were top officials of the State Department's Office of Counterterrorism like its Deputy Director Parker Borg. In a 2002 interview, Borg insisted that the Office of Counterterrorism 'declined [...] to consider the various groups in Central America, the Sandinistas or El Salvador groups [...] as being terrorists per-se'.[27] However, despite this objection, the Reagan administration continued a powerful reconstruction of the concept of insurgency and terrorist.

In considering the classification of Nicaragua as a sponsor of terrorism, one must also consider the Reagan administration's own policy. The United States' approach to Nicaragua met many of the same standards that it applied to blacklist Nicaragua as a state sponsor of terrorism. It supported insurgents: the Contras.[28] Those guerrillas violated the sovereign borders of multiple countries. The insurgents kidnapped, assassinated, sabotaged and smuggled illegal drugs and weapons. Even the head organizer of the Contra supply programme, Oliver North, was referred to by the director for the Office of Counterterrorism Robert Oakley as advocating the use of terrorist tactics as a legitimate counterterrorism option. In a 1992 interview, Oakley confirmed that North and National Security Advisor John Poindexter ran counterterrorism in Central America on their own and with little concern for international law, and it was a fear that he might be implicated in North's criminal actions that led Oakley to ask Secretary of State Shultz to allow him to step down early in the spring of 1986.[29]

Only a few months later did the Iran–Contra scandal embroil the United States in a shocking controversy that, at its core, involved sales of illegal weapons to Iran and illegal support operations for the Contras. These developments represented a glaring contradiction in US counterterrorism doctrine: it had exchanged weapons with a country it classified as a sponsor of terrorism (Iran) in support of a group it claimed were freedom fighters battling the forces of leftist international terrorism.[30] A central issue that caused this contradiction was, first, the tendency of Reagan to allow lower-level figures like North to operate with limited oversight and direction.[31] However, this apparent contradiction was also caused by the Reagan administration intentionally blurring the distinction between insurgent and terrorist and between state sponsorship of terrorism and state support for insurgencies.[32] The United States characterized support for leftist insurgency as tantamount to state sponsorship of terrorism, and Reagan's critics logically responded in kind to the United States' support for insurgents like the Contras. Generally, in insurgent/asymmetric conflicts, attacks on innocent people and other soft targets occur, and as a result, it is important that there be a reasonable distinction drawn between insurgent and terrorist because the two, as the post-2001 War on Terror demonstrated, are afforded different treatment. One is considered a lawful combatant, while the other is regarded as a criminal combatant, and the classification as illegitimate or criminal may justify the harsher treatment of both governments and individuals.

Neither the FMLN nor the Contras were necessarily terrorist groups, and neither Nicaragua nor the United States was necessarily a terror state in supporting each other. As uncomfortable as one might be about support for proxy guerrilla fighters in a programme of regime change, it still does not necessarily mean that the insurgent groups should be regarded as terrorist organizations. These were guerrilla insurgencies fighting nasty wars with long historical roots, and the United States and Nicaragua hoped to influence the end game of these conflicts. The distinction between insurgency and terror group is a very important one, but in the 1980s the United States blurred this difference as a tool for the achievement of its foreign policy goals.

State support for international terrorism, too, ignited a debate in the Reagan administration over the removal of the assassination ban enacted first during the Gerald Ford Administration.[33] The Reagan administration did officially reaffirm the ban in 1981; however, several developments during the 1980s caused a reasonable doubt as to the extent that the administration adhered strictly to this ban. In 1984, for example, revelations of a CIA assassination manual used in Contra training activities caused political turmoil as it suggested, during an election year, that the United States encouraged the use of assassination by the Contras.[34] As events of international terrorism increased alongside bloody conflicts in the developing world, George Shultz also advocated for a more aggressive approach to the problem. Following Reagan's outlaw state speech in 1985, he insisted that issues of international terrorism called for a re-evaluation of the assassination ban.[35] Likewise, Robert Oakley acknowledged that Oliver North openly advocated and, in some cases, pursued a myriad of actions that were not consistent with official policy doctrine. These included the use of terrorism against terrorists, as well as the potential pursuit of assassinations within other sovereign nations.[36] The Reagan administration's official policy supported the ban, but the issues of terrorism and insurgent war raised the question, and encouraged a discussion over past foreign policy doctrine.

Over the course of Reagan's presidency, the administration relied on elaborate legal arguments and intelligence sources to demonstrate that Nicaragua was a state sponsor of terrorism. Not entirely unlike the Bush administration's own argument prior to the invasion of Iraq in 2003, the Reagan administration created an elaborate rationale designed to promote the idea that Nicaragua represented an existential threat. Abraham Sofaer, the State Department's legal adviser, was one of several to insist that the use of pre-emption against state sponsors of terrorism was not an offensive action or a violation of the norms of sovereignty. Rather, Sofaer insisted that pre-emptive war against state sponsors of terrorism was defensive and a necessary adaptation that the international community had to make in order to address the more significant and unpredictable threat of international terrorism that emanated from sanctuary states.[37]

As in 2002–3, when the Bush administration put forth its own explanation for the invasion of Iraq, the Reagan administration constructed an elaborate set of reasons for Nicaragua's classification as a state sponsor of terrorism. The CIA, the Office of Public Diplomacy for Latin America and the Caribbean, as well as the State and Defense Departments, provided the backbone for the administration's argument. Intelligence gathered from the CIA and from other channels was crystalized in numerous reports that created a clear outline of the issue of state sponsorship. As early as 1981, the Reagan administration often suggested or implied that Nicaragua was a state sponsor of terrorism. This position formed the basis for its denial of economic aid in 1981. Early in Reagan's first term, the CIA, too, reported the role of Libyan and Palestine Liberation Organization (PLO) activity, as well as that of a series of terrorist groups within Nicaragua. Beyond the PLO, the administration also insisted that the Sandinistas provided safe haven and support for several other international terror groups. Among those identified were the Spanish group Euskadi Ta Askatasuna (ETA), the Italian Red Brigades, the Argentine Montoneros and the Uruguayan Tupamaros.[38]

As the United States' efforts against Nicaragua intensified, the Reagan administration increasingly suggested that the Sandinistas were a state sponsor of terrorism. In 1985, the administration's economic sanctions programme that it enacted in May was structured, in part, on a claim of Nicaragua's perceived terrorist threat.[39] By 1984–5, Nicaragua was included in the CIA publication *State Support for International Terrorism*, as well as in the State Department's annual report *Patterns of Global Terrorism*.[40] The administration also released several briefing books that directly linked Nicaragua to radical Middle Eastern or North African terrorists. Among these materials, *The Sandinistas and Middle Eastern Radicals* was a primary example of the Reagan administration's attempt to associate Nicaragua with the problem of international terrorism and to justify its interventionist policy.[41] These reports were among a series of materials that emerged in the mid-1980s demonstrating that state sponsorship of terrorism had played a more prominent role in the United States' approach to Nicaragua.

In 1985 and 1986, the Reagan administration's military efforts increased, amidst escalating hostility, and culminated in congressional authorization of lethal aid to the Contras in 1986. The administration built its argument for this escalation around the allegation of state sponsorship of international terrorism. By 1986, Reagan's policy was framed not just as another Cold War conflict but also as a pre-emptive war of regime change against a state sponsor of terrorism. The United States insisted that Nicaragua conform its government to the will of the United States by demanding it to throw down its arms and welcome the Contras into the government even as the United States redoubled its military support for these guerrillas. In addition to the use of military force, it also applied economic pressure designed to bring about the collapse or fundamental alteration of the Nicaraguan government. Throughout, the United States proceeded with little regard to the will of the international community or the basic principles of international law.

If a country is, indeed, a state sponsor of terrorism, the aggressive measures supported by the United States since the late Cold War are not entirely unreasonable. If a country's foreign policy is centred on acts of international terrorism, then such acts, the criminal targeting of civilians, do violate the international rights of sovereign citizens and states. Such a policy, if not simply a consequence of war, is a violation of international law and should warrant aggressive action by the international community. However, a problem with state terrorism since the late Cold War rests in how state sponsors of terrorism are identified and targeted. The process through which state sponsors are targeted has, at times, been directed unilaterally. The frequent identification and targeting of state sponsors on a unilateral basis encourages the tendency to use this practice for a political purpose and as a justification of offensive actions against other sovereigns. In two of the most significant cases – Nicaragua during the late Cold War and Iraq during the War on Terror – the United States made use of aggressive policies of regime change against the will of the international community and without substantial evidence against the accused.

The politicization of the counterterrorism programmes against state sponsors by the United States and other major powers has, I believe, contributed to an escalation of irregular conflict across the globe. This is due, in part, to approaches that were organized without appropriate international supervision or consensus. Indeed, both in the 1980s and in the post-9/11 world, the United States disregarded international oversight. The Bush administration lost the case before the UN Security Council in 2003, but disregarded international opinion.[42] Likewise, during its proxy war on Nicaragua, the Reagan administration simply ignored the proceedings at the United Nations' International Court of Justice (ICJ) in The Hague. Nicaragua argued that the United States acted in violation of its sovereignty and of international law. By 1986, the ICJ ruled in favour of the Nicaraguan government, but the Reagan administration ignored this body and continued to escalate its war of regime change.[43] The US Contra War finally abated as a result of the United States' own errors that culminated in the Iran–Contra scandal, due to the cunning of a young, newly elected Costa Rican president Óscar Arias Sánchez, who successfully organized the Treaty of Esquipulas (against the will of the United States) and helped end the Reagan administration's war against Nicaragua.[44]

Perhaps more than anything else, the modern international order was designed to prevent wars driven by the self-interested pursuits of individual nation states. Since the late Cold War, US counterterrorism policy has challenged this objective as it has led the way in asserting that the danger from state sponsors of international terrorism, often identified unilaterally, warrants aggressive interventionist policies designed to oust sovereign governments in regions of geopolitical significance. While there is a tendency to attribute this change to the policies of George W. Bush in the aftermath of the 9/11 terrorist attacks, the precedence for this strategy is, in fact, found in the late Cold War with the United States policy towards Nicaragua.

Notes

1 William Long, Colombia Storms Court; 7 judges among 89 Dead, *Newsday*, 8 November 1985, http://ntserver1.wsulibs.wsu.edu:2184/docview/285335049?accountid=14902 (accessed 15 June 2017).
2 'State Support for International Terrorism', May 1986, in: Folder 'Terrorism Info-General (3 of 4)', Box CPC-1, FBI 098, Craig P. Coy: Files, Ronald Reagan Presidential Library, Simi Valley, CA (henceforth RRL).
3 Ibid.
4 Brian Glyn Williams, *Counter Jihad: America's Military Experience in Afghanistan, Iraq, and Syria* (Philadelphia: University of Pennsylvania Press, 2017); Richard W. Stevenson, Ready to attack, *New York Times*, 18 March 2003, http://db15.linccweb.org/login?url=https://search-proquest-com.db15.linccweb.org/docview/92692527?accountid=45760 (accessed 15 June 2017).
5 Williams, *Counter Jihad*.
6 Lloyd E. Ambrosius, Woodrow Wilson and George W. Bush: Historical Comparisons of Ends and Means in Their Foreign Policies, *Diplomatic History* 30/3 (2006), 509–43.
7 A few significant contributors to the study of the Cold War roots of the War on Terror include the following: Williams, *Counter Jihad*; Paul Chamberlin, *The Global Offensive: The United States, the Palestinian Liberation Organization, and the Making of the Post-Cold War Order* (New York: Oxford University Press, 2012); Adrian Hänni, Discurso terrorista y la militarizacion del contraterrorismo estadounidense: Los anos de Reagan, *Relaciones Internacionales* 32 (2016), 97–117; Philip W. Travis, *Reagan's War on Terrorism in Nicaragua: The Outlaw State* (Lanham MD: Lexington Books, 2016); David C. Wills, *The First War on Terrorism: Counterterrorism Policy during the Reagan Administration* (Lanham, MD: Rowman and Littlefield, 2003); Odd Arne Westad, *The Global Cold War* (New York: Cambridge University Press, 2007); Mattia Toaldo, *The Origins of the U.S. War on Terror: Lebanon, Libya, and the American Intervention in the Middle East* (New York: Routledge, 2013).
8 Kissinger and Guzzetti, Memorandum of Conversation, 10 June 1976, in *The Digital National Security Archive* (henceforth DNSA), *Argentina, 1975–1980: The Making of US Human Rights* (Ann Arbor: Proquest, 2012). The Digital National Security Archive is operated by the National Security Archive located at George Washington University, Washington D.C., and operated by *Proquest*. This archive is available at subscribing university libraries and provides a thorough collection of recently available documents relating to the Dirty War. The Jimmy Carter and Gerald Ford Presidential Libraries also possess material relating to the Dirty War. Scholarly works dealing with the Dirty War include Paul H. Lewis, *Guerrillas and Generals: The Dirty War in Argentina* (Westport: Praeger, 2002); Federico Finchelstein, *The Ideological Origins of the Dirty War: Fascism, Populism in 20th Century Argentina* (New York: Oxford University Press, 2014); Gustavo Morello, *The Catholic Church and Argentina's Dirty War* (New York: Oxford University Press, 2015).
9 Southern Cone refers to the nations of Brazil, Uruguay, Paraguay, Chile and Argentina.
10 Department of State, Cable, 'Operation Condor', drafted August 18, 1976, and sent August 23, 1976, in *DNSA*, Argentina, 1975–1980.
11 David Binder, FBI Gets Tip in the Letelier Bombing Case that High Chilean Secret Policeman Flew to U.S. Last Month, *New York Times*, 23 September 1976. Orlando

Letelier was a former diplomat of the Chilean government led by Salvador Allende. Following Allende's ouster by the forces of militarist Augusto Pinochet Letelier fled to the United States.

12 'Department of State, Cable, "Operation Condor", drafted 18 August 1976, and sent 23 August 1976'. For primary source material on Operation Condor, see *The Digital National Security Archive*. This archive provides a thorough collection of recently available documents relating to Operation Condor. Scholarly works dealing with Condor include John Dinges, *The Condor Years: How Pinochet and His Allies Brought Terrorism to Three Continents* (New York: New Press, 2005); Patrice McSherry, *Predatory States: Operation Condor and Covert War in Latin America* (Lanham: Rowman and Littlefield, 2005); Stephen A. Rabe, *The Killing Zone: The United States Wages the Cold War in Latin America* (New York: Oxford University Press, 2015).

13 Edward Schumacher, Somoza, Ousted Nicaraguan Leader, is Ambushed and Slain in Paraguay, *New York Times*, 18 September 1980.

14 Telegram from Ambassador William Bowdler to the State Department, 'Nicaraguan Certification on Terrorism: The Somoza Assassination', in *DNSA*, NI01202, http://gateway.proquest.com/openurl?url_ver=Z39.88-2004&res_dat=xri:dnsa&rft_dat=xri:dnsa:article:CNI01202 (accessed 15 June 2017); Memorandum for Dr. Zbigniew Brzezinski, 'PRC Meeting on Central America', 1 August 1979, in DNSA, EL01327, http://gateway.proquest.com/openurl?url_ver=Z39.88-2004&res_dat=xri:dnsa&rft_dat=xri:dnsa:article:CEL01327 (accessed 15 June 2017).

15 Lawrence Pezzullo, interview by Arthur Day, *Foreign Affairs Oral History Project*, Association for Diplomatic Studies and Training, 24 February 1989.

16 Special Coordinating Committee Meeting, 12 January 1981, in *DNSA*, EL01364, http://gateway.proquest.com/openurl?url_ver=Z39.88-2004&res_dat=xri:dnsa:article:CEL01364 (accessed 15 June 2017).

17 Nina Serafino, Nicaragua: Conditions and US Interests, 19 November 1981, in *DNSA*, NI01409, http://gateway.proquest.com/openurl?_ver=239.88-2004&res_dat=xri:dnsa&rft_dat=xri:dnsa:article:CNI01409 (accessed 15 June 2017).

18 Economic Sanctions Against Nicaragua, 1 May 1985, in *DNSA*, NI02463, http://gateway.proquest.com/openurl?_ver=239.88-2004&res_dat=xri:dnsa&rft_dat=xri:dnsa:article:CNI02463 (accessed 15 June 2017).

19 National Security Council, 'National Security Security Decision Directive on Cuba and Central America', in Christopher Simpson, *National Security Decision Directives of the Reagan and Bush Administration: The Declassified History of U.S. Diplomatic and Military History, 1981–1991* (New York: Westview, 1995), 18, 53–4; Travis, *Reagan's War on Terrorism in Nicaragua*.

20 Memo from McFarlane to McCsc, 'Background Material on Terrorism', 15 August 1984, in *DNSA*, 'Terrorism and US Policy, 1968–2002', TE00715, http://gateway.proquest.com/openurl?url_ver=Z39.88-2004&res_dat=xri:dnsa&rft_dat=xri:dnsa:article:CTE00715 (accessed 15 June 2017).

21 Ibid.

22 'Terrorist Group Profiles', November 1988, viii, in *DNSA*, TE00967, http://gateway.proquest.com/openurl?url_ver=Z39.88-2004&res_dat=xri:dnsa&rft_dat=xri:dnsa:article:CTE00967 (accessed 15 June 2017).

23 Ibid.

24 State Support for International Terrorism, 1985, in *DNSA*, TE00857, http://gateway.proquest.com/openurl?url_ver=Z39.88-2004&res_dat=xri:dnsa&rft_dat=xri:dnsa:article:CTE00857 (accessed 15 June 2017).

25 Bureau of Diplomatic Security, U.S. Department of State, Lethal Terrorist Actions against Americans 1973–1986, in Robert A. Friedlander, *Terrorism: Documents of International and Local Control* (New York: Oceana, 1990).
26 Bernard Weinraub, President Accuses 5 'Outlaw States' of World Terror, *New York Times*, 9 July 1985, http://search.proquest.com/docview/425474442?accountid=14902 (accessed 15 June 2017). The full transcript of this landmark speech given by Reagan to the American Bar Association on 8 July 1985 is provided by the Ronald Reagan Library, https://www.reaganlibrary.gov/research/speeches/70885a (accessed 1 January 2020).
27 Parker Borg, interview by Charles Stuart Kennedy, *Foreign Affairs Oral History Project*, Association for Diplomatic Studies and Training, 12 August 2002.
28 For furthering reading on the US Contra War, see the following literature: Cythnia J. Arnson, *Crossroads: Congress, the President, and Central America, 1976–1993* (University Park: Penn State University Press, 1993^2); William LeoGrande, *Our Own Backyard: The United States in Central America, 1977–1992* (Chapel Hill: University of North Carolina, 1998); Greg Grandin, *Empires Workshop: Latin America, The United States, and the New Imperialism* (New York: Henry Holt, 2006); John Collins and Ross Glover, *Collateral Language: A User's Guide to America's New War* (New York: New York University Press, 2002); Travis, *Reagan's War on Terrorism in Nicaragua*.
29 Robert Oakley, Interview by Charles Stuart Kennedy and Thomas Stern, *Foreign Affairs Oral History Project*, Association for Diplomatic Studies and Training, 7 July 1992.
30 For an excellent overview of the Reagan administration's approach to terrorism, see Wills, *The First War on Terrorism*.
31 Ibid.
32 Robert Oakley, Interview by Charles Stuart Kennedy and Thomas Stern.
33 Doyle McManus, Assassination Ban May Not Apply in Anti-Terror Raids, *Los Angeles Times*, 13 July 1985, http://search.proquest.com/docview/292116773?accountid=14902 (accessed 15 June 2017).
34 Hedrick Smith, CIA Manual: A Policy Is Undermined, *New York Times*, 30 October 1984, http://ntserver1.wsulibs.wsu.edu:2184/docview/425209111?accountid=14902 (accessed 15 June 2017).
35 McManus, Assassination Ban May Not Apply.
36 Robert Oakley, Interview by Charles Stuart Kennedy and Thomas Stern.
37 Curtis Sitomer, Lawmakers Stress International Cooperation to Combat Terrorism, *The Christian Science Monitor*, 16 July 1985, http://search.proquest.com/docview/1400449442?accountid14902 (accessed 15 June 2017).
38 Nina Serafino, Nicaragua: Conditions and US Interests, 15–17; Patterns of Global Terrorism, 1984, in Folder 'Vice President's Task Force on Combatting Terrorism Statistics 2 of 2,' George Bush Vice Presidential Records, Task Force on Combatting Terrorism, General Office Files: Subject Files, OA/ID 15394, George Bush Presidential Library, College Station, TX (henceforth GBL).
39 Economic Sanctions against Nicaragua, 1 May 1985, in *DNSA*, NIO2463, http://gateway.proquest.com/openurl?url_ver=Z39.88-2004&res_dat=xri:dnsa&rft_dat=xri:dnsa:article:CNI02463 (accessed 15 June 2017).
40 Patterns of Global Terrorism, 1984; State Support for International Terrorism, 1985, in *DNSA*, TE00857, http://gateway.proquest.com/openurl?url_ver=Z39.88-2004&res_dat=xri:dnsa&rft_dat=xri:dnsa:article:CTE00857 (accessed 15 June 2017).

41 Defense Department Background Paper, Nicaragua's Military Build-up and Support for Central American Subversion, in Folder 'The Sandinistas and Middle Eastern Radicals,' Box 16, David S. Addington Files, RRL.
42 Stevenson, Ready to attack.
43 Paul Lewis, World Court Supports Nicaragua after US Rejected Judges' Roll, *New York Times*, 28 June 1986, http://db15.linccweb.org/login?url=https://search-proquest-com.db15.linccweb.org/docview/110933320?accountid=45760 (accessed 15 June 2017).
44 The Treaty of Esquipulas, also known as the Esquipulas II Accord, was an agreement made by the leaders of El Salvador, Costa Rica, Nicaragua, Honduras and Guatemala in August 1987 to bring an end to the conflicts in the region. The agreement was organized by President Oscar Arias Sánchez of Costa Rica. Arias won the Nobel Peace Prize for his efforts, which eventually brought an end to the conflicts in Central America. For further reading, see Travis, *Reagan's War on Terrorism in Nicaragua*; Philip Travis, Oscar Arias and the Treaty of Esquipulas, *Oxford Research Encyclopedia of Latin American History*, published online in August 2017.

Chapter 11

OUTLOOK

WRITING THE HISTORY OF MODERN INTERNATIONAL
TERRORISM – WHERE ARE THE PUZZLES?

Thomas Wegener Friis, Adi Frimark and Martin Göllnitz

Since 2001, most of the Western world has been conducting a self-proclaimed 'war on terror' trying to contain Islamic extremist terror and to target terrorist strongholds in the Middle East and Central Asia. The War on Terror has been fought with a wide range of tools from counter-extremism and counterterrorism efforts of the intelligence community to full-scale warfare. Regardless of the extent to which resources were utilized, the conflict between the West and Islamist extremists does not seem to have come to a foreseeable end. In this process, terrorists have struck Europe repeatedly in a number of bloody and media-efficient ways. In the past year, the truck attacks in Nice and Berlin, as well as the bomb blast at Brussels airport kept the terror issue on the European agenda. The terrorist attacks are regularly accompanied by populist demands to construct impenetrable border fences and to retract the right to move freely across the Schengen area.

The argument that the reintroduction of border gendarmeries would bring terrorism to a standstill overlooks the historical experiences in Europe. Just a few decades ago, in the 1970s and 1980s, Europe was hunted by a number of terrorist groups of both West European and Middle Eastern origin driven by either nationalist or socialist motives. The Irish Republican Army (IRA), Euskadi Ta Askatasuna (ETA), Tupamaros West Berlin and Munich, Wehrsportgruppe Hoffmann, Red Army Faction (RAF), Action Directe and Brigate Rosse were just some of the names that could make citizens shiver and extremists hope for a brighter tomorrow. The terrorist activities of these groups were predominantly focused against single countries, yet the groups also acted transnationally, participating in terror acts on foreign soil, transporting money or weapons, and leaving their home country to cool down, to train, or even to completely retire from a stressful career of international terrorism.[1]

A particularly interesting part of the internationalization of Cold War terrorism was the role of the Palestinian groups such as the Fatah, the Abu Nidal Organization (ANO) and certainly the Popular Front for the Liberation of Palestine (PFLP). In the slipstream of migration of Palestinian refugees to Western Europe, the different groups were able to operate more freely throughout the continent. Furthermore, some of the Palestinian groups were able to bond with European extremists. The authors argue that this new globalized strategy of some Palestinian groups made them more modern than their European contemporaries. Furthermore, the Palestinian groups raised the difficult issue of migration and international conflicts since they brought with them to Europe the conflict of Israel/Palestine and the will to force the question onto the international agenda. Black September made this point evident during the 1972 Olympics. The high degree of terrorist modernity makes the Palestinian groups some of the scientifically most rewarding cases for the research of terrorism.

Even though terrorism in the year 2020 is in some ways different from terrorism a few decades ago, we claim that it is never too late to learn a lesson, especially from terrorist groups that were able to step up their international engagement. Today, almost two decades after 9/11, it is high time that we tried to harvest the experiences that the Cold War era might offer for today's anti-terrorism effort. This chapter discusses the opportunities and the challenges that have to be met if one is to learn the lesson of the past.

The most fundamental problem when dealing with the question of terrorist groups in comparison to analysing 'normal' state players is the lack of a central government with agencies run by bureaucratic standards demanding documentation of their decisions in state archives. The illegal nature of terrorism makes the keeping of records not only practically impossible but also counterproductive to its means or even dangerous to the activist. Keeping absolute secrecy and applying 'need-to-know' principles are as essential to terrorist organizations as it is to intelligence services. In a few cases like the one of the Palestine Liberation Organization (PLO), which had safe havens in Jordan, Lebanon and Tunisia, it is possible to build up structures equivalent to the intelligence services of states. However, as the Israeli invasion of Lebanon (Operation 'Peace for Galilee') in 1982 proved, such a form of organization also made the PLO vulnerable.

The lack of a central archival collection documenting the terror activities from the inside makes it necessary to find alternative ways to acquire knowledge, namely from outside observers of the terrorist groups. Furthermore, the persistent work of the German journalist Thomas Scheuer also shows that even though oral history within this special field is obviously difficult, it can certainly be rewarding as well.[2] When terrorist groups operate transnationally, they unavoidably come into contact with a number of security and intelligence services that try to understand who these people are and if they plan to strike on their territory. However, the fact that the anti-terrorism efforts of the 1970s and, to some extent, the 1980s were largely a national affair means that looking through the prism of national intelligence services will by nature offer only a glimpse and from a narrowly defined perspective. When dealing with modern international players such as the Palestinians, paper trails can be found all over the European continent. It confronts the researchers with two big problems, namely the practical one that these files will be in a multitude of languages and the principal dilemma of archival access.

Granting access to intelligence documents of the 1970s and 1980s is for most Western intelligence services unnatural. Most countries in Western Europe are more than willing to use the argument of national security to protect their information against any intruders on their files. Eventually, this argument inadvertently not only serves to protect the terrorists of the past but also comes close to a state guarantee against learning for the future. Traditionally, the strength of Western democracies was to develop and to evolve. Secrecy for the sake of secrecy promotes ignorance, and in this fashion it is harmful to national security. As intelligence services are government agencies, it is eventually a political question whether future generations should be able to learn from the successes and errors of their predecessors.

Eastern Europe and international terrorism

Particularly in several of the Warsaw Pact countries, research about terrorist groups operating during the Cold War has taken its first steps forward due to the release of archival documents. The first and thus most prominent example was East Germany, whose archives were already made accessible in the early 1990s.[3] In the past years, the second strong player in Central Europe, Poland, has followed suit.[4] In other former socialist countries, individual studies have been conducted.[5] The access to archival material varies from country to country, as does the amount of time that the authorities of the communist regimes were given to cover their tracks.

To historical research of terrorism, the operative interest of communist intelligence offers several possibilities to understand terrorism better and on a broader empirical basis. Even though the reports of agents and the analysis of the services are an outside view, the unique combination of intimacy through the relations maintained with the organizations and the deeply rooted mistrust of the communist services to everything foreign – especially dangerous foreigners – has created important archival material. Despite parts of it having been destroyed, it provides an essential fundament for projects that are able to cross the language borders of Eastern Europe.

In general, the Eastern European research efforts still share a few weaknesses. First of all, from a practical point, the literature has largely been published in local languages, which makes the academic perception rather limited, and has led to parallel research on similar projects rather than a coordinated effort. Further, the research projects are dominated by a national scope reinforced by the national viewpoint of the used source material. Not only does this volume constitute a first step to make the insights of this documents based research available in English, but the chapters on state–terrorism relations in different Eastern European countries also bring up plenty of fruitful questions for comparative and transnational research to undertake in the future. The Eastern European research and the intelligence sources constitute important pieces of the greater puzzle, which needs to be laid in the years to come.

Western perspectives

The archival situation in Western Europe is still regrettably dominated by secrecy, and thus the actual knowledge about the operations of international terrorists and their relations with state actors is considerably weaker for this part of Europe. Western Europe constituted one of the main targets for terrorist groups, and the Western authorities and intelligence services have collected extensive information to confront the terrorist threat. On the other hand, their chances to recruit agents within the terrorist groups were smaller than those of the Eastern Europeans.

By means of logic and by today's standards, Western European agencies should have been focused on an effort to strictly oppose and fight terrorist organizations. However, as several chapters in this volume demonstrate, the scattered information points to a muddier picture than the rhetoric of the current 'war on terror'. As the Swiss case discussed in this volume demonstrates, the research in this area is only in its infancy. Among the additional countries that need to become the object of research based on archival sources, France deserves special attention. Several authors have claimed, with good arguments, that until the mid-1980s, France's approach towards international terrorism was guided by a *Sanctuary Doctrine*, trading tolerance of terrorists on French soil for their renouncement of violent attacks against French interests.[6] Nevertheless, the academic knowledge on the less-than-resolute French attitude towards international terrorism is still largely the same as summed up by the CIA back in 1985: 'Palestinian terrorist do not usually strike French targets. We suspect that this may be in return for French permission to operate in France, but we have only rumors to back up our suspicions.'[7]

One of the many incidents that give plausibility to this suspicion took place at Charles de Gaulle Airport in 1983, when French authorities apprehended the PFLP 'head and treasurer for Western Europe' Ghazi Massoud and the 'head' of the PFLP in Germany Mohammed Toman with 6 million Danish Kroner (more than US$600,000). The money likely came from a bank robbery carried out by a group of PFLP supporters in a Copenhagen suburb. However, the Danes were never certain because the French authorities denied them access to the money. According to the former Danish police chief inspector and adjunct lecturer at Cambridge University, Frank Madsen, who had a leading position at Interpol in Paris, the French refusal made sense if, and only if, they wanted to obstruct the investigations. If the money was proven to be stolen, the Danes would have demanded the two PFLP members be extradited, but, according to Madsen, the French authorities were keener on expelling them. As Madsen says, 'The resolution of the Paris end of the case, if one can call it a resolution, showed unequivocally that the fear that governments exhibit when faced with international terrorism supersedes any treaty obligations.'[8]

In less democratic states, the simple desire to keep unpopular policies secret from the public can make documents disappear forever, or at least for a very long time. However, in a democratic world, the argument that learning from the past – even when one's own role might not be glorious – should have some weight. The East Europeans used their good relation with international terrorist groups to obtain inside information on them. It is safe to presume that the Western Europeans did their best – even when the languages were difficult – to surveil the members of these organizations when they moved to their countries. After all, having a lead on information constitutes the essence of intelligence. Together with the already accessible East European ones, these West European puzzle pieces would be essential if Europe is to learn the lesson of the first decades of modern international terrorism.

Seized files

The Europeans are not the only ones called for if the future should obtain the chance to learn from the terrorist violence of the 1970s and 1980s. When writing about the Palestinian groups and modern international terrorism, access to Arab sources would be highly beneficial. These could naturally include interviews or oral history. In the following section, we will, however, focus on the potential of written Arab sources. Generally, the access to Arab intelligence sources is rather difficult. Even though assessments of and documentary information about the support of Arab intelligence services would certainly be interesting, it does not seem likely that these agencies are ready to share information with Western scholars in the near future. Neither does it seem plausible that Palestinian archives will declassify files on the subject. Scholars must thus hope to gain improved access to seized files. Two countries are particularly interesting, considering their potential to make such documents available to researchers: the United States and Israel.

In the past decade, the United States' global military engagement gave the country a golden opportunity to access the files of two important Middle Eastern players in the international terrorist violence of the latter half of the Cold War: Iraq and Libya. Documents from Iraq have been made available online by the Conflict Records Research Center (CRRC) at the National Defense University in Washington, DC.[9] In the *Saddam Hussein Collection* of 2015, there are several policy documents with relevance to the PLO in the 1970s and 1980s.[10] Still, a general investigation on how the Iraqi intelligence supported and handled their terrorist allies has not yet been carried out, at least not by academic researchers. The entanglement of the Iraqis was of course known at the time. In 1982, the CIA wrote:

> The focus of Iraq's support in the mid-1970s, according to [… (redacted)] Iraqi leadership statements, was anti-Syrian Palestinian groups fighting in Lebanon. These groups included the Arad Liberation Front, the pro-Soviet Popular Front for the Liberation of Palestine (PFLP) led by George Habash, the PFLP faction led by Wadie Haddad, the Democratic Front for the Liberation of Palestine (DFLP), the Palestine Liberation Front led by Abu Abbas, and the Palestine Popular Struggle Front. Iraq created the Black June Organization in 1976 to counter growing Syrian influence in Lebanon. Its leader, Sabri al-Banna (Abu Nidal) was a former member of Fatah who had been condemned by Fatah

after he tried to assassinate Yasser Arafat in 1974. Black June acted as Iraq's surrogate in wide-ranging acts of sabotage in Lebanon and Syria against the Assad government and in Baghdad's occasional wars with Arafat and the PLO. Aid was not limited to the Palestinians. The Italian Red Brigades, the West German Baader-Meinhof Gang and the Japanese Red Army trained in Iraq in the mid-1970s.[11]

Given this knowledge, it seems surprising that the opportunities offered by the Iraqi intelligence files have not yet been seized by terrorism scholars.

In the Israeli case, the documents of the PLO that the Israeli Defense Forces (IDF) captured during the invasion of Lebanon in 1982 (Operation Peace for Galilee) deserve our interest. While this collection of sources is not new, it is little known to the public, and many of the captured documents are still not available to researchers.[12] The accessible documents were translated from Arabic to Hebrew by the open sources intelligence unit (Hazav) of the IDF. The documents tell the story of a wide willingness of state actors to help the Palestinian organization by equipping them with weapons and training their members.

PLO members received training in various skills, ranging from civilian professions that can serve a dual purpose to pure military professions. A looted paper from August 1982 presents details about the conditions that nominees had to meet in order to become part of the Fatah Air Force. Courses were offered abroad at a non-mentioned location. Different skills were asked from the recruits if they intended to become pilots, flight engineers, flight technicians or meteorologists. An aviation cadet, for example, needed to hold a high school diploma in the humanities or in sciences, to be nineteen or twenty years old, physically healthy and medically approved by a committee of doctors, to be no less than 165 centimetres tall and be able to read and write English.[13]

Many of the courses took place in the Soviet bloc states, as well as in states that considered themselves part of the Eastern Bloc. For example, Yugoslavia offered a course on staff work and command; Eastern Germany allocated places in its military academy; various military courses were offered by the Soviet Union; Syria allocated places for different naval capabilities courses; and in Pakistan, Vietnam, Korea, Egypt, China, Libya, Hungary, Bulgaria, Yemen, India and so on, militants were trained in anti-aircraft weaponry, artillery, sabotage, armour, were provided officer courses and so forth.[14] Regarding the PLO's collaboration with the Eastern European states under communist rule, the content of the captured files corresponds very well with the archival material from Eastern Europe.

A rather surprising finding from the captured files concerns aid given to Palestinian terrorist organizations by Western states. A document written on 16 March 1982 lists combatants who were nominees for getting scholarships in order to receive professional education courses as mechanics, electricians and welders in Italy.[15] The knowledge acquired through these studies could be used dually: for civilian and military purposes. Some findings also point in the direction that some Western states were involved in helping to equip Palestinian terrorist organizations with weapons. One of the captured documents, holding detailed information about 'categories of arms that were used by Air Defense battalions and their origin', also lists states like Spain and France.[16]

Categories of arms	Origin	The way to get it
3 barrels 20 mm anti-aircraft	Spain	Lebanese Army
Anti-aircraft canons 37 mm	Russia	Syria/Fatah
Mortar	Russia	Fatah
500 machine gun, Mag, Bern	Western	Fatah
Regular and improved SAM 7	Russia	Fatah
Armoured personnel carrier and MX Tank 48	France	Lebanese Army

If these Western states have in fact been involved in such arms transfers, it might dampen their eagerness to make intelligence files on international terrorism accessible to research – even if their objective was to project terrorism away from their own population to other European countries or back to the Middle East. Likewise, the Israeli government has been less than eager to declassify documents for research on terrorism in the Cold War. Even though some documents are accessible at the Israel Intelligence Heritage and Commemoration Center in Herzliya, it is the conviction of the authors that they constitute only a part of the vast amount of documents that the IDF acquired during Operation Peace for Galilee, and so to speak the tip of the iceberg of the knowledge that could be gained. The next step should be a large declassification initiative.

Conclusions and perspectives

An overview of the possibilities for future research and the archival resources available can inspire both optimism and pessimism on the part of intelligence and terrorism research. For the pessimist, the past decade can be seen as a history of lost opportunities. In the war against terrorism, hard power has more often been the answer than brainpower and research. Even though the international terrorist violence of the 1970s and 1980s is likely to hold lessons to be learned, security bureaucracies and regulations have denied the Western European countries to harvest these fruits. For some countries, the past is likely to hold unpleasant truths, failed decisions and bad judgements, at least from a current perspective. For most intelligence agencies, it is tempting to make these stories disappear in secret vaults or maybe even better in the shredder; such a silent solution may even seem tempting to some politicians. For the tax-paying public and the victims of terrorism, ignorance should not be an appealing road.

The optimist would care less about the institutional obstructions and instead see the rich, newly gained knowledge, as well as the large potential for empirical, primary-source-based terrorism research. The biggest leap forward for researchers has been the effort to make Eastern European archival material available. Even though communist intelligence officers did their best during the collapse of their regimes to make sure the world stayed unaware of their deeds, they did not fully prevail. In the individual Central and Eastern European countries, research has come some way in the past decades, and the next step would be to coordinate the existing efforts and combine the collective institutional knowledge.

Terrorism studies are a notoriously difficult field to do sound empirical research, especially on larger international networks and over a long period of time. An especially rewarding research object would be the various Palestinian groups. Their ability to operate across borders, use friendly regimes, passive intelligence services, incite fear, raise money, and connect the dots on the European terrorist map of the time makes them appear much more modern than many of their contemporaries. In the case of the Palestinian organizations of the 1970s and 1980s, research could ideally end up using the files of the terrorists' allies in the Soviet bloc, the counterintelligence surveillance of Western European services and even Arab sources captured in Iraq, Libya or Lebanon. This puts researchers on the test, since a project to analyse the international terrorist activities of the 1970s and the 1980s is not only a question of the right methodology or approach but also a question of understanding most European languages, Arab and Hebrew – or to have researchers working together across borders. Terrorists were capable of doing this forty years ago, yet the intelligence community is still learning it. Certainly, researchers will be able to do it as well.

Notes

1. Christopher Daase, Die RAF und der internationale Terrorismus: Zur transnationalen Kooperation klandestiner Organisationen, in Wolfgang Kraushaar (ed.), *Die RAF und der linke Terrorismus* (Hamburg: Hamburger Edition, 2006), 905–29.
2. See, for instance, Thomas Scheuer, Unser Mann in Beirut, *FOCUS Magazin* 42 (2000), 52–60; Thomas Scheuer, Ich brachte die Waffen nach München, *FOCUS Magazin* 24 (1999), 54–7; Thomas Scheuer, Das letzte Geheimnis ..., *FOCUS Magazin* 27 (2016), 52–5.
3. See the article of Tobias Wunschik in this publication. See further Michael Müller and Andreas Kanonenberg, *Die RAF-Stasi-Connection* (Berlin: Rowohlt, 1992); Tobias Wunschik, *Die Hauptabteilung XXII: 'Terrorabwehr'* (Berlin: BStU, 1995); Tobias Wunschik, 'Abwehr' und Unterstützung des internationalen Terrorismus – Die Hauptabteilung XXII, in Hubertus Knabe (ed.), *West-Arbeit des MfS: Das Zusammenspiel von 'Aufklärung' und 'Abwehr'* (Berlin: Ch. Links Verlag, 1999), 263–73; Anne Sørensen, *Stasi og den vesttyske terrorisme* (Santa Barbara: Århus University Press, 2006); Tobias Wunschik, Gleiche Gegner, verwandte Methoden, unterschiedliche Strategien: Die Bekämpfung des Linksterrorismus in den beiden deutschen Staaten 1970–1989, in Beatrice de Graaf and Karl Härter (eds.), *Vom Majestätsverbrechen zum Terrorismus: Politische Kriminalität, Recht, Justiz und Polizei zwischen Früher Neuzeit und 20. Jahrhundert* (Frankfurt a. M.: Klostermann, 2012), 365–401; Jeffrey Herf, *Undeclared Wars with Israel: East Germany and the West German Far Left 1967–1989* (New York: Cambridge University Press, 2016); Matthias Bengtson-Krallert, *Die DDR und der internationale Terrorismus* (Marburg: Tectum Verlag, 2017); Jérôme aan de Wiel, *East German Intelligence and Ireland 1949-90: Espionage, Terrorism and Diplomacy* (Manchester: Manchester University Press, 2017).

4   See the article of Przemysław Gasztold in this publication. See further Przemysław Gasztold-Seń, Der Sicherheitsapparat der Volksrepublik Polen und die Rote Armee Fraktion, *Inter Finitimos: Jahrbuch zur Deutsch-Polnischen Beziehungsgeschichte* 9 (2011), 144–55; Przemysław Gasztold-Seń, 'Szakal' w Warszawie, *Pamięć.pl: Biuletyn IPN* 2 (2012), 32–6; Przemysław Gasztold-Seń, Międzynarodowi terroryści w PRL: historia niewymuszonej współpracy, *Pamięć i Sprawiedliwość* 22/1 (2013), 275–315; Przemysław Gasztold-Seń, Biznes z terrorystami: Brudne interesy wywiadu wojskowego PRL z bliskowschodnimi organizacjami terrorystycznymi, *Pamięć i Sprawiedliwość* 23/1 (2014), 165–216; Przemysław Gasztold-Seń, Between Geopolitics and National Security: Polish Intelligence and International Terrorism during the Cold War, in Władyslaw Bułhak and Thomas Wegener Friis (eds.), *Need to Know: Eastern and Western Perspectives* (Odense: University Press of Southern Denmark, 2014), 137–62; Przemysław Gasztold, *Zabójcze układy: Służby PRL i międzynarodowy terroryzm* (Warszawa: Wydawnictwo Naukowe PWN, 2017).

5   On Czechoslovakia see the article of Pavel Zacek in this publication. See also two articles by Daniela Richterova, The Anxious Host: Czechoslovakia and Carlos the Jackal 1978–1986, *The International History Review* 40/1 (2018), 108–32; and Strange Bedfellows: Intelligence Liaison between State and Non-state Actors: Czechoslovakia and the PLO. The latter article will be published in a forthcoming book that includes the proceedings of the 2015 conference *In the Shadow of the Cold War* held in Biała Rawska, Poland (Warsaw: IPN, 2020).
    On Hungary see the article of Balázs Orbán-Schwarzkopf in this publication. See further the source collection edited by Ágnes Hankiss, *Terroristák Budapesten: A kommunista állambiztonság és Európa* (Budapest: Hamvas Intézet, 2013), https://www.hamvasintezet.hu/wp-content/uploads/2018/10/terrorist%C3%A1k_beliv.pdf (accessed 1 January 2020); and an article about 'Carlos the Jackal' based on Hungarian and Polish sources by the journalist Gábor Mező, Terroristaparadicsom volt Budapest a nyolcvanas években, *PestiSracok.hu*, 28 March 2016, http://pestisracok.hu/terroristapar adicsom-volt-budapest-nyolcvanas-evekben (accessed 1 January 2020).
    On Bulgaria see the article of Jordan Baev in this publication. See further Evtim Kostadinov (ed.), *International Terrorism in the Bulgarian State Security Files* (Sofia, 2011); Christopher Nehring, Die Verhaftung Till Meyers in Bulgarien: Eine Randnotiz aus dem Archiv der bulgarischen Staatssicherheit, *Vierteljahrshefte für Zeitgeschichte* 63/3 (2015), 411–24.
    On Romania: The relations between the Securitate and 'Carlos the Jackal' during the Cold War were already made public by Liviu Tofan, *Şacalul Securităţii: Teroristul Carlos în solda spionajului românesc* (Iaşi: Polirom, 2013); Georg Herbstritt, *Entzweite Freunde: Rumänien, die Securitate und die DDR-Staatssicherheit 1950 bis 1989* (Göttingen: Vandenhoeck & Ruprecht, 2016), 227–33. See also the forthcoming article by Liviu Tofan, Carlos 'the Jackal' and the Romanian *Securitate*: It Takes Two to 'Tango'. The article will be published in the forthcoming book with the proceedings of the 2015 conference *In the Shadow of the Cold War*.
    On Yugoslavia see the article of Gordan Akrap in this publication.

6   See Jeremy Shapiro and Bénédicte Suzan, The French Experience of Counterterrorism, *Survival: Global Politics and Strategy* 45/1 (2003), 67–98; Michel Wieviorka, French Politics and Strategy on Terrorism, in Barry Rubin (ed.), *The Politics of Counterterrorism: The Ordeal of Democratic States* (Washington, DC: Paul H. Nitze School of Advanced International Studies, 1990), 61–90.

7 Talking Points for NIO: French Policy on the PLO, Office of European Analysis, Directorate of Intelligence, CIA, 29 October 1985, in: CREST, CIA General Records, 85T01058R000303580001-7, https://www.cia.gov/library/readingroom/docs/CIA-RDP85T01058R000303580001-7.pdf (accessed 1 January 2020).
8 Frank Madsen, *Transnational Organized Crime* (London: Routledge, 2009), 77.
9 See http://crrc.dodlive.mil/collections/sh (accessed 20 June 2017).
10 See Conflict Records Research Center (CRRC), Saddam Hussein Regime Collection, as of 25 September 2015.
11 Iraq: The Uses of Terror, An Intelligence assessment, Directorate of Intelligence, CIA, February 1982, in: CREST, CIA General Records, RDP83B00232R000100040005-4, https://www.cia.gov/library/readingroom/docs/CIA-RDP83B00232R000100040005-4.pdf (accessed 1 January 2020).
12 Already, shortly after their seizure, the first documents were published, including files about the links between Eastern Europe and the PLO. See Raphael Israeli (ed.), *PLO in Lebanon: Selected Documents* (New York: St. Martin's Press, 1983), 57–67. At the same time, West European intelligence services received information from their Israeli partners that carried the fingerprint of the documents seized during the Lebanon invasion. See PET-Kommissionens Beretning, Vol. 9 (Copenhagen, 2009), 308. In the mid-1980s, material from this intelligence coup was also published by Ray S. Cline and Yonah Alexander, first as a report to the U.S. Senate on state-sponsored terrorism and afterwards in a book for the general public. See Ray S. Cline and Yonah Alexander, State-sponsored Terrorism: Report prepared for the Subcommittee on Security and Terrorism for the use of the Committee on the Judiciary, United States Senate, June 1985 (Washington DC, Government Printing Office, 1985); Ray S. Cline and Yonah Alexander, *Terrorism as State-sponsored Covert Warfare: What the Free World Must Do to Protect Itself* (Fairfax, VA: Hero Books, 1986). Both, the report and the book, presented facsimiles of records, documenting the Palestinians receiving military training in the Soviet Union and Hungary.
13 Captured documents-August 1982, Hazav, 3.08.82/881/161, Israel Intelligence Heritage and Commemoration Center (IICC).
14 Captured documents-July 1982, Hazav, 14.07.82/881/101, IICC; Captured documents-July 1982, Hazav, 27.07.82/881/133, IICC.
15 Captured documents-August 1982, Hazav, 1.08.82/881/154, IICC.
16 Captured documents-July 1982, Hazav, 14.07.82/881/101, IICC.

ABOUT THE AUTHORS

Matthias Dahlke (PhD) works for the Minister-President of Land Brandenburg. He studied at Humboldt University Berlin and Panthéon Sorbonne Paris, did terrorism research in several European countries, and is the author of the book *Demokratischer Staat und transnationaler Terrorismus* (2011). He may be contacted at mdahlke@gmail.com.

Adi Frimark (PhD) is a lecturer and researcher at the Department of Political Studies at Bar-Ilan University, Israel, who specializes in security, intelligence and humanitarian aspects of conflict. She has worked extensively on European and national security research projects, including the development of project communication strategies and on end user requirements analysis. She may be contacted at adibellf@gmail.com.

Przemysław Gasztold (PhD) is a research fellow at the Historic Research Office of the Institute of National Remembrance in Warsaw and an assistant professor at War Studies University in Warsaw, Department of Security Threats and Terrorism. He received his PhD from Warsaw University, Faculty of Journalism and Political Science, in 2016. He is currently conducting research on the history of Polish Intelligence, on relations between communist Poland, the Middle East, and Africa, and on the ties between the Soviet bloc and international terrorism during the Cold War. In 2017 he published *Zabójcze układy: Służby PRL i międzynarodowy terroryzm* (Deadly Conspiracies: Polish Communist Intelligence Services and International Terrorism). His recent book *Towarzysze z betonu: Dogmatyzm w PZPR 1980–1990* (Comrades of Concrete: Dogmatism within the PUWP 1980–1990) was published in 2019. He may be contacted at przemyslaw.gasztold@ipn.gov.pl.

Martin Göllnitz (PhD) is a post-doc and assistant in the Department of History at the Philipps-University Marburg. From 2014 to February 2019, he worked as a scientific assistant at the German universities in Kiel and Mainz. He was also a visiting scholar at the Center for Cold War Studies (University of Southern Denmark). His major research fields are modern German terrorism history, the history of science and the history of political violence from the nineteenth to the twenty-first centuries. He is also interested in Scandinavian history, with a focus on nationalism and politically motivated murders. His latest monograph, *Der Student als Führer?* (The Student as Leader?), was published in 2018. He may be contacted at mgoellnitz@uni-marburg.de.

Marcel Gyr is a reporter at the Swiss daily newspaper *Neue Zürcher Zeitung* (since 2001). He is the author of *Schweizer Terrorjahre: Das geheime Abkommen mit der*

PLO (2016). He may be contacted at marcel.gyr@nzz.ch or through Threema (ID: Z5FUTETP).

Adrian Hänni (PhD) is a lecturer at Distance Learning University Switzerland, where he is responsible for the political history module, and a lecturer at the University of Zurich. He has also been a postdoctoral fellow at Leiden University, a Visiting Fellow at the Centre for the History of Violence at the University of Newcastle (Australia), and a Visiting Fellow at the German Historical Institute in Washington DC. His research interests include the history of propaganda, intelligence services, and terrorism with a focus on the Cold War era. In 2019, he edited the book *Über Grenzen hinweg: Transnationale Politische Gewalt im 20. Jahrhundert* (Across Borders: Transnational Political Violence in the Twentieth Century). His latest monograph, *Terrorismus als Konstrukt* (Terrorism as a Construct), was published in 2018. He may be contacted at adrian@adrianh.ch.

Tobias Hof (PhD) is Privatdozent of Modern and Contemporary History at the Ludwig-Maximilians-University Munich. Previously he has been DAAD Visiting Professor at the History Department of the University of Northern Carolina at Chapel Hill. His research focuses on the history of counterterrorism and terrorism, modern humanitarianism and fascism. His latest article 'From Extremism to Terrorism: The Far Right in Italy and West Germany' in *Contemporary European History* (2018) compares post-war Italian and West German right-wing terrorism. He is the author of the book *Staat und Terrorismus in Italien 1969–1982* (2011) and co-editor (with Prof. K. Larres) of *Terrorism and Transatlantic Relations: Cooperation and Divisions* (2020). He may be contacted at Tobias.Hof@lrz.uni-muenchen.de.

Ryszard M. Machnikowski (PhD) is an associate professor and the vice-dean for research and international affairs of the Faculty of International and Political Studies at the University of Lodz, Poland. He is an experienced expert consultant of the Polish government and the police force in Lodz, including the SWAT team in the City of Lodz (SPAP Lodz). The author of three books, Dr Machnikowski specializes in terrorism and security studies, transatlantic relations and problems of globalization. He may be contacted at ryszard.machnikowski@uni.lodz.pl.

Daniel Rickenbacher (PhD) is a research associate at the Concordia Institute for Canadian Jewish Studies in Montreal. He is working on a postdoctoral project, which investigates Middle Eastern terrorist and propaganda networks in Canada during the 1970s. Dr Rickenbacher studied General History, Political Science and Jewish Studies in Zurich, Basel and Jerusalem. From 2014 to January 2018, he worked as a scientific assistant at the Chair of Strategic Studies at the Swiss Military Academy at the ETH Zurich. His dissertation, defended at the University of Zurich in December 2017, deals with the evolution of pro-Arab propaganda networks in the United States and Western Europe from the First World War until the Cold War. His main areas of research are international conflicts, terrorism, Islamism, and anti-Semitism. He may be contacted at daniel_rickenbacher@yahoo.com.

About the Authors

Thomas Riegler (PhD), born 1977, studied history and politics at Vienna and Edinburgh Universities. He has published on a wide range of topics, including terrorism, film studies, and contemporary history. He is the author of *Terrorismus: Akteure, Strukturen, Entwicklungslinien* (Terrorism: Actors, Structures, Trends, 2009), *Im Fadenkreuz: Österreich und der Nahostterrorismus 1973-1985* (In the Cross Hairs: Palestinian Terrorism in Austria 1973-1985, 2010), *Tage des Schreckens: Die OPEC-Geiselnahme und der moderne Terrorismus* (Days of Fear: The OPEC Hostage-taking and Modern Terrorism, 2015), and *Österreichs geheime Dienste: Vom Dritten Mann bis zur BVT-Affäre* (Austria's Secret Services: From the Third Man to the BVT-Scandal, 2019). He may be contacted at rieglerthomas@hotmail.com.

Andrew Sanders (PhD) is an assistant professor of Political Science at Texas A&M University San Antonio. He is the author of *Inside the IRA: Dissident Republicans and the War for Legitimacy* (2011) and *The Long Peace Process: The United States of America and Northern Ireland, 1960-2008* (2019) as well as the co-author of *Times of Troubles: Britain's War in Northern Ireland* (2012). He may be contacted at Andrew.Sanders@tamusa.edu.

Thomas Skelton-Robinson studied history at the University of Glasgow, Birkbeck College (University of London), and the University of Cambridge. He has held various research positions, including researching for solicitors Mischcon de Reya in the libel case *David Irving vs. Penguin Books and Deborah Lipstadt* (1998–2000) and for Dr Wolfgang Kraushaar, Hamburger Institut für Sozialforschung/Stiftung zur Förderung von Wissenschaft und Kultur on the multi-volume project *The Red Army Faction and International Terrorism: A Chronology* (2011 onwards). He has published on Holocaust denial and on the connections between the Palestinian and West German left-wing terrorist movements. He may be contacted at ts-r@hotmail.co.uk.

Philip W. Travis (PhD) is an associate professor of History at the State College of Florida in Bradenton, Florida. He specializes in US international relations during the Cold War, and specifically with Latin America. Dr Travis received his PhD from Washington State University in 2014. He published his first academic monograph, titled *Reagan's War on Terrorism in Nicaragua: The Outlaw State*, in 2016. He may be contacted at travisp@scf.edu.

Thomas Wegener Friis (PhD) is an associate professor at the Center for Cold War Studies, the University of Southern Denmark, and a researcher in intelligence studies. He is one of the co-organizers of the Need to Know conference series, the Regional Editor of Intelligence, Security and Public Affairs, board member of the International Intelligence History Association and a member of the Scientific Committee of the Zagreb Security Forum. His main areas of research are intelligence and security, military history and foreign policy. His recent books include *Konflikt und Kooperation* (Conflict and Cooperation, 2019), *DDR-Spionage: Albanien bis Großbritannien* (GDR Espionage: From Albania to Great Britain, 2017), and *Spionage unter Freunden* (Espionage among Friends, 2017). He may be contacted at twfriis@sdu.dk.

SELECT BIBLIOGRAPHY

Theoretical literature and general works

Asal, Victor, Justin Conrad and Peter White, Going Abroad: Transnational Solicitation and Contention by Ethnopolitical Organizations, *International Organization*, 68/4 (2014), 945–78.

Bale, Jeffrey M., *The Darkest Side of Politics, Vol. 2: State Terrorism, 'Weapons of Mass Destruction', Religious Extremism, and Organized Crime* (New York: Routledge, 2018).

Bale, Jeffrey M., Terrorism or State 'Proxies': Separating Fact from Fiction, in: Michael A. Innes (ed.), *Making Sense of Proxy Wars: States, Surrogates and the Use of Force* (Dulles, VA: Potomac, 2012), unpaginated.

Bapat, Navin A., Understanding State Sponsorship of Militant Groups, *British Journal of Political Science* 42/1 (2011), 1–29.

Bergman, Ronen, *Rise and Kill First: The Secret History of Israel's Targeted Assassinations* (Random House: New York, 2018).

Byman, Daniel, *Deadly Connections: States that Sponsor Terrorism* (New York: Cambridge University Press, 2005).

Byman, Daniel, Passive Sponsors of Terrorism, *Survival* 47/4 (2005), 117–44.

Byman, Daniel and Sarah E. Kreps, Agents of Destruction? Applying Principal-Agent Analysis to State-Sponsored Terrorism, *International Studies Perspectives* 11/1 (2010), 1–18.

Kirchner, Magdalena, *Allianz mit dem Terror: Iran, Israel und die libanesische Hisbollah 1979–2009* (München: AVM, 2009).

Maoz, Zeev and Belgin San-Akca, Rivalry and State Support of Non-State Armed Groups (NAGs), 1946–2001, *International Studies Quarterly* 56/4 (2012), 720–34.

Richardson, Louise, State Sponsorship: A Root Cause of Terrorism?, in: Tore Bjørgo (ed.), *Root Causes of Terrorism: Myths, Reality, and Ways Forward* (New York: Routledge, 2005), 189–97.

San Akca, Belgin, Supporting Non-State Armed Groups: A Resort to Illegality, *Journal of Strategic Studies* 32/4 (2009), 589–613.

Seale, Patrick, *Abu Nidal: A Gun for Hire* (New York: Random House, 1992).

Siqueira, Kevin and Todd Sandler, Terrorists versus the Government: Strategic Interaction, Support, and Sponsorship, *Journal of Conflict Resolution* 50/6 (2006), 878–98.

Travis, Philip W., *Reagan's War on Terrorism in Nicaragua: The Outlaw State* (Lanham, MD: Lexington Books, 2016).

Eastern Europe, the Soviet Union and North Korea

Akrap, Gordan, *Information Strategies and Operations in Public Knowledge Shaping*, PhD Thesis, University of Zagreb, 2011.

Albats, Yevgenia, *KGB: State Within a State* (London: I.B. Tauris, 1995).

Andrew, Christopher and Vasili Mitrokhin, *The World Was Going Our Way: The KGB and the Battle for the Third World* (New York: Basic Books, 2005).

Andrew, Christopher and Vasili Mitrokhin, *The Sword and the Shield: The Mitrokhin Archive and the Secret History of the KGB* (New York: Basic Books, 2000).

Baev, Jordan, Infiltration of Non-European Terrorist Groups in Europe and Antiterrorist Responses in Western and Eastern Europe (1969–1991), in: Siddik Ekici (ed.), *Counter Terrorism in Diverse Communities* (Amsterdam: IOS Press, 2011), 58–74.

Baev, Jordan, *Bulgarian Arms Delivery to Third World Countries, 1950–1989: A Documentary Collection* (Zurich: CSS, 2006), http://www.php.isn.ethz.ch/lory1.ethz.ch/collections/coll_armstrade/introduction4f28.html?navinfo=23065 (accessed 1 January 2020).

Baev, Jordan, Bulgaria and the Armed Conflict in Central America, 1979–1989, in: Evgenii Pashentsev and Hector Luis Saint-Pierre (eds.), *Armies and Politics* (Moscow: RPR, 2002), 33–45.

Balantič, Polona, Jugoslavija in mednarodni terorizem v sedemdesetih letih: Dva primera neizročitve teroristov Zvezni republiki Nemčiji, Prispevki za novejšo zgodovino, *Contributions to Contemporary History* 55/1 (2015), 143–91.

Bengtson-Krallert, Matthias, *Die DDR und der internationale Terrorismus* (Marburg: Tectum Verlag, 2017).

Blumenau, Bernhard, Unholy Alliance: The Connection between the East German Stasi and the Right-Wing Terrorist Odfried Hepp, *Studies in Conflict & Terrorism* 43/1 (2020), 47–68.

Boyadzhiev, Todor, *Разузнаването* ['Reconnaissance'] (Sofia: Trud, 2000).

Dannreuther, Roland, *The Soviet Union and the PLO* (New York: Palgrave Macmillan, 1998).

Follain, John, *The Jackal* (London: Weidenfeld and Nicholson, 1998).

Gadowski, Witold and Przemyslaw Wojciechowski, *Tragarze śmierci: Polskie związki ze światowym terroryzmem* (Warszawa: Prószyński i S-ka, 2010).

Gallagher, Aileen, *The Japanese Red Army* (New York: Rosen, 2003).

Gasztold, Przemysław, Wars, Weapons and Terrorists: Clandestine Operations of the Polish Military Intelligence Station in Beirut, 1965–1982, *The International History Review*, published online on 26 September 2019, https://doi.org/10.1080/07075332.2019.1664609 (accessed 1 January 2020).

Gasztold, Przemyslaw, *Zabójcze układy: Służby PRL i międzynarodowy terroryzm* (Warszawa: Wydawnictwo PWN, 2017), 19–64.

Gasztold-Seń, Przemyslaw, Between Geopolitics and National Security: Polish Intelligence and International Terrorism during the Cold War, in: Wladyslaw Bułhak and Thomas Wegener Friis (eds.), *Need to Know: Eastern and Western Perspectives* (Odense: University Press of Southern Denmark, 2014), 138–48.

Gasztold-Seń, Przemyslaw, Der Sicherheitsapparat der Volksrepublik Polen und die Rote Armee Fraktion, *Inter Finitimos: Jahrbuch zur deutsch-polnischen Beziehungsgeschichte* 9 (2011), 144–54.

Ginor, Isabella and Gideon Remez, *The Soviet-Israeli War, 1967–1973: The USSR's Military Intervention in the Egyptian-Israeli Conflict* (New York: Oxford University Press, 2017).

Golan, Galia, Moscow and the PLO: The Ups and Downs of a Complex Relationship, in: Moshe Ma'oz and Avraham Sela (eds.), *The PLO and Israel: From Armed Conflict to Political Solution, 1964–1994* (London: St. Martin's Press, 1997), 121–40.

Golan, Galia, *The Soviet Union and the PLO* (Jerusalem: Hebrew University, 1976).

Grba, Stevan, *Razvoj vojnoobaveštajne službe od 1945. do 1985. godine: Razvoj oružanih snaga SFRJ, 1945–1985: Vojnoobaveštajna služba* (Belgrade: Vojnoizdavački i novinski centar, 1990).

Hänni, Adrian. Secret Bedfellows? The KGB, Carlos the Jackal and Cold War Psychological Warfare, *Studies in Conflict & Terrorism* 43/1 (2020), 69–87.

Hänni, Adrian, *Terrorismus als Konstrukt: Schwarze Propaganda, politische Bedrohungsängste und der Krieg gegen den Terrorismus in Reagans Amerika* (Essen: Klartext-Verlag, 2018).

Herf, Jeffrey, *Undeclared Wars with Israel: East Germany and the West German Far Left, 1967-1989* (Cambridge: Cambridge University Press, 2016).

Israeli, Raphael (ed.), *PLO in Lebanon: Selected Documents* (New York: St. Martin's Press, 1983).

Jander, Martin, Differenzen im antiimperialistischen Kampf: Zu den Verbindungen des Ministeriums für Staatssicherheit mit der RAF und dem bundesdeutschen Linksterrorismus, in: Wolfgang Kraushaar (ed.), *Die RAF und der linke Terrorismus*, Vol. 1 (Hamburg: Hamburger Edition, 2006), 696–713.

Kauffer, Rémy, Communism and Terrorism, in: Stéphane Courtois and Mark Kramer (eds.), *The Black Book of Communism: Crimes, Terror, Repression* (Cambridge, MA: Harvard University Press, 1999), 353–60.

Kopp, Magdalena, *Die Terrorjahre: Mein Leben an der Seite von Carlos* (Munich: Deutsche Verlags-Anstalt, 2007).

Kostadinov, Evtim, Tatyana Kiryakova, Jordan Baev and Kostadin Grozev (eds.), *International Terrorism in the Bulgarian State Security Files: Documentary Volume* (Sophia: The Committee for Disclosing Documents and Announcing Affiliation of Bulgarian Citizens to the State Security and the Intelligence Services of the Bulgarian National Armed Forces, 2010).

Lučić, Ivo, Bosnia and Herzegovina and Terrorism, *National Security and the Future* 2/3-4 (2001), 111–42.

Maeke, Lutz, *DDR und PLO: Die Palästinapolitik des SED-Staates* (Berlin: De Gruyter, 2017).

Malloy, Sean L., *Out of Oakland: Black Panther Party Internationalism during the Cold War* (London: Cornell University Press, 2017).

Nehring, Christopher, *Die Zusammenarbeit der DDR Auslandsaufklärung mit der Aufklärung der Volksrepublik Bulgarien: Regionalfilialen des KGB?* PhD Thesis, Heidelberg University, 2016.

Nehring, Christopher, Die Verhaftung Till Meyers in Bulgarien: eine Randnotiz aus dem Archiv der bulgarischen Staatssicherheit, *Vierteljahrshefte für Zeitgeschichte* 63/3 (2015), 411–24.

Oberdorfer, Don and Robert Carlin, *The Two Koreas: A Contemporary History* (New York: Basic Books, 2014).

Orbán-Schwarzkopf, Balázs, *Greys and Wolves in the Shadow of the Red* (Budapest: Hamvas Institute, 2016).

Persak, Krzysztof et al. (eds.), *A Handbook of the Communist Security Apparatus in East Central Europe 1944-1989* (Warsaw: Institute of National Rememberance, 2005).

Richterova, Daniela, The Anxious Host: Czechoslovakia and Carlos the Jackal 1978–1986, *International History Review* 40/1 (2018), 108–32.

Riegler, Thomas, 'Es muss ein gegenseitiges Geben und Nehmen sein': Warschauer-Pakt-Staaten und Terrorismusbekämpfung am Beispiel der DDR, in: Johannes Hürter (ed.), *Terrorismusbekämpfung in Westeuropa: Demokratie und Sicherheit in den 1970er und 1980er Jahren* (Berlin: De Gruyter Oldenbourg, 2015), 289–315.

Riegler, Thomas, Quid pro Quo: State Sponsorship of Terrorism in the Cold War, in: Bernhard Blumenau and Jussi M. Hanhimäki (eds.), *An International History of Terrorism: Western and Non-Western Experiences* (London: Routledge, 2013), 115–32.

Ruce světové revoluce: Carlos a jeho teroristická organizace v dokumentech Státní bezpečnosti, 1976–1989 ['Hands of the World Revolution: Carlos and His Terrorist Organisation in the Documents of the State Security, 1976–1989'], source collection forthcoming from the Prague publishing house Academia.

Simić, Mirko, *Istorijsko nasleđe vojnoobaveštajne službe: Razvoj oružanih snaga SFRJ, 1945–1985: Vojnoobaveštajna služba* (Belgrade: Vojnoizdavački i novinski centar, 1990).

Sørensen, Anne, *Stasi og den vesttyske terrorisme* (Santa Barbara: Århus University Press, 2006).

Tofan, Liviu, *Ș viuLI Securității: teroristul Carlos în solda spionajului românesc* (Bucarest: Polirom, 2013).

Vielhaber, David, The Stasi-Meinhof Complex?, *Studies in Conflict & Terrorism* 36/7 (2013), 533–46.

Volkogonov, Dmitry, *Etyudy o vremeni* (Moscow: Novosty, 1998).

Wiel, Jérôme aan de, *East German Intelligence and Ireland 1949–90: Espionage, Terrorism and Diplomacy* (Manchester: Manchester University Press, 2017).

Wunschik, Tobias, Die 'Bewegung 2. Juni' und ihre Protektion durch den Staatssicherheitsdienst der DDR, *Deutschland-Archiv* 6 (2007), 1014–25.

Wunschik, Tobias, Magdeburg statt Mosambique, Köthen statt Kap Verden: Die RAF-Aussteiger in der DDR, in: Klaus Biesenbach (ed.), *Zur Vorstellung des Terrors: Die RAF-Ausstellung*, Vol. 2 (Göttingen: Steidl, 2005), 236–40.

Wunschik, Tobias, *Baader-Meinhofs Kinder: Die zweite Generation der RAF* (Opladen: Westdeutscher Verlag, 1997).

Wunschik, Tobias, *Die Hauptabteilung XXII: 'Terrorabwehr'* (Berlin: BStU, 1995).

Western Europe and NATO States

Albanese, Matteo and Pablo del Hierro, *Transnational Fascism in the Twentieth Century: Spain, Italy and the Global Neo-Fascist Network* (London: Bloomsbury, 2016).

Arnson, Cythnia J., *Crossroads: Congress, the President, and Central America, 1976–1993* (University Park: Penn State University Press, 1993²).

Bale, Jeffrey M., *The Darkest Sides of Politics, Vol. 1: Postwar Fascism, Covert Operations, and Terrorism* (New York: Routledge, 2018).

Bell, Aaron T., A Matter of Western Civilisation: Transnational Support for the Salvadoran Counterrevolution, 1979–1982, *Cold War History* 15/4 (2015), 511–31.

Bird, Kai, *The Good Spy* (New York: Broadway Books, 2014).

Bohning, Don, *The Castro Obsession: U.S. Covert Operations against Cuba, 1959–1965* (Washington, DC: Potomac Books, 2005).

Bolender, Keith, *Voices from the Other Side: An Oral History of Terrorism against Cuba* (London: Pluto Press, 2010).

Boumaad, Abdelhak, *La Politique Américaine en Amérique Centrale: La Présidence de Ronald Reagan et le Nicaragua* (Lille: Atelier National de Reproduction des Theses, 1999).

Bülow, Mathilde von, *West Germany, Cold War Europe and the Algerian War* (Cambridge: Cambridge University Press, 2016).

Bülow, Mathilde von, Myth or Reality? The Red Hand and French Covert Action in Federal Germany during the Algerian War, 1956–61, *Intelligence and National Security* 22/6 (2007), 787–820.

Byrne, Malcolm, *Iran-Contra: Reagan's Scandal and the Unchecked Abuse of Presidential Power* (Lawrence, KS: University Press of Kansas, 2014).

Cadwalleder, Anne, *Lethal Allies: British Collusion in Ireland* (Cork: Mercier Press, 2013).

Carlton, David, *The West's Road to 9/11: Resisting, Appeasing and Encouraging Terrorism since 1970* (London: Palgrave Macmillan, 2005).

Cento Bull, Anna, *Italian Neofascism: The Strategy of Tension and the Politics of Nonreconciliation* (New York: Berghahn Books, 2012).

Chasdi, Richard J., Counterterror Failure: The Fadlallah Assassination Attempt, in: Richard Weitz (ed.), *Project on National Security Reform: Case Studies Working Group Report*, Vol. 2, March 2012, www.dtic.mil/get-tr-doc/pdf?AD=ADA558988 (accessed 1 January 2020).

Chauvin, Luc, French Diplomacy and the Hostage Crisis, in: Barry Rubin (ed.), *The Politics of Counterterrorism: The Ordeal of Democratic States* (Washington, DC: Paul H. Nitze School of Advanced International Studies, 1990), 61–90.

Coco, Vittorio, Conspiracy Theories in Republican Italy: The Pellegrino Report to the Parliamentary Commission on Terrorism, *Journal of Modern Italian Studies* 20/3 (2015), 361–76.

Cutonilli, Valerio and Rosario Priore, *I segreti di Bologna: La verità sull'atto terroristico più grave della storia italiana* (Milan: Chiarelettere, 2016).

Dahlke, Matthias, *Demokratischer Staat und Transnationaler Terrorismus: Drei Wege zur Unnachgiebigkeit in Westeuropa 1972–1975* (Munich: Oldenbourg, 2011).

Dahlke, Matthias, Das Wischnewski-Protokoll: Zur Zusammenarbeit zwischen westeuropäischen Regierungen und transnationalen Terroristen 1977, *Vierteljahrshefte für Zeitgeschichte (VfZ)* 57/2 (2009), 201–15.

Evans, Martin, *Algeria: France's Undeclared War* (Oxford: Oxford University Press, 2012).

Frangi, Abdullah, *Der Gesandte: Mein Leben für Palästina. Hinter den Kulissen der Nahost-Politik* (Munich: Heyne, 2011).

Gal Or, Noemi (ed.), *Tolerating Terrorism in the West: An International Survey* (London: Routledge, 1991).

Gaspardis, Paola, *Lo status dell'OLP nella diplomazia italiana* (Siena: Prospettiva Editrice, 2009).

Grandin, Greg, *Empires Workshop: Latin America, The United States, and the New Imperialism* (New York: Henry Holt, 2006).

Gyr, Marcel, *Schweizer Terrorjahre: Das geheime Abkommen mit der PLO* (Zurich: Verlag Neue Zürcher Zeitung, 2016).

Heitzer, Enrico, *Die Kampfgruppe gegen Unmenschlichkeit (KgU): Widerstand und Spionage im Kalten Krieg 1948–1959* (Köln: Böhlau, 2015).

Hof, Tobias, The Moro Affair – Left-Wing Terrorism and Conspiracy in Italy in the Late 1970s, *Historical Social Research* 38/1 (2013), 232–57.

Ingram, Martin and Greg Harkin, *Stakeknife: Britain's Secret Agents in Ireland* (Madison: University of Wisconsin Press, 2005).

Lammert, Markus, *Der neue Terrorismus: Terrorismusbekämpfung in Frankreich in den 1980er Jahren* (Boston: De Gruyter, 2017).

LeoGrande, William, *Our Own Backyard: The United States in Central America, 1977–1992* (Chapel Hill: University of North Carolina, 1998).

Ménage, Gilles, *L'oeil du pouvoir*, Vol. 3 (Paris: Fayard, 1999–2001).

Merlen, Eric and Frédéric Ploquin, *Carnets intimes de la DST: 30 ans au coeur du contre-espionnage français* (Paris: Fayard, 2003).
Naftali, Timothy, *Blind Spot: The Secret History of American Counterterrorism* (New York: Basic Books, 2005).
Punch, Maurice, *State Violence, Collusion and the Troubles: Counter Insurgency, Government Deviance and Northern Ireland* (London: Pluto Press, 2012).
Quemeneur, Tramor, La Discipline jusqu'au l'Indiscipline, in: Mohammed Harbi and Benjamin Stora (eds.), *La Guerre d'Algérie* (Paris: Laffont, 2004).
Rabe, Stephen A., *The Killing Zone: The United States Wages the Cold War in Latin America* (New York: Oxford University Press, 2015).
Report of the Congressional Committees Investigating the Iran-Contra Affair, with Supplemental, Minority, and Additional Views (Washington, DC: Government Printing Office, 1987).
Riegler, Thomas, Diplomatie und Terror: Die Operationen des PLO-Geheimdienstes 1979 in der BRD und in Österreich, *Journal for Intelligence, Propaganda and Security Studies (JIPSS)*, 8/1 (2014), 30–58.
Riegler, Thomas, The State as a Terrorist: France and the Red Hand, *Perspectives on Terrorism*, 6/6 (2012), 22–33.
Riegler, Thomas, *Im Fadenkreuz: Österreich und der Nahostterrorismus 1973 bis 1985* (Vienna: V&R unipress, 2010).
Schenk, Dieter, *Der Chef: Horst Herold und das BKA* (Hamburg: Hoffmann und Campe, 1998).
Seale, Patrick, *Abu Nidal: A Gun for Hire* (New York: Random House, 1992).
Shapiro, Jeremy and Bénédicte Suzan, The French Experience of Counter-terrorism, *Survival: Global Politics and Strategy* 45/1 (2003), 67–98.
Sidoti, Francesco, Terrorism Supporters in the West: The Italian Case, in: Noemi Gal Or (ed.), *Tolerating Terrorism in the West: An International Survey* (London: Routledge, 1991), 105–143.
Talbot, David, *The Devil's Chessboard: Allen Dulles, the CIA, and the Rise of America's Secret Government* (London: HarperCollins, 2016).
Urwin, Margaret, *A State in Denial: British Collusion with Loyalist Paramilitaries* (Cork: Mercier Press, 2016).
Wieviorka, Michel, French Politics and Strategy on Terrorism, in: Barry Rubin (ed.), *The Politics of Counterterrorism: The Ordeal of Democratic States* (Washington, DC: Paul H. Nitze School of Advanced International Studies, 1990), 61–90.
Wischnewski, Hans-Jürgen, *Mit Leidenschaft und Augenmaß: In Mogadischu und anderswo* (München: Bertelsmann, 1989).
Yousaf, Mohammad and Mark Adkin, *Afghanistan: The Bear Trap-The Defeat of a Superpower* (Havertown, PA: Casemate, 1992).
Zala, Sacha, Thomas Bürgisser and Yves Steiner, Die Debatte zu einem 'geheimen Abkommen' zwischen Bundesrat Graber und der PLO: Eine Zwischenbilanz, *Schweizerische Zeitschrift für Geschichte* 66/1 (2016), 1–24.

Stay Behind / Gladio

Ben Redjeb, Badis, The Central Intelligence Agency and the Stay-Behind Networks in West Germany: An Assessment, *British Journal of Humanities and Social Sciences* 14/2 (2016), 50–62.

Cogan, Charles, 'Stay-Behind' in France: Much Ado about Nothing?, *Journal of Strategic Studies* 30/6 (2007), 937–54.
Desmaretz, Gérard, *Stay-behind: Les réseaux secrets de la guerre froide* (Paris: Editions Jourdan, 2015).
Engelen, Dick, Lessons Learned: The Dutch 'Stay-Behind' Organization 1945–1992, *Journal of Strategic Studies* 30/6 (2007), 981–96.
Kemmerling, Markus, Kaltes Kriegsspielzeug, *Zoom: Zeitschrift für Politik und Gesellschaft* 4–5 (1996) ('Es muss nicht immer Gladio sein: Attentate, Waffenlager, Erinnerungslücken'), 6–9.
Keßelring, Agilolf, *Die Organisation Gehlen und die Neuformierung des Militärs in der Bundesrepublik* (Berlin: Ch. Links, 2017).
Lillbacka, Ralf, The Murder of Swedish Prime Minister Olof Palme; A Rebuttal of the 'Stay-Behind' Scenario, *Journal for Intelligence, Propaganda and Security Studies* 11/1 (2017), 112–25.
Matter, Martin, *P-26: Die Geheimarmee, die keine war: Wie Politik und Medien die Vorbereitung des Widerstands skandalisierten* (Baden: hier + jetzt, 2012).
Maurice, Charles, *Insane Killers Inc.: The Brabant Killers Mystery* (Rayem Press, 2018).
Meier, Titus J. *Widerstandsvorbereitungen für den Besetzungsfall: Die Schweiz im Kalten Krieg* (Zürich: NZZ Libro, 2018).
Nuti, Leopoldo, The Italian 'Stay-Behind' Network – The Origins of Operation 'Gladio', *Journal of Strategic Studies* 30/6 (2007), 955–80.
Nuti, Leopoldo and Olav Riste (eds.), Special Section: Preparing for a Soviet Occupation: The Strategy of 'Stay-Behind', *Journal of Strategic Studies* 30/6 (2007), 929–1024.
Richardson, John H. *My Father the Spy: An Investigative Memoir* (New York: Harper Collins, 2005).
Riegler, Thomas, *Österreichs geheime Dienste: Vom Dritten Mann zur BVT-Affäre* (Wien: Klever Verlag, 2019).
Riste, Olav, 'Stay Behind': A Clandestine Cold War Phenomenon, *Journal of Cold War Studies* 16/4 (2014), 35–59.
Riste, Olav, With an Eye to History: The Origins and Development of 'Stay-Behind' in Norway, *Journal of Strategic Studies* 30/6 (2007), 997–1024.
Schmidt-Eenboom, Erich and Ulrich Stoll, *Die Partisanen der NATO: Stay-Behind-Organisationen in Deutschland 1946–1991* (Berlin: Ch. Links, 2015).
Stejskal, James, *Special Forces Berlin: Clandestine Cold War Operations of the US Army's Elite, 1956-1990* (Philadelphia: Casemate Publishers, 2017).

INDEX

Abbas, Abu 167
Abbas, Ahmed 119
Abrams, Elliott 200
Abu Daoud 120
Abu El Heiga, Mohammed 209
Abu Gharbiya, Bahjat 98
Abu Maher 101–3, 108, 128, 136 n.71, 138 n.83
Abu Nidal Organization (ANO) 158, 190 n.35, 237
   attack on 'Jo Goldenberg' restaurant 4
   Austria's deal with 5, 12 n.24
   France's deal with 4–5, 11–12 n.24
Abu Sharif, Bassam 92, 96, 103, 106, 107, 110, 131 n.16, 132 n.32, 134 n.42, 136 n.65, 137 n.76, 138 n.83, 142 n.137, 164
Achille Lauro cruise attack 166, 167
Action Directe 19, 237
Action Organization for the Liberation of Palestine (AOLP) 128, 133 n.36, 150 n.239
Adair, Johnny 'Mad Dog' 59
Adams, Gerry 45, 54–6, 58, 59
Adams, Michael 102, 136 n.67, 137 n.76, 151 n.240
Adwan, Kamal 115, 116, 144 n.168, 145 n.180, 151 n.242
Aginter Press 3
Ahern, Bertie 57
Akca, Belgin San 10 n.10
AL-Ahram (newspaper) 151 n.243, 213, 215
Al Baath (newspaper) 215
Albrecht, Udo 137 n.73
Alexander, Yonah 246 n.12
Algeria 3, 179, 208, 213, 214
Algerian War of Independence (1954–62) 3

Al-Hadaf (magazine) 107, 116, 127, 151 n.244
al-Hout, Shafiq 119, 120, 132 n.29, 144 n.174, 146 n.193
Al-Jumhuriya (newspaper) 215
al-Kubasi Basil Raoud 117, 145 n.183
Allen, Richard 116, 144 n.174
Allende, Salvador 233 n.11
Allied Clandestine Committee (ACC) 22
al-Nahyan, Sheikh Zayid bin Sultan 107
al-Najjar, Mohammed Yousef 116, 145 n.180
al-Razd, Jihaz 120
al-Shamali, Fuad 65, 74–8, 82, 83, 210, 211, 213, 214
al-Yamani, Ahmed. *See* Abu Maher
al-Zomar, Osama Abdel 166
Ambrosius, Lloyd 224
American Federation of Labor and Congress of Industrial Organizations (AFL–CIO) 31
Ames, Robert 107, 117, 120, 121, 147 n.204, 197
Amman Agreement 126
Amos II, John W. 144 n.172
Amstein, André 64, 65, 76
Anabtawi, Hatim (of Nablus) 136 n.67
Anderson, Frank 121
Anderson, Terry 198
Andreotti, Giulio 159, 165
An Garda Siochana 58, 61 n.52, 62 n.86
An-Nahar (newspaper) 130 n.11
antagonistic supporters, of terrorist actors 10 n.8
Arab Commercial Bank 211–12, 214
Arab Lawyers Union (ALU) 213
Arab League 97, 108, 141 n.124, 207–8
   in Switzerland 210–12
Arab Nationalist Movement (ANM) 107, 140 n.116

Arafat, Yasser   178, 180, 181, 184
  Lodo Moro and   157–9, 161–2, 165–7
  Palestinian Fedayeen groups and   94, 97, 98, 107, 110, 120, 125, 127–9, 147 nn.203, 210, 149 nn.224–5, 231, 150 nn.233, 235
Argentina   225
Arguello, Patrick   92, 95
Arias Sanchez, Oscar   231, 235 n.44
Armenian Secret Army for the Liberation of Armenia (ASALA)   4
Arnson, Cythnia J.   234 n.28
Assad, Hafez   4, 196
Assad, Rifaat   4
Assmann, Karin   144 n.179
Athens News Agency   98
Auque, Roger   198
Aust, Stefan   137 n.73
Austria   25, 34 n.2, 36 n.12. *See also* Wischnewski Protocol
  ANO and   5, 12 n.24
  stay behind case study of   26–33
Austro-German agreements, with transnational terrorists. *See* Wischnewski Protocol
Auswärtige Amt (AA) (West German Foreign Office)   119
Avanguardia Nazionale   3, 17
Ayad, Abu. *See* Iyad, Abu (Salah Khalaf)
Azani, Eitan   193, 195, 204 n.2
Azhari, Ahmad   115, 144 n.168

Baader, Andreas   120
Bach, Gabriel   212
Baker, Albert   50
Bale, Jeffrey   1, 13 n.32
Barakat, Daoud   66, 69–71, 218
Barbie, Klaus   19, 72
Barlow, Gary   49
Barrett, Ken   57
Bar-Zohar, Michael   147 n.201, 189 n.29
Basler Zeitung (newspaper)   71, 80
Batatu, Hanna   13 n.31
'Battle of Karameh'   93
Baumann, Claude   99
Baumgarten, Helga   140 n.116
Baumgartner, Giorgio   163
BBC   78

Beaumont, Richard   109, 111
Belfast Telegraph (newspaper)   46, 49
Belgium   15, 33, 36 n.12, 213
  stay behind in incidents in   18–19
Ben-Itto, Hadassa   220 n.35
Bentoumi, Amar   214
Bergman, Ronen   117, 145 n.185
Berlusconi, Silvio   169 n.8
Bernath, François A.   78–82
Berne Group   106–7, 112–14, 140 nn.110, 112, 141 n.124, 143 n.159, 217
Berne Trial   212
Beuckels, Roger   19
Bezirksanwaltschaft Bülach (District Prosecutor's Office Bülach, Switzerland)   75
Bird, Kai   117, 120, 121, 140 n.113, 144 n.178, 145 nn.183–4, 189, 147 nn.200, 204, 210
Black September Organization (BSO)   77–8, 82, 90, 129, 158
  Italy and   155
Blair, Tony   45
Blankart, Franz   65, 66, 77
Blanket, The (online journal)   58
Bloody Sunday   48–9
BOAC hijacking   92, 131 n.16, 217
Boisard, Marcel   106
Boissier, Pierre   106–8, 139 n.105, 140 n.110, 141 n.121
Bologna massacre   163–7
Bonisch, Georg   188 n.7
Bonkoffsky, Christiaan   18
Bonnet, Yves   11 n.24
Borg, Parker   228
Böse, Wilfried   73
Bosonnet, Marcel   73
Bouhired, Djamila   213
Bouhouche, Madani   18
Bouteflika, Abdelaziz   214
Bouten, Guy   18
Bovin, Roger   102
Boyle, Harris   52
'Brabant Killers'   18–19
Brandt, Willy   101, 178, 180, 185, 187
Breen, Harry   58, 62 n.86
Bréguet, Bruno   72, 73, 104, 113, 114, 128, 218

Brigade mobile de la Gendarmerie (Luxembourg)   19
Britain   95-7, 100, 108-11. *See also* Palestinian Fedayeen groups
British Special Forces   27
British state and loyalist paramilitaries, in Northern Ireland. *See* collusion
Brown, Dean   97, 118, 149 n.228
Browne, Andrew   44
Brunshvig, Georges   212
B-Specials   51-2, 61 n.48
Buback, Siegfried   176
Buchanan, Robert   58, 62 n.86
Buckley, William   198
Bulgaria   242, 245 n.5
Bund Deutscher Jugend (League of German Youth)   19
Bundesanwaltschaft (Office of the Attorney General of Switzerland)   64-6, 72, 75-7
  Oversight Agency (AB-BA)   78, 79
Bundesarchiv (Swiss Federal Archives)   64
Bundeskanzlei (Federal Chancellery) (Switzerland)   66
Bundesnachrichtendienst (BND) (Germany)   19, 21
Bundespolizei (Swiss Federal Police, BUPO)   64, 65
Bundesrat (Swiss Federal Council)   35 n.2, 64, 69, 72, 77, 96, 142 n.134
Bunting, Ronald   55
Bunting, Ronnie   55
Bürgisser, Thomas   11 n.19, 67
Buser, Walter   67
Bush, H. W.   227
Bush administration over Iraq   224, 230, 231
Byman, Daniel   8, 10 n.8

Cabras, Paolo   162
Cadwallader, Anne   47, 52, 54, 58
Cairo Accord   126
Callan, I. R.   116
"Carlos the Jackal"   64, 72-4, 135 nn.49-50, 163, 164, 179, 245 n.5
Caroz, Yaacov   139 n.92
Carstens, Karl   188 n.7
Carter, Jimmy   182, 225

Casey, William   2, 200
Cassin, Vernon   121, 147 n.210
Casson, Felice   17
Castro, Fidel   224
Cavendish, Anthony   20, 27
Celio, Nello   102
Cellules Communistes Combattantes (CCC)   19
Centrale Suisse d'Assistance à la Palestine   213
Central Intelligence Agency (CIA)   1-2, 37 n.52, 39 n.92
  Easeful programme of   26
  on Iraq   241
  Palestinian Fedayeen groups and   117, 128, 147 n.210, 148 n.218, 150 n.231
  Salameh as source of   120-1, 123, 147 n.200
  stay-behind operations   20-1, 29-32
  Terrorism Review of   19
  Zarqa Crisis and   106-8
Centro Adestramento Guastatori (CAG)   16
Chamberlin, Paul Thomas   148 nn.213, 216, 150 n.235, 232 n.7
Chaussy, Ulrich   21
Chile   225
China   9, 105, 242
Christian Scientist Monitor (magazine)   105
Cicippio, Joseph   198
Clandestine Planning Committee (CPC)   22
Clarridge, Duan R.   144 n.179
Claude, Pierre Louis   211
Clegg, Lee   48
Clementi, Marco   161
Cline, Ray S.   246 n.12
Cobra special unit   179
Coco, Vittorio   172 n.71
Cogan, Charles   19
Colby, William   25, 39 n.92
Collins, John   234 n.28
collusion (Northern Ireland)
  counter-gangs and   50-4
  military killing and   47-50
  in 1980s   54-8
  significance of   43-4, 46

Colombia 223, 224
Colombo, Emilio 165
COMECON 6
Comité de Soutien au Peuple Palestinien (Committee for the Support of the Palestinian People) (Switzerland) 211
Comité de Soutien et d'Aide au Peuple Palestinien (Committee of Support and Help for the Palestinian People) (Switzerland) 213
Comité suisse de soutien au peuple palestinien (Swiss-Palestinian Support Committee) 74
Commissions of Investigations Act 52
Communist Party (KPD) (West Germany) 19
Communist Party of Labor (Switzerland) 211
Conflict Records Research Center (CRRC) 241
Contras 228
Cooley, John K. 105, 132 n.20, 142 n.137
Copeland, Miles 90
Corrigan, Owen 58
Cory, Peter 57, 58
Cossiga, Francesco 153, 163–6, 173 n.91
Costa Rica 223, 235 n.44
Council for the Advancement of Arab-British Understanding (CAABU) 102
Counterintelligence Corps (CIC), US Army 32
Counter Jihad (Williams) 224
Craxi, Benito 167
Curtis, Gunner Robert 48
Cusack, Jim 55
Cutonilli, Valerio 172 n.76
Czechoslovakia 26, 245 n.5

D'Andrea, Stefano 171 n.62
Dahbor, Amena 209
Dahlke, Matthias 130 n.10, 187 n.1
Daly, Miriam 55
Davies, Nicholas 46, 59
Dawson's Field Hijackings. *See* Zarqa Crisis
Deadly Connections (Byman) 8

Dead Men Talking (Davies) 46–7
De la stratégie judiciaire (Vergès) 213
delle Chiaie, Stefano 3
Democratic Front for the Liberation of Palestine (DFLP) 94
Denmark 39 n.92
de Silva, Desmond 57
Deslaire, Lucien 19
Detachment 'A' 37 n.58
   Mission Support Sites 21
Diehl, Digby 144 n.179
Dietl, Wilhelm 148 n.211
Digilio, Carlo 17
Dillon, Martin 46, 47, 59
Dingels, Hans-Eberhard 136 n.68, 180
Dinges, John 233 n.12
Diplomatische Dokumente der Schweiz (Diplomatic Documents of Switzerland) (DODIS) 67
Direction de la Surveillance du Territoire (DST) (France) 4, 5
Direction Générale de la Sécurité Extérieure (DGSE) (France) 4
Director of Public Prosecutions (DPP) (Britain) 49
Dirty War (Argentina) 225, 232 n.8
Dirty War, The (Dillon) 46
Dodge, David 198
Donaldson, Jeffrey 58
Douglas-Home, Alec 108, 122
Dozier, James 12 n.28
Drake, Richard 160
Dublin bombings 52
Dubois, Charles-Albert 102, 137 nn.78, 80
Dulles, Allen 26
Dunn, Richard 106, 107
Du Pasquier, Roger 215

Easeful guerrilla training programme 26
Eastern Europe and international terrorism 239
East Germany, CIA and stay-behind operations in 20
Eban, Abba 104
Egypt 93, 94, 97, 108–11, 142 n.135, 158, 210, 242
Eibl, Franz 189 n.27
Eichmann trial 212

Eidgenössisches Departement für
    auswärtige Angelegenheiten
    (Federal Department of Foreign
    Affairs, EDA)   66
Eidgenössisches Justiz-und
    Polizeidepartement (Federal
    Department of Justice and
    Police, EJPD)   65, 76
Eidgenössisches Politisches Departement
    (Federal Political Department)
    (EPD)   64–6, 69, 113–14, 138
    n.91, 141 n.121, 143 n.158
Elad, Shlomi   152 n.247
El Al hijacking (1968)   154–5, 157, 209
el-Dien, Youssef Azziz   110–12
Eliav, Lova   181
Ellenberger, Hans   68, 70, 75–6, 211, 215
El Salvador   226, 227, 235 n.44
Elten, Jörg Andrees   131 n.14, 137 n.76
Engelen, Dick   22
Ente Nazionale Idrocarburi (ENI)   156
Esquipulas II Accord. *See* Treaty of
    Esquipulas
Estado Novo   3
Euskadi Ta Askatasuna (ETA)   4, 7, 230,
    237

Fadlallah, Sheikh Muhammad   2
Fallaci, Oriana   132 n.19
Fanfani, Amintore   156
Farabundo Marti National Liberation
    Front (FMLN) (El
    Salvador)   224, 226
Fatah   4, 207–8, 237
    ascendency of   126–9
    Palestinian Fedayeen groups and   89,
    91, 94, 96, 114, 115, 119, 120,
    123–6, 130 n.9, 145 n.180, 147
    n.203, 149 nn.226, 231, 150 n.235
    support networks, in
    Switzerland   209–12
Fath (newspaper)   127
Federal Criminal Police Office (BKA)
    (West Germany)   177, 186
Ferraris, Luigi Vittorio   172 n.85, 173
    n.93
Finchelstein, Federico   232 n.8
Finland   26, 34 n.2
Finucane, Patrick   45, 46, 56–7, 59

Fioravanti, Giuseppe   163
Fischer, Albert G.   99, 135 n.56
Fisher, James   48
Fiumicino Airport incident   155, 157,
    158, 166
Flamigni, Sergio   160
Follain, John   12 n.24
Force Research Unit (FRU)   44, 45, 149
    n.224
Ford, Gerald   229
Foreign and Commonwealth Office (FCO)
    (UK)   98, 111, 114, 133 n.36
France   3, 19, 148 n.213
    deal with ANO   4–5, 11–12 n.24
    Hezbollah and   199
    Iran and   200–1
Franco, Francisco   3
Frangi, Abdallah   180, 186, 191 n.76
Freches, Carl   19
Frente Sandinista de Liberacion Nacional
    (FSLN) (Nicaragua)   224, 226
Freymond, Jacques   96, 102
Friedländer, Saul   82
Friedrich Ebert Foundation   175
Front de Libération Nationale (FLN)
    (Algeria)   3, 214
Fuller, Graham   117

Gaddafi, Muammar   157, 163, 165, 173
    nn.92, 94, 214
Gaddis, John Lewis   224
Gangs and Counter-Gangs (Kitson)   50
Ganser, Daniele   15–16, 33
Gautronneau, Vincent   11 n.24
Gelzer, Michael   68, 69, 75, 217
Gendarmerie (Belgium)   18
Generalunion Palästinensischer Studenten
    (GUPS)   210, 211
Genoud, François   72–5, 78, 83, 135 n.50,
    210, 211, 213–15, 217, 219 n.16
'German Autumn'   176, 179, 181, 183,
    185, 187
German Democratic Republic (GDR)   21
Germany   177. *See also* Wischnewski
    Protocol
Geschichte der Schweiz im 20. Jahrhundert
    ('The History of Switzerland
    in the Twentieth Century')
    (Tanner)   63

Giovannone, Stefano   153, 155, 161
Gladio (stay behind)   35 n.6
  assessment of   22–6
  case study of   26–33
  incidents of   16–22
Glass, Charles   198
Glenanne Gang   51–4
Glover, Ross   234 n.28
Gordigi, Wahid   199–200
Gould, Matilda   51
Gouttière, Christian   198
Graber, Armand   79
Graber, Pierre   64–6, 68, 74, 76, 78–81, 83, 90, 100, 103, 138 n.83, 142 n.134
Grandin, Greg   234 n.28
Grassi, Gero   161
GRCROOND stay-behind activities, of Austria   30
GRDAGGER organization   31
Great Synagogue attack   166, 167
Greece   3, 17, 33, 99, 131 n.11, 213
Green, John Francis   51, 52
Greenhill, Dennis   103, 104
Gregg, John   56
Groep Fonteijn. *See* TREVI network
Gruber, Karl   26
Guardian (newspaper)   55
Guatemala   235 n.44
Guevara, Che   224
Gusty Spence doctrine   59
Guzzetti, Cesar Augusto   232 n.8
Gyr, Marcel   11 n.19, 158

Haas, Kenneth   197
Habash, George   4, 208
  Lodo Moro and   153, 155, 158, 161, 163, 164
  Palestinian Fedayeen groups and   92, 94, 98, 105, 106, 126–8, 132 nn.18–19, 138 n.91, 139 nn.97–8, 101, 144 n.172, 150 n.235, 151 nn.242, 244, 247
Haber, Eitan   147 n.201, 189 n.29
Haddad, Wadie   74, 75, 92, 96, 106, 107, 128, 129, 130 n.9, 144 n.172, 152 n.250, 179, 207, 208, 214
Halevy, David   152 n.250
Hamill, Robert   57

Hammarskjöld, Knut   97–8
Hamshari, Mahmoud   116
Hankiss, Ágnes   245 n.5
Hänni, Adrian   232 n.7
Hariri, Hossein Ali Mohammed   199
Harvey, William   2, 17
Hawatmeh, Nayef   94, 126, 144 n.172
Hayman, Peter T.   117–18, 145 n.186
Heath, Edward   90, 108–9, 111, 128
Heenan, Mary   50
Heenan, Paddy   50
Hegi, Lukas   83
Heikal, Muhammad   109, 111, 113, 132 n.29, 142 n.137
Helms, Richard   26, 120, 123–6, 149 nn.224, 226
Henry, Roger   211–13
Herbstritt, Georg   245 n.5
Herf, Jeffrey   219 n.19
Hezbollah   2, 9, 193
  application of political violence   196–201
  bombing and hijackings of   194, 197–9
  on European soil   199–200
  foundation of   195
  as Iran's revolutionary proxy force, in Lebanon   193–6
  against Israel   201–2
  manifesto of   202
  operational infrastructure of   194–5, 204 n.2
  Shiite ideology and   204–5 n.9
Higgins, William   198
Hijazi, Mahmoud   139 n.92
Hismeh, George   94
Historical Enquiries Team. *See* Police Service of Northern Ireland
Hogg, Douglas   57
Honduras   223, 235 n.44
Höttl, Wilhelm   32–3
Hulme Jr., Derick L.   148 n.216, 149 n.227
Hungary   26, 242, 245 n.5
Hunt, Swanee   28
Hurst, Ian   46
Hussein, King of Jordan   77, 93, 97, 118, 121, 125, 126, 132 n.29, 134 n.41, 142 n.137, 146 n.189, 149 nn.226, 228

Iaselli, Questore 169 n.19
Ignatius, David 147 n.200, 181
Ijad, Abu. *See* Iyad, Abu (Salah Khalaf)
India 242
Inquiries Act (2005) (UK) 57
Interdepartementale Arbeitsgruppe '1970' (Interdepartmental Working Group '1970', IDA 1970) 64, 66–72, 76, 78, 79, 82
International Committee of the Red Cross (ICRC) 95, 99, 107, 114, 140 n.110, 141 n.121, 217
Iran 5, 179. *See also* Hezbollah
Iran-Contra affair 200, 228, 231
Iraq 134 n.41, 184, 224, 241
Irish Independence Party 55
Irish National Liberation Army 55
Irish Republican Army (IRA) 45, 58, 237
Irish Republican Socialist Party (IRSP) 55
Irwin, Alistair 47
I segreti di Bologna (*The Secrets of Bologna*) (Priore) 153
'Islamic Jihad Organization' 197. *See also* Hezbollah
Islamic Organization for the Liberation of Jerusalem 198
Israel 93, 99–101, 114, 133 n.34, 138 n.91, 140 nn.109–10, 165, 210
  Red Cross and 136 n.61
Israeli, Raphael 245 n.5
Israeli Defense Forces (IDF) 242
Israel Intelligence Heritage and Commemoration Center (Herzliya) 243
Issa, Abu 146 n.197
Italy 3, 16, 33, 34. *See also* Lodo Moro
Iyad, Abu (Salah Khalaf) 110, 132 n.29, 172 n.72

Jackson, Mike 45
Jackson, Robin 51–3
Jacobsen, David 198
Jagdverbände (hunter units) 25
Jarring, Gunnar 93
Jawher, Mousa Badawi 216
Jeanneret, François 72
Jenco, Lawrence 198
Jeschke, Axel 188 n.5

Jibril, Ahmed 63, 135 n.50
Johnson, U. Alexis 123
Joint Support Group (UK) 45
Jordan 158, 211, 213
  and fedayeen, relationship between. *See* Palestinian Fedayeen groups
Jordan, Hugh 57
Jordanian UNO mission bombing 70–1
Jost, Walter 97, 136 n.65, 141 n.132
Joubert, Christian 198
Joy, Peter 144 n.174
Joyce, Miriam 142 n.147, 150 n.235
jurisprudence rule principle 205 n.9

Kaddoumi, Farouk 64, 65, 67–8, 73, 74, 79–83, 90, 110, 151 n.243, 158, 165, 216
Kalak, Ezzedine 5, 80–1
Kampfgruppe gegen Unmenschlichkeit ('Fighting Group against Inhumanity') (KgU) 1, 21
Kanafani, Ghassan 107, 116, 144 nn.172, 174, 176, 216
Kaufman, Jean-Paul 198
Kazziha, Walid 140 n.116
Kemmerling, Markus 36 n.12
Kemptner, Thomas 198
Kerr, Gordon 45
Kerr, Malcolm H. 198
KGB 6
Khaled, Leila 92, 95, 97, 102, 109, 116, 128, 131 n.16, 217
Khider, Mohammed 212
Khider affair 212
Khomeini, Ayatollah 204–5 n.9
Kiewitt, Peter 178
Kilburn, Peter 198
Kirchner, Magdalena 13 nn.33
Kissinger, Henry 93, 95, 96, 103, 104, 120, 122–6, 133 n.34, 134 n.41, 148 n.216, 149 n.227, 225, 232 n.8
Kissinger Ban 130 n.5
Kitson, Frank 50, 53
Klein, Hans-Joachim 73
Klinghoffer, Leon 166
Kloten Airport attack 63, 66, 75, 95, 99, 136 n.56, 142 n.134
Kontrgerilla (Counter-Guerrilla) (Turkey) 21

Kopp 35 n.6
Kopp, Magdalena 72
Kostadinov, Evtim 245 n.5
Kram, Thomas 163, 164
Kreisky, Bruno 185–7, 190 n.35
  guests of 178–81
Kreutner, Jonathan 71
Kurdistan Workers' Party (PKK) 21

Laird, Melvin 95
Lambert, Brian Adam 46
Lanc, Erwin 184, 186
Landshut aircraft hijack 176, 177
Lang, Jörg 190 n.43
Larkin, Paul 46
La Stampa (newspaper) 17
Lausanne branch, of Comité de Soutien au Peuple Palestinien 211
LCPROWL APPARAT 19
Lebanon 12 n.24, 93, 106, 107, 144 n.168, 159, 213. *See also* Hezbollah
Leffler, Melvin 224
Legiao Portuguesa 3
Le Main Rouge ('The Red Hand') 2, 3
LeoGrande, William 234 n.28
Le Soir (newspaper) 131 n.14
Letelier, Orlando 225, 232–3 n.11
Le Temps (newspaper) 65
Lethal Allies (Cadwallader) 47, 52
Levavi, Arieh 138 n.91, 141 n.124
Lewin, Jeremy 198
Lewis, Paul H. 232 n.8
L'Hebdo (magazine) 72, 73
Libya 5, 99, 157, 172 n.83, 184, 208, 214, 242
  Italy and 165
Lillbacka, Ralf 34 n.2
Lister, David 57
Livingstone, Neil C. 131 n.14, 152 n.250
Lodo Moro 4, 153–4
  Bologna massacre and 163–7
  genesis of 154–9
  Moro kidnapping and 159–63
Lo Kuei-Po 105
Lorenz, Peter 176
Loughgall shootings (1987) 58
Low Intensity Operations (Kitson) 50
Lowry, Bill 58–9

loyalist paramilitaries, in Northern Ireland. *See* collusion
Lufthansa hijacking (1972) 129, 152 n.250
lukewarm supporters, of terrorist actors 10 n.8
Luxembourg 19
  bombings in 19
Lyttle, Tommy 55

McAliskey, Bernadette Devlin 54–6, 59
MacBride, Peter 48
McCann, Joe 47
McCaughey, William 52, 54
McConnell, Robert 52
McCowan, Mike 133 n.38
McDonald, Henry 55
McDonald, Jackie 54, 55
McEntee, Patrick 52
McEntee report 52
McFarlane, Robert 200
McIntyre, Anthony 58, 59
Mackay, Neil 45
McKerr, Gervaise 57
McKissack, Luke 133 n.38
McMichael, John 55
McSherry, Patrice 233 n.12
Madsen, Frank 240
Maeke, Lutz 119, 146 n.196
Maggi, Carlo Maria 17–18
Maginn, Loughlin 43, 44
Mahmud, Abu 184
Mahnaimi, Uzi 131 n.16, 134 n.42, 136 n.65
Malta 165
Mambro, Francesca 163
Marion, Pierre 4
Maronite Phalange (Lebanon) 2
Marz, Michael 188 n.8
Massoud, Ghazi 240
Matin dimanche 80
Mattei, Enrico 156
Matter, Martin 35 n.2
Maurice, Charles 18
Mayhew Patrick 48
Mehsen, Abdel 209
Meier, Titus J. 35 n.2
Meinhof, Ulrike 120

Meir, Golda 93, 94, 103, 104, 111, 122, 180
Meir Amit Intelligence and Terrorism Information Center 199, 201, 203
Ménage, Gilles 11 n.24
Merari, Ariel 152 n.247
Mercer, Johnny 47
Merlen, Eric 11 n.24
Miami Showband attack 52
Miceli, Vito 157
Micheli, Pierre 70, 74, 139 n.100, 141 n.124
Mickolus, Edward F. 131 n.14
Midgley, Eric 113
Milano, James 27
Mills, George 35 n.2
Ministry for State Security (MfS) (GDR) 6, 23
   SBO and 23–4
Mitrokhin Commission 154, 169 n.8
Mitterrand, François 11 n.24
Molden, Fritz 26, 33
Monaghan bombings 52
Montoneros 230
Moore, Chris 43
Moretti, Mario 160
Moro, Aldo 155, 156
   kidnapping of 159–63
Moro Commissions 160–2
Morrison, Danny 58
Mossad (Israeli Secret Service) 117, 131 n.14, 144 n.178, 145 n.184, 161, 162, 181
MI6 (British Secret Intelligence Service) 25, 114, 151 n.240
Mukhabarat (Egyptian Secret Service) 120
Mulvenna, Gareth 51
Munich massacre (1972 Summer Olympics) 181, 188 n.14, 211
Munich Oktoberfest bombing (1980) 21, 172 n.83
Murray, Andrew 47

Naan, Michael 47
Naqib, Fadle 144 n.178
Nart, Raymond 11 n.24
Nasser, Gamal Abdel 93, 94, 97, 108, 109, 111, 132 n.29, 141 n.126, 142 n.137, 217

Nasser, Kamal 115, 116, 145 n.180
National Liberation Front (FLN). *See* Front de Libération Nationale (FLN) (Algeria)
National Security Council (NSC) (US) 120, 125
   NSC–10/5 (US) 20
NATO 23, 26
   Northern Command 34 n.2
   secret armies 15–22, 33
   Supreme Headquarters Allied Powers Europe 22
Nazi War Crimes Disclosure Act 26, 28
Nehring, Christopher 245 n.5
Nelson, Brian 44, 50, 54, 56
   arrest and trial of 44–5
Nelson, Rosemary 57
neo-fascist theory and Lodo Moro 164
the Netherlands 36 n.12, 188 n.14, 213
Neue Zürcher Zeitung (NZZ) (newspaper) 64, 65, 69, 73, 74, 79
New Left 211, 219 n.19
New York Times (newspaper) 148 n.218
Nicaragua 235 n.44
   state terrorism during Cold War and 223–31
Nicaraguan Democratic Force 2. *See also* Contras
Nieri, Giuseppe 163
Nimeiry, Jaffar 110, 141 n.124
9/11 attack 224
19th of April Movement (M-19) (Colombia) 223
Nittel, Heinz 186
Nixon, Richard 93, 95, 120, 122, 124, 146 n.190, 149 n.227
Nordmann, François 65
North, Olive 228, 229
North Korea 105, 139 n.97, 151 n.242
Nuclei Armati Rivoluzionari 163
Nuclei for the Defence of the State (NDS) 17
Nuti, Leopoldo 17
Nutting, Anthony 128, 151 n.240

Oakley, Robert 228, 229
O'Ballance, Edgar 142 n.137, 151 n.242
Oberloskamp, Eva 12 n.27
Observer (newspaper) 18

O Connail, Daithi 56
O'Connell, Jack 97, 121
Office of Counterterrorism (US State Department) 228
O'Hagan, Daniel 48
Oktoberfest bombing. *See* Munich Oktoberfest bombing (1980)
Olah, Franz 30–1, 33
OPEC Ministerial Conference, attack on 179
Operation Banner 48, 61 n.33
Operation Condor 225, 233 n.12
Operation Falls Curfew 49
Operation Iceberg 28–9
Operation Motorman 49
Operation Peace for Galilee 196, 238, 242, 243
Operation Werwolf 25
Ordine Nuovo 17
Organisation Armée Secrète ('Secret Army Organization') (OAS) 3, 7, 211
Organisation Gehlen 19
Organization for Victims of Zionist Occupation 129
Organization of International Revolutionaries (OIR) 163
Österreichischer Wander-, Sport -und Geselligkeitsverein (OWSGV) 30–1, 33
Oudeh, Mohammad Daoud. *See* Abu Daoud

Paisley, Ian 55
Pakistan 13 n.31, 242
Palestine Liberation Organization (PLO) 4, 89. *See also* Lodo Moro; Palestinian Fedayeen groups; Switzerland
  Central Committee 127, 129, 150 nn.231, 238, 180
  proposals to Western Germany 181–3
Palestinian Fedayeen groups 89–91
  British and US contacts intensification and 114–22
  Jordan and 92–4
  PFLP's hijacking renunciation 126–9
  PFLP post Zarqa Crisis demands 111–14
  potential diplomatic opening and 122–6
  and Zarqa Crisis 122
    Britain 108–11
    CIA-backed connection 106–8
    course of 94–9
    imbroglio 103–4
    Israel and 99–101
    private initiatives 102–3
    Swiss soft power 105–6
    West Germany and 101–2
Palestinian National Council (PNC) 94, 190 n.55
Palestinian Rejection Front 158, 159
Palmers, Walter 177, 190 n.54
Paraguay 225
Parliamentary Commission to Inquire into Italian Terrorism 154
Parliamentary Commission to Inquire into the Kidnapping and Murder of Aldo Moro 154
passive support, significance of 8, 11 n.18
passive supporters, of terrorist actors 10 n.8
Pat Finucane Centre (PFC) 47, 50, 52
path dependence, concept of 188 n.13
Patterns of Global Terrorism (US annual report) 230
Pean, Pierre 219 n.16
Pedahzur, Ami 145 n.180
Pella, Giuseppe 156
Pentagon Field Manual 30–31 16
Pezzullo, Lawrence 226
Pham-Lê, Jérémie 11 n.24
Phillips, J. F. S 101, 102, 109–11, 114, 115, 133 n.36, 134 n.39, 135 n.50, 136 n.67, 137 n.76
'Physical Security Support Element-Berlin' (PSSE-Berlin) 37 n.58
Piazza Fontana bombing (1969) 17
Piccoli, Flaminio 155, 158
Pierson, Paul 188 n.13
Pifano, Daniele 163
'Pilgrim plans' 27
Pinochet, Augusto 233 n.11
'Pitchfork Murders' case 47–8
Pizza della Loggia bombing (1974) 17–18
Ploquin, Frédéric 11 n.24

Pohl, Willi   116, 137 n.73, 144 n.179
Poindexter, John   200, 228
Poland   239
Polgar, Thomas   22
Polhill, Robert   198
Police Service of Northern Ireland   50
Policia Internacional e de Defesa do Estado (PIDE) (Portugal)   3
Pompidou, Georges   122
Ponto, Jürgen   176
Popular Front for the Liberation of Palestine (PFLP)   6, 63, 72, 80, 90, 237. *See also* Palestinian Fedayeen groups; Switzerland
   Fatah's ascendency and   126–9
   post Zarqa Crisis demands of   111–14
   Zarqa Crisis and   216–18
Popular Front for the Liberation of Palestine-General Command (PFLP-GC)   158
Popular Front for the Liberation of Palestine-Special Operations Group (PFLP-SOG)   179
Popular Struggle Front (PSF)   98
Porter, Dwight   118
Portugal   3, 17, 33
Posner, Steve   130 n.5
Preston, Simon   27
Priore, Rosario   153, 155, 157, 160, 162, 163, 164, 172 nn.76, 83, 173 nn.92, 94
Protocols of the Elders of Zion   215
P-26 organization (Switzerland)   35 n.2
Public Prosecution Service (UK)   47
Punch, Maurice   46

Quandt, William B.   148 n.216
Quds Force (Brigades)   193–4, 204 n.2

Raab, David   109, 110, 131 n.13, 133 n.35, 137 n.80, 140 n.110, 141 n.124, 143 nn.153, 159
Rabe, Stephen A.   233 n.12
Rabin, Yitzhak   93, 94
Rachamim, Mordechai   75
Rahamim, Mordehai   209, 212
Ramirez Sanchez, Ilich. *See* "Carlos the Jackal"

Ranstorp, Magnus   200
Reagan, Ronald   6, 200, 223, 226–31
Red Army Faction (RAF) (West Germany)   6, 7, 120, 147 n.203, 159, 164, 237
Red Brigades (BR)   7, 12 n.28, 155, 159–61, 164–5, 230, 237
Reed, Frank   198
Reeve, Simon   148 n.211
Regier, Frank   198
Regime of the Colonels   3
Reilly, Thomas   48
Revolutionäre Zellen (Revolutionary Cells)   73
Revolutionary Armed Forces of Colombia (FARC)   224
Revolutionary Guard Corps   193, 196
Revolutionary Organization 17 November (17N)   3, 11 n.18
Richardson, John ('Jocko')   28
Richardson, John F.   28
Richardson, Louise   10 n.8
Richterova, Daniela   245 n.5
Riegler, Thomas   191 n.76
Riste, Olav   22
Ritchie, Charles   53
Rocca, Renzo   17
Rochat, André   98, 99, 100, 135–6 n.56
Rogers, William   93, 118, 140 n.109
Rogers Initiative   93, 94, 123, 126
Romania   245 n.5
Rondot, Philippe   4
Rosenwasser, Schmuel   139 n.92
Rothstein, Raphael   139 n.92
Royal Irish Regiment   53
Royal Ulster Constabulary (RUC)   44, 45, 51, 53, 54, 57
   DPP and   49–50
Rubin, Barry   144 n.168, 146 n.193
Rubin, Judith Colp   144 n.168, 146 n.193
Rückkehr in die Menschlichkeit (Klein)   73
Rumor, Mariano   157
Rundschau (Swiss television programme)   78
Rusk, Dean   146 n.191
Ruwayha, Walid Amin   133 n.38

Saadeh, Antun   210
sacrifice, principle of   205 n.9
Saddam Hussein Collection   241
Sadiq, Mohammed Ahmed   110, 142 n.137
Salameh, Ali Hassan   107, 110, 126, 127, 145 n.185, 147 nn.201, 210, 181–3, 189 n.29
   as CIA source   120–1, 123, 147 n.200
   role in Western Europe   147 n.203
Saleh, Abu Anzeh   155, 163, 169 n.19
Salvino, Guido   10 n.11
sanctuary doctrine   4, 240
Sandinistas   230
Sandinistas and Middle Eastern Radicals, The (US report)   230
Sands, Bobby   57
Santovito, Giuseppe   162
Sartawi, Issam   128, 133 n.36, 180–2, 184–6, 190 n.35
Satta, Vladimiro   162
Saudi Arabia   158, 179
Saville Report   47, 49–50
Sayigh, Yezid   150 n.238, 151 n.244
Scandinavia   25
Schaufelberger, Albert   227
Schauldemen, Harry W.   225
Schenk, Dieter   191 n.76
Scheuer, Thomas   238
Schiff, Zeev   139 n.92
Schiller, Margrit   147 n.203
Schleyer, Hanns Martin   176, 177, 182
Schmidt, Helmut   175–8, 188 n.7
Schmidt-Eenboom, Erich   37 n.52
Schröder, Gerhard   180, 189 n.27
Schutzstaffel (SS)   25
Schweizerische Depeschenagentur (SDA)   69
Schweizer Terrorjahre (Terror Years in Switzerland) (Gyr)   63–5, 78, 80, 83, 90
Scullion, John   51
SDRA8 (Belgium)   18, 19. *See also* Gladio (stay behind)
Seale, Patrick   12 n.24
2 June Movement   177
Seeyle, Talcott   93–4
seized files   241–3
Senior Review Group (SRG) (US)   122

September Crisis. *See* Zarqa Crisis
Service d'Action   19. *See also* Direction Générale de la Sécurité Extérieure (DGSE) (France)
Service de Documentation Extérieure et de Contre-Espionnage (SDECE) (France)   2
Service politique (of Geneva Cantonal Police)   82
Servizio Informazioni Forze Armate (SIFAR) (Italy)   2, 16
Servizio per le Informazioni e la Sicurezza Democratica (SISDE) (Italy)   164
Servizio per le Informazioni e la Sicurezza Militare (SISMI) (Italy)   4, 153, 164
   report   162
Seurat, Michel   198
Shankill Butchers, The (Dillon)   59
Shapiro, Jeremy   12 n.27
Shaw, Barry   49
Shepherd, J. A.   115, 144 n.168
Shultz, George   227–9
Sica, Domenico   164
Simonin, Pierre-Yves   66, 67
Simpson, Christopher   31
Sinn Fein   58
Sirhan, Sirhan Bishara   133 n.38
Sisco, Joe   103, 104, 118, 122, 123, 126, 146 n.190, 148 n.220
Six-Day War   211, 215
Skelton-Robinson, Thomas   82, 152 n.248
Skocpol, Theda   188 n.13
Skorzeny, Otto   25
Skorzeny plan   25
Skyjack Sunday. *See* Zarqa Crisis
Smallwoods, Raymond   54–6
Smidt, Wolbert   23
Smith, Michael   27
Smithwick, Peter   58
Smyth, Andrew   44
Social Democratic Party (SPD) (Germany)   19, 175, 178
Socialist International (SI)   179
Socialist Worker (newspaper)   45
Sofaer, Abraham   229
Somoza Debayle, Anastasio   225, 226

South Africa   8
Soviet Union   6, 134 n.41, 148 n.218, 157
    stay behind and   25
Spain   3, 16, 34, 177
Special Forces Berlin (Stejskal)   21
Special Operations Executive (SOE)   24–5
Special Reconnaissance Regiment
        (UK)   45
Spence, Gusty   51
Sportelli, Armando   157
'Spring of Youth' commando
        operation   116
Stakeknife (Hurst)   46
Stasi. *See* Ministry for State Security (MfS)
        (GDR)
State in Denial, A (Urwin)   47
State Support for International Terrorism
        (CIA report)   230
state support for terrorist actors   1–5
    classification scales and   10 n.8
    Cold War dimension of   5–7
state terrorism, during Cold War   223–31
State Violence, Collusion and the Troubles
        (Punch)   46
stay behind. *See* Gladio (stay behind)
Stay Behind Organisation (SBO)   21, 23.
        See also Gladio (stay behind);
        Bundesnachrichtendienst
        (BND)
Steen, Alann   198
Steiner, Yves   11 n.19, 67
Steinich, Annette   67
Stejskal, James   21, 37 n.58
Stethem, Robert Dean   199
Steven, Stewart   98
Stevens, John   44, 45
Stevens inquiry incident   44, 46, 57
Stobie, William   57
Stocker, James   132 n.21
Stoll, Ulrich   37 n.52
strategy of tension   3, 18, 21, 164
Strathearn, William   52
Stroessner, Alfredo   225
strong supporters, of terrorist actors   10 n.8
Strothmann, Dietrich   189 n.27
Struebig, Heinrich   198
suicide attacks   205 n.9
Sulzberger, Cyrus   156

Sunday Herald (newspaper)   45
Sunday Times (newspaper)   49
Susan, Bénédicte   12 n.27
Sutherland, Thomas   198
Sweden   26, 34 n.2, 188 n.8
Swinkels, Rudi   102
Swiss–Arab Society   211, 215
Swiss Federation of Jewish
        Communities   218
Switzerland   4, 12 n.24, 26, 35 n.2, 36 n.12
    Arab campaign and   215–16
    Arab League and Fatah support
        network in   209–12
    défense de rupture tactic in   213–15
    early Geneva PLO office and   68–71
    Palestinian Fedayeen groups
        and   95–100, 102–3, 109–14,
        141 n.124, 142 n.135
    and PLO, moratorium agreement
        between   74–7, 82–3
        controversy   63–8
        first-hand witness   78–82
        traces of   71–4
    soft power of   105–6
    Zarqa Crisis and PFLP terrorists
        release and   216–18
    Zurich-Kloten attack (1969) in   208–9
Symmes, Harrison   118, 121, 145
        nn.188–9
Syria   5, 134 n.41, 158, 196, 242
Szyszkowitz, Tessa   150 n.239

Tages-Anzeiger (newspaper)   65, 77, 218
Tanner, Jakob   63
'tartan gang' phenomenon   51
Taylor, Peter   116, 148 n.211
Technischer Dienst (TD)   19–20
'Terrorism Review', of CIA   19
Terrorist Group Profiles (US State
        Department publication)   227
Thain, Ian   48
Thalmann, Ernesto A.   113
Thatcher, Margaret   142 n.147
Thomas, Teresa Fava   146 n.189
Thornton, Chris   46
Toaldo, Mattia   232 n.7
Tofan, Liviu   245 n.5
Toman, Mohammed   240
Touqan, Abu Sameeh   127, 150 n.234

Tracy, Edward 198
Tramonte, Maurizio 18
Travis, Philip W. 232 n.7, 234 n.28, 235 n.44
Treaty of Esquipulas 231, 235 n.44
Trend, Burke 128, 151 n.240
TREVI network 189 n.14
Tribelhorn, Marc 131 n.12
Tribune de Genève (newspaper) 82
Tribune de Lausanne (newspaper) 77
Tripp, J. P. 133 n.37, 134 n.46
Tunisia 150 n.235
Tupamaros 230, 237
Turkey 33
Turner, Jesse 198
Turnly, John 55
TWA hijacking 92, 107, 133 n.34, 140 nn.110–11
Tyre suicide bombings (1982) 201

Ulster (*Sunday Times*) 49
Ulster Defence Association (UDA) 43, 50, 53
   collusion in 1980s and 54–8
Ulster Defence Regiment (UDR) 44, 52–4
Ulster Democratic Party 54, 56
Ulster Freedom Fighters (UFF). *See* Ulster Defence Association (UDA)
'Ulsterization' strategy 51
Ulster Special Constabulary 53
Ulster Volunteer Force (UVF) 51–4
'Underground Organisations' (Jeanneret) 72
United States 149 n.227, 165, 182. *See also* Central Intelligence Agency (CIA); Palestinian Fedayeen groups
   Nicaragua and 223–31
   stay behind operations and 35 n.6
unwilling hosts, of terrorist actors 10 n.8
Urwin, Margaret 47
US Contra War 231, 234 n.28
U Thant, General 214

Vereinigung Schweizerischer Nachrichtenoffiziere (Association of Swiss Intelligence Officers) (VSN) 82–3
Vergès, Jacques 72–3, 213–14
Very British Jihad, A (Larkin) 46
Vietnam 242
Vine, Richard David 140 n.110
von Crayen, Alexander 102, 103, 137 n.78, 138 nn.80, 83
von Crayen, Beatrix 137 n.78
von Moos, Ludwig 65

Waage, Hilde Henriksen 146 nn.190–1, 148 nn.216, 220, 149 n.228, 150 n.235
Walder, Hans 64
Ward, Peter 51
Warsaw Pact 6
Washington Special Actions Group (WSAG) 122
weak supporters, of terrorist actors 10 n.8
Wehrsportgruppe Hoffmann 237
Weinberger, Caspar 200
Weir, Benjamin 198
Weir, John 51–2, 54
Westad, Odd Arne 232 n.7
West Berlin, British stay-behind preparations in 20
West Germany 133 n.36, 135 n.49, 142 n.135
   stay behind in 19–20
   Zarqa Crisis and 95–7, 99–102, 109–10
Widgery inquiry 49
Wiegrefe, Klaus 188 n.7
Wieviorka, Michel 12 n.27
Williams, Brian Glyn 224, 232 n.7
Wills, David C. 232 n.7
Winkler, Willi 135 n.50, 152 n.250
Wischnewski, Hans-Jürgen 101–2, 136 nn.68, 71, 137 n.73, 190 n.35
Wischnewski Protocol 175–6
   in the aftermath of Vienna 185–6
   evaluation of 186–7
   Kreisky and guests and 178–81
   new PLO and 183–5
   1977 as peak of terrorism and 176–8
   PLO proposals to Western Germany and 181–3
Wood, Ian S. 55
Woods, Randall B. 39 n.92
Woog, Peter 212
'Wrath of God' 116

Wright, Billy 57
Wright, Mark 48
Würenlingen airplane crash 63–5, 75, 76

Yamani, Ahmed Zaki 176
Yariv, Aharon 116
Yedioth Ahronoth (newspaper) 153
yellow card principles 48, 49, 61 n.32
Yemen 242
Yom Kippur War 127, 156, 157
Yousef, Ibrahim 209
Youssoufi, Abderrahmane 213
Yugoslavia 242, 245 n.5

Zala, Sacha 11 n.19, 67
Zarqa Crisis 64–6, 68, 222 n.77
    Britain and 108–11
    CIA-backed connection and 106–8
    course of 94–9

    imbroglio 103–4
    Israel and 99–101
    PFLP terrorists release and 216–18
    private initiatives 102–3
    Swiss soft power and 105–6
    West Germany and 101–2
Zayed, Bassam 138 n.83
Zayn, Mustafa 106, 108, 140 n.110. *See also* Zein, Mustafa M.
Zein, Mustafa M. 107–8, 120, 121, 140 n.113, 141 n.121, 147 n.210. *See also* Zayn, Mustafa
Zernichow, Simen 146 nn.190–1, 148 nn.216, 220, 149 n.228, 150 n.235
Zhaglul, Fuad Saad 209
Ziegler, Jean 64, 67, 68, 74, 79–81, 83
Zionism 215

www.ingramcontent.com/pod-product-compliance
Lightning Source LLC
Chambersburg PA
CBHW072131290426
44111CB00012B/1854